D1240651

LIBRARY OF SECOND TEMPLE STUDIES

75

formerly the Journal for the Study of the Pseudepigrapha Supplement Series

Editor
Lester L. Grabbe

JUDAH BETWEEN EAST AND WEST

The Transition from Persian to Greek Rule (ca. 400–200 BCE)

A Conference Held at Tel Aviv University, 17–19 April 2007
Sponsored by the ASG (the Academic Study Group for Israel
and the Middle East) and Tel Aviv University

EDITED BY
LESTER L. GRABBE
AND
ODED LIPSCHITS

B L O O M S B U R Y
LONDON • NEW DELHI • NEW YORK • SYDNEY

Bloomsbury T&T Clark
An imprint of Bloomsbury Publishing Plc

50 Bedford Square   175 Fifth Avenue
London   New York
WC1B 3DP   NY 10010
UK   USA

www.bloomsbury.com

First published by T&T Clark International 2011
Paperback edition first published 2013

British Library Cataloguing-in-Publication Data
A catalogue record for this book is available from the British Library.

ISBN: HB: 978-0-567-04684-0
PB: 978-0-567-52626-7

Library of Congress Cataloging-in-Publication Data
A catalog record for this book is available from the Library of Congress

Typeset by Pindar NZ, Auckland, New Zealand

CONTENTS

CONTRIBUTORS

James Aitken is Lecturer in Hebrew, Old Testament, and Second Temple Studies in the University of Cambridge.

Israel Finkelstein is Professor of Archaeology of Israel in the Bronze and Iron Ages in the J.M. Alkow Department of Archaeology and Ancient Near Eastern Cultures at Tel Aviv University.

Lester L. Grabbe is Professor of Hebrew Bible and Early Judaism at the University of Hull.

Sylvie Honigman is Senior Lecturer of Ancient History in the Department of History at Tel Aviv University.

Aryeh Kasher is Professor Emeritus of the History of the Jewish People at Tel Aviv University.

Amos Kloner is Professor in the Department of the Land of Israel Studies and Archaeology at the Bar Ilan University in Ramat Gan.

Oded Lipschits is Associate Professor of Jewish History in the J.M. Alkow Department of Archaeology and Ancient Near Eastern Cultures at Tel Aviv University.

Menachem Mor is Professor of Jewish History and Dean of the Faculty of Humanities at the University of Haifa.

John Ray is Herbert Thompson Professor of Egyptology at the University of Cambridge.

Eveline van der Steen is Honorary Research Fellow in the School of Archaeology, Classics and Egyptology at the University of Liverpool.

Loren Stuckenbruck is Richard Dearborn Professor of New Testament Studies at Princeton Theological Seminary.

Oren Tal is Associate Professor of Classical Archaeology and Chair of the J.M. Alkow Department of Archaeology and Ancient Near Eastern Cultures at Tel Aviv University.

Lena-Sofia Tiemeyer is Lecturer in Old Testament/Hebrew Bible at the University of Aberdeen.

ABBREVIATIONS

AASOR	Annual of the American Schools of Oriental Research
AAWG	Abhandlungen der Akademie der Wissenschaften zu Göttingen
AB	Anchor Bible
ABD	David Noel Freedman (ed.) (1992) *Anchor Bible Dictionary*
AfO	*Archiv für Orientforschung*
AGAJU	Arbeiten zur Geschichte des antiken Judentums und des Urchristentum
AJA	*American Journal of Archaeology*
AJAH	*American Journal of Ancient History*
AJBA	*Australian Journal of Biblical Archaeology*
AJP	*American Journal of Philology*
AJS Review	*American Jewish Studies Review*
AJSL	*American Journal of Semitic Languages*
ALD	*Aramaic Levi Document*
ALGHJ	*Arbeiten zur Literatur und Geschichte des hellenistischen Judentums*
AnBib	Analecta biblica
AncSoc	*Ancient Society*
ANET	J. B. Pritchard (ed.) *Ancient Near Eastern Texts relating to the Old Testament*
AnOr	Analecta orientalia
ANRW	*Aufstieg und Niedergang der römischen Welt*
Ant.	Josephus, *Antiquities of the Jews*
ASORAR	American Schools of Oriental Research Archaeological Reports
ASTI	*Annual of the Swedish Theological Institute*
ATR	*Anglican Theological Review*
AUSS	*Andrews University Seminary Studies*
BA	*Biblical Archeologist*
BAR	*Biblical Archaeology Review*
BASOR	*Bulletin of the American Schools of Oriental Research*
BCH	*Bulletin de Correspondance Helléntique*

BETL	Bibliotheca Ephemeridum Theologicarum Lovaniensium
BHS	*Biblia Hebraica Stuttgartensis*
Bib	*Biblica*
BibOr	Biblica et orientalia
BiOr	Biblica et orientalia
BJRL	*Bulletin of the John Rylands Library*
BJS	Brown Judaic Studies
BO	*Bibliotheca Orientalis*
BSOAS	*Bulletin of the School of Oriental and African Study*
BTB	*Biblical Theology Bulletin*
BZ	*Biblische Zeitschrift*
BZAW	Beihefte zur *ZAW*
BZNW	Beihefte zur *ZNW*
CAH	*Cambridge Ancient History*
CBQ	*Catholic Biblical Quarterly*
CBQMS	*Catholic Biblical Quarterly* Monograph Series
CC	Corpus Christianorum
CEJL	Commentaries on Early Jewish Literature
CHI	*Cambridge History of Iran*
CHJ	W. D. Davies and L. Finkelstein (eds.) *Cambridge History of Judaism*
ConBOT	Conjectanea biblica, Old Testament
CP	*Classical Philology*
CPJ	V. A. Tcherikover, et al. (1957–64) *Corpus Papyrorum Judaicarum*
CQ	*Classical Quarterly*
CR: BS	*Currents in Research: Biblical Studies*
CRAIBL	*Comptes rendus de l'Académie des inscriptions et belles-lettres*
CRINT	Compendia rerum iudaicarum ad Novum Testamentum
CSCT	Columbia Studies in Classical Texts
DDD/DDD²	K. van der Toorn, B. Becking, and P. W. van der Horst (eds) *Dictionary of Deities and Demons in the Bible*: 1st edition 1995 (= *DDD*); 2nd edition 1999 (= *DDD²*)
DJD	Discoveries in the Judaean Desert
DSD	*Dead Sea Discoveries*
EI	*Eretz-Israel*
ESHM	European Seminar in Historical Methodology
ET	English translation
FAT	Forschungen zum Alten Testament
FGH	*Die Fragmente der griechischen Historiker* (Jacoby 1926–58).

FoSub	Fontes et Subsidia ad Bibliam pertinentes
FOTL	Forms of Old Testament Literature
FRLANT	Forschungen zur Religion und Literature des Alten und Neuen Testaments
GCS	Griechische christliche Schriftsteller
GRBS	*Greek, Roman, and Byzantine Studies*
HAT	Handbuch zum Alten Testament
HdA	Handbuch der Archäologie
HdO	Handbuch der Orientalisk
HR	*History of Religions*
HSCP	*Harvard Studies in Classical Philology*
HSM	Harvard Semitic Monographs
HSS	Harvard Semitic Studies
HTR	*Harvard Theological Review*
HUCA	*Hebrew Union College Annual*
IAA	Israel Antiquities Authority
ICC	International Critical Commentary
IDB	G. A. Buttrick (ed.) (1962) *Interpreter's Dictionary of the Bible*
IDBSup	Supplementary volume to *IDB* (1976)
IEJ	*Israel Exploration Journal*
IGLS	VII: *Inscriptions Grecques et Latines de la Syrie* (L. Jalabert, R. Mouterde and J.-P. Rey-Coquais (eds), Paris, 1929).
INJ	*Israel Numismatic Journal*
INR	*Israel Numismatic Research*
Int	*Interpretation*
IOS	*Israel Oriental Studies*
ITQ	*Irish Theological Quarterly*
JAAR	*Journal of the American Academy of Religion*
JANES	*Journal of the Ancient Near Eastern Society of Columbia University*
JAOS	*Journal of the American Oriental Society*
JBL	*Journal of Biblical Literature*
JCS	*Journal of Cuneiform Studies*
JEA	*Journal of Egyptian Archaeology*
JES	*Journal of Ecumenical Studies*
JHS	*Journal of Hellenic Studies*
JJS	*Journal of Jewish Studies*
JNES	*Journal of Near Eastern Studies*
JQR	*Jewish Quarterly Review*
JR	*Journal of Religion*
JRS	*Journal of Roman Studies*

JSHRZ	Jüdische Schriften aus hellenistisch-römischer Zeit
JSJ	*Journal for the Study of Judaism*
JSJSup	Supplements to *Journal for the Study of Judaism*
JSNT	*Journal for the Study of the New Testament*
JSOT	*Journal for the Study of the Old Testament*
JSOTSup	Journal for the Study of the Old Testament – Supplementary Series
JSP	*Journal for the Study of the Pseudepigrapha*
JSPSup	Journal for the Study of the Pseudepigrapha – Supplementary Series
JSS	*Journal of Semitic Studies*
JTS	*Journal of Theological Studies*
JWSTP	M. E. Stone (ed.) *Jewish Writings of the Second Temple Period*
KAI	H. Donner and W. Röllig *Kanaanäische und aramäische Inschriften*
KAT	Kommentar zum Alten Testament
LCL	Loeb Classical Library
LSTS	Library of Second Temple Studies
LXX	Septuagint translation of the OT
MGWJ	*Monatschrift für Geschichte und Wissenschaft des Judentums*
MT	Masoretic textual tradition (only the consonantal text is in mind when reference is made to pre-mediaeval mss)
NIGTC	New International Greek Testament Commentary
NovT	*Novum Testamentum*
NovTSup	Novum Testamentum, Supplements
NTOA	Novum Testamentum et Orbis Antiquus
NTS	*New Testament Studies*
OBO	Orbis Biblicus et Orientalis
OCD	S. Hornblower and A. Spawforth (eds) (1996) *The Oxford Classical Dictionary* (3rd edn)
OGIS	Dittenberger, W. (1903–5) *Orientis graeci inscriptiones selectae*
OLA	Orientalia Lovaniensia Analecta
OT	Old Testament/Hebrew Bible
OTL	Old Testament Library
OTP 1–2	J. H. Charlesworth (ed.) *Old Testament Pseudepigrapha*
OTS	*Oudtestamentische Studiën*
PAAJR	*Proceedings of the American Academy of Jewish Research*
PCZ	[= *P. Cairo Zenon*] C. C. Edgar (ed.) (1925–40) *Zenon Papyri I-V*

PEQ	*Palestine Exploration Quarterly*
P. Lon.	T. C. Skeat (1974) *Greek Papyri in the British Museum (now in the British Library): VII The Zenon Archive*
PVTG	Pseudepigrapha Veteris Testamenti graece
PW	Pauly-Wissowa, *Real-Encyclopädie der classischen Altertumswissenschaft* Wissowa, Georg, and Wilhelm Kroll (eds.) (1894–1972) *Paulys Real-Encyclopädie der classischen Altertumswissenschaft* (Stuttgart: J. B. Metzlersche Verlagbuchhandlung) = PW.
PWSup	Supplement to PW
RB	*Revue biblique*
RC	C. B. Welles (1934) *Royal Correspondence in the Hellenistic Period: A Study in Greek Epigraphy*
REB	*Revised English Bible*
REG	*Revue des études grecs*
REJ	*Revue des études juives*
RevQ	*Revue de Qumran*
RSR	*Religious Studies Review*
RSV	Revised Standard Version
SANE	Studies on the Ancient Near East
SAWH	*Sitzungsbericht der Akademie der Wissenschaften zu Heidelberg*
SBL	Society of Biblical Literature
SBLASP	SBL Abstracts and Seminar Papers
SBLBMI	SBL Bible and its Modern Interpreters
SBLDS	SBL Dissertation Series
SBLEJL	SBL Early Judaism and its Literature
SBLMS	SBL Monograph Series
SBLSBS	SBL Sources for Biblical Study
SBLSCS	SBL Septuagint and Cognate Studies
SBLSPS	Society of Biblical Literature Seminar Papers Series
SBLTT	SBL Texts and Translations
SC	Sources chrétiennes
SCI	*Scripta Classica Israelica*
ScrHier	*Scripta Hierosolymitana*
SEG	Supplementum epigraphicum graecum
SFSHJ	South Florida Studies in the History of Judaism
SFSJH	South Florida Studies in Jewish History
SHAJ	*Studies in the History and Archaeology of Jordon*
SJLA	Studies in Judaism in Late Antiquity
SJOT	*Scandinavian Journal of the Old Testament*
SNTSMS	Society for New Testament Studies Monograph Series
SP	Samaritan Pentateuch

SPA	*Studia Philonica Annual*
SPB	Studia postbiblica
SR	*Studies in Religion/Sciences religieuses*
SSAW	Sitzungsbericht der sachischen Akademie der Wissenschaften
STDJ	Studies on the Texts of the Desert of Judah
SUNT	Studien zur Umwelt des Neuen Testaments
SVTP	Studia in Veteris Testamenti pseudepigrapha
TAD 1–4	Bezalel Porten and Ada Yardeni (1986–99) *Textbook of Aramaic Documents from Ancient Egypt: 1–4* (Hebrew University, Department of the History of the Jewish People, Texts and Studies for Students; Jerusalem: Hebrew University).
TAPA	*Transactions of the American Philological Association*
TDNT	G. Kittel and G. Friedrich (eds.) *Theological Dictionary of the New Testament*
TLZ	*Theologische Literaturzeitung*
Trans	*Transeuphratène*
TSAJ	Texte und Studien zum antiken Judentum
TSSI	J. C. L. Gibson, *Textbook of Syrian Semitic Inscriptions*
TWAT	G. J. Botterweck and H. Ringgren (eds.) *Theologische Wörterbuch zum Alten Testament*
VC	*Vigiliae Christianae*
VT	*Vetus Testamentum*
VTSup	Vetus Testamentum, Supplements
WBC	Word Bible Commentary
WMANT	Wissenschaftliche Monographien zum Alten und Neuen Testament
WUNT	Wissenschaftliche Untersuchungen zum Neuen Testament
YCS	*Yale Classical Studies*
ZA	*Zeitschrift für Assyrologie*
ZAW	*Zeitschrift für die Alttestamentlichen Wissenschaft*
ZDMG	*Zeitschrift der Deutschen Morganländischen Gesellschaft*
ZDPV	*Zeitschrift des Deutschen Palästina-Vereins*
ZNW	*Zeitschrift für die Neutestamentlichen Wissenschaft*
ZPE	*Zeitschrift für Papyrologie und Epigraphik*
§	In a citation from Josephus, it refers to paragraph numbers in the text

PREFACE

This volume had its beginnings in the summer of 2001. John Levy, Director of the Academic Study Group for Israel and the Middle East (ASG – an organization interested in promoting cooperation between British and Israeli scholars), discussed with Lester Grabbe the possibility of helping to fund a conference. Preliminary discussions took place between Grabbe and Oded Lipschits about a conference at Tel Aviv University on the transition between the Persian and Greek periods in Judah. Then 9/11 intervened, and the meeting was put on hold. Finally, the conference was held in April 2007, with joint support from both the ASG and Tel Aviv University (including the Faculty of Humanities, the Chaim Katzman Archaeology Fund, the Chaim Rosenberg School of Jewish Studies, and the Sonia and Marco Nadler Institute of Archaeology). The editors and participants would like to express their grateful thanks to these organizations for their generous help and support.

Lester L. Grabbe, University of Hull
Oded Lipschits, Tel Aviv University
1 May 2010

Tuesday, 17 April 2007 – Gilman Building, 496

08.30–09.00:	Morning Coffee
09.00–Greetings:	Prof. Dina Porat, chair of the Chaim Rosenberg School of Jewish Studies
	John D. A. Levy, Academic Study Group on Israel and the Middle East
Opening Discussion:	The Goals of the Conference: Oded Lipschits and Lester Grabbe
09.15–10.45:	The Transition from the Persian to the Hellenistic periods – The Archaeological Perspective
Oren Tal:	Palestine in Transition – from Persian to Greek Rule – The Archaeological Perspectives
Gabriel Barkay:	The Beginning of the Persian Period and its End in the History of Palestine's Archaeological Research
Discussion	
10.45–11.15:	Break
11.15–12.45:	Archaeology of Jerusalem in the Persian and Early Hellenistic Periods
Israel Finkelstein:	Jerusalem in the Persian Period and the Wall of Nehemiah
Oded Lipschits:	The Size and Status of Jerusalem in the Persian and Early Hellenistic Periods
Discussion	
13.00:	Lunch Break
14.45–16.15:	The Greek, Babylonian and Egyptian Connection

Lena-Sofia Tiemeyer:	Will the Greek Texts Stand Up, Please!
John Ray:	The Alphabet that Never Was: An Egyptian Contribution to the Near East
Discussion	

16.15–16.45:	Coffee Break

16.45–17.30:	A session in honour of Prof. Aryeh Kasher for his 72nd Birthday
A. Kasher:	Further Thoughts on Josephus' Report of Alexander's Campaign to Palestine

17.30–18.30:	Summary Discussion of the First Day
Lester Grabbe and Oded Lipschits	

Wednesday, 18 April 2007 – Gilman Building, 496

08.30–09:00:	Morning Coffee

09.00–10.30:	The Imperial and the Local
Lester Grabbe:	Hyparchs, *Oikonomoi* and Mafiosi: The Governance of Judah in the Ptolemaic Period
Eveline van der Steen:	Empires and Farmers: How Imperial Politics Affect Local Organization
Discussion	

10.30–10.45:	Break

10.45–12.45:	Samaria and the Samaritans between Persian and Hellenic Rule
Menachem Mor:	The Samaritans' Transition from the Persian to the Greek Period
Yuval Shahar:	The Samaritan Temple on Mount Gerizim: Archaeological Identification and Social Identity
Discussion	

13.00:	Lunch Break

14.00–15.45:	A Tour in the Diaspora Museum
15.45–16.00:	Coffee Break
16.00–17.30:	Idumea and the Coast between Persian and Hellenic Rule

Moshe Fisher: Yavneh-Yam as a Case Study of the Southern
                       Israeli Coast between Persian and Hellenic
                       Rule (5th–2nd centuries BCE)
Amos Kloner: The Introduction of the Greek Language and
                       Culture in the Third Century BCE According to
                       the Archaeological Evidence in Idumaea
Discussion

17.30–18.15:   Summary Discussion of the Second Day
Lester Grabbe and Oded Lipschits

Thursday, 19 April 2007 – Naphtali Building, Venecuela Auditorium
08.30–09.00:   Morning Coffee

09.00–10.30:   Ideology and its Context
Sylvie Honigman: King and Temple in 2 Maccabees: the Case for
                       Continuity
Loren Stuckenbruck: 1 Enoch 10 and the Conversion of Humanity
Discussion

10.30–10.45:   Break

10.45–12.15:   The Question of National Identity
James Aitken: Judaic National Identity.
Jill Middlemas: The Novella and Identity: The Case of Esther
Discussion

12.30–Lunch Break

14.15–Final Discussion
Lester Grabbe and Oded Lipschits
15.30:   A Tour of Apollonia-Arsuf with Prof. Israel
                       Roll, Prof. Moshe Fischer and Dr Oren Tal

INTRODUCTION

Lester L. Grabbe

The purpose of the conference was to explore not only the events but the character of the period in which Judah changed from a Persian province into a territory under Greek rule. The period is roughly defined as 400 to 200 BCE, for convenience, but more important are the events and developments that affected the Jews at this crucial time. A couple of papers in fact fall outside these chronological limits. Participants were given the general aims and subject of the conference but allowed to develop their own individual topics. In a set of papers of this quantity a variety of topics and approaches is inevitable. Individually, each has its own interests and concerns, yet all together they begin to sketch an age in which the Jewish community and the Jewish religion developed and changed in important ways. In the past, it has often been argued that the Greek conquest formed the watershed in Jewish history. On the other hand, there are reasons to see the Persian period as the seminal period in Jewish history, because most of the elements important in later Judaism originated then (Grabbe 2004: 359–60). Nevertheless, the early Greek period saw considerable movement, change, and development, partly because of the peculiar history of the Hellenistic kingdoms.

The following section summarizes the individual papers. After that comes a discussion of the main themes cutting through the various essays. In some cases, an essay or essays are part of a wider debate, meaning that some indication of this debate may be given.

Summaries of Papers

According to James Aitken, two questions deserve discussion about 'Judaic National Identity'. One has to do with the period 400–200 BCE: how far is it a transition period or a time of innovation or catalyst for earlier ideas? The second is whether Hellenism in particular had substantial influence on the nature of Judah or Judaism. These questions partly arise from periodization. Writing history always involves dividing into periods, and this division always involves a particular emphasis or focus. Different ways of dividing have been tried – to get away from the traditional Persian, Hellenistic, Seleucid, Maccabaean, etc. – but they always create their own problems. There has been a tendency to emphasize the Hasmonaean period, so that the 'pre-Hasmonaean' becomes a precursor to developments under the Maccabees rather than a period to be analyzed on its own. A central problem for the period 400–200 BCE is the lack of evidence or sources. Whether any biblical books fall into this period is a matter of debate, but we can reasonably put some biblical books plus some other literary sources during this time. This gives us a perspective for change, but interpretation is not simple (e.g. the question of levirate marriage or marriage to foreigners). *Ben Sira* is widely accepted as dating to the end of this period, but if we did not know or suspect the date, would we guess that it was written during the Hellenistic period? Several recent authors discuss Jewish identity (Mendels, S. Schwartz, Goodblatt), and see it centred on the temple and shared beliefs. But it is not immediately evident that there was a Judaic identity in the Persian period since the term 'Yehud' or 'Judah' is an administrative designation rather than the traditional biblical Israel. Considering the continuing use of 'Israel' internally, Judah might have originally been only an external determinant. In addition, the mixed nature of the population might have raised problems for identity, since the leading families ('the returnees') would have seen themselves as a distinct group. Taking Ben Sira as an example, he gives a picture of a Jewish *ethnos* with its focus on Jerusalem. Ben Sira presents what might be called 'Zion nationalism' (Goodblatt's term), with his emphasis on the temple and Jerusalem as God's residence. Simon II in ch. 50 is presented as both protector and benefactor, and therefore the effective head of state, incorporating traces of a foundation legend. Planting is also a theme, connected with the flourishing of Wisdom (ch. 24) and the high priest, a flourishing that is also evident in the allusions to the bones of dead ancestors. The prophecies will be renewed through them, but they also serve as a claim on ownership of the land, their resting in the land as a marker of possession. In sum, the issues presented include the realization that identity of a national group may not have started from within the group but from external political factors. In time, the circumstances of Jews in the Diaspora, and the political machinations over control of Coele-Syria led to greater attention on certain issues. For some, the responsibility of the state to its wider 'ethnic' groups across the Mediterranean helped to forge an identity, while for others the time of change from Ptolemies to Seleucids encouraged a restatement of Jewish identity. The themes of national identity had already begun in the Persian period but they seem to have sprung up with new vigour by the beginning of the second century.

In this respect perhaps the Hellenistic period is of great importance since the rivalry between the Hellenistic kingdoms stimulated a Jewish search for its own identity.

Israel Finkelstein examines the question of Jerusalem in the Persian Period and the Wall of Nehemiah. In his view, the archaeology of Jerusalem in the Persian (and Early Hellenistic) period – the size of the settlement and whether it was fortified – is crucial to understanding the history of the province of Yehud, the reality behind the Book of Nehemiah and the process of compilation and redaction of certain biblical texts. It is therefore essential to look at the finds free of preconceptions (which may stem from the account in the Book of Nehemiah) and only then attempt to merge archaeology and text. A considerable number of studies dealing with Jerusalem in the Persian period have been published in recent years. Although the authors were aware of the results of recent excavations, which have shown that the settlement was poor and limited to the eastern ridge (the City of David), they continued to refer to a meaningful, fortified 'city' with a relatively large population. All the scholars who dealt with the nature of Jerusalem in the Persian period based their discussion on the biblical text, mainly on the description of the reconstruction of the city-wall in Nehemiah 3. Intensive archaeological research in Jerusalem in the past 40 years has shown that:

1. The southwestern hill was part of the fortified city in the late Iron II and the Late Hellenistic periods.
2. The southwestern hill was not inhabited in the Persian and Early Hellenistic periods. The Persian and Early Hellenistic settlement should therefore be sought on the southeastern ridge – the City of David.

In the City of David, too, the evidence is fragmentary. Most finds from the Persian and Early Hellenistic periods were retrieved from the central part of the ridge, between Areas G and D of the Shiloh excavations. In the case of the City of David, too, the negative evidence is as important as the positive. No Persian or Early Hellenistic finds were retrieved in the southern tip of the ridge and from the area between the Temple Mount and Area G of the Shiloh excavations. The maximal size of the Persian and Early Hellenistic settlement was ca. 240 (N-S) × 120 (E-W) m, that is, ca. 20–25 dunams. Calculating the population according to the broadly accepted density coefficient of 20 people per one built-up dunam – a number which may be too high for what seems to have been a sparsely settled ridge – one reaches an estimated population of 400–500 people; that is, about 100 adult men.

Two finds in the field have been perceived as indications for the course of Nehemiah's city-wall: a wall excavated by Kenyon on the crest above the eastern slope of the City of David and a structure unearthed by Crowfoot on the western side of that ridge. Yet, both finds cannot be dated to the Persian period. Also, there is no indication for the renovation in the Persian period of the ruined late Iron II city wall. Therefore, there is no archaeological evidence for the city-wall of Nehemiah. Had it not been for the Nehemiah 3 account, no scholar would have argued for a Persian-period city-wall in Jerusalem. Another clue that Nehemiah 3 does not reflect Persian-period realities may be found in the archaeology of two of the three well-identified and excavated (rather than surveyed) sites mentioned in the list – Beth-zur and Gibeon. Beth-zur yielded only limited Persian period finds and Gibeon was not inhabited between the sixth century and the late-Hellenistic period.

So what is the historical reality behind the description of Nehemiah's rebuilding of the walls of Jerusalem? Scholars have noted the independent nature of the list in Nehemiah 3 as compared to the rest of the 'Nehemiah Memoir', but are divided on the question of whether Nehemiah used an earlier or a contemporary source that was kept in the Temple archives, or whether a later editor inserted the text into the Book of Nehemiah. Taking into consideration the archaeological evidence presented in this paper, an existing source from the Persian period, which described a genuine construction effort at that time, is not a viable option. We are left, therefore, with the following possibilities:

1. That the description in Nehemiah 3 is utopian; it was based on the geographical reality of the ruined Iron II city-wall but does not reflect actual work on the wall.
2. That a Persian-period author used an early source, which described the late 8th-century construction or a pre-586 renovation of the Iron II city-wall and incorporated it into the Nehemiah text.
3. That the description was inspired by the construction of the Late Hellenistic, Hasmonaean city-wall.

In 'Hyparchs, *Oikonomoi*, and Mafiosi: The Governance of Judah in the Ptolemaic Period', Lester L. Grabbe notes that there are no new sources for the Ptolemaic period. Almost all of what we have is material that was discovered, and much of it published, by the early twentieth century. All we can do is interpret what has been long known. A study of the context in which Judah existed is important for a possible understanding of her existence in the Ptolemaic empire. First, we need to be aware that the Ptolemies were pragmatic rather than dogmatic. Their concern was to collect as much revenue as possible. In Egypt, they set up a system that had a conventional configuration to it, but even here there is evidence that it was less systematic and more flexible than is sometimes appreciated. Secondly, they seem to have been willing to allow rather different administrative arrangements in the territories outside Egypt than those in Egypt itself. Thirdly, the Ptolemies were quite tolerant of the continuation of native customs and practices (e.g. the use of Demotic in the lower levels of the administration and the continuation of the Egyptian judicial system for Egyptians). Finally, this leads to the conclusion that we should not necessarily expect in Judah a replication of the system in Egypt itself. The question is, what indications do we have of the particular system in use in Palestine? In deciding this question we also need to keep in mind that no hard and fast distinction can be made between official systems and informal systems. Or, to put it another way, informal systems of governance might be as important as, or perhaps even more important than, the formal ones. For the administration of Palestine we have the following points arising from the sources:

- Hecataeus of Abdera indicates that the priests – the high priest in particular – were responsible for regulating, judging, and generally administering the community.
- The Zenon papyri show that local dignitaries of Syria and Palestine often had official or unofficial positions or at least possessed a confident independence in relation to the Ptolemaic officialdom. The most important was Tobias who headed a military colony, perhaps encompassing both cavalry and footsoldiers, in the 'land of Tobias'. The local man Jeddous (probably a Hebrew name and thus possibly in Judah) is ready to resist Zenon's man sent to collect a debt or to take the surety for it, while two Idumaean brothers are happy to try to extort money even from the *dioikētēs* of all Egypt.
- In the Tobiad Romance, the high priest represents the community to the Ptolemaic government and is responsible for paying a sum of money to Ptolemy (likely the regular taxes of Judah).
- The inscriptions of Ptolemy II show that a number of the normal Egyptian officers were a part of the administrative scene in Syria and Palestine, including the *oikonomos* (finance officer), the *kōmarchēs* (village head), and a higher *dioikōn tas kata Surian kai Phoiniken prosodous* (supervisor of the revenues in Syria and Phoenicia, though this last might be the same as the *dioikētēs* or the head of financial matters in Egypt).
- Judaic coinage in the early part of the third century (prior to about 269 BCE) might indicate a certain autonomy on the part of Judah in the early Ptolemaic period.
- The decree of Antiochus III shows that Judah was allowed to have a form of government to which it was accustomed. This included the native institution of the *gerousia* (council of elders). (The high priest is not specifically mentioned, which is a bit of a puzzle, but there are several possible explanations.)

The precise administrative arrangements for Palestine can only be conjectured, until direct primary evidence is found. But the information we
have so far indicates the following picture: Syria-Palestine, including
Judah, was incorporated into the Ptolemaic system of administration.
This emphasized the maximization of revenue, short of eroding the tax
base. Officials were appointed to oversee production and collect taxes.
For certain sorts of revenue the tax-farming rights were auctioned off. Yet
some of the traditional arrangements of the native peoples were allowed
to continue, and natives of the area were involved in all but perhaps the
highest levels of administration. For Judah, this meant that the high priest,
the priests as a whole and the *gerousia* were in some way a part of the
Ptolemaic administration of Judah. The high priest may have held certain
Ptolemaic offices, such as *oikonomos*, at various times during Ptolemaic
rule. We have indications, however, that alongside the official administration was an informal set of governance structures in which local strongmen
had a lot to say in how things were run. These structures may have had an
official status (e.g. in the case of Tobias), but in other cases the natives no
doubt acted like mafiosi. In either case, the local people seem to have had
a significant say in how their region was administered within the overall
Ptolemaic guidelines.

In 'King and Temple in 2 Maccabees: The Case for Continuity', Sylvie
Honigman points out that *2 Maccabees* is usually considered as illustrating a decisive shift in the history of Judaea, since it allegedly describes,
for the first time, the cultural conflict between Judaism and Hellenism.
However, the present paper contends that the terms *Ioudaismos* and
Hellenismos are used in *2 Maccabees* in a sense quite distinct from their
modern meanings. Modern readers implicitly share the belief that the
neologism 'Ioudaismos' was formed in imitation of 'Hellenismos', not
only in morphology, but also in content. In fact, the reverse is much more
plausible. As a native Judaean, the author of *2 Maccabees* must have
condensed traits of familiar experience in the term 'Ioudaismos', while
ascribing to 'Hellenismos', a derivative meaning, in order to create a
contrast which might be relevant in terms of his original worldview. As
the present paper argues, the daily reality epitomized in the neologism
Ioudaismos in *2 Maccabees* is the socio-political order that had been current in the temple state of Judaea since early Persian times, and which still
prevailed under the Seleucid dynasty. More precisely, *Ioudaismos* means
all that contributes to the regular operation of the temple, with a particular
emphasis on the material aspects. In this sense, *Ioudaismos* includes the
political and economic relations between the foreign king and the temple
of Jerusalem – in particular, the royal subsidies to the cult, the royal gifts,
and the tax exemptions granted by the king – which means that theology
and royal ideology are closely interrelated. The term *Hellenismos*, in this

view, encapsulates all the phenomena which the author sees as hindrances to the 'normal' operation of the traditional order. If we accept these two basic definitions, it becomes readily apparent that the cultural set according to which the author of *2 Maccabees* vilifies Antiochos IV is the 'traditional' royal ideology which had defined relations between (foreign) king and local temple ever since Persian times. From this perspective, the problem with Antiochos IV was that he was a 'wicked' king, and not that he was a 'Greek' king. To be sure, *2 Maccabees* offers some innovative statements as compared to the traditional worldview. However, the boldness of these statements can be properly assessed only if we admit that the author's worldview was basically traditional – by which is meant the situation inherited since the constitution of Judaea as a temple state under the Persians. Accordingly, the discussion is divided into two parts. Through an inquiry into the worldview of the author of *2 Maccabees*, the first shows that the socio-political and, hence, religious, order, described under the label of *Ioudaismos* in *2 Maccabees* was that inherited from Achaemenid rule.

Starting from the revised definition of the term *Hellenismos* in *2 Maccabees*, the second part reviews various phenomena which first appeared in Judaea after Alexander's conquest, suggesting that some changes are sometimes too hastily ascribed to the impact of 'Hellenization'. The discussion first offers a historiographical survey of the notion of 'cultural transfer' aimed at contextualizing the modern use of 'Hellenization'. The theoretical model which underlies its use, that of 'acculturation', has been heavily criticized. In effect, it presupposes a unidirectional influence, from one culture to the other, especially in cases of power imbalance – and relations between Greek settlers and natives in the Hellenistic East were indeed analyzed in this way – and focuses on the stronger side, from which the influence stems. In other words, the very label 'Hellenization' defines the Hellenic side of the relationship as the primary term of reference. It is the Greek definition of its own culture – *paideia* – which is taken as a reference point for the investigation of the impact of the cultural encounter between Greeks and non-Greeks in the Hellenistic East. Because of its biases, the model of 'acculturation' is now commonly replaced with that of 'interculturation', or 'cultural receptivity', which stresses the dynamics affecting the 'receiving' society, and not the 'giving' one. Studies in 'interculturation' have further shown that receiving cultures selectively borrow items which meet their own need: such 'needs' may be material, or symbolic. Moreover, they accept that various groups within the receiving culture may either borrow distinct items, or appropriate the same item in distinct ways. In consequence, we can no longer apprehend the process of 'Hellenization' in Judaea through the prism of Greek *paideia*, and the supposed cultural conception of their own identity by contemporary Greeks.

Therefore, an essential preliminary step to any study of the cultural impact of the establishment of a Graeco-Macedonian order in the Near East in general, and in Judaea in particular, is to identify in a more accurate way which items were borrowed from Greek culture, and to determine which needs, especially social and cultural, they met. Not all the changes which took place in the aftermath of Alexander's conquest need result from Greek cultural influence, even if we take this phrase in a broad sense and include in it, for example, the use of money, banking, or the mental traits associated with financial accounting in the Greek world. (1) The political and military instability which characterized the Hellenistic world triggered the first signs of disintegration of the 'embedded' society of Judaea into a 'complex' one, which resulted in the emergence of individualistic trends. Signs of this evolution are found in the emergence of an opposition to the high priest, and in the emergence of the religious 'sects'. Incidentally, the presentation of the events of the 160s adopted in *2 Maccabees* recaptures the way the social consequences of regional instability were beginning to be translated into theological terms. In this text, the high priest has clearly lost the exalted status he enjoyed in the Persian era (Mal. 2.6-7); (2) D. Schwartz has argued that the Exile period, and the subsequent creation of diaspora communities, had prompted a progressive spiritualizing of the notion of God's sovereignty. This theological trend was certainly given new inflections under the impact of Greek culture, but it originated in much earlier times. It would certainly have continued to evolve even without the influence of the Hellenistic schools of philosophy, since it met a real social need: the demographic expansion of the diaspora communities in early Hellenistic times.

Finally, the beginnings of conversion illustrate how old and new trends may be interwoven. The mass conversion of the Idumaeans and the Ituraeans, while assimilating the idea that a group may change its initial destiny during the course of its life, actually still exhibits a mentality typical of a segmented society, for which the various parts of the whole territory and its whole population need to be organically related to each other and to the cultic and ritual system. This kind of blatant contradiction in one and the same deed is, of course, typical of a transitional phase.

Aryeh Kasher makes a number of points in his 'Further Thoughts on Josephus' Report of Alexander's Campaign to Palestine (AJ, XI 304–347)':

1. According to main Graeco-Roman sources (i.e. Arrian, Plutarch and Curtius Rufus), Alexander's conquest of Syria and Palestine was carried out according to a well-thought military plan, and was represented as such in details by Alexander himself in a detailed speech before his headquarters, immediately after the victory in the battle of Issus (late October or early November 333 BCE). Following Arrian, the most

prominent and reliable source on Alexander, the campaign to Syria
and Palestine was by no means a marginal one, nor an incidental episode, but an outcome of a brilliant military strategy planned carefully
by a real genius. Alexander gave up the idea of pursuing the defeated
Persian army into the depth of Babylonia and Persia, in order to avoid
the dangerous possibility of a counter attack in his rear from the
direction of Syria, Phoenicia and Palestine. He preferred first to secure
his control of the eastern basin of the Mediterranean Sea (including
the conquest of Egypt), and only then to invade into the depth of the
Persian Empire. He was also eager to put his hands on the Persian war
treasury, which was kept in Damascus, hoping of course to solve his
severe logistical problems.

2. The presence of Macedonian troops in Palestine (including territories
    east of the Jordan River) is indirectly proved from different traditions
    on the establishments of the Hellenistic cities there, and the examples
    of Samaria, Pella, Dion and Gerasa are self-evident. The initiative
    of settling military colonies in those places was probably first taken
    by Perdiccas, one of Alexander's generals who was later counted
    among his heirs (the so-called Diadochi). Perdiccas intended to
    safeguard his hold of the region by settling down Macedonian troops
    in sensitive strategical sites, and thus to prevent unexpected uprisings.
    However, such insurrections broke out in the absence of Alexander
    while engaged in the conquest of Egypt, as well as in the foundation
    of Alexandria and in his royal visit to the famous Temple of Amon-Ra
    in the western desert oasis of Siva. Not by chance, this was also the
    timing of the outbreak of the Samaritan revolt against Alexander, so
    well echoed by Curtius Rufus and other sources.

3. The most important military goals laid upon the shoulders of
    Paramenion, the chief commander of Alexander at the time, was to
    take care of the regular food supplies to the Macedonian army that was
    engaged in the siege of Tyre. This Phoenician city was undoubtedly
    the most important and rather the main basis of the Phoenician fleet
    in the service of the Achaemenids. We shall not err in maintaining
    that the capture of the Tyre was a top military and political mission in
    Alexander's campaign to the East, and indeed this explains the enor-
    mous and long efforts to carry it out in seven months (January–July
    332 BCE).

4. A strict comparative analysis of Josephus' version of the Jewish-
    Samaritan conflict at the time (*Ant.* 11.297–303, 321–25) with the
    biblical evidence proves that they are obviously two different literary
    traditions, not identical at all, but complementary to each other. It is
    now clear that the Samaritan satrap Sanballat, who was mentioned
    in the Bible, could by no means be identified with the Sanballat

mentioned by Josephus. This very conclusion was first postulated by I. Spak already in 1911, but was generally rejected because of the common view that underestimated Josephus as a historian and discredited his report.

5.   By contrast, the total disqualification of Josephus' version, because of quasi-historical and literary contradictions, no longer stands the test of source criticism.

6.   The papyrological and numismatic evidence from Wadi Daliyeh clearly denote the existence of more than one Sanballat, so that Josephus' story was by no means anachronistic, as postulated by many scholars in the past.

7.   Alexander was not able to move towards Egypt immediately after the conquest of Gaza, since he was badly wounded and had in addition to be logistically prepared for the crossing of the Sinai desert in summertime. He must have done it in the autumn, when the heat was reduced. In any case, he could by no means cross the Sinai desert in seven days without taking prior care of water supplies and food for his army, not to mention that he personally was badly wounded by a stone missile in his shoulder! This is sufficient reason to think that he actually had also enough time to pay a visit to Jerusalem, a city which could ignite his intellectual curiosity by Greek philosophers like Hecataeus of Abdera who was counted among his devoted companions to the East.

8.   The meeting of Alexander with the Jewish high priest can pass very well the test of historic analysis.

9.   Alexander's political change when preferring an alliance with the Jews was the main cause that pushed the Samaritans into revolt.

10. Jews seemed to have profited from the annexation of some border territories to Judaea, approved by Alexander.

Summing up: it is worth pouring more credibility on Josephus' evidence on Alexander's campaign to Palestine, which is quite a misty chapter in the historic political transition from the Persian rule to the Greek one.

Amos Kloner gives 'The Introduction of the Greek Language and Culture in the Third Century BCE, According to the Archaeological Evidence in Idumaea'. During the fourth century, Aramaic was the lingua franca of Idumaea, which has now yielded 1,600 (unprovenanced) Aramaic ostraca, alongside well over 60 found in a proper archaeological context. Of the 1,300 names, about a third are Arabic, more than a quarter are Idumaean, another quarter West Semitic, and the rest Judahite and Phoenician (with about 1 per cent other ethnicities). About the same proportions are found in Maresha itself. Evidence for the use of Aramaic is found for the fifth to second centuries BCE, but Greek appears alongside Aramaic from the early third century (or possibly even the late fourth). Of the 950 coins found at Maresha, 135 are Ptolemaic (12 from Ptolemy I, 78 from Ptolemy II, and 26 from Ptolemy III to VIII). The burial caves of Hellenistic Maresha form a ring round the Lower City (outside the city limits). All the inscriptions in the burial chambers were written in Greek, which raises the major question: why did the local population (including Idumaeans) choose to use Greek rather than Aramaic for their burial inscriptions? All the dates in the Tombs 1 and 2 appear to be from the late Ptolemaic period (probably Ptolemy V, regnal years 1–5) and the Seleucid period. They are similar to Ptolemaic-period tombs at Alexandria and have mainly Greek sepulchral elements. Of particular interest is a burial tomb from Khirbet Za'aquqa in what was evidently a village or farmhouse. It contained about 20 separate graffiti, from which 33 names could be read. The onomasticon is purely Greek with no identifiable regional characteristics (such as Idumaean, Arab, or Judahite names) and may be ascribed to Greek settlers who arrived in the early Hellenistic period – a date supported by both the material culture remains found in the tomb and the one date found in the graffiti, which is the twelfth year of Ptolemy II (272/271 BCE). During the three or four generations the tomb was in use, there is no sign of intermingling with local Idumaeans or other Semitic groups. This seems to be evidence for a completely Hellenized population. At the beginning of the third century BCE the Greek language had become widely used among the local populations of Idumaea, as attested by the names inscribed in the tombs of Marisa and Za'aquqa. Greek presumably reached Marisa directly from Alexandria, and it is amazing how quickly it became used in the daily life of Idumaea.

Oded Lipschits discusses 'Jerusalem between Two Periods of Greatness: The Size and Status of the City in the Babylonian, Persian and Early Hellenistic Periods'. His aim is to present the archaeological material from Jerusalem to consider its size and status in the sixth and fifth–fourth centuries, and in the Early Hellenistic period. In the years between 586 and 167 BCE Judah was a small province under the rule of great empires. Jerusalem became again the *Birah* of the province only in the middle of the fifth century BCE. In contrast with the rich and well-recognized architectural remains from the seventh as well as from the second centuries BCE, not many building-remains from the Persian and early Hellenistic periods have been uncovered in Judah or Samaria. This is the case even in sites where abundant pottery sherds, stamp impressions, figurines and other typical Persian period finds were uncovered. Under the Assyrian, Babylonian and Persian rule there was a marked process of attenuation in urban life in Judah. The administrative and urban centres that survived those periods were small and weak in comparison with their state before the sixth century or after the second century BCE. We should also accept Stern's claim that the scarcity of building-remains from the Persian period does not reflect the actual situation at that time, but is the outcome of incomplete archaeological data. The topographical nature of the south-eastern hill in Jerusalem requires that buildings be built on bedrock, which requires previous buildings to be removed. This is why archaeological remains of the sixth–third centuries have been found mainly in pockets or dumps down the valley.

The 586 BCE destruction of Jerusalem appears prominently in the excavations over the site. The force of the destruction and the degree of demographic decline with regard to the city are there to see. The city remained desolate and deserted for the next 50 years, evidently as a result of Babylonian policy. Although the Persians supported trade cities along the coast, they did not encourage urban centres in the hill country. Not many building-remains from the Persian period have been found in the boundaries of Yehud. As in many other sites, also in most of the excavated areas at the city of David, many finds from the Persian period (pottery sherds and stamp impressions) were discovered. However, in most cases these finds were not linked to any clear stratum or architectural finds. The dating of the few finds on the Western Hill (especially the *yehud* stamp impressions) leads to the conclusion that it was uninhabited during the Persian and Early Hellenistic period. Most of the pottery sherds and stamp impressions from the City of David dated to the Persian period were discovered, however, during Kenyon and Shiloh's excavations along the eastern slope: in Area G, Area E, Area D, and in the excavations of Reich and Shukron south of Area D. Only area G of Shilo's excavations revealed many finds from the Persian period that are also related to architectural remains. In this area, Shiloh identified a clear stratum (Stratum 9) on top of Stratum 10A (the stratum of the Babylonian destruction), and under Strata 8–7 that are dated to the Hellenistic period. In Area E three different stages of Stratum 9 were distinguished. The dating, the location, and the long line along the eastern slope of the ridge of quarrying refuse are all indications of the missing Persian period wall. The finds on the ridge of the City of David and on the slopes provide evidence for a poor but existing settlement in the Persian period.

Despite the relatively massive finds, the information available to us about the Persian period is still very scant, and there is no possibility of characterizing the nature of this occupation. The major find uncovered outside of the line of fortification built on the rock at the top of the eastern slope and its stratigraphic context has not been proven. As against other assumptions it seems to me that the remains from the Persian period were spread all along the City of David, and the areas where these finds were not discovered are the areas where intensive building activities were conducted during the Hellenistic-Roman and later periods. This is also the case as regards the Ophel. In this large area between the Temple enclosure and the City of David very intensive building activities were conducted in later periods, and the area was cleaned to the bedrock more than once. The minimum built-up area in the Persian period should be calculated, therefore, as covering only the City of David, about 350 m from north to south and about 80–100 m from east to west (ca. 28–30 dunams). To this must be added the 20 dunams of the Ophel, as the main built-up area. If we will use the accepted density coefficient of 25 people per one built-up dunam, one reaches an estimated population of 1,000–1,250 people. Jerusalem did not become a real urban centre before the Hellenistic period: the 'return to Zion' was a slow and gradual process. In this case it is no wonder that no such wall was discovered and securely dated to the Persian period, but the absence of the find should not serve the argument that the story in Nehemiah is a fiction. This would be too hasty.

Menachem Mor discusses 'The Samaritans in Transition from the Persian to the Greek Period', i.e. about 350 to 200 BCE. The main source is Josephus' *Antiquities* (11.302–407), with the assumption that despite all the difficulties, Josephus has a trustworthy historical resonance in the parts that concern the Samaritans. There are also valuable archaeological finds. The focus will be on four main areas:

1. The building of the Samaritan temple. Josephus testifies that it was built by Sanballat with the permission of Alexander the Great. One Delos inscription is dated to the mid-third century BCE. The *Prayer of Joseph* from Qumran, dated to the second century BCE, seems directed at the Samaritan temple. The Elephantine papyri show that government approval was needed for erection of a temple. However, Josephus is mistaken that Alexander approved the building of the temple; rather, Sanballat took advantage of the unstable situation to erect the temple, without seeking anyone's approval. The recent volumes by Y. Magen (with H. Misgav and L. Tsfania [2004] and Magen 2008a; 2008b) argues from archaeology that the Samaritan temple was built in 445 BCE by Sanballat the Horonite. The main argument against Magen is the argument from silence, the silence of the book of Nehemiah about any such temple. The coins prove only that Gerizim was a sacred site, not that a temple stood there. The archaeological finds do not support any exact date for the founding of the temple. The leaders of the Elephantine community address their letter to Bagohi the governor and to Delaiah and Shelamaiah (sons of Sanballat). If there was a Samaritan temple, would not they have addressed it to its high priest? Finally, the inscriptions published by Magen, et al., are all from the Hellenistic period.

2. The Samaritan leadership. During this time Samaria was governed by the Sanballat family, with Sanballat I in the time of Nehemiah and Sanballat III as the last government. The latter persuaded his son-in-law

Manasseh (who was in line for the Jerusalem high priesthood) not to
leave his daughter by promising him a temple on Gerizim. The victories of Alexander allowed the temple to be built. Alexander brought
the Sanballat governance of Samaria to an end with the appointment
of Andromachus as governor, but the Samaritans revolted and killed
him. Alexander punished them heavily, as partially attested by the
Wadi Daliyeh papyri: the Samaritans had lost political autonomy.
3. Part of the punishment was expulsion of the inhabitants of the city
    of Samaria. Most of them went to Shechem, which was an unwalled
    city and sparsely inhabited in the Persian period (though a Persian
    military outpost at the time). The sudden growth of the city in the
    fourth century BCE can be put down to this transfer of population from
    Samaria.
4. Land disputes with the Jews. Josephus quotes Hecataeus of Abdera
    to the effect that Alexander gave Samaritan territory to the Jews. This
    issue has been much debated because it has a remarkable parallel
    with the gift of three Samaritan provinces to Judaea by the Seleucid
    Demetrius II (*1 Macc.* 10.30; 11.30–36). Josephus refers to friction
    between Jews and Samaritans in the time of Onias (*Ant.* 12.156).
    Does Josephus distinguish between Σαμαρεύς and Σαμαρείτις?
    Some have argued that he meant the inhabitants of the city of Samaria,
    but there is evidence that he uses both terms for the Samaritan sect.
    The evidence dates the events to the time of Onias II (240–218
    BCE). Onias hoped for the change of regime from the Ptolemies to
    the Seleucids. The defeat of Seleucus II and the visit of Ptolemy III
    to Jerusalem meant that Onias lost his position as a tax collector.
    Similarly, Ptolemy IV probably removed Joseph Tobiad as tax col-
    lector and gave the office to his son Hyrcanus. During this time the
    Samaritans remained loyal to the Ptolemies and were rewarded by
    having the three border districts returned to them.

John Ray examines 'The Alphabet that Never Was: A Possible Egyptian
Influence on the Near East'. Surprisingly little Egyptian influence on
Hebrew Bible literature has been discovered up to the present. A recent
suggestion is to find 'ibis' in Job 38.36. This might be relevant for the
origins of the alphabet. Although the Egyptian writing system contains
many ideograms, it also has 25–30 signs that stand for sounds – a sort of
alphabet. Papyrus Saqqâra 27 is a Demotic papyrus that pictures different
birds; each bird is in a bush that begins with the same sound ('letter') as
the bird, and the bird flies to a location also beginning with that sound.
The editors suggested that this included the original order of the Egyptian
alphabet and had been written to help, in some way, apprentice scribes.
The first bird in the list seems to be the ibis (*hb* in Egyptian), which

gives a remarkable parallel to Plutarch's statement that the Egyptian 'alphabet' had the ibis as its first letter. Flinders Petrie had already found a list in Tanis that gave the hieroglyphic 'letters' in the same order as the Saqqâra list. The order of the first three letters is H, R/L, Ḥ, giving the name HLḤ alphabet (instead of ABC). The remains of what seems to be a 'hieroglyphic dictionary' (Papyrus Carlsberg 7) gives the ibis as its first entry and seems to give the same order of the other letters as found in the Saqqâra text. Yet these texts are all late, from the Greek or Roman periods. Is this 'alphabet' really Egyptian? Joachim Quack has recently demonstrated that this Egyptian alphabet has the letters in the same order as the original Epigraphic South Arabian script. What is more, the Egyptian lists omit the letter *f*, a letter very characteristic of Egyptian but absent from ESA. A text found in Beth-Shemesh (in 1933 but only recently deciphered) and a Ugaritic text (*KTU* 9.426) turn out to have alphabets of the HLḤ type. These texts take the HLḤ alphabet back to the second millennium BCE. The question is where it originated. If it originated in Arabia as some think, why would the Egyptians use it in the late period when the normal Semitic and Greek alphabets were widespread in their environment? And what more natural letter to begin with than the ibis, sacred to the scribal god Thoth? But what of the missing *f*? Oddly, it may be because no bird began with an *f* in Demotic. The occurrence of the HLḤ alphabet in Arabia, Beth-Shemesh, and Ugarit could be explained by sea trade routes.

In 'Empires and Farmers', Eveline van der Steen explores the impact that power changes within a region or country have on the local population. The information available from the Islamic conquest and especially in the eighteenth to early twentieth centuries is much more extensive than that from the Persian and Hellenistic periods. It will help us to understand the possibilities and may allow us to draw conclusions about the earlier changes in power, such as the transition from Persian to Greek rule. The Islamic invasion may have been relatively peaceful. The decline of towns had apparently begun in the Byzantine period and continued under Islamic rule, but the large increase in small sites in the early Islamic period is the result of the Islamic conquest. Large-scale changes in territory were not unusual in the tribal history of the Near East, from a variety of causes. The change from the Umayyad to Abbasid government in 750 resulted in a general decline of Palestine and increase in the nomadic element. In the factional fighting in Palestine during the transition from the Abbasid to the Fatimid dynasty, the Tay tribes established a powerbase. Tay tribes were involved in fighting during the Crusader invasion, and in the change from the Mamluks to the Ottomans, most of the tribes were ruling only limited territory in Palestine. The Ottoman Empire reached its zenith in the sixteenth century. Palestine and Jordan were densely populated and productive in agriculture, though a decline set in at the end of the sixteenth century. The Jordanian tribes were often rebellious. Increased taxes led to a serious decline at the beginning of the eighteenth century, with depletion of villages and agricultural production. Attempts were made to take power in different parts of Palestine. Zaher al Umar in Galilee in the first half of the eighteenth century, extended his rule because of the demand by European traders for local cotton. But he came to be seen as a rebel by the Ottoman government and was killed. He was succeeded by Ahmed Al-Jezzar who was the official Ottoman governor. He turned Palestine into a well-organized province and curbed the power of the Bedouin. But his rapacious financial squeezing led to a decline of the region and even revolts. Around 1800 his successor Saleiman Pasha changed to a kind of laissez faire politics which protected the large towns and trade routes but allowed the Bedouin tribes to exploit other areas which ceased to be under effective government control. With the Wahabi invasion the Ottomans turned to Muhammad Ali Pasha. He stopped the Wahabis but then took over Palestine and expanded his rule. His suppression of the local Bedouin tribes brought them under control but destroyed part of the local economy. But it also allowed peasant agriculture to flourish. Eventually, some of the Bedouin tribes revolted but were suppressed. At the beginning of the twentieth century various tribal confederations were attempting to establish power against a weakening Ottoman Empire. World War I brought many out on the Allied side against the Ottomans, and being on the winning side brought rewards.

These examples illustrate two forms of power changes. One ignores the local population and structures; the other attempts to use them for their own ends. Alongside this are changes from within (by local rulers) and changes from without. The two patterns do not coincide since outsiders sometimes make use of the local situation and tribes. Interestingly, power changes that suppressed the Bedouin tribes often led to increased settlement and agricultural activity. But in the long run, power changes that ignored local structures led to general decline. The existing social and tribal structures were exploited in the various internal power changes within the Islamic Empire. This was clearest during World War I when both the Ottomans and the British tried to gain the support of local tribes. The 'winning tribes' changed the local structure to their advantage. Those who said the land was different from the people have often changed local organization to encourage increased production and growth in villages and farmsteads. But when the 'conquerors'' demands became greater, as they usually did, the people often revolted or fled across the borders, and the apparent prosperity disappeared.

Loren Stuckenbruck ('Early Enochic Tradition and the Restoration of Humanity: The Function and Significance of *1 Enoch* 10') investigates a passage from the *Book of Watchers* (*1 Enoch* 1–36) that is often referred to as a 'conversion of all nations'. The general view remains that this passage predicts the conversion of the Gentiles already in the third century BCE. The questions that arise from this statement will be examined within a three-fold framework: (1) The nations in the Hebrew Bible: passages speak of coming to Jerusalem for instruction, to walk in God's paths (Isa. 2.3), bring gifts to Jerusalem (Isa. 18.7) and be subservient to Israel and recognize Yhwh (Isa. 45.14-15), and even worship Yhwh in Jerusalem (Isa. 66.23; Ps. 22.27), and so on. The implication is that Israel will become the head of the nations, with the divine presence in Jerusalem; however, it is never suggested that the nations will be 'converted' or become part of the chosen people; (2) The role and function of 10.21 in the Book of Watchers: *1 Enoch* 6–11 seems to be Noachic, a distinct element in the *Book of Watchers*. It associates the time of Noah with eschatalogical time, which is bound up with the fate of the fallen angels. It is their teachings and actions that lead to sin and bad activities on the part of humans. The mass of humanity was created by God and to be distinguished from the demonic aspects of the world. Hence, humans as such will participate in the 'new heavens and the new earth' to come in the eschaton, of which the new beginning after the flood was an archetype. The author is not simply equating the objectionable aspects of culture with Alexander the Great's successors; the demonic is broader than this; (3) *1 Enoch* 10.21 in the Enoch tradition and in Second Temple literature: in *1 Enoch* 11–16 the concept is extended into the Enochic tradition, but in 17–36 the focus comes more onto human participation in sin, with the fallen angels tradition becoming less prominent. The second century BCE traditions (*Apocalypse of Weeks*, *Epistle of Enoch*, and the *Animal Apocalypse*) refer to a turning of the Gentiles, drawing on ideas from both *1 Enoch* 5 and 10, while the Watchers have all but disappeared from the tradition. Human responsibility for sin is emphasized. Although the *Animal Apocalypse* shows Gentiles negatively, towards the end of the vision the nations go through a three-stage reconciliation towards Israelites, obeying their commands, gathering together in 'the house', and a final transformation into 'white bulls'. The conversion of the Gentiles takes place through a divine act of recreating the human race. This text was addressing the wider challenges for Jewish self-definition being posed by Hellenization. It is only one of several texts from the third century BCE that envisaged the conversion of Gentiles.

Oren Tal considers '"Hellenistic Foundations" in Palestine'. Because we lack direct evidence of Ptolemaic and Seleucid foundations, it has been conventional to rely on name changes to indicate a new foundation. Ptolemaïs (versus the original name of Acco) is a good example; another is Scythopolis (versus Beth-Shean). Other possible sites are Philoteria

(Beth-Yeraḥ) and Philadelphia (Rabat-Ammon). Joppa seems to have been refounded when the city struck coins with a ligatured monogram indicating the name Iope. Other cities apparently founded anew – as indicated by coinage – were Gaza, Ascalon (Ashkelon), and Dora (Dor). Considering that Jerusalem was the only Ptolemaic mint issuing silver fractions on the Attic weight (under Ptolemy I and II), it may also have been refounded about 301 BCE. Victor Tcherikover first defined the *polis* in relation to Hellenistic Palestine. He believed that the coastal cities became *poleis* under the Ptolemies, but Gideon Fuks argued that this change of status came about only under the Seleucids. Fergus Miller, on the contrary, found evidence for *poleis* only in the Roman period. According to Fuks, the numismatic evidence contradicts Miller's interpretation. Fuks' theory that the right to strike autonomic coins was a centralized Seleucid policy would mean that only a few cities were *poleis*: Ptolemaïs, Ascalon, and Gaza. The other cities that minted coins had an unclear status. Since autonomic coins were used only within their cities and the immediate locality, the new issue of autonomic coinage by a municipality was a reflection of a change in status. But this does not demonstrate adoption of Greek customs or the existence of a Greek (re)foundation. What about other epigraphic evidence? The title *agoranomos* on lead weights and other objects is an indication, but most royal edicts relate to hierarchical structure and not status of the city. From an archaeological point of view, new fortifications were built in some sites in the Hellenistic period and in others existing fortifications were refurbished. In each case they followed local building traditions, and Greek elements (if present at all) tend to be limited to decoration. This lack of buildings in the Greek style supports Miller's position. The Hellenistic and Palestinian *poleis* have their own content different from the classical *polis*; similarly, the roots of the *polis* are different from the ancient Near Eastern urban settlements. To summarize, in most cases the Hellenistic foundation in Palestine was the refoundation of an existing urban settlement. Many of these were coastal sites (Jerusalem was an exception) and most had an Achaemenid past rather than being a new foundation.

The article, 'Will the Greek Texts Stand Up, Please?', by Lena-Sofia Tiemeyer, provides a brief overview of the various prophetic texts that are normally viewed as stemming from the late Persian and early Hellenistic period (400–200 BCE). Its primary aim is to elucidate and evaluate the criteria used to date these texts. Three chief criteria have been used: linguistic features (including characteristics of Late Biblical Hebrew [LBH] and Greek loans), historical references (including Greek place names and references to Greece and to post-Alexander events), and context. A recent criterion is that relating to eschatology and apocalyptic, which are generally associated with the Hellenistic period or later. We have a relatively scanty knowledge of early Hellenistic Judah because of lack of contemporary sources from Judah itself. Jerusalem was captured four times under Ptolemy I, and Judah belonged to the Ptolemaic empire for a century, during which time there were five 'Syrian Wars' between the Ptolemies and the Seleucids. The rest of the article provides a survey of texts alleged to be Hellenistic by at least some scholars:

Isaiah: It has been suggested that the Oracles Against the Nations (18–25) were partially updated to match events in the Hellenistic period. The Isaiah Apocalypse (24–27) has been dated over a period from the eighth to the second centuries BCE, based on the five criteria of (1) eschatology versus apocalypse; (2) identification of the city destroyed in 24.10-12; (3) the identification of Leviathan and the Sea Monster (27.1); (4) the interpretation of 25.10 and the destruction of Moab; (5) the references to Assyria and Egypt (27.12-13). Is it 'proto-apocalyptic' or full-blown apocalypse? Are the references to Assyria and Egypt coded symbols for the Seleucid and Ptolemaic realms? Allusions to events 'discovered' in the text range from the fall of Babylon to Cyrus or to Alexander, the destruction of Samaria by the Macedonians about 331 BCE, the fall of Moab to the Nabataeans in the early third century BCE, and the razing of Samaria by John Hyrcanus in 107 BCE. A recent argument puts Third Isaiah (56–66) at the end of the fourth century, relating references to the sabbath and the destruction of the temple (64.10) to Ptolemy I's capture of Jerusalem in 302/301 BCE. Yet the arguments to date the chapters to the period later than the sixth century are not convincing, especially the explanation of 64.9-10. Agatharchides of Cnidus described the capture of Jerusalem but not its destruction.

Ezekiel: There are significant differences between the MT and LXX of the book. If the LXX is earlier – as many think – its translation in the third century would suggest that the MT was a Greek-period development, though not every oracle in the book would be this late. Some have seen specific references to the Hellenistic period in Ezekiel 7.

Zechariah 9–14: Several different Hellenistic backgrounds have been proposed: (1) time of Alexander the Great; (2) wars of the Diodochi; (3) Ptolemaic province of Judah; (4) period of the invasion and conquest of Judah by Antiochus III; (5) time of the Maccabaean revolt. Given the wide diversity of interpretation, based on supposed historical allusion, can this method of dating be satisfactory?

Joel: A good deal depends on whether one thinks the book is a unity or to be divided into two main redactional layers. The key passages are 4.6 (ET 3.6), 4.17 (ET 3.17), and 4.19 (ET 3.19). It also has been dated to the time of Ptolemy I.

Themes and Topics

NB: please note that in the following discussion, references to articles within the present volume are indicated by putting the author's surname in small caps.

All the essays in this volume relate in one way or the other to Judah in the late Persian or early Hellenistic period, but some focus on particular themes with a wider context while others are more specifically about Judah. Both types of essays are ultimately relevant in understanding Judah and the Jews in this time.

Judah in the Transition Period

One way of trying to understand Judah in this transitional period from Persian to Greek rule is by looking at other periods of Palestinian history: a major comparison would be Palestine under Islamic rule (VAN DER STEEN). The long history of Islamic control shows many examples of two main power changes. The first would ignore the local population and structures and impose rule from the centre; the other would attempt to exploit the local situation for its own ends. On the whole, those that ignored the local situation led to decline over time, whatever the seeming immediate benefit. For example, suppressing the Bedouin tribes often increased settlement and agricultural production for a time, but in the long run it caused a decline in the region. This happened in the eighteenth and early nineteenth centuries. In the other scenario, in which the local peoples and structures might be enlisted by both insiders and outsiders, the local people themselves might respond by making changes that increased their advantages. This happened during World War I when both the British and the Ottomans courted the local tribes. But when the demands of the overlords became too great (for instance, when tax demands were too high), the people might revolt or flee, causing a drastic decline in the local prosperity. The implications are not spelled out by VAN DER STEEN, but we can make our own deductions. One of them is that the Ptolemies wanted to maximize income but were also careful not to erode their tax base (GRABBE). This seems to be one of the reasons that they used tax farmers. The Ptolemies also worked with local people and maintained local systems as long as they worked. This is why the high priest continued to have a high profile in Judah.

Many questions about Judah during the Ptolemaic period remain unanswered. One of these is the question of how the region was administered (GRABBE). Surprisingly, we know much more about the Ptolemaic administration in Egypt than in Palestine, mainly because of the abundant finds of papyri in the former region. One general policy pursued by the Ptolemaic government was to avoid interfering with arrangements that seemed to work. This suggests that the administration known from the Persian period was likely to have continued under Ptolemaic rule. This indeed seems to be the case, from our limited sources (which are not generally as reliable as the relevant papyri in the Egyptian homeland). This suggests that there was considerable autonomy at the local level but also for the region as a whole.

Whether Judah or the Coele-Syrian region was organized as a province is not known. There are no references to a governor as such, though one might be inferred from one or two sources. With regard to Judah itself, it appears that the main figure was the high priest, who not only held the leading religious post but also seems to have acted as the chief administrator in the eyes of the Ptolemaic government. Unfortunately, we have no primary documents that relate to the high priest in that role, but a number of secondary sources (Hecataeus of Abdera, the Tobiad Romance, Josephus) accord the high priest the task of acting as the Jewish representative to the Ptolemies and the Ptolemaic representative to the inhabitants of Judah. Yet it appears that he was assisted by a 'council' (*gerousia*) made up of the leading priests, nobles and ranking elders. Whether he collected the taxes directly, to be forwarded to the next layer of the Ptolemaic administration is not certain, but there are indications that he indeed did so.

The weakness of our literary (mostly secondary) sources for Palestine are nevertheless evident in light of some inscriptional data. These indicate that an economic official (*oikonomos*) for the region existed and that under him were similar officials for the various sub-regions. Unfortunately, we have no clear indication of what sub-regions existed, but it is reasonable that Judah was one (unless it was itself divided into more than one sub-region). The important point is that none of our literary sources contain any suggestion of these officials, leaving us with a blank slate when it comes to knowing exactly how the system worked and also showing us the limits of relying on Greek and Jewish literary sources of the period. No doubt the Ptolemaic government was mainly concerned that it received its appropriate amount of taxation. But as noted above, literary sources indicate that the high priest was responsible for collecting and handing over the taxes. Perhaps he held – at least, some of the time – the office of *oikonomos*. Of course, we might be witnessing a certain amount of evolution of the system in the differences between sources.

A good example to illustrate some of the difficulties in trying to evaluate sources can be found in the story Josephus gives us about Alexander's visit to Jerusalem (KASHER). An evaluation of the story brings into play the whole panoply of source analysis, literary licence and Jewish memory versus Greek memory. One of the problems we have is relating administrative documents to literary sources. The Egyptian papyri have yielded many of the former, but Jewish literature is mainly made up of literary narratives. This story of Alexander also raises questions of pro-Jewish propaganda. See below for a further discussion of this account.

Hellenism and Hellenization

One of the most emotive subjects in much writing on Jews and Judaism of this period is that of Hellenism. It is also a subject on which there are strong opinions that are not necessarily backed up with evidence. A full treatment of the subject is naturally beyond the scope of this Introduction, but some of the issues arising out of the articles in the present volume are briefly discussed here (for a more detailed treatment of Hellenism, with extensive bibliography, see Grabbe 2008: 125–65 [ch. 6]).

We first have the question of the terms *Ioudaismos* and *Hellenismos* (HONIGMAN). Both of these terms occur in *2 Maccabees* and have normally been considered as marking a sign of cultural conflict. Since *Hellenismos* is a known term in Greek usage, commentators have usually begun their discussions with it. Yet we have to keep in mind that the Jewish author had his own concerns and outlook. It seems rather that the one who composed *2 Maccabees* began with the term *Ioudaismos*, which included the temple cult, the Jewish way of doing things, the Seleucid concessions to Jewish customs, royal support and the like (which also means that the theology of *2 Maccabees* is closely interrelated to traditional royal ideology). He then defined *Hellenismos* in the light of that concept. To his mind this meant everything that hindered or attacked any aspect of *Ioudaismos*; that is, it was not primarily concerned with aspects of Hellenistic culture but with measures or actions against 'Judaizing', regardless of what this had to do with Hellenization. This is important because the criticism of Antiochus IV was not primarily based on antipathy to Greek culture but to actions of the king that were regarded as those of 'the wicked king'. Judah had a long history of rule under both native and foreign kings, and a strong ideological element was the labelling of kings as 'good' or 'bad'. The image and criticism of Antiochus IV could just as easily been given under Achaemenid rule as Greek. Antiochus was not condemned because he was Greek but because he was 'a bad king'.

This leads to a second consideration, namely, that the Jewish engagement with Hellenization was one of 'interculturation' (HONIGMAN). As so often with a subordinate people confronted by a new dominant culture, the Jews adopted from the Greeks what they found useful, whether material or symbolic. They were not being overwhelmed with an 'acculturation' (or 'cultural imperialism') process, as so often assumed in past treatments. It is important to catalogue what items of Greek culture were actually taken over and in what way, because the borrowed cultural aspects might well be adapted or appropriated in particular ways. They borrowed, not because of being forced but because those elements that they took over served to meet their own needs, both social and cultural.

The changes among the Jews at this time were by no means all due to Greek cultural influence. Part of what we see is not the result of 'Hellenization' as such but the consequence of the evolution of Jewish society, which might be described in anthropological terms as the move from a 'segmentary' to a 'complex' society (HONIGMAN). A consequence of this was the development of more individualized trends. These trends included the rise of 'sects' in the wake of challenges to the authority of the high priest. Another was a progressive spiritualizing of the concept of God's sovereignty, perhaps a consequence of the flourishing Jewish diaspora. A third trend was the mass conversion of neighbouring peoples, the Idumaeans and Ituraeans, though it shows an attitude still based on the segmentary society. This could indicate that Judahite society was still in a transitional phase of development.

The Hellenistic foundations in Palestine provide an interesting instance of how complicated the situation of Hellenization was (TAL). It is not always easy to determine whether or when a Greek foundation had been created, though autonomous coinage is one indication. Most *poleis* were refoundations of urban settlements that had already existed in the Persian period. The vast majority were coastal sites, though there were exceptions, such as Jerusalem. Yet the architecture of administration and other official buildings was not usually Greek, except perhaps in decoration, but the style and mode of construction known locally. There were few new Hellenistic foundations in Palestine.

Language and Literature in the Transition Period
A significant feature of Hellenization was language. Several of our contributors touched on the language issue. We can take it for granted that the common language in Palestine during this period was Aramaic, which is well attested, yet we also have evidence of Greek. KLONER points to the situation in Maresha/Marisa where Aramaic is known from the fifth to second centuries, but Greek is also documented alongside Aramaic from at least the third century and possibly the fourth. Furthermore, the burial inscriptions (dating from the late Ptolemaic and Seleucid periods) are always in Greek. The inscriptions (all in Greek) in the tomb at Khirbet Za'aquqa (a village or farmstead near Maresha) contain 33 names, all of which are purely Greek with no indication of local identification, over several generations. This suggests a Greek population, probably a colony of some sort. Yet the use of Greek among the local Idumaean population is also attested from the early third century, as noted.

Another linguistic innovation in the Hellenistic period occurs in the area of the Egyptian hieroglyphic alphabet (RAY). This is the so-called

HLH alphabet. A text from Beth-Shemesh has recently been identified as being written in this alphabet. Yet it is also known from a Ugaritic text, which makes its origins in the second millennium. The alphabetic order is the same as the Epigraphic South Arabian script, which might give it an Arabian origin. This raises the question of why it was being used at a time when the Semitic and Greek alphabets were widespread in the region. There might be something about the coming of the Greeks that stimulated this usage, which would make it another illustration of the novel developments arising from this.

A variety of Jewish literature, including some of the biblical books, seems to have arisen during the late Persian or early Hellenistic period. One contribution surveys the biblical prophetic books that have been thought to originate during this time (TIEMEYER). Isaiah 18–25 seems to have been updated to take account of events in the Hellenistic period. Isaiah 24–27 has been dated ranging from the fall of Babylon to the razing of Samaria about 107 BCE. However, the arguments for dating Third Isaiah (56–66) later than the sixth century are unconvincing. The Greek version of Ezekiel is often thought to be earlier than the Hebrew text, which would put both in the Greek period. Ezekiel 7 is often seen as referring to the Hellenistic period. Zechariah 9–14 has been dated to such a wide range of dates, from Alexander to the Maccabees, that alleged historical allusions seem questionable. For Joel the question of unity is an important one; it has been dated to the time of Ptolemy I.

From the perspective of Jewish theology, there was also innovation, which can be discussed with regard to *1 Enoch* 10.21, a passage widely interpreted as envisaging the conversion of Gentiles (STUCKENBRUCK). The idea that non-Jews would recognize Yhwh and worship him is not completely new, since some passages in the Hebrew Bible seem to have this in mind (e.g. Isa. 18.7; 45.14-15; Ps. 22.27). Yet at a time when Judah and its inhabitants were under foreign domination, not only *1 Enoch* 10.21 but other texts seem to believe that the Gentiles would eventually stand alongside the Jews in honouring and obeying the true God. It may be that this text was addressing the wider challenges for Jewish self-definition being posed by Hellenization. The Hellenistic age would certainly have raised the question in the mind of pious but self-reflective Jews.

Jewish Identity

The question of Jewish identity has exercised modern scholars – perhaps rather more so than ancient Judahites. The literature of this period (Ezra-Nehemiah, Chronicles, Zechariah, Malachi) often identifies the people with Israel, yet references in non-Jewish literature and Jewish writings aimed at outsiders refer exclusively to 'Ιουδαῖοι (or *Yĕhûdîm*), variously translated as 'Jews', 'Judaeans', and 'Judahites', and Jewish writings also often use the term (Nehemiah, Esther). This term centres on those who lived in Yehud/Judah/Judaea, but it is also clearly an ethnic term that applies to people who originated in Judah but lived elsewhere, perhaps for generations. Thus, the colony at Elephantine is known as 'Judahites' (*Yĕhûdāyā*'), and 'Ιουδαῖοι is the term used widely in the Egyptian and other Greek papyri for the people who had lived there for centuries (see further Grabbe 2008: 153–5). Such ethnic terms and identifications were common in the ancient world.

James AITKEN suggests it is not clear that there was a Jewish identity in the Persian period since 'Yehud' was an administrative term. True, there had long been a 'kingdom of Judah' in the same area (note also the use of the term 'Judaeans/Judahites' for the members of the Elephantine community). The question, however, is how subjects of the kings of Judah saw their identity (also the members of the Elephantine community). The issue of identity may not be so much a matter of internal concerns but external political factors: it may be that rivalry between the Ptolemies and Seleucids stimulated the search for an identity. Also, a large diaspora community which still looked to Judah and Jerusalem as its 'home' or 'mother city' would have contributed.

AITKEN refers to Hecataeus of Abdera who gives us our first description of the Jews in the Greek period. The authenticity of this quotation has been questioned recently, but when all the facts are considered, the passage seems most probably an actual statement by Hecataeus of Abdera (Grabbe 2008: 113–19, 283–6). Here we have the Jews described as an *ethnos* but also as a 'colony' of people who are said to come from Egypt. The centre of their polity is a temple, and the nation is led by priests, with a high priest as head of state. Likewise, Ben Sira emphasizes the temple and Jerusalem as God's dwelling place. This indicates that religion was already an issue with regard to the Jews at the time.

When the issue of religion comes into it, however, things become more complicated. Ethnicity and religion often went together, in that certain ethnic groups were thought to favour a particular god. Indeed, this is implied in Hecataeus' statement that the Jews worshipped the 'heaven that surrounds the earth'. Thus, religion and ethnicity could go together, but this is not to say that Iudaoios was a religious term at this time. The question of when this came about – when Ioudaios could be used only to indicate religion – is much harder to say. The issue is raised by STUCKENBRUCK in his discussion of *1 Enoch* 10. If this passage predicts the conversion of the Gentiles already in the third century BCE, do they become Jews? Many passages in the Hebrew Bible think of the nations as eventually worshipping Yhwh, yet there is no suggestion that they became a part of the chosen people. But already beginning with passages probably dating to the third century and continuing on into the second century (such as the *Animal Apocalypse*), the conversion of the Gentiles to Yhwh worship is envisaged. STUCKENBRUCK argues that this is part of the challenge of Jewish self-definition posed by Hellenization. The conversion of the Idumaeans and the Ituraeans to Judaism is also no doubt a stage on the path, though HONIGMAN suggests that this identification of people and cult is characteristic of a society that still existed in segmented form.

In conclusion, the religious issue was associated with the matter of Jewish identity from at least the third century BCE, and the concept of conversion emphasized the religious side even further. One who was not a Jew could become a Jew by adopting Judaism. Yet an ethnic overtone was and continues to be present when one is automatically a Jew if born of a Jewish mother (though in this period the key parent may have been the father: Cohen 1999).

Relating Text and Archaeology
Archaeology is an important component of any description of what was happening to Judah in this period. It is unfortunate that the archaeology data for this era are not always as easily available as in some other periods, whether in the ground or in scholarly works accessible to non-archaeologists. But what we have is very valuable (see Lipschits 2005; Lipschits et al. 2007; Grabbe 2004: 22–53; 2008: 27–50). The archaeology is a primary source, providing much needed first-hand information. This not only complements literary sources but also serves as a necessary check on the literary accounts. Naturally, the artifacts have to be interpreted, but so do the literary sources: the hermeneutical question applies to both sorts of source, as is well illustrated in a number of the contributions to the present volume.

Perhaps the most controversial paper is likely to be that of Israel FINKELSTEIN who argues that the lack of archaeological evidence for Nehemiah's wall is decisive: there was no such wall. Rather, the list in Nehemiah is to be ascribed to an earlier or later period, most likely the time of the Maccabees. The settlement of Jerusalem covered only 20–25 dunams, with perhaps up to 500 people in total. Many specialists in the Persian period will find this hard to accept. First, the wall is central not only to Nehemiah 3 (which may be a later insertion) but also to the next chapter, Nehemiah 4. Secondly, it calls into question the existence of a Nehemiah Memorial. Nehemiah 3 can be isolated from the Memorial, but not ch. 4. Is the present lack of archaeological evidence definitive? Oded LIPSCHITS argues that it is not.

LIPSCHITS accepts FINKELSTEIN's point about the lack of archaeological evidence, but he draws attention to the general situation with Persian-period finds on the southeastern hill of Jerusalem. In most cases, the artifacts are not clearly associated with a stratum or architectural feature. He argues that Persian-period remains were scattered over the City of David area but that later building activities removed them in certain sections. In his view the city of Nehemiah covered approximately 42 dunams, with a population of 1000, or possibly even double that if the Ophel was inhabited as it probably was. Thus, we cannot negate so easily Nehemiah's wall on the basis of current lack of archaeology. On the other hand, we should not expect a massive wall as in the Middle Bronze, late Iron, or later Hellenistic-Roman fortifications. It might have been more symbolic than anything and was not needed for defence. But Jerusalem would go through a phase of intensive building after this, making the current lack of finds for this period explicable. The argument that absence of finds makes Nehemiah's wall a fiction is too hasty, in his judgement. Many biblical scholars would agree with him, but the lack of material evidence for Nehemiah's wall remains a puzzling and frustrating situation.

The connection of text and archaeology can be well illustrated in KLONER's study. In the Idumaean city of Maresha/Marisa, archaeology has turned up a great deal of information about the houses and burial places of the inhabitants that tell us how the people lived and buried their dead. Since the tombs included many inscriptions, archaeologists have also had a place in adding to the inscriptional data. Coin finds indicate the tombs were used during the Ptolemaic period from the time of the 1st Ptolemy and well into the Seleucid period. The tombs have resemblances to Ptolemaic-period tombs in Egypt. A discussion of the inscriptions is given above (under 'Language and Literature').

Josephus and Events under Alexander
Two contributors discussed events under Alexander that were based on Josephus' account: M. MOR, on the building of the Samaritan temple, and A. KASHER, on Alexander's visit to Jerusalem. As readers might expect, I am not convinced in either case, as I already argued more than 20 years ago (Grabbe 1987; also 2005). Nevertheless, it is important to examine the arguments.

First, with regard to Alexander's visit to Jerusalem, there has been a strong consensus of present-day scholarship against such a visit (outlined with bibliography in Grabbe 2008: 274–8). Why? Is it some prejudice against Josephus? In this case, the main reasons are not a disinclination to believe Josephus but the simple recognition that no early source on Alexander mentions anything like this. Yet it is inconceivable that any Alexander historian who knew of the incident would have omitted it. We are not dealing with a case of modern anti-Semitism; on the contrary, the ancient Greek writers would have been fascinated by an episode in which Alexander did something so contrary to his normal demeanour. One cannot imagine that Arrian or Quintus Curtius or Plutarch or any number of other early writers on Alexander would all have been silent. Arrian, on the other hand, tells us:

> Alexander now determined to make his expedition to Egypt, Palestinian Syria (as it is called) had already come over to him, except for a eunuch named Batis, who was master of the city of Gaza. [Arrian, *Anabasis* 2.25.4]

It is not a matter of guesswork: Arrian makes the plain statement that by the end of the siege of Tyre, all the rest of Syro-Palestine had submitted, except for Gaza. If Jerusalem had also been an exception, Arrian would have clearly told us. On the other hand, the story in Josephus and other sources is a prime pro-Jewish story. It is precisely the sort of propaganda that might have been invented by Jewish apologists. And, as is clear, the story appears almost entirely in Jewish sources.

More of a historical problem is the question of a Sanballat in connection with the end of the Persian empire (MOR). Josephus mentions only one Sanballat, not in connection with Nehemiah but at the time of Alexander. This was identified as Sanballat III by Frank Cross (1998), who had already argued for a Sanballat II on the basis of finds from Wadi Daliyeh. Now, J. Dušek (2007: 321–31) has made the case that even no Sanballat II exists; rather, seal WP 22 refers to Delaiah, which makes the Sanballat the figure of Nehemiah ('Sanballat I'). MOR's reasons for a Sanballat III are essentially those of Frank Cross against whom I had argued in 1987 (though I had accepted the existence of a Sanballat II, not otherwise attested, on the basis of the Wadi Daliyeh finds). Yet the Sanballat of Josephus looks remarkably like the Sanballat of Nehemiah, just transposed several generations. The story of Manasseh and Nikaso is a version of the story found in Neh. 13.28. And what about Jaddua, the high priest of Josephus' story? Is he different from the Joiada of Neh. 13.28? (There are a number of variant spellings of the names in Josephus manuscripts where they are not clearly distinguished.) The fact that Josephus gives names to the unnamed figures of the biblical text does not change the basic outline.

Two pieces of data might be seen as providing evidence for a third Sanballat. Among the Samarian coins are several with the letters *sn* (Meshorer/Qedar 1999). The suggestion of the editors that this is an abbreviation of the name *Sanballat* is a reasonable one since another coin seems to have the name written out almost in full (Meshorer and Qedar 1999: 27, 93). Dušek, however, argues for a different reading: *sn'by* (2007: 530). Thus, the question of which Sanballat – if any at all – is named in the coins is a fraught one. Meshorer and Qedar choose 'Sanballat III' (1999: 27); however, Hanan Eshel suggests that the coins fit better with 'Sanballat II' (1999: 10), while as just noted Dušek argues for a different reading. In the Wadi Daliyeh papyer, some governors are named as witnesses (Gropp 2001; Dušek 2007: WDSP = Wadi Daliyeh Samaritan Papyri). We appear to have 'before [H]ananiah governor of Samaria' (קדם פחת נניה[ח] שמרין) *qdm [□]nnyh p□t šmryn* [WDSP 7.17; also perhaps in WDSP 9.14); the name, however, may be '['A]naniah' (נניה[ע] *'nnyh*). Another apparent reference to a governor is possibly to someone named 'Joshua', though only one or two letters of the name are preserved in the photograph: '[before Josh]ua son of Sanballat and Hanan the prefect' (ל יש[וע בר סנאבלט וחנן סגנא]) *[lyš]w' br sn 'bl□ w□nn sgn'* [WDSP 11r.13]). If this reading is correct, it may be the same as the reading on seal impression WD 23 (Leith 1997: 184–7; Dušek 2007: 50–52), which has a few letters, perhaps 'to Josh[ua]' (ל יש[וע] *lyš[w']*). On the other hand, Dušek (2007: 262–4) notes that there is no evidence that the individual (whatever his name) in WDSP 11r.13 who is 'son of Sanballat' is governor or indeed holds any administrative post.

What is clear, though, is that we have no evidence that those explicitly labelled 'governor' were members of the Sanballat family. The assertion that the government of Samaria was kept in the Sanballat family throughout the Persian period is simply conjecture and nothing more. It is circular reasoning to conjecture a Sanballat III as governor at the time of Alexander and then use that conjecture as evidence that a line of Sanballatide governors existed in the late Persian period. The fact is that Sanballat III is an invention by conflating various sources rather than reading them critically, as I pointed out more than two decades ago (Grabbe 1987). Josephus clearly knew little about the Persian period, filling it mainly with the texts of 1 Esdras and the Greek Esther; however, because he knew the correct sequence of at least some of the Persian kings, he attempted to create a more 'scientific' narrative by arranging his sources around this kinglist. It is true that he also had some other material, but we do not know his source(s), nor to what extent he reproduced his source(s) and to what extent he has adapted and reworked his source(s) to create his own narrative.

One of the points made by MOR is that the archaeological argument for a temple on Gerizim in the mid-fifth century is not proved. As a non-archaeologist, I am not in a position to comment on that, other than to say that most archaeologists I have consulted seem to believe the excavator's opinion (set out in Magen 2008a; 2008b; Magen et al. 2004) is correct. It should be noted that when MOR wrote his article, the volumes of Magen and also of Dušek were not available (I thank Professor Mor for bringing Magen's 2008 volumes to my attention). This is a debate that will no doubt continue. Like so many other topics, it illustrates how some very basic facts about the transition from Persian to Greek rule are still disputed and new information seems to complicate rather than resolve the issue.

Conclusions

The present volume can contain only a portion of the public and private – individual and group – exchanges made in our conference. Yet no conference can hope to encompass the fullness and complexity of this important transition period from Persian to Greek rule. To the extent that one can come to conclusions from such a diverse range of papers and opinions, we can draw attention to the following:

- Hellenism and Hellenization constituted a complex process, but the Jews neither rejected them, nor were overwhelmed by them. They took over what was useful, in some cases adapting the elements to their needs.
- The Greek language was the normal language of Jews outside Palestine, and it had a place in Palestine. It did not displace Aramaic, which remained the common language in the region, but Greek colonies and Greek foundations used Greek.
- A number of Greek foundations (*poleis*) are known, mainly on the coast, but also Jerusalem. But outside Judah there were other Greek settlements, such as in Maresha/Marisa and Samaria.
- The exact form that Ptolemaic administration took in Palestine is still uncertain, but the Ptolemies were pragmatic and continued to operate pre-existing systems that worked. The indications are that the high priest had a major function as representative of the community in Judah to the Ptolemaic court.
- The unsettled nature of the region allowed certain entrepreneurial Jewish individuals and families (such as the Tobiads) to establish themselves and flourish, providing an informal level of government alongside the official.
- The value of archaeology for understanding this period was well demonstrated in the papers. Relating archaeology and text for historical reconstruction is, however, a complex process, as the debates on Nehemiah's wall and on the history of the Samaritan community illustrate.

1

Judaic National Identity

James K. Aitken
University of Cambridge

The Problem

There are two questions underlying the theme of this volume that are pertinent for discussion. The first is how far the apparent transition period between the Persian and Hellenistic periods in Judah can really be seen either as one of innovation or instead as a time of continuation, witnessing the flourishing of ideas that have their origins in the earlier Persian period. The second question is whether external influences, most often amalgamated under the term Hellenism, had any substantive influence on the nature of Judah and the Jewish religion in this period. We must first discuss, therefore, these two questions and the problem of reconstructing a period for which we have so few sources, before turning to our chosen topic of national identity, which will serve as a test for these reflections.

Periodization

The issue of periodization in Jewish history is particularly acute for this era, and it is an issue that Lester Grabbe has discussed succinctly (Grabbe 2000: 317–19). The many books whose historical period begins with the time of Alexander the Great establish, by their very subject division, the Hellenistic period as one of constitutive or formative importance without considering the broader historical range. Thus, books on early Jewish history will often begin either with the Persian period of administration over Israel (e.g. Grabbe 1994) or later with the new political climate of Alexander the Great (e.g. Hayes and Mandell 1998). Although the period of Alexander the Great has traditionally been seen as a new political era and an important time for Greek history, for the history of the Jews it is perhaps not a time of any great change, the rule over Palestine passing from Persia to the Ptolemies through the hands of Alexander without any noticeable effect on the conditions there. Changing portrayals of

Alexander in some recent biographies that portray him in a less than idealistic fashion or at least as someone without a clearly defined agenda,[1] and a
move away from an imperial or colonial view of the Hellenistic kingdoms
(Sherwin White and Kuhrt 1993), has led to a diminution in the importance
placed on the Hellenistic period. The ideal portrait of Alexander as a great
statesman and 'evangelist', in works such as Hammond's tellingly entitled
The Genius of Alexander the Great (1997), has been countered by the
portrayal of an Alexander that sought personal fame and autocracy. What
used to be seen as the start of a new age, with Greek expansionism and
the idealization of a Greek culture – Hellenism – is seen in more realistic
terms. Reflective of this is an Alexander displaying the classic symptoms
of an alcoholic (O'Brien 1992), or as a butcher (Bosworth 1996), who
"spent much of his time killing and directing killing, and arguably, killing
was what he did best" (Bosworth 1996, v). Even if the likely exaggeration
in such portrayals were tempered, the era should not be seen as glorious as
sometimes portrayed. It was still significant, even if Alexander was more
a destroyer of the old world of the Persian Empire than the founder of a
new world. For our purposes it is significant, as it downplays the idea of
a Hellenistic ideal spreading as intentional propaganda, rendering it less
unified and less tangible.

For the Jews, it was probably not until the latter half of the third century,
nearly a century after Alexander's death, that a real change began with
the Syro-Palestinian wars and the eventual transference of Palestine from
Ptolemaic to Seleucid control. Even then, it was not the political climate
that really changed, decrees indicating that the treatment of Jews largely
remained unchanged throughout the period,[2] and we can imagine for
day-to-day life there was little noticeable effect. But we might be able
to discern a development in Jewish thought, as we shall see, that might
have grown more organically through particular influences or political
situations. Nevertheless, to begin a history with Alexander is a convenient
point in time, and it allows some scholars to make observations on the
consequent increase in Greek influence in the East from the new Empire.
This can be overstated, though, since for Palestine at least there had been
Greek influence in the Persian period, represented in the form of coins
and pottery, and this does not seem to have grown exponentially after
Alexander the Great.

---

1   See the essays in Bosworth and Baynham 2002. For critical portrayals, note Schachermeyr
1949; Badian 1958; Will 1986; Bosworth 1996; Green 1992; Worthington 2003. Fraser (1996) discusses inter alia the impression created by sources that attribute many city foundations to Alexander,
and presents a sober picture of the few that we can confidently say he did found.

2   Decrees recorded in Josephus, and attested in such inscriptions as the Hefzibah stele, and the
new 'Heliodorus inscription', suggesting a change in the policy of temple administration.

The relative scarcity of evidence that we have in comparison to the Maccabaean period ensures that attention and space are devoted to the Maccabees and the Hasmonaean dynasty. Indeed, a work such as the Revised Schürer (following the German original) begins with the reign of Antiochus IV and the Maccabaean era (175 BCE), either because this was a decisive time for Judaism or because solid evidence only begins then (e.g. Schürer, revised by Vermes et al., 1986–87). As a decisive time it also seems to be the chosen period for Simon and Benoît (1968). The problem is not that the earlier period before the Maccabees is overlooked by studies, but that the inevitable interest in the Maccabaean period prevents an independent analysis of this earlier time. Walbank's history includes a chapter on 'Religious Developments' in which the Maccabaean revolt appears to be given space disproportionate to its historical importance (1992: 222–26; cf. Green 1993). Walbank telescopes history somewhat in suggesting that the revolt 'helped to create the conditions in Palestine which made it fertile soil for the rise of Christianity two hundred years later' (1992: 222), perhaps influenced too much by Hengel (1969).

Periodization of history is necessary and helpful, but the terms by which we describe the divisions and the reasons for our choices can be determinative for the historiography. As Finley has reminded us, periods can also be divided differently, according to whether we are interested in social or political history, linguistic or literary (1975: 60–74, esp. 64–6; cf. Finley 1985). Certainly developments within Judaism, such as that of angelology (Grabbe 2000: 224–25, 317–19), can indeed be traced back to the Persian period, and a history of these beliefs should be constructed on a broad schema, while others, such as responses to political conditions, should be based around the political circumstances of Seleucid rule, the Maccabees and Roman governance. No division is better or preferable to another, but each reflects a different interest and each should be written about with an awareness of the existence of the other. The validity of a particular scheme is rarely discussed. It is not a matter, however, of seeking a different historical division than the traditional 'Hellenistic', but rather of being aware of the consequences of our divisions. The designation of the period between Qohelet and the early apocryphal books as 'pre-Maccabaean' involves the danger already mentioned of seeing the period as inevitably leading to the Maccabaean crisis (as it serves in Hengel 1969). It can result in the alleged causes of the Maccabaean crisis being sought in the third century, which, whether true or not, has to be argued and not assumed. An alternative, merely temporal, designation such as Judaism in the fourth and third centuries (cf. the sub-title of Stone and Satran 1989) is unhelpful, since that is an artificial time construct. It has the advantage of not prioritizing a social or political interest for designating the period, but by the same token it has the disadvantage of not being a period that is dictated by the events in the Hellenistic period or in Jewish history.

For Hellenistic history there is some justification in the period beginning with Alexander the Great as a dividing point, but it is not so clear-cut for Jewish history. Lack of evidence makes any judgement precarious for Jewish history, but there seems little initial change in the third century. Indeed, if works such as the early portions of 1 Enoch were composed in the early Hellenistic period, then they would have to have their intellectual roots in the Persian. It is likely that the second to first centuries BCE (and the Roman period) were more important for developments in Judaism, paving the way for formative rabbinic Judaism, not so much owing to the establishment of a so-called 'independent' Jewish state under the Hasmonaeans, but owing to wider social, political and geographical factors.

In looking at this particular period we nonetheless are challenged by our selection of sources. In considering this era we are drawn away from a biblical centrism in sources and encouraged to use sources that are in all probability contemporaneous with, or slightly later than, those of the later biblical books. Greek writers such as Hecataeus and Eupolemus, pseudepigraphic works such as 1 Enoch and perhaps Jubilees, and apocryphal books such as Ben Sira, Tobit and perhaps Judith, all shed light on this time-frame and on the final editing and composition of the Bible.

External Influence

Our central problem is lack of evidence for the very period under consideration, especially given the debate in biblical scholarship regarding the dating of biblical books. Depending on which scholar one consults, some, all or none of the biblical books are to be dated to the period of 400–200 BCE. The sources that might fit into this period have been carefully catalogued and described by Grabbe (cf. Grabbe 2000; 2001; 2004). But if some developments are to be traced back to the Persian period, how are we to determine the precise influences that are operating and the time period within which certain changes took place? A particular problem is the adoption by successive ruling powers of social and political structures, literary forms and ideologies. The customs of the Persians were adopted by Greeks and Macedonians. The Ptolemies adopted from Egyptians and Greeks. And the Greeks themselves had adopted features earlier from the ancient Near East. This means that any comparative analysis or attempts to suggest influence upon literature from another culture has to be handled cautiously, since features can be found in many different societies. While we might attribute influences to Hellenism, they could equally derive from comparable features in other cultures. Corley, for example, has identified many comparable passages to those from Hebrew literature on friendship, but does not venture to suggest which are influential (Corley 2002). It was in fact an intentional political stratagem to 'naturalize' one's authority in local terms (Kuhrt and Sherwin-White 1991), and the Jews may well have participated in similar conventions (cf. Rajak 2002a; Aitken 2000). Berquist raises the problem of identity by introducing the problem of the multiple social levels that have to be considered (2006: 53–66), noting the degrees to which both imperialization and decolonization operate. For Jews, their identity would have been both Persian and Yehudite (2006: 63).

In addition to the difficulty of identifying a particular source of an idea, at times it is more a matter of inference than indisputable evidence that allows us to suggest a degree of influence. If, for example, we did not know that Ben Sira was written in the second century BCE (owing to the translator's preface and the naming of the high priest Simeon), is there anything in the text that could allow us to place it in the Hellenistic era? In other words, are any of the supposed Hellenistic features typical of Greek or late Egyptian ideas, or do we infer that they are Greek because that is when the book was written? Similarities in thought to Theognis (as argued by Middendorp 1973; and Sanders 1983) could be accounted for as mere proverbial material; the praise of the fathers could be a biblical summary rather than a Hellenistic encomium (as argued by Lee 1986), and ideas that seem typical of Greek philosophy (e.g. Hengel 1969) may be little more than conventional (see Mattila 2000). Even Ben Sira's supposed conservatism in opposition to Hellenism can only be explained if we know the date of the book first. This is not to deny that there was major change in the period, but that it can more easily be identified in the archaeological record (military presence, commerce, language, pottery, architecture, diet; see, e.g., Sharon 1991; Stern 1989; Newman 2005) than in the literary.

Our preoccupation with the Hellenistic period as one of formative influence, perhaps owing to a certain Greek idealism in western thought (Aitken 2004: 341), has sought explanations within that climate without always identifying the essential elements. Comparisons need to be made and historical reconstructions require a certain imagination, but if we cannot be sure even with a book such as Ben Sira, whose date we can be reasonably confident on, there may be much that we are missing in sources that we cannot date so easily.

Approaching the Period

In looking at the transition period from Persian to Hellenistic rule, we are confronted by the serious lack of evidence, especially literary, in the third century BCE in comparison to other regions and other time periods. There seems to be a good deal of evidence for Judah in the fourth century (see in particular Lipschits et al. 2007), and then again from the second. Nevertheless, important in this regard is the apparent stability of populations in the Persian and early Hellenistic periods, the real expansion and administrative changes taking place only under the Hasmonaeans (Lipschits and Tal 2007, 33–52). As a result we might be able to speculate from the fourth century that conditions changed little. To place it in perspective, we in fact find a remarkable quantity of data for Jews in Egypt in the third century, thanks in large part to the survival of Jewish inscriptions and papyri, as well as Ptolemaic papyri mentioning Jews or people with Jewish names. Literary references from Egypt to Jews also survive, and the Septuagint translation of the Pentateuch is a Jewish Egyptian source from the period. The contrast with the evidence from Judah is stark. It is only at the end of this period, namely from the end of the third century or the beginning of the second, that our evidence begins for Judah. At which point it appears to be a flourishing period of literary activity, although this might only appear so in hindsight and owing to chance survival.

Although our literary evidence is limited for the particular period, we can with reasonable confidence place a number of biblical sources at one end of the time-frame, and a number of other literary sources at the other. From this we are able to gain a perspective on the change. Change, however, is rarely linear, and, as already noted, can vary from facet to facet. Indeed, changes can be reversed, especially in response to other ideologies – counter-reformations, if you like. Therefore, it is not a simple matter of seeing what was before and after, but of identifying fault lines or issues of tension and discovering their partial realizations. A classic case of this is the issue of marriage that arises in a number of sources. It is not clear what was the precise practice of levirate marriage or of marriage to foreigners, but the book of Ruth touches on both and indicates, albeit in a manner that leaves us uncertain as to the author's intentions, that there was tension over the issue (following here a Persian period dating for this work; Zevit 2005). Such tensions can also be seen in marriage to foreigners in Ezra-Nehemiah, and the problem of levirate marriage is already clear in Genesis 38 and might account for the need for clarification in Deuteronomy. Marriage issues continue too in the book of Tobit. Some of these issues are only fully resolved in rabbinic literature (for which see Satlow 2001).

Judah and Identity

The question of nationalism and identity in antiquity and the relation between the two terms have received some attention in recent years (e.g. Hall 1997, on ethnicity), particularly under the influence of sociological theory. There are a number of theoretical issues that need to be considered (as discussed in detail by Goodblatt 2006: 1–27), but for now, attention will be on the sources.[3] Possible models for understanding the Persian period have been proposed by Berquist (2006), but most studies of Jewish nationalism have taken a broad focus, covering a large period of history with most attention being placed on the transition from Hellenistic to Roman rule, leading up to the Roman revolts (e.g. Mendels 1997; Schwartz 2001; Goodblatt 2006) rather than on the Persian period (so too the earlier study: Farmer 1957). For Mendels, the nationalism in the early Hellenistic period is to be seen in the creative re-writing of history by Jewish authors and the modification of the biblical accounts. This they did in response to the broader political context within the Hellenistic Kingdoms. While other nations could in some way associate themselves with the Hellenistic kings, the Jews could not since their beliefs were anathema to imperial demands. As a result the Jews developed a strong national identity in opposition to the Hellenistic kingdoms, incorporating the wish for a Jewish state centred on the temple, land, monarchy and army. For Schwartz, nationalism too is focused on the temple as the prime religious institution for the Jews, and Jewish identity is built upon cultural norms. Important within Schwartz's analysis seems to be a shared belief of origins that are distinct from their neighbours. Goodblatt's book, as his predecessors', says very little on the Persian period, with greater attention paid to the Hasmonaean period and after. Shared ancestry, culture and customs were unifying identity features for Jews in antiquity, so that even with hellenization and other external forces, the underlying identity in Judaism remained, and beliefs in the land and the institutions continued. Goodblatt sees this in terms of the preservation of the Hebrew language, the reading and preservation of the Bible, the role of the priestly class, the importance of the temple ('Zion nationalism'), and the place of the land ('Israel nationalism' and 'Judah nationalism'). He does not apparently distinguish between identity as a shared construction of common roots (national saga) and identity as genuinely sharing common roots.

It is not immediately self-evident that there was an identifiable Judaic identity in the Persian period. Although Judah was the name of one of the tribes of Israel and an Iron Age kingdom of Judah appears to have existed, it was not an obvious choice of name for the post-exilic district. It might have been a Persian designation for the district within the province, as

---

3 We should also heed the words of Kramer (1997), who describes recurring themes in the historical literature on nationalism, and replicates a key characteristic of the historiography by stressing that the complexity of nationalism and its interpreters resists every simplifying, comprehensive definition. The historical accounts never escape from the political and cultural contexts in which all historical narratives are produced.

indeed is implied by the title in the Bible and Aramaic papyri of *pechah* of
Judah for the Persian (appointed) governor. Nevertheless, the title Yehud
seems to have prevailed, appearing in the Elephantine papyri ("nobles
of Judah") and on coins, not only in the Persian period but also in the
Hellenistic period where coins continue to bear the title in Hebrew (sometimes paleo-)script of Aramaic Yehud or Hebrew Yehudah (see Meshorer
1967: 36–8; Kindler 1974; Jeselsohn 1974). The Yehudin in Elephantine
and later Jewish self-designations of *Ioudaioi* do imply that the origins of
Jewish identity lie in an attachment, whether real or constructed, to this
province (so Grabbe, contra Thompson). That this might be originally an
external determinant is implied by the continuing use and importance of
the title Israel in Jewish sources in contrast to the preference for Judah in
non-Jewish sources. Thus, it is possible that there was no clear identity
initially associated with the term Judah beyond its possible administrative
designation. Nevertheless, the fact that it becomes the term on the coins
might suggest that it already had meaning for the inhabitants. This could
be reinforced by the fact that the palaeo-Hebrew script is used on such
coins at the end of the Persian period, implying a national or religious
sentiment (so Naveh 1998: 91–2), although it is still possible that the script
was in general use at that time.

Certainly we should not underestimate the trauma that might have been
caused by the Babylonian destruction of Jerusalem, and the long-lasting
effect it might have had on the people. Weinberg has emphasized the
psychological and sociological devastation that would have struck both
those deported and those left behind (1992). Post-exilic writings imply an
attempt at establishing social and religious issues for the community, but
the lack of specific institutions would have impeded a centrifugal movement for establishing such identity. Indeed, the continued ambivalence
towards the Jerusalem temple, seen in the delays in rebuilding it, means
that even later on in the fifth century BCE that institution, so central later,
was not an option (Williamson 2004: 39–40). One strategy adopted by
those attempting to establish a national identity might well have been the
invention of the myth of the empty land (see, e.g. Barstad 1996).

An important example of the construction of identity has been noted
by Millar, who uses later evidence to suggest a shared understanding from
earlier. He identifies how the author of *1 Maccabees*, amid the description
of conflicts and resistance to 'Hellenism', can in the first chapter recall
'a communal historical consciousness and a national culture' (Millar
2006: 3, on *1 Macc.* 1.1-9). 1 Maccabees continues the tradition of biblical
historiography, picking up where Ezra-Nehemiah and Chronicles left off,
not so much earlier. He proposes that the older culture continued from the
pre-Greek past, and while undeniably influenced by Hellenistic elements,
in many ways largely remained unchanged. Throughout Syria, broadly

defined, the culture continued, even if in many places we cannot be sure precisely what that older culture was (Millar 2006: 4–7). We are perhaps not as optimistic as Millar in being able to describe Judah more precisely than other parts of Syria, but the essential point remains. Within historical memory there was a good deal of continuity, and the very reactions we find in the second century arise from an established sense of identity. A common tradition could be appealed to by authors, and this presupposed a common understanding, whether based on historical reality or not.

If we are to see a high degree of literacy in this period, as Goodblatt implies (2006), then a case could be made that the biblical text and the Hebrew language itself were forces behind establishing national identity. It is not certain, however, how far we should derive conclusions from the large number of Qumran manuscripts, a collection that is surely a product of a learned minority than representative of general levels of literacy (see Hezser 2001: 476–78; contra Wise 1992: 143–47). Likewise, the biblical injunction to teach the commandments (e.g. Deut. 4.9) need not be proof that people did actually have a high degree of literacy. The evidence of graffiti, or 'occasional inscriptions' (Millard 1972), is indeterminate as to who actually wrote it (Young 1998: 240). Indeed the large number of graffiti inscriptions from Gerizim (mostly likely from the Persian and Hellenistic periods), written in Hebrew (both palaeo-Hebrew and standard Aramaic-script), Aramaic and Greek (see Magen et al. 2004), do not necessarily point to large numbers of the population being able to either read or write. These inscriptions are uniformly well written and we may infer that there were professional scribes writing the dedications for the people.

Another reason for problems in establishing identity in the early Persian period is the mixed nature of the peoples involved. The leading families (the 'returnees') would have seen themselves as a distinct group from those that remained in the land and the problems associated with this are to be seen in Ezra 9 and Nehemiah 13. They are in this regard reflecting similar attempts to establish an identity that we find in other cultures, be it the tale of the Doric invaders, or the purification of the Hyksos in Egyptian and Ptolemaic sources. The book of Chronicles later aimed at turning attention to the Temple, and, as we see in parts of Jeremiah, providing a much more unified picture. Part of the movement to clarify Judaic identity was certainly to focus on local Jewish figures such as the portrayal of Zerubbabel in Haggai and Ezra 1 in contrast to the role accorded the Persian official in Ezra 5–6. The editing of the book of Ezra in this regard seems to be the first signs of such a movement to create a clear Jewish status.

Looking at the issues today we can see the movement towards focus on the Temple, which was probably the fiscal centre, shared inheritance and land as natural outcomes of reading the Pentateuch and interpreting Jewish history. However, we should look at it afresh to see how these connections were formed and articulated. For this purpose one area will be discussed that has been overlooked in the discussions of national identity and that once more focuses our attention on Jewish attachment to the land. It is seen to be located within a different context and suggests different roots for the notions, even though we already see land concerns in the Holiness Code and Ezra-Nehemiah. The development of Jewish institutions and the increasing importance of the role of the high priest and the judiciary were no doubt central to the formation of a national identity. How it was expressed in some writers, though, and the reasons for their expressions, need to be explained.

Ben Sira at the Turn of the Second Century

Ben Sira, writing in the 190s BCE or earlier, is obviously an important source for reflecting the socio-historical conditions at the end of our time period and during a significant era of the transfer of control of Coele-Syria to Seleucid rule. More often than not, Ben Sira has been portrayed in scholarship in theological terms. He has been viewed as presaging in his writing the Maccabaean crisis and a religious decline, and reaffirming Jewish identity in the face of Hellenistic influence.[4] Ben Sira is nevertheless also important for the possible light his work sheds on the political interests of his time, including the earlier Ptolemaic period, and in particular on Jewish self-identity. The only non-biblical figure the book names is the high priest Simon son of Onias (*Sir.* 50.1), who died in 196 BCE, but the book also alludes to damage to the city (*Sir.* 50.1-4) no doubt incurred during the fifth Syrian War (cf. Josephus *Ant.* XII 138–44). The editing of the book should therefore be placed, at least in part, in the 190s BCE, and the author can be seen as reflecting views of the late third and early second century BCE. It is therefore one of the most important sources for establishing views in this little-known period, the era of the transfer of control of Coele-Syria to Seleucid rule, and it is one of the first sources we have for bridging the gap of the transition period.

As an example of his value as a source, the book corroborates evidence that we can piece together from elsewhere regarding the socio-economic conditions of third-century Judah. Economic growth, particularly in terms of wealth being found in the hands of particular families is a feature of the time (see, in general, Schwartz 1994). The tale of the Tobiads (Josephus

---

4   Expressed already by Smend (1906) and dominant in current scholarship (e.g. Skehan and Di Lella 1987). For preliminary criticism, see Aitken 2000.

Ant. 12.154-236) portrays large-scale tax farming by wealthy and influential Jewish families, working in close cooperation with and receiving the support of Ptolemaic Egypt.[5] The Zenon archive likewise mentions a Tobias, a man of considerable wealth and influence (*CPJ* 1.1, 1.4; cf. Jeddous in *CPJ* 1.6), and attests to successful trade between Egypt and Judah at this time. This would all have been supported by the decrees of Ptolemy II Philadelphus in 261 BCE (Bagnall 1976), which seem to have extended local tax rights to the village level and increased the level of taxation.

The relevance to Ben Sira is that a reflection of this changing economic situation can account for the emphasis within the book on the social conditions. The style of the book as proverbial literature masks the historical relevance, and the connections with the contemporary situation are rarely made.[6] However, the book does present a highly mercantile society, in which business can be used for unlawful gains (*Sir*. 26.20–27.2), especially when the rich have the power of persuasion and force (*Sir*. 13.4-7). It is recognized that the rich have a greater role in society than the poor (*Sir*. 13.21-23), and can even affect political positions (*Sir*. 10.8). Nonetheless, almsgiving is still a recognized need with the society (*Sir*. 29.8-13). At the same time, it is within this setting a developing class of scribe appears to arise, independent enough to engage in a range of activities from travelling (*Sir*. 34.9-12), perhaps for business reasons,[7] to advising in the royal courts (e.g. *Sir*. 4.7; 39.4).[8] They are for the most part stewards, though, a class that are not poor or labourers (*Sir*. 38.31-34) but are not necessarily connected with the priestly class either. We may infer from Ben Sira that the economic and social conditions have allowed people of independent means, educated but without manual skills to emerge and have a role within society. Ben Sira himself seems to have been one example, and the growing diaspora, where teachers and scribes would not have at all been supported by the temple, must have encouraged such positions, as well as sustained them economically. Those who translated the Septuagint in the third century, if they had come from Judah, would have been of this type,

---

5   On the tale of Tobiads see inter alia Gera 1998, who demonstrates some of the fictional elements behind it.

6   Tcherikover (1959: 146–48) does make connections in passing, although his models are not necessarily to be followed today. Camp and Wright (2001) bring together all the passages on wealth and poverty, but then reflect them through the lens of honour and shame discourse. As a result, the relevance for the socio-economic conditions of the time is neglected. Wischmeyer (1995) also gathers much material together but without integrating it into what we know of the historical context. Wright (1997) is more successful at drawing out historical conclusions from Ben Sira.

7   Although the presentation of travel is standard in Hellenistic writings, this does not detract from the possibility that it also represents the reality of the Ptolemaic empire.

8   The standard work on Ben Sira's presentation of the scribe is still Stadelmann 1981.

as indeed most likely was Ben Sira's grandson in the later second century (*Sir.* prologue, ll. 27-36). Perhaps too were some of those who moved to Qumran, after the initial settlers of priestly origin. This class of educated people, neither labourer, nor necessarily having a priestly function, would have seen their position within the wider Ptolemaic and Seleucid empires in which they worked. This could mean that they also sought answers to the problem of Judaic identity.

Ben Sira and Judaic Identity

Ben Sira's emphasis on Zion and the temple is well known, and falls into Goodblatt's category of Zion nationalism. The residence of Wisdom in Jerusalem and the Temple (see ch. 24) reinforces this image and suggests that the city is God's chosen residence. The nationalistic prayer in ch. 36 (in recent studies considered genuine; see Palmisano 2006) calls for defeat of enemies, divine visitation on Zion and the restoration of prophecies for the land. Then in the Praise of the Fathers many of these themes are picked up in the establishment of the temple under David and Solomon, and in the portrayal of the defence of Jerusalem against attack, expressed in the times of Hezekiah, Nehemiah and the contemporary high priest Simon. In each case, the king is supported by a prophet, suggesting the ideal balance between royal governance and prophetic insight (noted by Mack 1985).

The praise of the high priest Simon in ch. 50 especially has political overtones that have sometimes been overlooked in discussions of the function of the priesthood in this period.[9] Wright, for example, suggests that the models for Ben Sira's rulers are God himself and the idealized kings of Israel's past (2007: 88). He downplays any possible connections with Hellenistic kings, arguing that one of the most important Hellenistic ideas, the king as benefactor, is absent from the book, and that although some of the acts of the high priest could be considered as benefactions, the author does not call them that. In short, he does not take the opportunity to make explicit such an important ideological term of Hellenistic kingship (Wright 2007: 81–2). It could be argued, however, that the theme is so strong that the term, however εὐεργεσία would be translated into Hebrew, is not necessary. Simon, whose predecessors are likewise each recalled in the book as taking care of the city (Hezekiah, Zerubbabel, Nehemiah),

---

9   They are downplayed by Rooke (2000: 263–64), who sees his functions as merely religious, focused on the sanctuary. Mulder 2003 has drawn out the biblical parallels but not the contemporary social situation. The roles ascribed to the priest, however, within the context of the time would have recalled these functions without their being named. A more sensitive treatment is given in Rajak 2002b.

is presented as an established ruler, both a protector and benefactor and therefore the effective head of the Jewish state. First, he provides for the restoration of the city (*Sir.* 50.2-3, acting as a εὐεργέτης) and then serves as its protector (50.4, as a σωτήρ 'he considered how to save his people from ruin and fortified the city against siege'). The comparison with the ideal function of a Hellenistic ruler could not be lost on those familiar with the Hellenistic political climate at the time. Elsewhere I have suggested there are the traces of a foundation legend in this passage too, and therefore at this time of the beginnings of Seleucid governance of the region, emphasis is placed both on a new beginning and also on the reassertion of Jewish self-governance. The reality is that there was probably hardly any change for the majority of the population after the Seleucid defeat of the Ptolemies at Panium in 200 BCE. Antiochus III might have granted special rights (Josephus *Ant.* 12.145-6; recorded in *Sir.* 50.1-4), but these were mostly reaffirming the status quo. Nevertheless, it was an opportunity from the Jewish side for writers to express and reaffirm their own self-understanding, and to reinvigorate awareness of a national consciousness. And this Ben Sira does.

Ben Sira is not alone in his interests, suggesting the themes in his work reflect wider concerns of the time. A quite different type of writer is Hecataeus of Abdera (c. 300 BCE), one of the few literary sources for our set period, and the section preserved in Diodorus Siculus (book 40) is usually taken as authentic in contrast to those excerpts in Josephus (see Bar-Kochva 1996), although it might all ultimately derive from Jewish sources. His excursus on the Jews presents a number of details regarding the land in addition to some well-discussed issues of Jewish governance. Already in Hecataeus we have the picture of a Jewish *ethnos*, with its focus on Jerusalem. We need to be careful with vocabulary, since it is not certain how far Diodorus adhered to Hecataeus' wording, and it is recognized that there is much of the Diodorean style in the excursus. It is easy to dismiss much of what we read in Hecataeus as either a confused and conflated reading of biblical history or as repeating the features of Greek foundation legends without serious concern over the true story of Jewish history and the current people. The passage is typical of foundation stories in which barbaric lands are occupied. Moses leads the new settlement, which is called a colony (ἀποικία). This term is usual for a Greek settlement initiated by a mother city, even though the Jews were foreigners who were expelled from Egypt – a slight contradiction in the account.[10] It is not a typical Jewish description of resettlement in the land

---

10   Some of the vocabulary of colonization in Jewish literature has been discussed by Mélèze-Modrzejewski (1993: 65–92).

of the Patriarchs, but it does reflect a central focus for identity in Judah, built around the Temple and priesthood. It also draws attention to the role of the land and its occupation, a theme prominent in both 1 Enoch and Ben Sira.

In addition to the prominent role of the Temple in Ben Sira, there is another theme, that of planting, that can be shown to be of importance.[11] Planting as a theme in Ben Sira is closely connected with the flourishing of Wisdom (ch. 24) and the High Priest (ch. 50), in which the centrality of Wisdom to the cult is presented in Edenic language (Hayward 1991). The actual word 'to plant' is used with reference to Jeremiah, drawing upon the language of Jeremiah (Jer. 1.10):

> *Sir.* 49.7
> For they had afflicted him;
> yet he had been consecrated in the womb as prophet,
> to pluck up and afflict and destroy,
> and likewise to build and to plant (וכן לבנת לנטע).

This equates the rebuilding, which is mentioned with reference to Hezekiah, Nehemiah and Simeon, with planting, and in part accounts for the flourishing of the Temple. It links the prophetic tradition with the belief that the land will flourish again, the building of the city of Jerusalem intimately connected with its planting like crop. The allusion to Jeremiah though is not a chance biblical citation, since the agricultural themes, already seen in the temple depiction, continue in the reference to the Twelve Prophets:

> 49.10 May the bones of the twelve prophets revive from where they
> lie, for they comforted the people of Jacob and delivered them
> with confident hope.

The Hebrew here is partially damaged, but it seems to correspond to the wording found in *Sir.* 46.11-12:

> The judges also, with their respective names, those whose hearts did
> not fall into idolatry and who did not turn away from the Lord – may
> their memory be blessed!

---

11 Planting has of course become a popular theme in recent scholarship, with special reference to Qumran and Jubilees: Fujita 1976; Tiller 1997; Swarup 2006.

12 May their bones revive from where they lie, and may the name of
those who have been honoured live again in their sons!

The passages are more, however, than a presentation of the fertility of the
land. For Ben Sira picks up an interest in burial places, seen in the books
of Judges (e.g. Judg. 10.1-5; 12.8-15) and Joshua (24.30), and develops
a biblical theme of the importance of the graves of the ancestors. It is not
clear precisely in what way he wishes the bones to revive (especially as in
v. 12 the name is what is to live on). That the renewal of prophecy might
be in mind in the reference to the Twelve Prophets could be supported by
comparison with the portrayal of Samuel, which naturally follows on from
the mention of the Judges:

> *Sir.* 46.20
> Even after he had fallen asleep he prophesied and revealed to the king
> his death, and lifted up his voice out of the earth in prophecy, to blot
> out the wickedness of the people.

The passage alludes to Saul's consulting Samuel via the witch of Endor
(1 Sam. 28.8-19), and takes it as a form of prophecy arising from the earth
itself, presumably the place where Samuel is buried. The same issue is
brought in with regard to Elisha's dead body (cf. 2 Kgs 13.21):

> *Sir.* 48.13
> Nothing was too hard for him, and when he was dead his body
> prophesied.

This interest in the role of the dead is further brought to mind by the
secondary burial of Joseph, remembered at the end of the Praise of the
Fathers.

> *Sir.* 49.15
> And no man like Joseph has been born, and his bones are cared for
> (פקד).

It is particularly striking, as noted by Kugel (1994: 129), that the one
piece of information we are given about Joseph is this: that his bones were
taken care of[12] (i.e. transported from Egypt to Israel). It is an allusion to

---

12   The verb used in the Hebrew of Ben Sira 'to care for' (פקד) is the same as that in Exod.
13.19, and seems to have been a technical term for care for the dead (see Bloch-Smith 1992:
220–21). The same verb is picked up by Ben Sira and used in the subsequent verses: in 49.16 of

the original request by Joseph (Gen. 50.22-26), which was fulfilled in the time of Moses (Exod. 13.19), that his bones be taken and buried in the land of Israel. In the biblical story, the bones of Joseph are in due course taken to Shechem as a means of establishing the inheritance of Joseph's sons (Josh. 14.32). Later Jewish tradition makes much of the legend of the bones of Joseph, but focusing more on the reasons why they had not been transported before and on the problems of finding their location in Egypt (see Kugel 1994: 128–55). Certainly in the earlier history of Judah there was a cult of the dead (Bloch-Smith 1992), but the explanation for the focus in Ben Sira's writing, which reflects nothing of the later traditions, should be sought elsewhere.

It is possible that Ben Sira had in mind the most famous Hellenistic transportation and burial of bones, namely that of Alexander the Great. It is recorded by a number of historians how Alexander's body, after his death in Babylon, was diverted at Damascus from its destination of Macedon to Egypt, to ensure for Ptolemy (probably Ptolemy I Soter: see Strabo, *Geography* xvii.794) a propitious succession. The precise details are contradictory in the ancient records,[13] but it seems clear that the body was first laid to rest in Memphis and then under Ptolemy I, or perhaps Ptolemy II Philadelphus (293–246 BCE) soon after the death of Ptolemy I, was moved to Alexandria. To have the possession of the body was to have royal power and prestige (Diodorus 18.36.6-7; cf. Erskine 2002: 171–75). It was even thought that the corpse had magical powers, as had that of Oedipus, and that possession of it would bring success to any city in which it lay (Aelian, *Varia Historia* 12.64). A cult of Alexander-*Ktistes* ('founder of the city') soon developed in the district of his tomb, which was henceforth referred to as *sema* or *soma* (see Strabo *Geography* xvii.793).[14] This could be interpreted as the background for Ben Sira's attention to Joseph's bones in two respects. First, although the belief that possession of bones in a city or country endowed a special power and status to the rulers of that country was already known in biblical times, as seen in the account in Joshua (14.32) of the placing of the bones in Shechem, it was a prominent issue in the Hellenistic era owing to the rivalry over Alexander's body. Second, if Ben Sira has Alexander in mind, he is presenting his land as favoured in opposition to Alexandria and the land of the Ptolemies. Such

Shem, Seth and Enosh, and then in 50.1 of the Temple in Jerusalem. A direct connection seems to be drawn between the treatment of these patriarchs and the Jerusalem Temple in Ben Sira's own day.

13   For discussions, see Hammond and Walbank 1988: 120; Fraser 1972: 1.15-16; Schlange-Schöningen 1996.

14   The cult of the tomb probably started early on, but became prominent in Roman times (e.g. Suetonius *Life of Augustus* 18). See Spencer 2002: 169–70.

an antitype would serve Jewish nationalistic sentiments as well as imply an anti-Ptolemaic agenda, if there was any at the time.

In conjunction with the other passages discussed, this verse places an emphasis on the power of the dead ancestors, and particularly in their bones as they lie in the earth, and that through these ancestors the prophecies will be renewed. We seem to have here an emphasis on the ancestors as historical predecessors and guarantors of the future, and attention given to their lying in the very earth, which will bear fruit. The relocating of Joseph's bones is important as a statement on the possession of the land. It may be compared with the *sema* of Alexandria, in which a clear statement was made by laying to rest in his own city the body of Alexander. At a time when the Ptolemies and the Seleucids were vying for possession of the region, it has some political force if Ben Sira claims the land as Jewish. While the Hellenistic kingdoms sought 'spear-won land', Ben Sira claims land by ancestral burial.

Conclusions

After the exile, Judah was in a new political situation, reduced in size and lacking temple and monarchy. It is possible that the trauma of the conquest and exile left their mark in the national conscience, that it took time for Jews to emerge with a new national identity. We lack evidence from that crucial period between the fourth and second centuries, but seeing the issues that were at the forefront of either end of that transition period provides us with a glimpse of the concerns at the time.

In this case, the example of Ben Sira was taken as a book reflective of concerns in the late third century and the beginning of the second. His focus on the land and its restoration draws upon biblical themes, but suggests that early post-exilic issues regarding purity and population of the land have continued, if in modified form, in this time. It does not mean that the issues are precisely the same as earlier, but that the land was a key matter of demarcation in Judaean identity. Although throughout this period the wider political conditions for the Jews did not change, each successive foreign power most likely continuing the administration and rights of their predecessors, this does not mean the wider political context is unimportant. The identity of a national group may not only be self-generated within a group but can be stimulated by external political factors. In time, the circumstances of Jews in diaspora, and the political machinations over control of Coele-Syria led to greater attention on certain issues. For some, the responsibility of the state to its wider 'ethnic' groups across the Mediterranean helped to forge an identity, while for others the time of change from Ptolemies to Seleucids encouraged a restatement of Jewish identity. The themes of national identity had already begun in the Persian period but they seem to have sprung up with new vigour by the beginning of the second century. In this respect perhaps the Hellenistic period is of great importance (as Mendels also tries to show) since the rivalry between the Hellenistic kingdoms stimulated a Jewish search for Judaean identity.

2

GEOGRAPHICAL LISTS IN EZRA AND NEHEMIAH IN THE
LIGHT OF ARCHAEOLOGY: PERSIAN OR HELLENISTIC?

Israel Finkelstein
Institute of Archaeology
Tel Aviv University

The geographical lists in Ezra and Nehemiah have served as the backbone
for the reconstruction of the history of Yehud. But do they really represent
the Persian period? Scholars took their dating for granted because this
is what the text says. But with no extra-biblical sources to support this
notion, this conventional wisdom is gripped by circular reasoning. The
only way out of this trap is to consult archaeology. Yet, archaeology has
never been systematically and independently utilized in order to verify the
background of these lists. In what follows I wish to discuss two lists – the
construction of the city-wall of Jerusalem in Nehemiah 3 and the List of
Returnees in Ezra 2.1-67; Neh. 7.6-68 – in the light of archaeology.

The Wall of Nehemiah

Knowledge of the archaeology of Jerusalem in the Persian (and Early
Hellenistic) period – the size of the settlement and whether it was fortified – is crucial to understanding the history of the province of Yehud, the
reality behind the Book of Nehemiah and even the process of compilation
and redaction of certain biblical texts (on the latter see, e.g. Schniedewind
2003; 2004: 165–78; Edelman 2005: 80–150). Indeed, a considerable
number of studies dealing with Jerusalem in the Persian period have
been published in recent years (e.g. Carter 1999; Eshel 2000; Stern 2001:
434–36; Edelman 2005; Lipschits 2005; 2006; Ussishkin 2006). Although
the authors were aware of the results of recent excavations, which have
shown that the settlement was limited to the eastern ridge (the City of
David), they continued to refer to a meaningful, fortified 'city' with a
relatively large population.

The Current View

Carter argued that Jerusalem grew from a built-up area of 30 dunams in the Persian I period to 60 dunams 'after the mission of Nehemiah' (1999: 200) and estimated the peak population to have been between 1250 and 1500 people (ibid.: 288).

Eshel (2000) reconstructed the history of Jerusalem in the Persian period almost solely according to the biblical texts, arguing that the 'Jerusalem of Nehemiah was a small town . . . nevertheless it had eight gates . . . much more than the real need of the town at that time' (ibid., 341). Regarding the rebuilding of the walls, following Nehemiah 3, Eshel envisioned a major operation, which involved many groups of builders.

Stern began the discussion of the archaeology of Jerusalem in the Persian period with a sentence based solely on the biblical text: 'Persian period Jerusalem was bounded by walls erected by Nehemiah' (2001: 434). At the same time he acknowledged that 'only a few traces have survived of the city wall of Nehemiah along the course described in the Bible (ibid.: 435, referring to a segment of a city-wall which was dated by Kenyon to the Persian period (below)).

Edelman (2005) saw the construction of the walls by Nehemiah as a turning point in the history of Yehud – marking the transfer of the capital from Mizpah to Jerusalem. She described a major construction effort in Jerusalem under Persian auspices in the days of Artaxerxes I – an effort far greater than the reconstruction of the city-walls, that also included the Temple and a fort (2005: 344–48).

Ussishkin declared that 'the corpus of archaeological data should be the starting point for the study of Jerusalem . . . This source of information should take precedence, wherever possible, over the written sources, which are largely biased, incomplete, and open to different interpretations' (2006: 147–48). Reviewing the archaeological data, he rightly concluded that the description in Nehemiah 3 must relate to the maximal length of the city-walls, including the western hill. But then, solely according to the textual evidence in Nehemiah 3, he accepted that the Persian period settlement was indeed fortified: 'When Nehemiah restored the city wall destroyed by the Babylonians in 586 B.C.E., it is clear . . . that he restored the city wall that encompassed the Southwestern Hill, as suggested by the "maximalists"' (Ussishkin 2006: 159; also 160).

Lipschits's reconstruction of the history of Jerusalem in the Persian period (2006) revolved around the rebuilding of the city-wall by Nehemiah. Though 'there are no architectural or other finds that attest to Jerusalem as an urban center during the Persian Period' (Ibid.: 31), 'the real change in the history of Jerusalem occurred in the middle of the fifth century B.C.E., when the fortifications of Jerusalem were rebuilt. Along with scanty archaeological evidence, we have a clear description of this event in the Nehemiah narrative . . .' (ibid.: 34). Lipschits described Jerusalem as a 'city' of 60 dunams, with a population of ca. 1,500 inhabitants (ibid.: 32; also 2003: 330–31; 2005: 212; see a different number, 3,000 people, in 2005: 271).

Obviously, all the scholars who dealt with the nature of Jerusalem in the Persian period based their discussion on the biblical text, mainly on the description of the reconstruction of the city-wall in Nehemiah 3.

The Finds

Intensive archaeological research in Jerusalem in the past 40 years has shown that:

1. The southwestern hill was part of the fortified city in the late Iron II and the Late Hellenistic periods (for the Iron II see Geva 2003b: 505–18; 2003c; Avigad 1983: 31–60; Reich and Shukron 2003; for the Late Hellenistic period see Geva 2003b: 526–34; Wightman 1993: 111–57).

2. The southwestern hill *was not* inhabited in the Persian and Early Hellenistic periods. This has been demonstrated by excavations in the Jewish Quarter (Avigad 1983: 61–63; Geva 2003b: 524; 2003c: 208), the Armenian Garden (Gibson 1987; Geva 2003b: 524–25), the Citadel (Amiran and Eitan 1970) and Mt Zion (Broshi 1976: 82–83). Apart from a few possible isolated finds (Geva 2003b: 525), there is no evidence of any activity in any part of the southwestern hill between the early sixth century and the second century BCE. The Persian and Early Hellenistic settlement should therefore be sought on the southeastern ridge – the City of David.

In the City of David, too, the evidence is fragmentary. Most finds from the Persian and Early Hellenistic periods were retrieved from the central part of the ridge, between Areas G and D of the Shiloh excavations (Shiloh 1984: 4). The Persian period is represented by Stratum 9, which fully appears, according to Shiloh (1984: 4, Table 2) in Areas D1 (Ariel, Hirschfeld and Savir 2000: 59–62), D2 and G (Shiloh 1984: 20), and which is partially represented in Area E1. But even in these areas the finds were meagre and poor; most of them came from fills and quarrying refuse. Persian-period sherds and a few seal impressions were found in Reich and Shukron's Areas A and B, located in the Kidron Valley and mid-slope respectively, ca. 200–250 m south of the Gihon Spring; they seem to have originated in the settlement located on the ridge (Reich and Shukron 2007).

Stratum 8 stands for the Early Hellenistic period. It is fully represented only in Area E2, partially represented in Areas E1 and E3, and scarcely represented in Areas D1 and D2 (Shiloh 1984: 4, Table 2). In this case, too, the finds are meagre. They are composed of three *columbaria* (De Groot 2004) and a structure that yielded the only assemblage of Early Hellenistic pottery from Jerusalem (in Area E1 – Shiloh 1984: 15).

In the case of the City of David, too, the negative evidence is as important as the positive. No Persian or Early Hellenistic finds were found in Area A on the southern tip of the ridge. It is significant to note that in Area A1, Early Roman remains were found over Iron II remains (De Groot, Cohen and Caspi 1992). In Kenyon's Site K, located on the southwestern side of the City of David, ca. 50 m to the north of the Siloan Pool, Iron II sherds were found on bedrock, superimposed by Late Hellenistic finds (Kenyon 1966: 84).[1]

As for the northern part of the ridge, the Persian and Early Hellenistic periods were not represented in B. and E. Mazar's excavations to the south of the southern wall of the Temple Mount, which yielded Late Hellenistic and mainly Early Roman finds superimposed over Iron II buildings (E. Mazar and B. Mazar 1989: XV–XVI). It is also significant that Persian and Early Hellenistic finds were not reported from B. Mazar's excavations near the southwestern corner of the Temple Mount (B. Mazar 1971). A few finds, but no architectural remains or in situ assemblages of pottery, were retrieved by Crowfoot in the excavation of the 'Western Gate', (Crowfoot and Fitzgerald 1929) and by Macalister and Duncan (1926) in the excavation immediately to the west of Shiloh's Area G. The 8–10 m thick dump-debris removed by Reich and Shukron on the eastern slope of the City of David, near the Gihon Spring (Reich and Shukron 2007; also 2004), yielded ceramic material from the Iron II and 'late Second Temple period', but no Persian and Early Hellenistic pottery. Reich and Shukron interpret this as evidence that Area G, located upslope from their dig, was uninhabited at that time. Finally, it is noteworthy that sifting of debris from the Temple Mount recovered almost no Persian period finds (compared to a significant number of finds from the Iron II and from the Hellenistic-Early Roman periods – Barkay and Zweig, 2006).

Reich and Shukron (2007) also noted that 75 of the 85 *Yehud* seal impressions from the Shiloh excavations published by Ariel and Shoham (2000) originated from Areas B, D and E. They concluded that the settlement of the Persian and Early Hellenistic periods was restricted to the top

---

1   Shiloh's Area K, located on the ridge 90 m to the north of Area A, in roughly the same line as Kenyon's Site K, was excavated to bedrock. The earliest remains date to the Early Roman period. In this case a large-scale clearing operation, which could have destroyed the earlier remains, seems to have taken place in the Roman period (also Kenyon 1965: 14; 1966: 88 for her excavations nearby).

of the ridge, south of Area G (see a somewhat similar view in Ariel and Shoham 2000: 138).

All this seems to indicate that:

1. In the Persian and Early Hellenistic periods activity on the Temple Mount was not strong (compare the Iron II finds to the south of the southern wall of the Temple Mount to the negative evidence for the Persian and Early Hellenistic periods and see Barkay and Zweig 2006), and in any event did not include intensively inhabited areas;
2. The northern part of the ridge of the City of David was uninhabited;
3. The southern part of the ridge was probably uninhabited as well.

The Persian and Early Hellenistic settlement was confined to the central part of the ridge, between Shiloh's Area G (which seems to be located on the margin of the inhabited area) and Shiloh's Areas D and E. The settlement was located on the ridge, with the eastern slope outside the built-up area. Even in this restricted area, a century of excavations, by a number of archaeologists, failed to yield even a single (!) house or proper floor from the Persian period, and only one structure from the Early Hellenistic period was found. The idea that the settlement was eradicated because of later activity and erosion (e.g. De Groot 2004: 67) must be rejected in the light of the reasonable preservation of the Late Hellenistic and Iron II remains.

The maximal size of the Persian and Early Hellenistic settlement was therefore ca. 240 (N-S) × 120 (E-W) m, that is, ca. 20–25 dunams (contra to the idea of a 60-dunam settlement [excluding the Temple Mount] in Carter 1999: 200; Lipschits 2006: 32; and a 30-acre settlement [possibly including the Temple Mount] in Avigad 1993: 720). Calculating the population according to the broadly accepted density coefficient of 20 people per one built-up dunam (Finkelstein 1992 and bibliography)[2] – a number which may be too high for what seems to have been a sparsely settled ridge (ibid.) – one reaches an estimated population of 400–500 people; that is, ca. 100 adult men.[3] This stands in sharp contrast to previous, even minimal, estimates of 1,250, 1,500 or 3,000 inhabitants (Carter 1999: 288;

---

2   This coefficient is based on ethno-archaeological and ethno-historical data, which stand against Zorn 1994. Zorn reached inflated numbers which do not fit the demographic data on pre-modern societies. His error may have stemmed from the assumption that all buildings at Tell Nasbeh were inhabited at the same time; the truth of the matter is that no stratigraphic sequence has been established for the settlement, which was inhabited continuously for centuries, throughout the Iron and Babylonian periods!

3   King and Stager (2001: 389) are the only scholars to speak about a small settlement with 'a few hundred inhabitants'; at the same breath they accepted the description of the construction of the city-wall by Nehemiah as historical (see below).

Lipschits 2006: 32; 2005: 271; 'a few thousands' in Avigad 1993: 720), estimates which call for a large settlement of 75–150 dunams – more than the entire area of the City of David.[4]

These data fit well the situation in the immediate environs of Jerusalem, where the number of spots with archaeological remains dropped from 140 in the Iron II to 14 in the Persian period (Kloner 2003a: 28*; 2001: 92; 2003a: 30* for the Early Hellenistic period). They also fit the general demographic depletion in the entire area of the province of Yehud – a maximum of 20,000–30,000 people in the Persian period according to Carter (1999: 195–205) and Lipschits (2003: 364), ca. 15,000 according to my own calculations (Finkelstein forthcoming) – about a third or a fourth of the population of that area in the late Iron II (Carter 1999: 247 based on Broshi and Finkelstein 1992; Ofer 1993).

Nehemiah's Wall

Archaeologists have accepted the description of the reconstruction of the wall in Nehemiah 3 as a historical fact, and have been divided only about the course of the fortifications. The minimalists restricted them to the City of David, and the maximalists argued that the description included the southwestern hill (see summary in Ussishkin 2006). Two finds in the field have been perceived as indications for the course of Nehemiah's city-wall: one on the crest above the eastern slope of the City of David and the other on the western side of that ridge.

Kenyon (1974: 183–84) argued that because of the collapse of the late Iron II city-wall and buildings on the eastern slope of the ridge as a result of the Babylonian destruction, the city-wall of Nehemiah was built higher up, at the top of the slope. In her Square A XVIII (adjacent to Shiloh's Area G) she identified a short segment in the city-wall that had first been uncovered by Macalister and Duncan (1926) – a wall that was later unanimously dated to the Late Hellenistic period (see literature on the First Wall above) – as the city-wall built by Nehemiah. Her dating of this segment of the wall was based on pottery found in a layer dumped against its outer face; this pottery was dated by Kenyon (1974: 183) to the fifth to early third centuries BCE (the sixth to fifth centuries BCE in ibid.: caption to Pl. 79). Shiloh, too, argued – without any archaeological evidence – that the city wall was built 'on the bedrock at the top of the eastern slope' (1984: 29; also Avigad 1993: 720). Stern (2001: 435) accepted Kenyon's

4 Not to mention Weinberg's estimate, based on his interpretation of the biblical text, of 15,000 people in Jerusalem and 150,000 in Yehud in the time of Nehemiah (1992: 43 and 132 respectively).

identification and dating of this segment as Nehemiah's wall. Ussishkin (2006: 160), on the other hand, suggested that Nehemiah reconstructed the Iron II wall, which runs on the lower part of the eastern slope of the City of David.

The only piece of information from the western side of the City of David comes from Crowfoot's 1927 excavations. A massive structure that had been founded on bedrock, under thick layers of later occupations and debris, was identified as a Bronze Age gatehouse that continued to be in use until Roman times (Crowfoot and Fitzgerald 1929: 12–23). Albright (1930–31: 167) identified Crowfoot's 'gatehouse' with the Dung Gate of Nehemiah 3.13, while Alt (1928) proposed equating it with the Valley Gate of Nehemiah 3.13.

Yet, both finds – the wall uncovered by Kenyon and the structure unearthed by Crowfoot – cannot be dated to the Persian period.

Kenyon's identification of Nehemiah's wall was based on (yet unpublished) pottery found in a small sounding, in a fill or a dump thrown against the outer face of the wall (1974: Pl. 79). As rightly argued by De Groot (2001: 78), such a layer cannot be used for dating a city-wall. This material could have been taken from any dump on the slope and put there in order to support the wall (for the same situation in the Outer Wall of Gezer, see Finkelstein 1994: 278). Excavations immediately to the west of this spot by E. Mazar (2007a) did not unearth architectural remains of the Persian and Early Hellenistic periods. But they made clear that this segment is part of the Late Hellenistic city-wall, first uncovered by Macalister and Duncan (1926; see in details Finkelstein et al. 2007).

Ussishkin (2006) has recently dealt in detail with the structure excavated by Crowfoot and identified by him as a gatehouse. Ussishkin has cast doubt on the identification of the structure as a gate, and convincingly argued that it probably dates to the Late Hellenistic or Early Roman period (2006: 159; see also Kenyon 1964: 13).

To sum up this issue, there is no archaeological evidence for the city-wall of Nehemiah. The wall in the east dates to the Late Hellenistic period and the structure in the west – regardless of its function – also post-dates the Persian period. Had it not been for the Nehemiah 3 account, no scholar would have argued for a Persian-period city-wall in Jerusalem. Three early city-walls are known in the City of David, dating to the Middle Bronze Age, the late Iron II and the Late-Hellenistic period. All three have been easy to trace and have been found relatively well preserved. No other city-wall has ever been found and I doubt if this situation will change as a result of future excavations.[5]

---

5   Theoretically, one could argue that Nehemiah 3 relates to the walls of the Temple compound.

One could take a different course and argue, with Ussishkin (2006), that Nehemiah merely rebuilt the ruined late-Iron II wall. Yet, in the many sections of the Iron II wall that have been uncovered – on both the southwestern hill and the southeastern ridge – there is no clue whatsoever for a renovation or reconstruction in the Persian period. In the parts of the late-Iron II city wall uncovered on the southwestern hill, the first changes and additions date to the Late Hellenistic period (Avigad 1983: 65–72; Geva 2003b: 529–32). No such reconstruction has been traced in the long line of the Iron II wall uncovered in several excavations along the eastern slope of the City of David south of the Gihon spring. Archaeologically, then, Nehemiah's wall is a *mirage*.

This should come as no surprise, judging from what we do know about the Persian period settlement systems in Yehud in particular and the entire country in general. To differ from the construction of the Iron II and Late-Hellenistic fortifications in Jerusalem – which represent a well-organized territorio-political entity with significant wealth and population, evidence for high-level bureaucracy and clear ideology of sovereignty – the small community of several hundred inhabitants of Persian-period Jerusalem (that is, not many more than 100 adult men), with a depleted hinterland and no economic base, could not have possibly engaged in the reconstruction of the ca. 3.5-km-long(!) Iron II city-wall with many gates (accepting Ussishkin's reconstruction) (2006). And why should the Persian authorities allow the reconstruction of the old, ruined fortifications and make Jerusalem the only fortified town in the hill country? The explanations of scholars who have dealt with this issue – that this was made possible because of the pressure of the Delian League on the Mediterranean coast, revolt in Egypt, etc. (summaries in Hoglund 1992: 61–4, 127–28; Edelman 2005: 334–40; Lipschits 2006: 35–8) – seem far-fetched, given the location of Jerusalem, distance from Egypt, international roads, coastal ports or other strategic locations (Lipschits, ibid.). Indeed, Persian-period fortifications are known only along the coastal plain (Stern 2001: 464–68).

The Reality behind Nehemiah 3

So what *is* the historical reality behind the description of Nehemiah's rebuilding of the walls of Jerusalem?

Scholars have noted the independent nature of the list in Nehemiah 3 as compared to the rest of the 'Nehemiah Memoir' (Torrey 1910: 225; Williamson 1985: 200; Blenkinsopp 1988: 231; Throntveit 1992: 74–5;

Yet, the description of a city-wall with many gates and towers does not comply with this possibility.

Grabbe 1998: 157), but are divided on the question of whether Nehemiah used an earlier or a contemporary source that was kept in the Temple archives (Kellermann: 1967: 14–17; Williamson 1985: 201; Throntveit 1992: 75; Blenkinsopp 1988: 231), or whether a later editor inserted the text into the Book of Nehemiah (e.g., Torrey 1896; 37–8; 1910: 249, who identified the editor with the Chronist; Mowinckel 1964: 109–16, who opted for a post-chronist redactor). Taking into consideration the archaeological evidence presented in this paper, an existing source from the Persian period, which described a genuine construction effort at that time, is not a viable option. We are left, therefore, with the following possibilities:

1. That the description in Nehemiah 3 is utopian; it was based on the geographical reality of the ruined Iron II city-wall but does not reflect actual work on the wall. The text may describe a symbolic act rather than an actual work, similar to symbolic acts connected to the founding of Etruscan and Roman cities. And it may correspond to an ascriptive, ideal-type of a city that ought to include a wall (cf. Odyssey 6.6-10).[6]
2. That a Persian-period author used an early source, which described the late eighth-century construction or a pre-586 renovation of the Iron II city-wall and incorporated it into the Nehemiah text.
3. That the description was inspired by the construction of the Late Hellenistic, Hasmonaean city-wall.

The first possibility is difficult to accept. The detailed description of the construction of the city-wall and the prominence of the story of the wall throughout the Nehemiah Memoirs renders it highly unlikely. Moreover, the description in Nehemiah 3 – which includes reference to many gates, towers, pools and houses – seems to refer to a true reality of a big city; in the light of what has already been said, the late Iron II and Hasmonaean periods are the only options.

The second possibility should probably be put aside: A) There is no evidence – historical or archaeological – of major work on the Iron II city-wall in the late seventh or early sixth centuries, and it is doubtful if a source from the late eighth century would have survived until the fifth or fourth centuries without being mentioned in any late-monarchic biblical source. B) Most names of gates, towers and pools in the list do not correspond to the many such names in late-monarchic biblical texts.[7]

---

6 I am grateful to my colleague and friend Irad Malkin for drawing my attention to these possibilities.

7 Except for the Tower of Hananel and the Horse Gate, mentioned in Jer. 31.38 and 31.40

The third option would put Nehemiah 3 with what scholars see as late redactions in Ezra and Nehemiah, which can be dated as late as the Hasmonaean period (Williamson 1985: xxxv; Wright 2004). The usage of words such as the province *Beyond the River* (עבר הנהר – Neh. 3.7), *pelekh* and פחת (Neh. 3.11) does not present difficulty for such a late dating, as they appear in late Jewish sources (for עבר הנהר see *1 Macc.* 7.8 – Rappaport 2004: 281; for *pelekh* in the rabbinical literature [without entering the discussion on the meaning of the word] see Kohut 1926: 346; Demsky 1983: 243; for פחת see Dan. 3.27).

Dating this text to the Hasmonaean period[8] may correspond to the importance given to the figure of Nehemiah in the first two chapters of *2 Maccabees* (as the builder of the Temple!), which Bergren (1997) interpreted as an attempt to bolster the figure of Judas Maccabaeus, the hero of *2 Maccabees*, by comparing him to Nehemiah – a prominent figure in the restoration, a builder, a political leader, a zealot for the low and a paradigm of piety (ibid.: 261–62).[9] Nehemiah could have been chosen as such a model for the Hasmonaeans because he represented a non-Davidide, non-Zadokite leadership.

Clues that Nehemiah 3 does not reflect Persian-period realities may be found in the archaeology of two of the three well-identified and excavated (rather than surveyed) sites mentioned in the list – Beth-zur and Gibeon.

The archaeology of Beth-zur (Neh. 3.16) in the Persian period has been debated. Funk (1993: 261), Paul and Nancy Lapp (1968: 70; P. Lapp 1968a: 29) and Carter (1999: 157), argued that the site was very sparsely, in fact, insignificantly inhabited in the Persian and Early Hellenistic periods. Funk noted that the 'interpretation of the Persian-Hellenistic remains at Beth-zur is dependent in large measure on the extant literary references . . .' (1968: 9). Based on a single locus (!), Stern (2001: 437–38; see also 1982: 36) adhered to the notion of a significant activity at the site in the Persian period. Reich (1992) argued in the same line according to an architectural analysis. The published material from the excavations (Sellers 1933; Sellers et al. 1968) includes only a limited number of finds – sherds, vessels and coins – that can safely be dated to the Persian period

respectively. The Fish Gate and the Valley Gate appear in 2 Chron. (33.14 and 26.9 respectively), but not in late-monarchic texts.

8   According to Nehemiah 3, the population of Jerusalem included 3,044 men, a number which translates to a total of 12,000–15,000 inhabitants (Weinberg 2000: 316). If this number has any credibility, it fits a city of ca. 600 dunams – the size of Jerusalem in the late Iron II and the second century BCE.

9   Ben Sira (49.13), an early second-century author, also emphasizes the role of Nehemiah as a builder. This reference may indicate the existence of a pre-Hasmonean tradition about Nehemiah as a builder; it cannot be used as a proof for the construction of a wall in the Persian period.

(Stern 2001: 437), while most forms belonging to the Persian-period repertoire are missing altogether. Hence, though archaeology may have revealed traces of some Persian-period activity at the site, it is clear that it was an important place only in the late Iron II and the late Hellenistic periods. It should be noted that Beth-zur – supposedly the headquarters of half a district in the province of Yehud – did not yield even a single Yehud seal impression (over 530 have so far been recorded – Lipschits and Vanderhooft 2007b: 3).

It is noteworthy that during the wars of the Macabbees Beth-zur was located on the border of Judaea and seems to have changed hands several times. It was fortified by Judas Maccabaeus (*1 Macc.* 4.61), held by Lysias (*1 Macc.* 6.7), fortified by Bacchides (*1 Macc.* 9.52) besieged by Simeon (*1 Macc.* 11.65) and fortified by him (*1 Macc.* 14.33). One can argue that in the Persian period Beth-zur belonged to the province of Yehud and that it became a border stronghold in the early Hellenistic Period, but there is no evidence for such a change in any source and it seems highly unlikely.

Gibeon (Neh. 3.7) did not yield unambiguous Persian-period finds either. Without going into the debate over the dating of the Gibeon winery and inscriptions – late monarchic or sixth century (see summary in Lipschits 1989: 287–91) – the *mwsh* seal impressions and wedge-shaped and reed-impressed sherds found at the site (Pritchard 1964: Figs 32.7, 48.17) attest to a certain activity in the Babylonian or Babylonian/ early Persian period. Yet, typical Persian-period pottery and Yehud seal impressions were not found (for the latter see Lipschits 2005: 180). Late Hellenistic pottery and coins dated to the days of Antiochus III and John Hyrcanus are attested at Gibeon (Pritchard 1962: 163). According to Pritchard, there is 'only scant evidence of occupation from the end of the sixth century until the beginning of the first century BCE' at Gibeon (1993: 513). Still, in an attempt to provide evidence for the Gibeon of Neh. 3.7 he argued that 'scattered and sporadic settlements' did exist there during the Persian and Hellenistic periods (Pritchard 1962: 163). Stern rightly interpreted the Gibeon finds as evidence for only sixth century and possibly early Persian period activity at the site (1982: 32–3; 2001: 433; Lipschits 2005: 243–45 – sixth century).[10] Another clue for dating Nehemiah 3 may be found in the Yehud seal impressions. The distribution of Groups 1–12 (Vanderhooft and Lipschits 2007), which date to the Persian period, does not fit the territory described in this chapter.[11] In the highlands, these seal

10   Three other sites in the list which are well identified yielded both Persian and Hellenistic finds: Jericho (Stern 1982: 38; Netzer 2001 respectively), Zanoah (Dagan 1992: 92) and Tekoa (Ofer 1993: Appendix IIA: 28). Keilah poses a problem, as thus far surveys of the site seem to have yielded only Persian-period pottery (Kochavi 1972: 49; Dagan 1992: 161).

11   I refer to the main concentrations of the seal impressions. The presence or absence of a

impressions are concentrated in Jerusalem and its surroundings, including Ramat Rahel, with only a few (six items) found in the highlands to the north of Jerusalem. No seal impression of this type was found south of Ramat Rahel. In the east, seal impressions of these types were retrieved at Jericho and En-Gedi (six items) – a reasonable reason for the inclusion of this area within the borders of Yehud.[12] Nehemiah 3 mentions the districts of Jerusalem and Beth-haccherem (most probably Ramat Rahel – Aharoni 1979: 418), Mizpah in the north, Beth-zur in the south and Keilah in the upper Shephelah, in the southwest. Therefore the two sources of information – the distribution of the Persian period Yehud seal impressions and Nehemiah 3 – describe different situations in the history of Yehud-Judea. If it indeed reflects realities of the Hellenistic period, it may be meaningful that it does not mention a district in the Gezer/Lod area, which implies that it predates the annexation of these cities to Judaea in 140s BCE.

There are several problems regarding the Hasmonaean option for the background of Nehemiah 3. First, the toponyms in the description of the First Wall in Josephus's *Wars* 5, 4.2 – especially the 'gate of the Essens' (as well as names of gates mentioned by Josephus elsewhere) – are different from the toponyms in Nehemiah 3. But the change may be assigned to post-Hasmonaean, mainly Herodian times. A more severe problem is the prominence of the story on the construction of the city-wall throughout the Nehemiah Memoirs. Accepting a Hasmonaean reality behind the city-wall account in Nehemiah would therefore call for a drastic new approach to the entire Book of Nehemiah.

The List of Returnees
Scholars have debated the relationship between the two versions of the list (Ezra 2.1-67; Neh. 7.6-68), the historical authenticity of this source, its date, whether it represents one wave of returnees or a summary of several immigrations, and its value for estimating the population of Yehud (for the latest discussions see Carter 1999: 77–8; Edelman 2005: 175–76; and especially Lipschits 2005: 158–68 with extensive bibliography).

Twenty places are mentioned in the list. They are located in the highlands of Benjamin, the vicinity of Jerusalem (to Bethlehem in the south), and the areas of Lod in the west and Jericho in the east. The location of three of these places – Netophah, Nebo (Nob) and Senaah – is not

---

single item means nothing, as shown by the impressions found in Babylon and Kadesh-barnea (Vanderhooft and Lipschits 2007: 21 and 27 respectively).

12   In the west they were found at Gezer and Tel Harasim in the western Shephelah (four items altogether) – places clearly outside the borders of Yehud until the expansion of the Hasmonaean state in the days of Jonathan and Simeon; none was found in the many sites of the upper Shephelah.

sufficiently well established, while the rest are well (or reasonably well) identified and hence their archaeology can be consulted.

Sites Excavated

For *Jerusalem* and *Gibeon* see above. Gibeon is mentioned in late monarchic biblical sources – in the list of towns of Benjamin (Josh. 18.25), unanimously dated to the late seventh century BCE (Alt 1925; Na'aman 1991 with previous literature) and in the Book of Jeremiah (28.1; 41.16).

Bethel was fully settled in the late Iron II (Kelso 1968: 36–7). A wedge-shaped and reed-impressed sherd found at the site (Kelso 1968: Pl. 67,8) and a Babylonian seal bought from the villagers of Beitin (Kelso 1968: 37; Stern 1982: 31) seem to indicate that the site continued to be inhabited in the sixth century BCE (and see below for the reference in Zech. 7.2). Kelso (1968: 37, 38) suggested that the town was destroyed in the second half of the sixth century.

No unambiguous evidence for a Persian-period occupation was found at Bethel; there were no architectural remains, no pottery and no seal impressions. Moreover, the foundations of the Hellenistic walls penetrated into the Iron II remains (Kelso 1968: 36) with no Persian period layer in between. The excavators speculated that a Persian-period settlement may have been located under the built-up area of the village of Beitin, near the spring, in the southern part of the site (Kelso 1968: 38), but such a settlement should have left a clear ceramic imprint at the site. The only such clue is a tiny sherd identified by Illiff as part of a fifth-century BCE Greek lekythos (Kelso 1968: 80, Pl. 37, 10).[13]

A prosperous Hellenistic settlement was uncovered at Bethel (Kelso 1968: 36, 40, 52; Lapp 1968b).

Bethel is mentioned in a large number of late-monarchic biblical sources, such as the list of towns of Benjamin (Josh. 18.22) and the description of the days of Josiah (2 Kings 23). Papyrus Amherst 63 mentions deportees brought by the Assyrians, who were probably settled at Bethel (Steiner 1991). If the mention of Bethel in Zech. 7.2 refers to a place (e.g. Meyers and Meyers 1987: 382–83; and is not part of a name of a person – e.g. Ackroyd 1968: 207), it testifies to the fact that the site was inhabited in the late sixth century. Bethel is mentioned in the list of forts built by Bacchides (*1 Macc.* 9.50).

Hadid is safely identified in the mound of el-Haditheh northeast of Lod.

---

13   I wish to thank Oren Tal for checking this sherd and confirming its date as suggested decades ago by Illiffe.

Salvage excavations at the site indicate that the late Iron Age settlement extended over the main mound and its northwestern slope (Brand 1998: 27–9). The excavation yielded two seventh-century BCE Neo-Assyrian cuneiform tablets (Na'aman and Zadok 2000). The site was occupied in both the Persian and Hellenistic periods (Brand 1997; for the Hellenistic settlement see also Nagorsky 2005).

Hadid is mentioned in connection with the history of the Hasmonaeans; it was fortified by Simon (*1 Macc.* 12, 38; 13, 13; Jos., *Ant.* XIII, 203, 392).

Jericho. Tell es-Sultan was intensively settled in the seventh century BCE. Yehud seal impressions and attic vessels (Vanderhooft and Lipschits 2007; Stern 1982, 38 respectively) indicate that the site was inhabited in the Persian period. The late Hellenistic settlement was located at Tulul Abu el-Alayiq to the southwest of Tell es-Sultan (Netzer 2001).

Jericho is mentioned in the late-seventh century BCE list of towns of Benjamin (Josh. 18.21). It is referred to in various Hellenistic sources – the Zenon papyri, 1 and *2 Macc.*, Diodorus, and Strabo (Tsafrir, Di Segni and Green 1994: 143).

Lod. The mound of Lod has never been properly excavated; in fact, its exact extent under the Arab town is not very clear (see Gophna and Beit-Arieh 1997: 88). Still, enough finds have been unearthed to show that Lod was inhabited from Neolithic to Ottoman times (ibid.). Excavations at Neve Yarak, a neighbourhood of modern Lod situated near the ancient mound, yielded Iron II, Persian and Hellenistic finds (Rosenberger and Shavit 1993; Feldstein 1997; Khalaily and Gopher 1997; Arbel 2004). It is quite clear, then, that the site was inhabited in all three periods discussed in this paper.

Lod is mentioned in *1 Macc.* 11.34 as one of the three toparchies added to the Hasmonaean territory in 145 BCE.

Sites Surveyed

Bethlehem. The ancient mound occupies the eastern sector of the ridge overbuilt by the town of Bethlehem. It seems to have been fully occupied in the Iron II (see list of spots with Iron II finds in Prag 2000: 170–71). A recent survey of parcels of land still available for research to the east of the Church of Nativity revealed Iron II and Byzantine sherds (Prag 2000); no other period is mentioned.

The only quantitative survey at the site was conducted by Ofer (1993: Appendix IIA, 13), who collected 26 rims from the late Iron II, two rims from the Persian period, and one or two rims from the Hellenistic period. Beyond indicating periods of occupation, these data are insufficient for reconstructing the size of the site and the intensity of activity in the various periods of habitation.

Bethlehem is mentioned in the LXX version of the list of towns of Judah (Josh. 15.59a) which dates to the late seventh century BCE (Alt 1925; Na'aman 1991) and in the Book of Jeremiah (41.17).

Anathoth. Early studies did not locate pre-Roman remains at the village of Anata (Blair 1936; Albright 1936). Hence the location of biblical Anathoth was sought at two sites in the vicinity of the village.

Ras el-Kharubeh was both surveyed and excavated (for early research see Bergman 1936). The modern excavation yielded a small number of sherds (40 altogether) from the late Iron II, sherds from the Persian period (about 25 per cent of the material from the dig), and a large number of sherds from the late Hellenistic period. The site was found to be eroded and sparsely inhabited (Biran 1985: 209–11). A survey conducted at the site yielded Iron II and Hellenistic sherds, but no Persian-period finds (Dinur and Feig 1993: 358).

Another site suggested for the location of biblical Anathoth is Khirbet Deir es-Sidd, which was also excavated by Biran (1985: 211–13). It was strongly inhabited in the late-Iron II, but did not yield Persian-period finds. Only a few Hellenistic-Roman sherds were found. A survey conducted at the site yielded a large number of sherds, 70 per cent of which were dated to the Iron II. Persian-period sherds were found in a tomb. Hellenistic sherds were also present (Dinur and Feig 1993: 379).

A thorough, modern survey of the village of Anata (Dinur and Feig 1993: 359–60) has shown that it is built on an ancient site. Hence there is no reason to seek the location of Anathoth elsewhere. The survey yielded 242 sherds, 35 per cent of which date to the Iron II and 10 per cent to the Hellenistic period. The Persian period is not represented.[14]

The mention of Anathoth in the Book of Jeremiah attests to its being settled in late-monarchic times.

Azmaveth is safely identified with the village of Hizma northeast of Jerusalem. The site was surveyed twice. Kallai (1972: 185) reported sherds from the Roman period and later. A more thorough and modern survey was conducted by Dinur and Feig (1993: 372–73), who reported sherds from the Iron II, Persian and Hellenistic periods.

Kirjath-Jearim is safely identified in the mound of Deir el-'Azar, above the village of Abu-Ghosh. A large collection of pottery from the site, stored by the Antiquities Authority, was studied by the author in 1992. It includes

14 As an editor of the volume in which Dinur and Feig and Feldstein et al.'s surveys were published, the author went over the pottery of all sites. This includes the sites reported here, Anata, Hizma, Kh. el-Kafira, Kh. el-Burj, er-Ram, Jaba and Mukhmas.

440 sherds, of which 310 date to the Iron II, 1 to the Persian period, 49 to the Persian or Hellenistic period, 23 to the Hellenistic period, and 11 to the Hellenistic or Roman period. The number of sherds collected at the site is sufficient to state that it was strongly inhabited in the late Iron II, very sparsely inhabited – if at all – in the Persian period and inhabited in the Hellenistic period.

Kirjath-Jearim is mentioned in the late seventh century BCE list of towns of Judah (Josh. 15.60; 18.14) and in the Book of Jeremiah (26.20).

Chephirah is safely identified with Kh. el-Kafira northwest of Jerusalem. The site was surveyed twice. Vriezen (1975) collected a large number of Iron II sherds and several Persian and Hellenistic sherds (ibid. Figs. 4: 23–25 and 5 respectively). Feldstein et al. (1993: 209–11) surveyed the site thoroughly and collected 243 sherds, of which 81 per cent date to the Iron II. A few sherds were tentatively dated to the Persian period and 13 per cent were assigned to the Hellenistic and Roman periods. It is clear from these data that the main period of occupation was the Iron II, that activity at the site in the Persian period was weak, and that occupation intensified in the Hellenistic period.

Chephirah is mentioned in the late seventh century BCE list of towns of Benjamin (Josh. 18.26).

Beeroth. The location of Beeroth was debated in the early years of research (summary in Yeivin 1971: 141–42), but was later safely fixed at the site of Khirbet el-Burj on the outskirts of the modern Jerusalem neighbourhood of Ramot (ibid.). The site was surveyed and partially excavated in a salvage operation.

Kallai (1972: 186–87) was the first to conduct a modern survey at the site. He reported Iron II pottery and a single wedge-shaped and reed-impressed sherd that should probably be dated to the sixth century BCE. Feldstein et al. (1993: 231–33) conducted a more modern and thorough survey at the site and collected 212 sherds, of which 74 per cent date to the Iron II, a few to the Persian period, 9 per cent to the Persian or Hellenistic period and 8 per cent to the Hellenistic period.

A salvage excavation was conducted at the site in 1992 (Onn and Rapuano 1994). Most of the finds belonged to medieval times, but evidence was revealed for a settlement that was occupied from the Iron Age through the Hellenistic period.

It is clear from this data that the settlement was at its peak in the Iron II, that activity in the Persian period was weak and that a certain recovery occurred in the Hellenistic period.

Beeroth appears in the late seventh century BCE list of towns of Benjamin (Josh. 18.25). It is possibly mentioned in *1 Macc.* 9.4 as Βερεα. (Jos. Ant. 12.422 writes Βηρζεθ, but see discussion in Rappaport 2004: 233).

Ramah is unanimously identified with the village of er-Ram north of Jerusalem. Only one modern survey was conducted at the site – by Feldstein et al. (1993: 168–69). They collected a large number of 359 sherds, of which 20 per cent date to the Iron II, 2 per cent to the Persian period and 13 per cent to the Hellenistic period. This means that the site was strongly inhabited in the Iron II, that it declined in the Persian period, and that it recovered in the Hellenistic period.

Ramah appears in the list of towns of Benjamin (Josh. 18.25) and in the Book of Jeremiah (31.15; 40.1).

Geba is safely identified with the village of Jaba northeast of Jerusalem. The site was surveyed twice. Kallai (1972: 183) reported sherds from the Iron II and the Persian period. Feldstein et al. (1993: 177–79) conducted a more thorough survey at the site and collected 284 sherds, of which 23 per cent date to the Iron II and 22 per cent to the Hellenistic period. It seems, therefore, that the site was strongly inhabited in both the Iron II and the Hellenistic period. It was probably deserted (or very sparsely inhabited) in the Persian period.

Geba appears in the late seventh century BCE list of towns of Benjamin (Josh. 18.24).

Michmash is safely identified with the village of Mukhmas to the northeast of Jerusalem. The ancient site – Khirbet el-Hara el-Fauqa – is located on the northern edge of the village. The site was thoroughly surveyed by Feldstein et al. (1993: 185–86), who collected 643 sherds (!), of which 14 per cent date to the Iron II, 10 per cent to the Persian period and 19 per cent to the Hellenistic period. This means that the site was strongly inhabited in all three periods discussed here.

Michmash served for a while as the seat of Jonathan the Hasmonaean (*1 Macc.* 9.73; Jos. *Ant.* 13.34).

Ai of the List of Returnees is a riddle. The site of et-Tell was not inhabited after the Iron I. Assuming that there is a connection between the Ai of the Book of Joshua (as a name originally derived from an etiological story) and the Ai of the List of Returnees, the only sites which may provide an archaeological reality behind this place-name are the village of Deir Dibwan, or better (from the preservation of the name point of view) Khirbet el-Haiyan, located on the southern outskirts of Deir Dibwan.

Deir Dibwan is a large village that has never been properly surveyed. Feldstein et al. (1993: 183–84) managed to collect 20 sherds there, among them a single sherd from the Iron II and all the others from the Roman period and later. This is insufficient to reach conclusions regarding the settlement history of the site.

Khirbet el-Haiyan was both excavated and surveyed. Excavation at the site revealed evidence for occupation starting in the Roman period (Callaway and Nicol 1966: 19). Kallai (1972: 178–79) collected sherds from the Roman period and later. Feldstein et al. (1993: 183) retrieved

112 sherds at the site, of which 32 per cent were dated to the Hellenistic or Roman period.

These data are not sufficient for this discussion. It seems logical to suggest that Ai of the List of Returnees should be sought at Deir Dibwan.

Ono. Gophna, Taxel and Feldstein (2005) have recently shown that Ono cannot be identified with Kafr Ana, a site that was not occupied from the Chalcolithic to the Byzantine period. Instead, they suggested identifying Ono at the site of Kafr Juna, located 1 km to the northeast of Kafr Ana. Surveys conducted there yielded a large number of Iron II, Persian and Hellenistic sherds (ibid.).

Discussion

Table 2.1 summarizes the finds at the sites mentioned in the List of Returnees.

Table 2.1 Summary of periods represented at the sites mentioned in the List of Returnees, including intensity of occupation (V = evidence for activity, but data not sufficient to specify intensity of activity)

	Iron II	Persian	Hellenistic
Jerusalem	Strong	Weak	Strong
Bethlehem	V	Weak	Weak
Gibeon	Strong	— (except for sixth century)?	Weak
Anathoth	Strong	—	Medium
Azmaveth	V	V	V
Kirjath-Jearim	Strong	Weak	Medium
Chephirah	Strong	Weak	Weak
Beeroth	Strong	Weak	Medium
Ramah	Strong	Weak	Medium
Geba	Strong	—?	Strong
Michmash	Strong	Medium	Strong
Bethel	Strong	— (except for sixth century)?	Strong
Ai (if Kh. Haiyan)	—	—	V?
(if Deir Dibwan)	V		
Lod	V	V	V
Hadid	V	V	V
Ono	Strong	Strong	Strong
Jericho	V	V	V

Three to five places mentioned in the list (including places which were thoroughly excavated), were not inhabited in the Persian period, and at other sites activity was meagre. Places which are not mentioned in the list are also worth mentioning. The best marker for importance of Judaean sites in the Persian period is the number of Yehud seal impressions found in the course of their excavations (I refer to Types 1–15 in Vanderhooft and Lipschits 2007, Types 13–15 may date to the early Hellenistic period). The sites with the largest number of such seal impressions are Ramat Rahel, Jerusalem, Mizpah, Nebi Samuel, Jericho and En Gedi. Mizpah, En Gedi and Beth-haccherem (most probably Ramat Rahel – Aharoni 1979: 418) do not appear in the list, and the list does not include any name which can fit the location of Nebi Samuel. In other words, four of the six sites with the largest number of Yehud seal impressions are absent from the list – another indication that the list does not fit the reality of the Persian period.

The concentration of Yehud seal impressions of Types 13–15 (Vanderhooft and Lipschits 2007) in the area north of Jerusalem is also noteworthy. In this area Impressions 13–14 mark a growth from ca. 5.5 per cent of the seal impressions in the early group (Types 1–12, of the Persian period), to 11 per cent in the middle group. This may indicate an expansion of the province, or at least of the Jewish population, to the north, to include the highlands around Mizpah, in the late-Persian/early Hellenistic period.

Finally, it is evident that the number of returnees which appear in the list (see discussion in Lipschits 2005: 161–62) – if taken as reflecting a real demographic reality – does not fit the depleted population of Yehud in the Persian period (for the latter see Carter 1999: 195–205; Lipschits 2005: 270; Finkelstein forthcoming).

All this is sufficient to argue that the list of returnees cannot be seen as an authentic record of the places where returnees settled in the Persian period. The archaeology of the list contradicts the ideas of both those who accept the list as genuinely representing the early settlement, immediately after the return (e.g. Galling 1951; Myers 1965: 14–17), or in the days of Nehemiah (Blenkinsopp 1988: 83), and those who see it as summarizing several waves of returnees up to the days of Nehemiah (summary in Lipschits 2005: 159–60, n. 91). Based on a demographic estimate for Persian-period Yehud, Lipschits (2005: 160–61) rejected the notions of large-scale deportations at the end of the Iron II and significant waves of returnees thereafter, and suggested that the list is a literary compilation that could have been based on several censuses that were undertaken during the Persian period (for other scholars who proposed a similar solution see references in ibid: 160, n. 92). The results of this investigation make this suggestion too untenable.

There are several ways to decipher the reality behind the List of

Returnees. According to the first, it reflects a late Iron II situation, possibly focused on a vague memory of the main areas from which people were deported, or the main areas to which they returned in the sixth century BCE. Another possibility is that the list has no historical value at all, and simply mentions important settlements of the late Iron II, in areas that were included in the province of Yehud. A third explanation could be that the list was compiled in the late Hellenistic (Hasmonaean) period and reflects the settlement reality of that time, against the background of a vague memory of the territory of the province of Yehud with the addition of the area of Lod. The latter possibility would also fit the demographic reality hidden behind the list.

It is noteworthy that seven of the places in the list are mentioned in the Books of Maccabees, including important places in the history of the Hasmonaeans such as Beeroth, Michmash and Hadid. The appearance in the list of Lod, Hadid and Ono is also significant, as the district of Lod was added to Judea only in 145 BCE (*1 Macc.* 11.34) – another clue that the list may depict second century BCE realities.

Conclusion

Archaeology seems to indicate that Nehemiah 3 and the List of Returnees cannot be dated to the Persian period. Though there are several possibilities to decipher the reality behind these lists, dating them to the second century BCE seems the most logical and less difficult one.

Regarding Nehemiah 3, the archaeological finds indicate that in the Persian and Early Hellenistic periods Jerusalem was a small village with a depleted population, incapable of engaging in large-scale building operations. In addition, there is no archaeological evidence for any reconstruction or renovation of the Iron II fortifications in the Persian period. Taking these data into consideration, there are three ways to explain Nehemiah 3.1): (1) that it is a utopian list; (2) that it preserves a memory of an Iron Age construction or renovation of the city-wall; (3) that the list is influenced by the construction of the First Wall in the Hasmonaean period. The latter option seems to pose lesser difficulties.

Regarding the List of Returnees, several sites mentioned in it were not inhabited in the Persian period, or were very sparsely settled. Moreover, important Persian-period places are not mentioned in the list. This leaves two main options for understanding the reality behind the list. According to the first, it portrays a late Iron II situation. According to the second, it was compiled in the late Hellenistic (Hasmonaean) period and represents the settlement conditions of the time.

Dating the actuality behind Nehemiah 3 and the List of Returnees to the Hellenistic period calls for a re-evaluation of the date of the Books of Ezra and Nehemiah, but this is beyond the scope of this article.

Concluded October 2007

Acknowledgement

Oded Lipschits and David Ussishkin read parts of this manuscript and provided me with valuable comments; I am grateful to both of them. Needless to say, the responsibility for the ideas presented in the article rests with me only.

3

HYPARCHS, *OIKONOMOI* AND MAFIOSI: THE GOVERNANCE
OF JUDAH IN THE PTOLEMAIC PERIOD

Lester L. Grabbe[1]
University of Hull, England

Those of us who work in the Persian period often bemoan our lack of information and the major gaps in our knowledge of Persian history. One might expect that things will be different once we reach the Greek period. After all, we have Greek historians writing about Alexander's exploits and those of his successors, and does not Egypt provide an abundance of papyri? This is true, but it masks some significant problems that historians of Ptolemaic Judah must face. Although several accounts of Alexander's conquests have been preserved, the interior of Palestine gets little mention. Similarly, although we have a detailed record of much of the time of the Diadochi, the Greek accounts of the rest of third-century history are sporadic. As for the vaunted papyri, they tend to relate to Egypt proper, with little on such peripheral areas as Palestine and Syria. For example, the basic question of whether there was a governor of Syria-Palestine or of its individual divisions, or whether these areas were governed directly from Alexandria, cannot be answered definitively.

Administration in Egypt

We have most information about Egypt proper (Bagnall 1976: 3–5). Especially important as primary sources are the *Revenue Laws* of Ptolemy II, *P. Tebtunis* 8 and *P. Tebtunis* 703.[2] It has been argued that

---

1 The original version of this paper served as the base text for some sections of Grabbe 2008. The original format has been kept, but the data within it have been updated. More information on some aspects of it can be found in Grabbe 2008.

2 The *Revenue Laws* were published by Grenfell 1896; for a recent English translation see Bagnall and Derow (2004: 114); for a translation of the central sections, see Austin (2006: 296–97).

the Ptolemies had largely continued the system of Pharaonic rule (Welles 1949), though this is a complicated issue. A simplified model contains three levels (Thomas 1978: 188–89; Manning 2003: 137). At the very top (reporting to the king, of course) were the διοικητής (finance minister) who was responsible for much of the administration of the country because the arrangements were primarily aimed at securing sufficient and regular revenue. Over the *chora* (countryside) of Egypt was the ἐπιστράτηγος, an office that has been much debated (Thomas 1975; 1982). There was also the ὑπομνηματογράφος (recorder) and the ἐπιστολογράφος (registrar). At the next level, the basis of the administration was the nome. The country was divided up into 40-odd nomes. Each nome had a nomarch who was responsible for basic administration. Alongside him was the οἰκονόμος who was responsible for finances. The third administrative officer in each nome was the βασιλικὸς γραμματεύς (royal scribe). Because these were originally equal in authority, it gave a means of providing a check on the authority of each officer. However, the στρατηγός, who originally held a military post, came to take on increased power and responsibility in the civic area until he became the chief administrator in each nome, a development that began already in the third century. At the bottom was the village administration, with the κωμάρχης (village headman) and the κωμογραμματεύς (village scribe).

Each of the higher officers had various officials reporting to him. For example, under the *dioikētēs* were ὑποδιοικηταί or subordinate finance officers and at the 'ground level' were other specialized officials, such as the γενηματοφύλακες (guards over the threshing) and the σιτολόγοι (guards over the royal stored grain). In order to assure its revenues the government made use of tax-farmers (τελῶναι) to act as underwriters (Rostovtzeff 1941 vol. 2: 328–31; Harper 1934). At an annual auction tax-farmers would bid for the right to guarantee the revenue for a particular region, whether large or small. They would put up sureties to support their bid. If the income fell short of the bid, they had to make it up from their own resources, but if it exceeded the bid, they kept the excess or at least a good portion of it. Although the tax-farmers took a certain risk, it was clearly a lucrative enterprise in the long run. Most years they would have made money, or there would be no point in taking part in the auction. From the Egyptian government's point of view, the tax-farmers took the risk, while the government could operate in confidence that an assured level of income would be coming into the coffers. They could no doubt have gained a higher income over time if they had simply collected the

---

Tebtunis Papyri 8 was published in Grenfell et al. (1902: 66–9), but see more recently Bagnall 1975; and 703 in Hunt and Smyly (1933: 66–102).

taxes for themselves, but they traded this chance of a higher income for the security of a regular steady income.

The tax-farmers were not tax collectors. The collection of taxes was the duty of the state agents (λογευταί, ὑπερεταί). This was probably to the long-term benefit of the state, since over-zealous collection by those with an interest in maximizing income would eventually wear the peasants down and reduce revenue in the long run. With their income assured, the Egyptian officials could take a more equitable approach to the collection of the taxes. On the other hand, the tax-farmers were not just passive by-standers, waiting to see whether the income would come in or not. They were intimately involved in overseeing the particular agricultural or industrial activity on which the tax was based and also in seeing that the state officials did their job in the collection of the tax in question (Harper 1934).

One might think that we could simply transfer this system to Palestine, yet there are several reasons why one cannot. First, one of the indelible points arising out of Bagnall's study (1976) is the variety of administrative arrangements under the Ptolemies, especially in the Ptolemaic possessions outside Egypt. For example, Philocles, king of Sidon, held a Ptolemaic office (Hauben 1987; 2004). A second reason has already been hinted at: the above system in Egypt is overly simplified. In fact, a rather less tidy and more complicated set of arrangements existed, at least part of the time and over at least part of Egypt. For example, it has been debated whether there was more than one *dioikētēs*, since some have interpreted one text (SB 7377) as showing several *dioiketai* over Egypt at the same time (Thomas 1978). If so, the suggestion that it was a short-lived set of arrangements is reasonable, but it illustrates our lack of certainty even in a basic area. We also know that not every nome was overseen by a nomarch; in some cases it was a toparch or even sometimes an *oikonomos* (Samuel 1966). Usually the toparch was subordinate to the nomarch but apparently not always. Also, the Thebaid was divided into several nomes, with the nomarch over all of them (Thomas 1978: 192–93). A further complication is that, as noted above, the *stratēgos* gradually took over most of the powers of the nomarch who was reduced to the level of a minor financial officer by the middle of the second century BCE (Thomas 1978: 194).

A third reason relates to the language and ethnic situation of the bureaucracy. Although Greeks and the Greek language operated at the highest levels of the administration, Egyptians using Greek operated in the middle level, and Demotic was widely used at the lower levels. A number of sources indicate that the Egyptians formed a substantial part of the administrative apparatus already in the early Ptolemaic period. Drawing on the papyri from Hibeh, A. E. Samuel (1970: 451) concluded with regard to the early Ptolemaic administration:

> Indeed, not only does the opportunity to join seem to have been
> equal, but the opportunity to rise seems to have been there as well. I
> see no differentiation in the types of jobs held. Non-Greeks became
> nomarchs, basilikoi grammateis [royal scribes], and filled a variety
> of important offices. The ranks of the local bureaucracy seem to have
> been filled indifferently by Greeks or non-Greeks.

Many examples can be found of Egyptians in relatively high administrative offices. One example is the *oikonomos* Horos and his assistant
Harmachis (Clarysse 1976). Indeed, M. R. Falivene (1991: 222) points
out that Demotic documents suggest that the highest tax officials before
Ptolemy II were not Greek. The only requirement for working in the
bureaucracy was knowledge of the dominant language, Greek. Even this
was not the barrier it might seem, since facility in the language did not
necessarily mean fluency. Individuals who held official office had Greek
scribes to produce letters in official epistolary style (Clarysse 1976: 206).
On the other hand, many Egyptian scribes were fluent in Greek and made
few or no mistakes (Clarysse 1993). As D. J. Thompson notes, the 'imposi-
tion of conformity on diverse ethnic communities was never an interest
of the Ptolemaic state' (1984: 1074), and although she was speaking
specifically of ethnic communities in Egypt itself, how much more was it
the case with ethnic communities in the Ptolemaic possessions.

The Lagids were pragmatic and opportunistic. Uniformity was not
the aim but arrangements that worked and that provided the revenue
expected by the crown. Where previous systems had existed, they might
be continued, though possibly with some modification. The pragmatism
is well illustrated by the variety of different internal arrangements even
in Egypt itself and also by the use of native Egyptians and the Demotic
language in the administration in Egypt.

Sources with Regard to Judah

Unfortunately, we have no spectacular new finds. Those acquainted with
this historical period will find familiar sources. Yet a careful perusal of them
gives us some useful hints towards the administrative situation in Palestine.

Zenon Papyri
One of the main contributions of the Zenon papyri to Jewish history is
the figure of Tobias, head of a cleruchy (military settlement) and a major
local figure in Palestine. This seems to provide a dimension of realia to
the literary figure in both Nehemiah and, especially, the Tobiad Romance
(see below). The question of whether Joseph Tobiad even existed could

once have been debated, but it is now unlikely that he is entirely the stuff of fiction. Tobias is the head of a cleruchy that served as reserves for the Ptolemaic army (*PCZ* 59003; Durand 1997: text 3; *CPJ* 1.1: 6–7, 19: Τουβίου ἱππέων κληροῦχος). Although not a lot is said directly about Tobias, much can be inferred from the situation described and the occasionally telling phrase or reference in the documents.

It has been suggested that both a cavalry unit and a band of foot soldiers made up his cleruchy (*CPJ* 1: p. 120; Durand 1997: 51–2). Tobias's stature is shown by a number of indications. There are references to the 'land of Tobias' (*P. Lon.* 1930; *CPJ* 1.2d: 16; Durand #6: 176: ἐν τῆι Τουβίου), showing a considerable territorial area of influence. Tobias makes a gift of slaves to Apollonius the finance minister (*PCZ* 59076; *CPJ* 1.4; Durand 1997: #30) and of exotic animals to the king himself (*PCZ* 59075; *CPJ* 1.5; Durand 1997: #29). This shows a man confident of his position in society but also ready to deal as a loyal subject with Ptolemy and his ministers in the higher echelons of society.

There are also other local figures in the Zenon papyri. Two are of particular interest. One is a villager named Jeddous (*PCZ* 59018; *CPJ* 1.6; Durand 1997: #23). Since his name is evidently Hebrew, he could well be from Judah, but not necessarily. If he holds an office, it is not given, but he seems to be a substantial individual in a position of (official or unofficial) power in his own region (Durand [1997: 159] suggests that he was a *kōmarchēs*). He apparently owed money to Zenon who wrote a letter demanding either payment or the pledge on which the loan was based to be given to his man Straton. Instead, Jeddous attacked the messengers and threw them out of the village. Whether or not he held an office, he felt that he had a sufficient power base to defy the representatives of the Egyptian government.

One document contains a copy of extended correspondence relating to two brothers in Idumaea, named Kollochoutos and Zaidēlos, and some escaped slaves (*PCZ* 59015 verso; Durand 1997: #42). Zenon had apparently bought slaves (on behalf of Apollonius) from one of the brothers, but when these slaves were taken back to Egypt, they escaped and returned to their former master. After they were tracked down, the Idumaeans agreed to return them but only after a payment of 100 drachmas, probably a fair percentage of the original purchase price. The correspondence recorded in the extant document is Zenon's attempt to enlist the aid of various local officials and others in getting the slaves back. What this illustrates is the willingness of local people to defy an official representative of the Egyptian government. It suggests that the brothers (or their family) probably had a local position of power which they considered strong enough to serve them in holding out for what Zenon thought was nothing less than extortion.

Hecataeus of Abdera

Hecataeus' description of the Jewish community in Palestine has been widely accepted as genuine, at least as far as the data in Diodorus are concerned. This view has recently been challenged by separate studies on rather different grounds. D. W. Rooke has attempted to dismiss Hecataeus' account by arguing that 'there are too many question marks over its historical reliability' (2000: 250). After admitting that there are several points of contact with Judaic tradition, she then states that 'a good deal of the information has been presented in a way which gives quite a different picture from that which is given by the tradition itself' (2000: 248–49). This is true but also seems to be an argument in favour of its authenticity rather than against it. Notice some considerations about the account:

1. The general description of Egypt in Hecataeus' *Aegyptiaca* (*On Egypt*) has deficiencies, but these are those characteristic of even the best Greek accounts of the time (Burstein 1992). His was probably better than that of Herodotus (Book 1). Only those with access to the native records could have written a proper history of Egypt, but even with all its faults Hecataeus has things of value to tell us about Egypt. In the same way, his description of the Jews (which is probably taken from his *Aegyptiaca*) has weaknesses. While his knowledge was clearly derived in part from common Egyptian views about the origins of the Jews, it is also possible that he gained knowledge from contact with some Jews directly.

2. In spite of some unflattering comments about the origins of the Jews, Hecataeus has some authentic information about the Jewish community in Palestine:
    *   Hecataeus knows that they live in Judah and have Jerusalem as a main city.
    *   Moses was the leader of the Jews out of Egypt.
    *   A temple exists there with a priesthood headed by a high priest who supposedly traces his roots back to Moses.
    *   The high priest rules the country instead of a king.
    *   They have a written law going back to Moses.
    *   They do not use images in their worship.

    It would be simplistic to ignore this and take the view that it is a question of all or nothing. Indeed, with the exception of a misunderstanding or two, the account is remarkably accurate, especially considering that it comes from a non-Jew and one who has no special regard for the Jews. This suggests that his source of information (whatever it was) contained some authentic information – perhaps even a good deal of authentic information – on the Jews.

3. These comments about authenticity relate only to the passages in

Diodorus. The passages in Josephus – after much debate – now seem to be a later composition by a Jewish writer (Bar-Kochva 1996).

R. E. Gmirkin (2006: 34–71) has recently argued that the description in Diodorus is not from Hecataeus but from the Roman writer Theophanes, 250 years later in the time of Pompey the Great. The main arguments are that the account of the Jews in Diodorus 40.3 differs from the comments from the *Aegyptica* on the Jews in 1.28 and that the context in 40.3 is the conquests of Pompey, of which the main historian was Theophanes. Let us consider these arguments in turn:

Although Gmirkin gives a rather lengthy treatment of Diodorus 40.3, he says hardly anything about Diodorus 1.28-29. The statement in book 1 of Diodorus is in fact very short:

> Now the Egyptians say that also after these events a great number of colonies were spread from Egypt over all the inhabited world. To Babylon, for instance, colonists were led by Belus . . . They say also that those who set forth with Danaus, likewise from Egypt, settled what is practically the oldest city of Greece, Argos, and that the nation of the Colchi in Pontus and that of the Jews, which lies between Arabia and Syria, were founded as colonies by certain emigrants from their country; and this is the reason why it is a long-established institution among these two peoples to circumcise their male children, the custom having been brought over from Egypt. [translation from LCL]

It is is difficult to see how this 'seriously contradicts' the account in 40.3, as Gmirkin alleges. All Diodorus says in 1.28 is that a variety of nations, the Jews among them, originated as 'colonies' (οἰκίσαι) from Egypt. In 40.3 the 'foreigners' are expelled because of a plague which is ascribed to neglecting the Egyptian gods for the deities of the foreigners. Among those expelled are Moses and those who go with him to Judaea but also Danaus and Cadmus who went to Greece, but the Jews are described as a 'colony' (ἀποικία) headed by Moses. Circumcision is not mentioned in 40.3, but why should it be? In both cases, we would expect Diodorus to be paraphrasing Hecataeus rather than quoting him verbatim. It is possible that Hecataeus mentioned the Jews in more than one context, but it would not be surprising if Diodorus drew only on a single account in his two separate passages.

The assertion that Theophanes is the source of the passage in 40.3 would be difficult to establish in any case since we have only a few excerpts from Theophanes (*FGH* 188). Gmirkin's argument that Diodorus 40.1–2 comes from Theophanes is guesswork since the authorship of the passage is not identified. It would be a reasonable hypothesis to ascribe this to Theophanes, but it would still be a hypothesis. Unfortunately, Gmirkin simply assumes this hypothesis rather than trying to prove it. But to ascribe 40.3 to Hecataeus is not a hypothesis: it is based on the plain statement within the passage itself that this is what 'Hecataeus' says. Granted, the writer is said to be 'Hecataeus of Miletus', but this is a natural mistake to make by a scribe (perhaps by Photius who preserves the passage or possibly even a slip of the pen by Diodorus himself). But it would be rather unlikely for an original Theophanes to be replaced by 'Hecataeus of Miletus' in the process of textual transmission.

We thus return to our original starting point: Hecataeus of Abdera has provided us with a description of the Jewish community around 300 BCE. What source or sources he used are unknown. Even if the information goes back to a native informant in one way or another, however, it still represents an outsider's interpretation rather than that of a Jew. For one thing, it appears to have been assimilated to the image of the *patrios politeia* or image of the Greek 'native constitution' (Mendels 1983). The picture given is, therefore, precisely what we would expect of someone in Hecataeus' position.

For the administration of Judah, the one point that stands out from Hecataeus' account is the place of the high priest, the priests, and the temple. The high priest is the leader of the community, not only religiously but also in other aspects of the community and civic life: training for and conducting warfare, dividing land among the settlers, rearing children and so on. The priests are to be judges in major disputes. The temple seems to be the centre of the community. Although this implies that it has a place beyond the purely religious, any civic functions are not spelled out. If priests are acting as judges, did they do this in the temple or elsewhere? The description is no doubt idealized.

If this is an idealized picture, how useful is it as a description of Judah at the time? Has Hecataeus simply said what he thinks would fit his stereotype of the Jews? There is clearly some stereotyping, but Hecataeus does not seem to be a whole-hearted admirer of the Jews. He sees them as having an 'unsocial and intolerant mode of life' (40.3.4). This suggests that he is passing on the information he has, as far as he understands it. As noted above, it is remarkable the extent to which his account matches our knowledge of the Jews where we have information. Therefore, it seems perverse to reject out of hand his statements for which we do not currently have confirmation. A proper critical evaluation is what is needed.

The Tobiad Story
The story of the Tobiads seems to provide an essential perspective on governance and administration in Judah in the third century BCE (Josephus, *Ant.* 12.4.1-11 §§154–236). As it stands, it is problematic. There is no

question that any historical data have been buried in a legendary account that exaggerates and distorts, telling an entertaining tale but one that is not always believable. This has led some to dismiss the Tobiad story as 'not an accurate historical account, but a piece of propaganda written by a Jew of Ptolemaic Egypt in the second or first century' (Gera 1998: 57–58). Yet when we move from the Tobias of the Zenon papyri in 259 BCE to the Hyrcanus who has a huge deposit in the Jerusalem temple about 180 BCE (*2 Macc.* 3.11) – a period of about 80 years – we should hardly be surprised to find a figure filling the gap who made a name for himself in the context of the Ptolemaic empire. In other words, while Joseph Tobiad might bear the marks of exaggeration and even legend, a member of the Tobiad family who gained wealth and power by exploiting his connections with the court is what we would expect to find at this time. Since Tobias in 259 BCE was a mature but not necessarily an old man, while by 180 BCE Hyrcanus would have been getting on in life, we probably need postulate only one generation between them, though two is certainly possible.

As noted above, tax-farming was a way to make a lot of money in a short period of time, especially if one was both clever and lucky. Joseph could have been a regional tax-farmer who became notorious because he was collecting from his own friends and neighbours, as it were. It is extremely unlikely that Ptolemaic Syria and Phoenicia would have yielded 16,000 talents of silver in tribute a year – a figure sometimes ascribed to the whole of the Ptolemaic empire at this time.[3] For Joseph to offer to double the revenues (from 8,000 to 16,000 talents) would also go contrary to the general Ptolemaic policy, which was to keep a steady income without eroding the tax base on which it was established. To double the income by strong-arm methods would create chaos and loss of revenue in the long run. But for Joseph to be a successful tax-farmer in the Palestinian area would be in keeping with the situation of his family and the context in which it operated.

D. Gera rightly notes that Joseph Tobiad is presented as collecting taxes, whereas the tax-farmers in Egypt did not do so. However, several considerations need to be kept in mind: (1) the tax-farming model from mainland Greece was for tax-farmers to collect the revenue; (2) the tax-farmers in Egypt, although leaving collection to agents of the state, were hardly passive by-standers, but supervised the tax-producing activity from start to finish (Harper 1934); (3) there is evidence that tax-farmers

---

3 According to Jerome's *Commentariorum in Danielum* 3.11.5, the income from Ptolemy II's Egypt was 14,800 silver talents. His source was probably Porphyry, and Prophyry himself seems to have good sources for the Greek history of his time. But this sum is likely to be exaggerated, considering that Egypt yielded 700 talents under the Persians (Herodous 3.91).

collected taxes in the Ptolemaic possessions outside Egypt (Bagnall 1976: 20–21). We have a letter of Heracleitus to Zenon that tells of an attempt to export some slaves without a licence through Tyre (*PCZ* 59093; Durand 1997: #45; Tcherikover 1937: 68–72), apparently by an agent named Apollophanes. The "tax-farmers" (*telōnai*) in Tyre seized the slaves, suggesting that they not only guaranteed the level of customs duties but also took a direct hand in collecting them. Thus, the picture of Joseph not only guaranteeing the taxes but also collecting them is not unbelievable, even if we cannot be absolutely certain how it worked in practice in Palestine at this time.

A question concerns the figure of 20 talents that the high priest paid yearly to the Ptolemaic king (*Ant.* 12.4.1 §§158–59). It has been assumed that this was simply the annual tribute for Judah (e.g. Momigliano 1931–32: 612). Recently, it has been argued that this was some sort of traditional payment by the high priest ('some sort of Temple tax') but was not connected with the taxation of Judah as such (Rooke 2000: 259). Is it only a matter of guesswork or is there any way to delineate the precise nature of this payment? The basic problem is that it occurs in a literary text. Literary texts often seem to be unreliable in numbers such as this. Also, such texts cannot usually be trusted to use terms in a proper technical sense. Josephus refers to the high priest Onias as having 'the governorship of the people' (τοῦ λαοῦ τὴν προστασίαν). This might suggest that the high priest held a formal office (*prostasia*) in the Ptolemaic administration, perhaps having to do with finance, and that this office was subsequently transferred to Joseph Tobiad (Momigliano 1931–32: 612; Marcus 1943: 84–85 n.d.). The difficulty is that literary writers may not have used such technical terms properly; even Polybius is not consistent in the use of such terms (Bagnall 1976: 41–2; 213–15).

Recent study on the tax system of the Ptolemies may allow us to say more on the question. Although our sources give varying figures for the tax revenue of Ptolemaic Egypt, B. P. Muhs (2005: 10–11) has shown that the salt tax (a capitation tax) of about 250 BCE was 1.5 drachmas for a man and 1 drachma for a woman. Using Muhs' figures, we would calculate a population of about 96,000 to pay 20 talents from this poll tax alone. This figure for the population of Judah at this time seems high, considering that the population during the Persian period was probably only about 30,000 at its height (Lipschits 2003: 324–26, 355–60). But there were most likely other obligations. In Egypt proper these included corveé labour. Whether corveé applied in Judah is not clear, but that there were other taxes is likely. We should also consider that the tribute for the entire Transeuphrates (Syro-Palestine and Phoenicia) plus Cyprus during the Persian period was said to be 350 talents of silver (Herodotus 3.91). This suggests that Josephus' 20 talents paid annually by the high priest comes to a reasonable figure for the annual tax revenue from Judah in the middle of the third century BCE.

Decrees of Ptolemy II

Among the Rainer papyri in Vienna is one with parts of two decrees by Ptolemy II Philadelphus issued about his 24th year (260 BCE).[4] The legible parts read as follows (Bagnall and Derow 2004: #64):

> [Col. 1 = left col., lines 1–10] – to the *oikonomos* assigned in each hyparchy [*huparcheia*], within 60 days from the day on which the [ordinance] was proclaimed, the taxable and tax-free [livestock] . . . and take a receipt. And if any [do not do as] has been written above, [they shall be deprived of] the livestock and shall be [subject to the penalties] in the schedule. [Whatever] of the livestock was unregistered up to the proclamation of [the ordinance shall be free of taxes] for former years, of the pasture tax and crown tax and the other penalties, but from the 2[5]th year they shall pay the sum owing by villages . . . As for those . . . who make a registration in the name of another, the king will judge concerning them and their belongings shall be confiscated. Likewise . . .
>
> [Col. 1, lines 17–21]Those holding the tax contracts for the villages and the komarchs [*komarchas*] shall register at the same time the taxable and tax-free livestock in the villages, and their owners with fathers' names and place of origin, and by whom the livestock are managed. Likewise they shall declare whatever unregistered livestock they see up to Dystros of the 25th year in statements on royal oath.
>
> [Col. 1, lines 23–28]And they shall make each year at the same time declarations and shall pay the sums due as it is set out in the letter from the king, in the proper months according to the schedule. If any do not carry out something of the aforesaid, they shall be liable to the same penalties as those registering their own cattle under other names.
>
> [Col. 1, lines 29–32]Anyone who wishes may inform (on violations), in which case he shall receive a portion of the penalties exacted according to the schedule, as is announced in the schedule, and of the goods confiscated to the crown he shall take a third part.
>
> [Col. 1, line 33 – col. 2 = right col., line 11]By order of the king: If anyone in Syria and Phoenicia has bought a free native person or

---

4   On this inscription, see Liebesny 1936; Rostovtzeff 1941: I, 340–51; Lenger 1964: ##21–22; Bagnall and Derow 2004: #64.

has seized and held one or acquired one in any other manner – to the *oikonomos* in charge in each hyparchy within 20 days from the day of the proclamation of the ordinance. If anyone does not register or present him he shall be deprived of the slave and there shall in addition be exacted for the crown 6000 drachmas per head, and the king shall judge about him. To the informer shall be given . . . drachmas per head. If they show that any of the registered and presented persons were already slaves when bought, they shall be returned to them. As for those persons purchased in royal auctions, even if one of them claims to be free, the sales shall be valid for the purchasers.

[Col. 2, lines 12–15]Whoever of the soldiers on active duty and the other military settlers in Syria and Phoenicia are living with native wives whom they have captured need not declare them.

[Col. 2, lines 16–26]And for the future no one shall be allowed to buy or accept as security native free persons on any pretext, except for those handed over by the superintendent [τοῦ διοκοῦντος] of the revenues in Syria and Phoenicia for execution, for whom the execution is properly on the person, as it is written in the law governing farming contracts. If this is not done, (the guilty party) shall be liable to the same penalties, both those giving (security) and those receiving it. Informers shall be given 300 drachmas per head from the sums exacted.

This inscription tells us a number of things. First, we know that Syria and Phoenicia were divided into hyparchies which seem to have been units for purposes of collecting revenue. Also, we know that *oikonomoi* or financial officers of the Ptolemaic government operated in Syria and Phoenicia. This had already been conjectured by Tcherikover (1937: 43). There is also a reference to the 'superintendent' (ὁ διοικῶν) of the revenues in Syria and Phoenicia (col. 2, lines 18–19), but it is not clear whether this person is different from the *dioikētēs* or chief financial officer of Egypt. There are references to the tax-farmers for the individual villages, who work with the village head (κωμάρχης) to collect the revenue. This suggests that some of the administrative apparatus in Egypt also operated in Syro-Palestine. Yet surprisingly by the year 260 BCE certain basic procedures were not yet in place. Also, we cannot take the references here to the full panoply known from Egypt.

Decree of Antiochus III

Antiochus III defeated Scopas, the general of Ptolemy V, about 200 BCE. According to Josephus, Antiochus III issued a decree which lists the temple personnel and relieves some of their taxes temporarily so the temple can be repaired from war damage. The decree is as follows (the sections in square brackets being further discussed below):[5]

> King Antiochus to Ptolemy, greeting. Inasmuch as the Jews, from the very moment when we entered their country, showed their eagerness to serve us and, when we came to their city, gave us a splendid reception and met us with their senate [γερουσία] and furnished an abundance of provisions to our soldiers and elephants, and also helped us to expel the Egyptian garrison in the citadel, we have seen fit on our part to requite them for these acts and to restore their city which has been destroyed by the hazards of war, and to repeople it by bringing back to it those who have been dispersed abroad. In the first place we have decided, on account of their piety, to furnish them for their sacrifices an allowance of sacrificial animals, wine, oil and frankincense to the value of twenty thousand pieces of silver, and sacred *artabae* of fine flour in accordance with their native law, and one thousand four hundred and sixty *medimni* of wheat and three hundred and seventy-five *medimni* of salt.
>
> [And it is my will that these things be made over to them as I have ordered, and that the work on the temple be completed, including the porticoes and any other part that it may be necessary to build.]
>
> The timber, moreover, shall be brought from Judaea itself and from other nations and Lebanon without the imposition of a toll-charge. The like shall be done with the other materials needed for making the restoration of the temple more splendid. And all the members of the nation shall have a form of government in accordance with the laws of their country, and the senate [γερουσία], the priests, the scribes of the temple and the temple-singers shall be relieved from the poll-tax and the crown-tax and the salt-tax which they pay.
>
> [And, in order that the city may the more quickly be inhabited, I grant both to the present inhabitants and to those who may return before the month of Hyperberetaios exemption from taxes for three years.]
>
> We shall also relieve them in future from the third part of their tribute, so that their losses may be made good. And as for those who were carried off from the city and are slaves, we herewith set them free, both them and the children born to them, and order their property to be restored to them.

---

5   Quoted in Josephus, *Ant.* 12.3.3–4 §§138–46 (translation from Thackeray, et al. 1926–65: 7.71–75).

This document has generally been taken as authentic, even if those documents in §§145–46 and §§148–53 are rejected.[6] We should expect such a decree from a conqueror, and a number of considerations argue for its existence. First, there is the statement in *2 Maccabees* 4.11 about 'the royal concessions to the Jews, secured through John the father of Eupolemus', the only logical context being the time of Antiochus III's conquest. Second, it fits the general situation in Syro-Palestine at the time. A subordinate people is often ready for a change, in hopes of a bettering of their condition, if ruled by a particular power for a long period of time. Third, the last section of the decree fits the general approach of Ptolemy II's decree in the Rainer papyrus, suggesting not only a common administrative approach and style but also a common administrative policy towards those being governed. The basic agreement in style and content with other Seleucid documents (accepted even by one so exacting as Gauger), has been well demonstrated, and the contents are not intrinsically unlikely.[7] Antiochus also interacts with his minister Ptolemy, just as he does in the Hefzibah stela quoted below. Fourth, there is little that looks like Jewish propaganda here. Antiochus remits certain taxes temporarily to help in rebuilding the damaged city, as one might expect. He does not deliver fantastic sums of money nor treat the Jews in any special way, as one might expect in falsified letters.

These positive points do not remove all the problems. Establishing authenticity in a document preserved by later scribal tradition is never easy. Some alteration is inevitable simply through scribal error and adaptation. It takes only a small number of changes to completely alter the tenor of a document.[8] There are two problems which remain, despite the positive

6 See most recently Gauger 1977: especially pp. 19, 23–4, 61–3, 136–39. Although Gauger argues against the other two documents in the context (*Ant.* 12.3.3-4 §§138–53), he thinks the Antiochus edict to Ptolemy is authentic, though adapted for its context by Josephus. The main linguistic study of the text is Bickerman 1935; 1946–48; 1955. For other studies, see Hengel 1974: 1:271–72 (+ notes); Marcus 1943: 7:743–66.

7 On the style, see Gauger and Bickerman in the previous note, and also compare the original decrees of Ptolemy II and Antiochus III quoted in this paper. Although some tax concessions are made to the Jews, they are only temporary, to allow repair of the temple and city. There is nothing of the wholesale exemption of temple personnel from tax or special privileges bestowed on the Jews as found in other royal decrees which are likely to be examples of Jewish propaganda (e.g. some of the decrees in Ezra; on them see Grabbe 2006a; also Grabbe 2006b).

8 This is well demonstrated in the debate over Jewish citizenship in Alexandria in the first century. Josephus quotes an alleged document of the emperor Claudius showing that the Jews had equal citizenship rights with the Greeks (*Ant.* 19.5.2 §§280–85). We now have an authentic document of Claudius' which may well be the original on which Josephus's document is based (see *CPJ* 2: pp. 36–55 [text #153]). Only a few minor changes have completely altered the message of the decree from one denying citizenship to the Jews to one affirming it! Miriam Pucci ben Zeev (1998: 295–326) thinks that there are two different decrees here, however, which remains a possibility.

arguments: the first is that in contrast to the normal style of royal Seleucid documents, two sections (§§141 and 143) are in the first person singular, making them the most suspect.[9] These are set off in square brackets above. The second is the failure to mention the high priest. There are several possible explanations for this: Antiochus may have wanted to concentrate on the institutions (the 'senate') or groups rather than individuals; Simon may have opposed Antiochus (but then why was he allowed to continue in office?); there was no high priest at the time of the invasion, or perhaps the high priest was killed in the fighting over Jerusalem, and Simon came to the office only after Antiochus had entered the city. These are only suggestions, but lack of mention of Simon, while a puzzle, is not fatal to the decree's authenticity.

Antiochus III and the Stratēgos *Ptolemy son of Thraseas*

After the Seleucid takeover of Syro-Palestine in 200 BCE, we know that Ptolemy son of Thraseas was '*stratēgos* and high priest over Coele-Syria and Phoenicia' (*OGIS* #230). He had been an official of Ptolemy V (Polybius 5.65.3) but evidently had changed sides and gone over to Antiochus III (Gera 1987; 1998: 28–34). One could infer that this Ptolemy already held the office of *stratēgos* over Coele-Syria and Phoenicia under Ptolemaic rule, a reasonable inference but not at all certain. The post could well have been created by Antiochus as the best way to control the newly conquered region. Thus, this does not prove a governor over all Syro-Palestine under the Ptolemies. Ptolemy son of Thraseas is also mentioned in an inscription found in Palestine in Hefzibah, near the city of Beth-shean.[10]

> (D) To King [Antiochus (III)], memorandum from Ptolemy the *strategos* and high priest; [concerning any disputes that may arise]: I request that written instructions be sent [so that] disputes arising in [my] villages and involving peasants [with] each other should be [settled] by my agents, but those arising with peasants from [the] other villages should be investigated by the *oikonomos* [and the official] in charge [of the district (*topos*)], and if / [they concern murder] or appear [to be] of greater significance they should be referred to the *strategos* in Syria [and] Phoenicia; the garrison commanders [and

9   Gauger 1977: 19, 23–4, 61–3, 136–39. Despite Bickerman's able defence of the document, his attempt to salvage the text at this point is ingenious but unconvincing. It is better simply to recognize that two passages have probably been subject to scribal reworking at some point.
10   Landau 1966; Fischer 1979; Bertrand 1982; Austin 2006: #193; Gera 1987; 1998: 20–34.

those] in charge of the districts (*topoi*) should not [ignore] in any way those who call for their [intervention]. The same letter to Heliodous.

. . .

(F) To the Great King Antiochus (III) memorandum [from Ptolemy] the *strategos* [and] high priest. I request, King, if you so please, [to write] to [Cleon] and Heliodorus [the] *dioiketai* that as regards the villages which belong to my domain, crown property, and the villages which you instructed should be registered, / no one should be permitted under any pretext to billet himself, nor to bring in others, nor to requisition property, not to take away peasants. The same letter to Heliodorus.

(G) King Antiochus (III) to Marsyas, greetings. Ptolemy the *strategos* and high priest reported to us that many of those travelling / are forcibly billeting themselves in his villages [and] many other acts of injustice are committed as they ignore [the instructions] we sent about this. Do therefore make sure that not only are they prevented (from doing so) but also that they suffer tenfold punishment for the harm they have done . . . The same letter to [Lysanias], Leon, Dionicus.

In this inscription Ptolemy does not appear to be over all Syria and Phoenicia but only a portion of it, since reference is made to villages not under his control. Also, mention is made of the '*stratēgos* in Syria and Phoenicia', as if this is someone other than Ptolemy. Ptolemy himself was evidently put in charge over the whole area at a later time.

Yehuda Coinage

An interesting phenomenon is the continuation of coinage for Judah during the early part of the Ptolemaic period, until about 269 BCE (Barag 1994–99). The small silver coinage that had been characteristic of the late Persian period soon ceased in the Egyptian realm after the death of Alexander, to be replaced by bronze coinage. Apparently Judah was the only region in which such currency was issued after 301 BCE (Barag 1994–99: 29). The coin types include one with the head of Ptolemy I and *Yhdh* in Paleo-Hebrew letters; another with the head of Ptolemy I and the legend *Yhd*; three variants with the head of Ptolemy I, the head of Berenice I, and *Yhd*; two variants with a young bare-headed man (the youthful head of Ptolemy II during his co-regency with Ptolemy I?) and *Yhd*; and a type with the heads of Ptolemy I and Berenice I on one side and Ptolemy II and Arsinoe II, with *Yhd*, on the other. The reason why Judah retained its own right of coining during this period is unknown. There was no doubt strong central control over the mint, but equally this right of their own coinage also suggests a certain privilege on behalf of the Jews, perhaps as a reward of some sort or to encourage Judah to cooperate with the Ptolemies.

Discussion

We have some idea of how the administration in Egypt worked during the third century. There are still questions, and it was more flexible and complicated than sometimes represented, but we have quite a bit of information in the papyri. It would be very tempting simply to transfer this system to Palestine and assume that the Egyptian government would appoint the equivalent of a nomarch, an *oikonomos*, and royal scribe – or even a *stratēgos* – over Judah. There are several problems with such an approach. First, Bagnall shows that a variety of administrative arrangements were made in the Ptolemaic possessions outside Egypt; also, the Zenon papyri make no mention of such officers in connection with the area of Judah; further, the Ptolemies were quite happy to continue previous arrangements if they seemed to be working, which could include leaving native systems of administration in place (though naturally under Egyptian control).

We do have some indication of some offices in Syro-Palestine. The decree of Ptolemy II mentions that an *oikonomos* had been assigned to each hyparchy. There is also a possible reference to *toparchs*, those over a district. These are typical Egyptian arrangements. We do not know if there was a single *stratēgos* over the whole of Syrio-Palestine. The existence of such an office seems to be attested during the reign of Antiochus III, but this does not guarantee its existence under the Ptolemies. The 'superintendent of the revenues in Syria and Phoenicia' is named at one point, but this might be simply a reference to the *dioikētēs* over the whole of Egypt. It has been suggested that Syro-Palestine was administered by the *dioikētēs* (so Wilcken, *apud* Tcherikover 1937: 74 n. 62).

We have to keep in mind that the regions of Coele-Syria and Palestine had a long history on which to draw. For example, the Phoenician cities had been actors – at times, important actors – in the eastern Mediterranean for more than a millennium. They had proved themselves adaptable over the centuries, but they also managed to maintain a certain amount of autonomy much of the time (see Grainger 1991 for the situation under the Ptolemies). Similarly, the Jews had hardly forgotten that they had been an independent nation, even if that had been centuries earlier. This means that informal systems of government and administration in society were likely to have continued, even when they were considered superseded by the ruling power. These informal systems of governance might be as important as, or perhaps even more important than, the formal ones.

One of the things that becomes apparent when reading the Zenon papyri is that some of the natives were not afraid to express their independence. We already know of Tobias who clearly had a local position of power and influence and evidently exercised this with Ptolemaic blessing in the 'land of Tobias'. If the Tobiad legend is to be believed, Tobias' son (or grandson) Joseph gained even more power with an official post of tax-farmer cum collector in a wider region of Coele-Syria (the whole of the region according to the legend but probably exaggerated). But it is not just Tobias and Joseph, who in any case seem to have made an effort to cooperate with the Ptolemaic officials.

We also have the story of Jeddous who owed money to Apollonius (*PCZ* 59018; *CPJ* 1.6; Durand 1997: #23). Zenon sent two local officials to either collect the debt or seize the pledge offered as a guarantee of repayment. Jeddous threw them out of the village, and they returned empty handed. Jeddous could hardly have defied the agents of the *dioikētēs* of all Egypt if he had not been head of the village and probably with a power base encompassing a larger region. Among the Zenon correspondence are further letters about a couple of brothers in Idumaea (*PCZ* 59015 verso; Durand 1997: #42) who had apparently sold some slaves to Zenon. These were taken to Egypt but later escaped and returned to their former masters, the two brothers in Marisa. In a blatant case of extortion the brothers offered to restore the slaves if they were paid 100 drachmas. Again, we see a situation in which what seem to be local strongmen are willing to defy officials of the central government. This picture is supported by the fact that Judah continued to have its own coinage during the first decades of Ptolemaic rule.

Finally, we should mention sources that contain hints of different arrangements for the governance of Judah. Hecataeus of Abdera puts a good deal of emphasis on the position and authority of the high priest but also indicates the priests as a whole were in positions relating to administration and the justice system. The Tobiad Romance suggests that the high priest was responsible for paying the annual tribute of Judah to the Ptolemies. The decree of Antiochus III makes mention of the *gerousia* and the priests (though strangely omitting the high priest) and notes that the Jews were permitted to continue their traditional form of government. All this suggests that the Ptolemies were satisfied to allow previous arrangements to continue in Judah as long as the revenues were forthcoming. The system seems to have been a compromise, with various Ptolemaic offices in place (though possibly filled by natives) but with the high priest, the priests and the *gerousia* still having an important place in the administration.

Conclusions

There are few new sources for the Ptolemaic period. Almost all of what we have is material that was discovered, and much of it published, by the early twentieth century. All we can do is interpret what has been long known.

A study of the context in which Judah existed is also important for a possible understanding of her existence in the Ptolemaic empire. First, we need to be aware that the Ptolemies were pragmatic rather than dogmatic. Their concern was to collect as much revenue as possible but without damaging the revenue base. In Egypt they set up a system that had a conventional configuration to it, but even here there is evidence that it was less systematic and more flexible than is sometimes appreciated. Second, they seem to have been willing to allow rather different administrative arrangements in the territories outside Egypt from those in Egypt itself, no doubt taking account of the fact that the Palestinians did not have the tradition of close official supervision such as was customary in Egypt. Third, the Ptolemies were quite tolerant of the continuation of native customs and practices (e.g. the use of Demotic in the lower levels of the administration and the continuation of the Egyptian judicial system for Egyptians). Finally, this leads to the conclusion that we should not necessarily expect in Judah a replication of the system in Egypt itself.

The question is what indications we have of the particular system in use in Palestine. In deciding this question we also need to keep in mind that no hard and fast distinction can be made between official systems and informal systems. Or, to put it another way, informal systems of governance might be as important as, or perhaps even more important than, the formal ones. We have clear indications that at the local level powerful families and strongmen often controlled or ran things, regardless of whether this was done with official sanction or not. One can compare the *mafia* tradition in Sicily.

For the administration of Palestine we have the following points arising from the sources:

- Hecataeus of Abdera indicates that the priests – the high priest in particular – were responsible for regulating, judging, and generally administering the community.
- The Zenon papyri show that local dignitaries of Syria and Palestine often had high official positions or at least possessed a confident independence in relation to the Ptolemaic officialdom. The most important was Tobias who headed a military colony, perhaps encompassing both cavalry and foot soldiers, in the 'land of Tobias'. The local man Jeddous (probably a Hebrew name and thus possibly in Judah) is ready to resist Zenon's man sent

to collect a debt or to take the surety for it, while two Idumaean brothers are happy to try to extort money even from the *dioikētēs* of all Egypt.

- In the Tobiad Romance the high priest represents the community to the Ptolemaic government and is responsible for paying a sum of money to Ptolemy (most likely the regular taxes of Judah). It also shows the continuation of local power in the Tobiad family, again with official sanction.
- The inscriptions of Ptolemy II show that a number of the normal Egyptian officers have a part in the administrative scene in Syria and Palestine, including the *oikonomos* (finance officer), the *kōmarchēs* (village head), and a higher *dioikōn tas kata Surian kai Phoinikēn prosodous* (supervisor of the revenues in Syria and Phoenicia, though this might be the same as the *dioikētēs* or the head of financial matters in Egypt). The Hefzibah Inscription indicates that toparchs may also have been appointed over districts.
- Judaic coinage in the early part of the third century (prior to about 269 BCE) might indicate a certain autonomy on the part of Judah in the early Ptolemaic period.
- The decree of Antiochus III shows that Judah was allowed to have a form of government to which it was accustomed (πολιτευέσθωσαν πάντες οἱ ἐκ τοῦ ἔθνους κατὰ τοὺς πατρίους νόμους). This included the native institution of the *gerousia* (council of elders). (The high priest is not specifically mentioned, which is a bit of a puzzle, but there are several possible explanations).

The precise administrative arrangements for Palestine can only be conjectured, until direct primary evidence is found. But the information we have so far indicates the following picture: Syrio-Palestine, including Judah, was incorporated into the Ptolemaic system of administration. This emphasized the maximization of revenue, short of eroding the tax base. Officials were appointed to oversee production and collect taxes. For certain sorts of revenue the tax-farming rights were auctioned off. Yet some of the traditional arrangements of the native peoples were allowed to continue, and natives of the area were involved in all but perhaps the highest levels of administration. For Judah, this meant that the high priest, the priests as a whole, and the *gerousia* were in some way a part of the Ptolemaic administration of Judah. The high priest may have held certain Ptolemaic offices, such as *oikonomos*, at various times during Ptolemaic rule. We have indications, however, that alongside the official administration was an informal set of governance structures in which local strongmen had a lot to say in how things were run. These structures may have had an official status (e.g. in the case of Tobias), but in other cases the locals no doubt acted like mafiosi. In either case, the local people had a significant say in how their region was administered within the overall Ptolemaic guidelines.

4

KING AND TEMPLE IN *2 MACCABEES*: THE CASE FOR CONTINUITY

Sylvie Honigman,
Tel Aviv University

A generation or two ago, scholars of the Hellenistic period presented the conquest of the Achaimenid empire by Alexander the Great as the major turning point in the history of the ancient Near East.[1] The settlement of Greek immigrants was presumed to have opened up an era of economic, social and cultural dynamism in the whole region. However, there was a debate as to whether the natives also benefited from the new opportunities. Some scholars claimed that native élites could easily make their way into Greek society, since the Greeks at this time, defined their identity in cultural terms, and regarded anyone who adopted the Greek language and way of life as one of them. Acquiring Greek *paideia* allegedly made someone Greek. Other scholars objected that, far from merging, native and Greek societies simply co-existed side by side, and native élites enjoyed the new opportunities only to a very limited extent.[2] Whichever side they took in this controversy, everyone agreed about one point: 'Hellenization' was the keyword for understanding the social, economic and even political processes that affected the Eastern part of the Hellenistic world in these days. In short, Hellenization was held responsible for the pervading changes that local societies underwent after Alexander's conquest – even

---

1 I shall write 'Temple' with a capital letter exclusively to refer to our modern – Jewish and Christian – relation to the temple of Jerusalem. I will refer to it without a capital letter when trying to recapture the ancient conception of it. Even though I certainly admit that the temple of Jerusalem was as sacred and unique for ancient Judaeans as it is for modern Jews and Christians, I wish to emphasize that, in Persian and Hellenistic times, the religious situation of Judaea was not distinct from that of any other temple state. Therefore, I will use a 'normalized' spelling to refer to the temple of Jerusalem, as I would for any other temple. This principle will also apply to my spelling of 'high priest'.

2 Compare, e.g., the enthusiastic narratives of Tarn and Griffith 1952 and Wilcken 1931. On the side of the sceptics, Préaux 1978.

though not everyone agreed that these changes were overwhelmingly positive.

Not surprisingly, perhaps, the earliest attacks on this prevailing view came from Marxist circles. Acculturation to Hellenism was said to be a 'superstructure', which could not account for the economic processes of the time. Whatever the validity of their detailed arguments, Marxist scholars were the first to point out that the transition from the Achaimenid empire to the Hellenistic kingdoms was characterized by a basic continuity in economic and administrative structures.[3] Other, non-Marxist, schools of thought followed suit. The aftermath of decolonization in Europe, and the Vietnam war in the USA, further prompted a thorough revision of earlier tenets about the benefits of Alexander's conquest for Near Eastern societies. The 'Gröningen workshop' began implementing a fruitful interdisciplinary approach, gathering together students of the Persian and the Hellenistic worlds.[4]

Under the impact of these combined approaches, the concept of continuity between Achaimenid and Hellenistic times has now become the prevailing working premise in studies of Hellenistic times.[5] The field of ideology was soon added to that of economic and administrative structures. It is now widely acknowledged that Alexander and the various Hellenistic dynasties which followed him took over the imperial culture of the Achaimenids in its broad lines.[6] The main aspect of this re-appraisal of Hellenistic royal ideology concerns the relations between kings and native élites. Contrary to the view articulated by Christian Habicht in 1958, it is now accepted that the societies of the various Hellenistic royal courts included members of these native élites.[7] Similarly, the Hellenistic kings maintained good relations with the various priestly classes, and honoured local temples by performing the religious duties incumbent on them.[8]

3   Kreissig 1978 on agrarian issues; see further Kreissig 1977. See also the various papers by P. Briant collected in Briant 1982.

4   Gröningen workshop: see the proceedings of their meetings published in the series *Achaimenid History*. Among the prominent names in the workshop, one finds P. Briant (see previous note), A. Kuhrt, and S. Sherwin-White.

5   A convenient overview is given by Briant 1990. One important exception concerns the monetization of the economy and tax policy. See Le Rider and de Callataÿ (2006: 105–114, 245–77) and Manning (2010: 1–2).

6   See Sherwin-White and Kuhrt 1993.

7   Habicht 1958. Habicht's view was criticised by Sherwin-White and Kuhrt (1993: 121). See further pp. 144ff. and 150–52.

8   One typical example of the historiographical shift is provided by recent interpretations of the priestly decrees of Canopus (237 BCE; *OGIS* 56, transl. Austin 271) and the Memphis decree (the Rosetta stone, 186 BCE; *OGIS* 90, transl. Austin 283). Earlier views saw the inclusion of an elaborated Egyptianized royal titulature together with the wide-ranging gifts granted to the temples by the king in the later text as evidence that the 'weakening' Ptolemaic king was 'compelled' to

One side-effect of this new historiographical orientation has been the demotion of the once crucial concept of 'Hellenization' in studies of the encounter between Greek and native populations in the Hellenistic East. As just recorded, the basis for good relations between the two sides at the highest level of society is now sought in the continuity with Achaimenid royal ideology, while aspects of inter-ethnic intermingling among lower classes are apprehended through new concepts, like 'multiculturalism'.[9] The new conceptual models have made earlier references to Greek *paideia* irrelevant. General arguments against the concept of 'acculturation' from the field of post-colonial studies have further contributed to the demotion of 'Hellenization' in general, and Greek *paideia* in particular, as explanatory factors for the dynamics of inter-ethnic encounters.

Scholarship on Judah/Judaea in the Persian and Hellenistic eras has not stood aside from the re-appraisals currently debated in historiography dealing with these two periods from a more general perspective. The new approaches have been assimilated, but at a slower rate than in studies bearing on other geographical and cultural areas. In the balance between the 'typical' and the 'particular', Judah has long been too systematically presented as an exception.[10] The documentation available for this cultural area in the so-called 'Second Temple period' is indeed exceptional in nature, both in extent and content, which has been one of the reasons for this circumspect attitude towards the debates led elsewhere. Not only does the literary corpus of biblical and post-biblical texts[11] allow scholars to treat specific issues that have no counterpart elsewhere (or so it is alleged), but this corpus largely explains the inclination among the students of Judaea to keep to the now conservative view that Alexander's conquest did indeed constitute a decisive turning point. A large part of the literary corpus of this period was written in Greek by native authors, and the influence of Greek literary culture and thought is also unmistakable even in works which were written in Hebrew and Aramaic. Hellenistic influences have also been pointed out in most of the many religious innovations of the time which form the background to the emergence of both Rabbinic Judaism and Christianity.

make 'concessions' to the Egyptian priests. One of the earliest revised readings was offered by Koenen 1983. See further Koenen 1993.

9 See Johnson 1992.

10 The case of scholarship on Judah/Judaea is not absolutely isolated: see the once consensual tendency among students of Hellenistic and Roman Egypt to conceive of their subject as 'exceptional'. See Préaux 1950 and 1953; revised view in Lewis 1984. The exceptional nature of the documentation – documentary papyri – was, in this case also, responsible for this conviction.

11 Which has consequences, of course, for the sociology of the scholars working on Judah: beside archaeologists and historians, theologians add a distinctive field of training, making interdisciplinary dialogue more complex than elsewhere.

To be sure, there is a tendency among students of Judaea to point to a different event as the major turning point in the history of Judaea in Second Temple times. Although, it is claimed, the aftermath of Alexander's conquest laid down the basic trends, the effects of 'Hellenization' were really capitalized on only with the constitution of an 'independent' kingdom under the 'national' dynasty of the Hasmonaeans in the second century BCE. Most scholars tend to locate the roots of Rabbinic Judaism and Christianity in this time.[12] However, the identification of this event as a second major turning point, no less – and perhaps even more – important than Alexander's conquest, merely duplicates the problem. In the last few decades, historiography in general has become suspicious about the concept of abrupt breaks, and historical studies are now far keener to emphasize continuities. Just as the grounds for turning Judaea into an exception by maintaining that Alexander's conquest did have a major impact on its subsequent history appear to be increasingly ill-based, so the statement that the achievement of political independence under the Hasmonaeans constituted a major break overlooks important aspects of continuity.

The view that the history of Judaea was exceptional may not derive merely from the exceptional nature of the sources. It may also, more worryingly, be a clear case of the end of the story – the emergence of Rabbinic Judaism and Christianity – unduly influencing the reconstruction of its beginning. Since the issue at stake is tracing back the roots of the two religious trends which most affected the course of subsequent Western history, the religious innovations have been over-emphasized from a rather deterministic perspective, while instances of continuity have been disregarded as insignificant residues. The present paper intends to show how our understanding of the events that affected Judaea in the 160s BCE may benefit from a perspective which stresses aspects of continuity from the Persian period down to Hasmonaean times and beyond. More precisely, the paper will be concerned not so much with reconstructing the cultural dynamics of the events themselves, as with analysing the way they are presented in *2 Maccabees*.

According to the accepted view, *2 Maccabees* is precisely the text which presented the conflict between the Seleucid dynasty and local leaders in cultural terms for the first time, and made use of newly coined words to articulate its own perception of the facts: *Ioudaismos* is explicitly

---

12   See Aitken in this volume. For radical statements of this view, the papers by Edelman, Davies, and Niehr in Edelman (ed.) 1995b. Edelman contends that the very emergence of 'Judaism' was a Hasmonaean phenomenon, the local religion of Judaea down to 143 being a late form of 'Yahwism', the former phase corresponding, in religious terms, to a phase of 'inclusive monotheism', and the latter, to 'exclusive monotheism'. On Davies, see below.

contrasted with *Hellenismos* and *Allophylismos* or 'foreignism', as it is called by Daniel Schwartz.[13] However, the present paper will contend that these terms have been understood inappropriately as conveying the same connotations for the author of *2 Maccabees* as for modern readers. All modern interpretations tacitly take it as their premise that the neologism *Ioudaismos* was formed in imitation of *Hellenismos*, not only in morphology, but also in content. In fact, the reverse is much more plausible, as far as content is concerned: it is the term *Hellenismos* that derives its meaning from *Ioudaismos*. As a native Judaean, the author of *2 Maccabees* must have condensed traits of familiar experience in the term *Ioudaismos*, while ascribing to *Hellenismos* a derivative meaning, which would allow him to create a contrast between the two which could be meaningful in terms of his locally rooted worldview. Moreover, modern readings tend to assume that these terms, as they appear in *2 Maccabees*, reflect an objective, unproblematic description of reality, and not the particular view of the author. This unreflecting approach is becoming untenable, at a time when the newly emerging historiographical consensus holds that there never was such a thing as a 'normative Judaism', but that there were a variety of 'Judaisms' from the outset, deriving from a variety of earlier 'Yahwisms'.[14] Thus the time has come to ask how the terms of *Ioudaismos* and *Hellenismos* are specifically contextualized in *2 Maccabees*.

As the present paper will argue, the reality captured in the neologism *Ioudaismos* in *2 Maccabees* is the dominant socio-political order which had been established in the polity of Judah/Judaea in the early Persian period, and which still prevailed under the Seleucid dynasty. This socio-political order was organized around the temple of Jerusalem, which functioned as its main political, religious and economic centre. The high priest acted first and foremost as the main representative of the local community vis à vis the imperial political and administrative structure. I shall provisionally describe this polity as a 'temple state', or, more appropriately, as a 'temple community'.[15] The term *Hellenismos*, in this view, encapsulates all the phenomena that the author sees as hindrances to the 'normal' operation of the traditional order – 'traditional', that is,

---

13   *2 Macc.* 4.10-17; Schwartz (1992: 11).

14   See the convenient overview by Davies (1995: 145–51).

15   Temple state' is the accepted phrase. However, I prefer to talk of a 'temple community', since I am reluctant to describe ancient political entities as 'states'. In effect, the use of the latter term entails too many confusions with the modern, industrial and post-industrial, political formation that we inescapably think of when using this word. It should be made clear that, by 'temple community', I do not mean to endorse the description of the socio-political organization of Judah which has been labelled as a '*citizen* temple community' (*Bürger-Tempel-Gemeinde*) by Joel Weinberg. See his essays collected and translated in Weinberg 1992. A good summary of Weinberg's view is provided by Blenkinsopp 1991. Further, Bedford 1991.

from the time that Judah/Judaea had become a temple community in Persian times. If we accept these two basic definitions, it becomes readily apparent that the cultural context within which the author of *2 Maccabees* vilifies Antiochos IV, derives from the 'traditional' royal ideology which had been defining relations between (foreign) king and local temple ever since Persian times. This Persian royal ideology, in turn, derived from earlier models which seem to have been common to the whole ancient Near East for centuries. From this perspective, Antiochos IV is censured in *2 Maccabees* for behaving as a 'wicked king' by the standards of this traditional royal ideology, and not for behaving as a 'Greek'. To be sure, *2 Maccabees* offers some innovative statements as compared to the traditional worldview. However, the boldness or otherwise of these statements can be properly assessed only if we admit that the author's worldview was basically traditional.

The following discussion will be divided into three parts. The first part will discuss in more general terms some basic concepts on which the subsequent discussion of the concepts of *Ioudaismos* and *Hellenismos* in *2 Maccabees* will be based: in particular, the relation between the concepts of 'religion' and 'culture', and 'acculturation' and 'Hellenization'. The second part will read *2 Maccabees* from the perspective of continuity. The contention that the socio-political, and hence, religious, order, described under the label of *Ioudaismos* in *2 Maccabees* was that inherited from pre-Hellenistic times, will be discussed in detail. This contention does not, of course, try to imply that the Judaean society was altogether static in Hellenistic times. However, it is questionable whether all the phenomena which seem to be first manifested in Judaea after Alexander's conquest are to be taken systematically as consequences of 'Hellenization'. To take one example: war was endemic in Hellenistic times – and warfare can be expected to entail disruptions, and hence changes. However, it would be absurd to describe all the effects of war as manifestations of 'Hellenization' only because the participants in these wars were Greeks. The third and last part of the present paper will therefore address the issue of change, in an attempt to suggest alternative ways of accounting for its various manifestations. Thus some phenomena may even gain by being described as *adaptations* of old patterns of thinking and behaviour to new conditions, rather than revolutionary changes that can only be explained by admitting external influences. As for 'genuine' changes, some may result from the impact of political, military and economic developments, that is, processes which are only loosely connected with the proper effects of 'Hellenization'.

Ioudaismos *as a complex socio-religious system*

'Culture' vs. 'religion': 'Judaeans' vs. 'Jews'

The issue of 'Hellenization' cannot be dealt with without clarifying related concepts: Hellenization of whom and what are we looking at? Of Judaeans or Jews? Of a 'culture', or a 'religion'? Or perhaps both? There has been a lively debate in recent scholarship as to whether the population of Judaea should be referred to as 'Judaeans' or 'Jews', and when the transition from one label to the other should be located in time. The debate is, of course, sharpened by the fact that both the Hebrew/Aramaic terms *yehudi/yehud* and the Greek *Ioudaios* can be translated both ways. The issue at stake in this debate, beyond the semantics, is whether ancient 'Judaism' was a 'culture' or a 'religion', and when, if at all, the transition from the former to the latter took place. Discussions about these two related issues are particularly muddled, since the concepts of 'culture' and 'religion' are not always defined very clearly, let alone used in a consistent way from one scholar to the next. Additional issues complicate this matter still further, particularly the question of whether or not there was a 'normative' Judaism to which the other forms should be opposed as 'marginal' or even 'sectarian' forms. Alternatively, perhaps we should speak of 'Judaisms' in the plural only – leaving open the issue of what was the common denominator which made them forms of 'Judeaism' in the first place.[16] Discussions about Hellenization are certainly part of this larger debate: the question at stake is whether or not 'Hellenization' played a part in the transition from one set of terms and concepts to the other, and whether it applied only to the later phase (Judeaism as a religion), or to both.

The debate around dating the 'transition' from 'Judaeans' to 'Jews' raises problems which cannot be easily addressed on the basis of the premises underlying it. To begin with, the very attempts at dating the transition imply a belief in sharp turning points.[17] More problematically, the link implicitly made between the designation of the population of Judaea as 'Judaeans' and the description of Judaism as a 'culture' on the one hand, and between their designation as 'Jews' and the description of Judaism as a 'religion', on the other, threatens to leave the whole population of Judaea without a culture once they are called 'Jews' and Judaism is described as a 'religion'. Scholars have been aware of this danger, but the solutions proposed have only increased the questionable tendency to interpret the concept of 'religion', in this context, in a restricted sense.

With a few exceptions until recent times, scholars working on Second

---

16   See Davies 1995.
17   See, e.g, the papers quoted above, n. 11.

Temple Judaism have used a very narrow definition of religion. The latter is understood as a set of beliefs, which together constitute a faith. An extreme example of this standpoint is offered by Philip Davies' discussion of the emergence of Judaism as a religion. Davies' starting point is his contention that there never was a unified 'Judaism', only a plurality of 'Judaisms'. This stance obliges him to confront the problem of how to define 'Judaism' as a 'genus' forming the 'common denominator' of the various particulars, his 'Judaisms'. The solution he apparently puts forward is to distinguish between a 'Judaean culture' and 'Judaisms'. In his view, the early Hellenistic period was still the time of 'Judaean culture'; that is, the culture of the people settled in Judaea, which is experienced in an unreflecting way, since it 'has not yet been conceptualized'. 'Culture', therefore, gathers the elements of a society that the insiders themselves take as a matter of fact, and do not feel the need to think about. In the transitional phase, intellectuals begin proposing definitions of their own culture. This reflective time constitutes a transitional phase between culture and religion, which Davies calls 'Juda-ism', the hyphenized spelling stressing its definition as 'the idea of a Judaean way of life'. Since the initial 'Judaean culture' was from the outset 'defined in different ways by different Judaeans', it follows that its transformation into a religion can only be plural, i.e. the 'Judaean culture' gave way to various 'Judaisms'. Logically, according to Davies, 'Judaism' and 'Judaisms' relate to 'Jews', and not Judaeans, inasmuch as they represent an option, or rather, a set of options, open to people who do not necessarily originate in the Judaean society which constituted the original *Sitz im Leben* of this way of life.[18]

The definitive transition from (hyphenized) Juda-ism to (non-hyphenized) Judaism was achieved with the Hasmonaeans. However, Davies considers that while the Hasmonaeans created 'the matrix for a "Jewish worldview"', in imposing their form of Judaism – the 'Judaism of the victors', as he calls it, in which 'circumcision, diet, sabbath, holy books' were 'dominant characteristics' – Judaism (in the singular) as a full-fledged religious system of national scope developed only much later, with Rabbinic Judaism.[19] While Davies' approach is certainly stimulating, the details of his argument fall short of solving all problems. Its sequential reconstruction, in particular, is questionable. First of all, it is not clear why a 'culture' must necessarily turn into a 'religion' simply because it becomes reified. Besides, 'culture', as anthropologists and historians have now recognized, is not a unified thing, and cannot be presented as constituting the homogeneous common denominator from which the

---

18   Davies (1995; 152–53) for the various quotations.
19   Davies (1995: 173–77).

various 'Judaisms' later evolved. Second, there can be little doubt that the form of Judaism which was consciously adopted from the time of the Hasmonaeans and which is itemized in *2 Maccabees*, had its roots in earlier times. In other words, Juda-ism co-existed with Judaism for quite a long time (not to mention 'Judaean culture'), with the dates of the beginning and end of the process remaining quite elusive. Third, it is hard to accept that 'Jews' had to wait as late as the emergence of Rabbinic Judaism in the second century CE in order to enjoy 'a full-fledged religious system'. Finally, it is questionable whether 'Judaisms' can be defined as a mere set of 'intellectual systems expressed by individual authors', that is, a set of 'options'. This amounts to defining religion, at best, as a set of beliefs.

Thus attempts at defining a clear sequence of evolution from 'Judaeans' to 'Jews', and from 'culture' to 'religion', and locating the 'transition' from one to the other in both cases, create awkward paradoxes. First of all, evolution was not only necessarily gradual, it also stretched over a very long span of time. While most scholars would admit this, the way out of this deadlock is, in my view, to be sought elsewhere: in a wider definition of the concept of 'religion', a definition which sets 'culture' and 'religion' as complementary, and not opposite, terms. In my own discussion, I shall speak of 'Judaeans', but I have no qualms about talking of 'Judaism' and defining it as a 'religion', or, better still, as a 'religious system'.

Defining religion: rites versus beliefs

The concept of religion worked out by anthropologists is quite different from those which underlie most studies of Second-Temple Judaism. These, with few exceptions, put the stress on beliefs and faith. To put it in a nutshell, anthropologists perceive religion in a way which is very close to Davies' concept of culture. Thus, Clifford Geertz has defined religion as a cultural system.[20] On the basis of Geertz's definition, Simon Price has emphasized that religion, as a cultural or socio-cultural system, is best apprehended through its ritual system, and not its set of beliefs.[21] To be sure, rites may articulate beliefs, and beliefs may be related to rites. However, there are two differences between these two kinds of definitions. First of all, the notion of 'beliefs' is used in a sense much broader than 'faith'. To quote Bob Becking's definition, which is inspired by cultural anthropology: 'Texts, rituals and iconic representations of the divine are expressions of the belief of a society or of the most powerful group in a

---

20 Geertz 1973a [1966].
21 Price (1986: 1–40).

society. The idea "belief" in the last clause has more to do with "world view" and "ideology" than with "faith" in a restricted religious sense.'[22]

While anthropological definitions of religion as a ritual system have been widely accepted among students of Greek and Roman religions,[23] these have had a limited influence on the scholarship of Judaism in Hellenistic times. This discrepancy requires explanation, all the more since biblical scholars, as the example of Becking shows, have been much keener to turn to anthropology for the study of Yahwism(s) – as the earlier phases of the religion of the people settled in the geographical area covered by Persian Judah and Hellenistic Judaea are now commonly referred to. The perspective of hindsight may partly be held responsible for this gap between classicists and students of Hellenistic Judaism, whereas, again, the gap between students of Biblical Yahwism and students of ancient Near-Eastern religions has now been largely bridged. Hellenistic Judaism eventually led to the invention of a new, fully spelled-out, religious system by the rabbis of the second century CE, as well as to the emergence of the Christian religious system. The latter, as has been increasingly recognized in recent scholarship, is rooted in religious currents which formed part of Judaean society in Hellenistic times. These currents rejected the temple-centred worldview in more or less radical ways, and emphasized beliefs. As a consequence, scholars studying the Judaean 'religion' in Graeco-Roman times tend to devote most attention to the emergence of new beliefs and the gradual transformation of old ones.

The definition of Judaism as a 'monotheism' in Hellenistic and later times is certainly the main reason why scholars conceive of Hellenistic Judaism as 'different' from the religions of surrounding peoples, and thus neglect the methodological discussions held about other ancient religions. However, stressing the opposition between 'monotheism' and 'polytheism' is precisely a case of defining religion through its faith, and not its rites. To be sure, Greek and Roman authors repeatedly claim that 'Jews were different', and their attitude has undoubtedly encouraged modern scholars to see Judaism as exceptional in its own time. However, what ancient authors meant to say in stating that Judaism was different is quite distinct from what most modern scholars understand. Greek authors of

22 Becking (1999: 258). The concept of 'belief system', which has been borrowed from cultural anthropology by biblical scholars in order 'to (re-)conceptualize the religious ideas in a given text' (Becking 1999: 256) posits an approach to religion very similar to that adopted here. However, since the word 'belief' too easily creates confusion, I will speak of religion as a 'ritual system'. For a thorough criticism of a narrow definition of religion as well as the view that religion is about beliefs see Asad (1993: 27–79).

23 In an inflated bibliography, see, beside Price 1986, Schmitt-Pantel and Bruit-Zaidman 1992; Parker 1998; Beard, North and Price 1998; Scheid 2001 and 2005.

Hellenistic times emphasized the Judaeans' belief in a single deity because this 'detail' echoed an issue familiar in Greek philosophical thought, for these authors were trained in philosophy. Thus it is no coincidence that the Judaeans were described as philosophers in their works. However, this approach hardly singled out the Judaeans, since other peoples from the East (Indian Brahmans and Persian Magi) were also labelled philosophers.[24] As for rites, we can guess that the mockery by Greek authors of the Judaean observance of their sabbatical rest-day and dietary rules was nothing particularly out of the ordinary. There is no reason to believe that the rationalist philosophers who mocked these rites as being superstitions would have spared the ritual customs of Greek cities which proved as counter-productive as, say, the sabbatical rest in a time of war. For example, we know that on two celebrated occasions the Spartans arrived at the battlefield too late, because the departure of the army was delayed by the festival of the Hyakinthia.[25]

While Hellenistic speculations about philosophical peoples left Roman authors indifferent, the latter did pay a great deal of attention to the rites of foreign peoples. We know that Jews were set apart from the rest of humanity because of their refusal to share the meals of others. However, it is once more questionable whether this attitude, which Roman authors deplored, really did single them out. Similarly hostile statements were made against Egyptian zoolatry, the practice of human sacrifices in Druidism, castration in the cult of the Great Mother from Pessinous, not to mention the hostile tone pervading Livy's account of the Bacchanalia affair that shook Rome and Italy in 186 BCE (Livy, 39.8-19). Livy complacently detailed the horrendous deeds which were slanderously ascribed to the worshippers of the cult of Bacchus – a Greek cult! In short, all ritual practices which were seen as deviant from a Roman standpoint attracted derogatory comments. The main victims of this sport were undoubtedly the Egyptians, and not the Jews.[26] In short, the testimony of Greek and Roman authors cannot seriously be adduced in support of the modern view that monotheism, i.e., a specific aspect of its set of beliefs, was what made Judaism distinct.

If, on the contrary, the stress is laid on rites, and not on beliefs, the contrast between Greek, Roman and other ancient religions on the one hand, and Second Temple Judaism on the other, becomes much less sharp. This shift of emphasis has immediately tangible consequences for our understanding of the events that shook Judaea under Antiochos IV. To be sure, the introduction of a foreign deity into the temple of the local deity

---

24   On Barbarian philosophers, see Diogenes Laertius 1.6-11. On Brahmans, further, Strabo 15.59.
25   Herodotos, 7.206 (the Thermopylai) and 6.106 (Marathon).
26   Smelik 1984.

in Jerusalem following Antiochos' order constituted a desecration, that is, the ultimate pollution. However, there can be no doubt that the 'Greek' king was perfectly aware of the significance of this step. Replacing one deity with another without performing the appropriate rites would have been just as gravely polluting for a Greek sanctuary as it was in Jerusalem. Greek religious systems, just like the Judaean one, believed that this sort of impious deed would bring destructive consequences for the community.[27] Thus Antiochos IV's behaviour cannot be explained as a miscalculation deriving from different religious sensitivities.

So what is the concept of an ancient religion from an anthropological perspective? Beyond the specificity of each religious system – be it Greek, Roman, Egyptian, Judaean or Babylonian – common factors can be pointed out. Above all, religion was not an autonomous field in ancient societies. Rites had two basic functions. First, rites were precisely those means by which societies articulated their conception of their own internal order, social hierarchy and the place and rôle of everyone in the social order. Secondly, rites both enabled and translated the relation between the society, as a microcosm, and the whole universe, as the macrocosm ruled by the god(s). Basic harmony was posited between the two scales of the micro- and macrocosms, and the rites, as long as they were properly executed, fostered – or restored – this harmony. This conception of the efficacy of rites was shared by virtually all the various religious systems found around the Mediterranean basin and the Fertile Crescent as far as Mesopotamia.

If religion is understood as a ritual system whose *raison d'être* is to articulate the way a specific society experiences reality, separating 'religion' from other fields of daily life, such as politics, economy and war, becomes a nonsense. Inasmuch as these aspects are part of a society, the ritual system is intimately related to them as well. By this, I do not simply mean that specific rites were performed in the context of politics, war or in order to ensure the fertility of the fields. If religion is a ritual *system* encompassing reality, its relationship with the various fields of reality needs to be seen as an organic interconnection.

Religion did not form an autonomous field in Judaean society of Second

---

27   See Christiane Sourvinou-Inwood's remarks (1990: 296 and 301): '[T]he ownership of sanctuaries was perceived as belonging to the human, and not the divine, sphere, which is why sanctuaries could change hands without it being felt that any disrespect to the gods had been committed.' *However,* 'All Greeks were bound to respect other cities' sanctuaries and cults if they did not wish to offend the gods. The "law" of the Greeks as reported in Thucydides 4.9.2 [. . .] was that whichever *polis* had control over a land also owned its sanctuaries, and *they should worship as far as possible according to the rites that were customary there before the change of ownership*' (emphasis added).

Temple times any more than elsewhere. Admittedly, the local religious system distinguished between sacred and secular spheres, either in terms of space, time or activities, but so did all religious systems at this time. The relevant point lies elsewhere, in the deep interconnections between sacred and profane activities which made up the received worldview. Even though cultivated fields were located in secular space (as opposed to the precinct of the temple which delineated sacred space), the territory in which individuals belonging to the Judaean community lived[28] needed to be kept unpolluted, since its fields grew the crops from which the offerings of first-fruits were brought to the sacred space of the temple every year. The level of purity required from the priests was naturally much stricter than that required from Israelites, since the priests performed the sacred rites in the name of the community. However, Israelites also needed to keep pure, since they gathered into the precincts of the temple at the three yearly festivals, and ate the Passover lamb they had ritually sacrificed there. These few examples illustrate how the religious sphere was deeply interconnected with the economic and social ones.[29] The socio-political field was no less affected. In earlier times, the behaviour of the ruler reflected on the whole community: disasters befell the whole people because the king had misbehaved. At least from Persian times on, the prosperity of the fields of the Judaeans was dependent on the behaviour of common people towards the deity and temple (e.g. Haggai 1.5-6).

The definition of religion just put forward invites us to ask anew what the author of *2 Maccabees* had in mind in coining the term *Ioudaismos*. Before we can tackle this question, however, further definitions need to be clarified, since the answer partly depends on them: the definitions of 'culture' and 'acculturation' – or, more appropriately, 'cultural interaction', or 'interculturation' – of which 'Hellenization' is simply a specific form.[30]

'Culture', 'acculturation', 'interculturation' – and 'Hellenization'
The definition of 'culture' which prevailed in the 1960s and 1970s is best epitomized in the work of Clifford Geertz. The latter defined culture as 'an historically transmitted pattern of meanings embodied in symbols, a system of inherited conceptions expressed in symbolic form by means of which men communicate, perpetuate and develop their knowledge about

---

28   The territory, far from being a homogeneous and objective sequence of space, is identified with the people living in it. On this concept of space, see Wright 2006. The concept of time was equally subjective: Japhet 1994 and 2006.

29   The organic link between the temple and the economic prosperity of the community is explicitly articulated in many texts. See, e.g., Haggai 1.4-6, 9-12.

30   For a long-term survey of the definitions of the term 'culture' in connection with the concept of 'Hellenization', see Friedman 1990.

and attitudes towards life'.[31] This view came under attack in the 1980s. Geertz was criticized for conceiving of a culture as a homogeneous entity, whose boundaries could be clearly delineated.[32] Current views describe the concept as both more complex and more dynamic. Each group within a society, and, at a different level, each individual, appropriate the stock of symbols and cultural forms available in the society in a different manner, and interpret it in their own interests.[33]

This new emphasis on the question of agency (i.e. the role of concrete people) in the formation and evolution of a specific culture has impinged on recent understandings of the phenomenon of 'cultural transfer'. Models of increasing complexity have been proposed to analyse the latter. The model of 'acculturation' long dominated Western scholarship. This model presupposed a unidirectional influence, from one culture to the other, especially in cases of power imbalance – and relations between Greek settlers and natives in the Hellenistic East were indeed analysed in this way – and focused on the stronger side, from which the influence stems.[34] In accordance with this model, the concept of 'Hellenization' was used in a way that defined the Hellenic side of the relationship as the primary term of reference. Hence, attention was paid primarily to the way Greeks themselves conceived of their own culture and ethnicity, since it was assumed that this Greek self-definition was the one automatically taken over by local Near Eastern cultures. Greek self-definition was therefore thought to provide the means of understanding how local populations in areas which came to form the Hellenistic East re-conceived their own culture and ethnicity. The insistent reference to the concept of *paideia* found in Athenian orators of the fourth century BCE (above all, Isocrates), together with the importance of the gymnasium as a social institution in Greek cities of post-classical times, led scholars, through the 1960s at least, to emphasize the role of Greek *paideia* in the encounter between Greeks and non-Greeks in the Hellenistic East. The prevailing view was that the Greeks themselves conceived of their collective identity in cultural, and not ethnic, terms, from the fourth century onwards. That is, a 'Greek' was an individual who spoke Greek and behaved as a Greek, and not necessarily someone of Greek descent. Thus social opportunities were readily open to members of the native élites, who only needed to learn Greek, and receive a Greek education to be accepted into the Greek

31   Geertz (1973a [1966]: 89).
32   Geertz 1973b.
33   See Chartier 1985. Chartier's paper reacted to Darnton 1984, a book which had made the best of Geertz's theory. On the revised view of culture, see further Barth 1989.
34   I am here using the useful overview offered by Miller (1997: 244–46), from whom I borrow many phrases, including 'models of cultural transfer'.

colonial society. Sceptical voices raised in the 1970s objected that the phenomenon of Hellenization was marginal, and that in general, two cultures,
Greek and the various native cultures, co-existed all over the Hellenistic
East without mingling. However, the view of both the supporters of the
former view and its opponents was based on the model of 'acculturation'.
Needless to say, both sides also conceived of 'culture' as a whole endowed
with clearly defined boundaries.[35]

The model of 'acculturation' is no longer defensible. As a result, it is
no longer possible to apprehend the process of 'Hellenization' in Judaea
through the prism of Greek *paideia*, and the supposed cultural conception
of their own identity by contemporary Greeks.[36] After the flaws of the
'acculturation' model had led to its rejection as a conceptual tool, various
other models followed. One of the earliest alternatives suggested was the
'centre–periphery' model, and the associated concept of 'emulation'. This
model was denounced, in its turn, for its imperialistic connotations, and
replaced with the notion of 'interculturation', or 'cultural receptivity'.
Whatever their specific nuances, the models currently in use all stress the
dynamics affecting the 'receiving' culture, and not the donor one (as was
the case with the 'acculturation' model). Beside this search for an acceptable way of conceptualizing 'cultural transfer', two further premises have
been widely taken on in recent studies. First, studies in 'interculturation'
have shown that receiving cultures selectively borrow items which meet
their own needs: such 'needs' may be material, or symbolic. Secondly, the
revised definition of 'culture' as an open arena in which social tensions
are given expression has led scholars to pay attention to the fact that
distinct groups within a receiving society both borrow distinct items and
appropriate the same items in different ways.[37]

---

35   See above, n. 1. Surprisingly, the view that Greek ethnicity was based on *paideia* in late
Classical and Hellenistic times has regained favour recently in Hall (2002: 172–228).

36   To take the issue from the other side, it has been suggested, correctly in my view, that the
discourse about *paideia* in Athenian orators (beginning with the Funeral Oration of Pericles in Thuc.
2.35-46, and down to Isocrates) was strictly instrumental to Athenian imperialism. See Saïd 2001.
Moreover, the emphasis on *paideia* in the Athenian public discourse of the fourth century was not
followed by any humanistic opening up of Athenian citizenship in the fourth century, to say the
least. See Lape 2004, for a re-reading of Menander's comedies in this perspective. Lape shows
that the Athenians of the second half of the fourth century retained their ideology of pure descent,
which had been expressed through the myth of autochthony since the early fifth century. Menander's
characters fall in love with young girls, but no marriage is eventually concluded which infringes
the civic laws jealously protecting the genealogical purity of the civic body. See in particular her
introductory chapter.

37   A good example of the current approach is given by Margaret Miller's analysis of the
borrowing of cultural items from the Persian empire in fifth-century Athens (Miller 1997). Under
the heading of 'cultural receptivity', her study illustrates both the phenomenon of 'selective borrowing' and the mechanism of differential appropriation of the cultural symbols borrowed. Miller

This current understanding of the phenomenon of interculturation invites us to re-consider the process of cultural changes that Judaean society underwent in the Hellenistic era. First, the contention that the meaning of *Hellenismos* in *2 Maccabees* derived from that of *Ioudaismos*, and not the reverse, naturally follows from the now commonly accepted view that the active role, in instances of cultural transfer, was mainly played by the receiving society, or, more accurately, by *agents* from within the receiving society, and not by agents from the donor society. Next, the connotations associated with *Hellenismos* in the author's mind need not be similar to those that Isocrates ascribed to this term – or those that modern scholars ascribe to Isocrates. Third, the connotations associated with the term *Hellenismos* by the author of *2 Maccabees* need not be similar to those shared by Jason, the 'Hellenized' high priest, and his followers. In the same way, the term *Ioudaismos* in *2 Maccabees* needs to be seen as encapsulating a *specific* meaning, which precisely reflects the attitude – more precisely, as we shall see in a moment, the worldview – of the author himself. The word *Ioudaismos* is not to be taken as an objective description of reality.

In view of the definitions of religion and culture just presented, it is implausible that, in coining the term *Ioudaismos*, the author of *2 Maccabees* had only 'faith', or 'culture' *in the narrow, modern sense of the word*, in mind. This is not to deny that the very coining of the term represents an intellectual revolution.[38] As a reification of the social, political and religious order on the basis of which Judaean society was organized, this neologism undoubtedly reflects a capacity for abstraction which points to a deep influence of the Greek way of thinking. However, the term is one thing, its content is another. Inasmuch as religion did not constitute an autonomous field either in Judaean, or, for this purpose, in Greek society, the term *Ioudaismos* must reflect this state of affairs. It must, therefore, signify the interconnected structure of the society it is intended to describe or, more accurately, the interconnected structure of the society as the author of *2 Maccabees* saw it.

traces the behaviour of Athenian aristocrats, 'middle class' individuals, and the public sphere of the democratic state. See, in particular, ch. 10. See further the remarks by Mitchell (2006: 415), with further bibliography, n. 29.

38   Whether the neologism was our author's or whether he merely used a word which was in the air, is immaterial for our concern. The term was certainly new, and this is the important point.

Ioudaismos *in* 2 Maccabees*: The case for continuity*

The worldview of 2 Maccabees

Determining the precise connotation of '*Ioudaismos*' in *2 Maccabees* requires a close reading of the text which cannot be included here. The remarks below summarize the conclusions of a detailed study I intend to present elsewhere.

Studies of *2 Maccabees* have emphasized that the narrative displays a Deuteronomistic view of history: the scheme of sin-punishment-judgement and salvation gives the narrative its basic structure.[39] This scheme is commonly referred to as the 'theology of retribution'; it certainly underlies the narrative. However, the notion of 'theology' cannot be understood as a complex of 'faith' alone in a religious system centred on a temple. *2 Maccabees* obviously reflects a far more encompassing and coherent worldview than mere questions of faith. In particular, the scheme that informs the narrative raises issues of a clearly political nature.

The worldview of the author of *2 Maccabees* is unquestionably centred on the temple: the temple cult is what holds the community together in the first place, and determines its fate. More accurately, the community, centred on the temple, is dependent on two figures for its welfare. First of all, it is dependent on the behaviour of the high priest in fulfilling his responsibilities: the neglect of the cult by the high priest Jason and other priests who prefer to attend the exercises at the gymnasium at the expense of their duties jeopardizes the welfare of the community (4.14). However, the high priest is not alone. The narrative consistently creates an organic link between his figure and that of the king: good, pious high priests not only ensure peace and prosperity for the community (as Onias did; 3.1-3) and successfully avert pending disasters (3.4-40), they also bring good kings in their wake (Seleukos IV, in Onias' case; 3.3). Wicked high priests (Menelaos and Jason), on the contrary, bring disasters on the community, because they inescapably draw a wicked king (Antiochos IV) in their wake. The disasters that befell the community *under* wicked high priests, and *through* the agency of the wicked king, are spelled out in detail in the text.

The main scandal denounced in *2 Maccabees* is obviously the disruption of the temple cult through the defilement of the altar by the

---

39 George Nickelsburg identifies five steps in the narrative: 1) *The blessing* of Jerusalem under Onias (3.1-40); 2) *The sin* of Hellenization under Jason and Menelaos (4.1–5.10); 3) *Punishment* through Antiochos' reprisals (5.11–6.17); 4) The *turning point* of the deaths of the martyrs and prayers of the people (6.18–8.4); 5) And *judgment and salvation*, as materialized in Judas's victories (8.5–15.36). See Nickelsburg (2003 [1971]: 668) and (1981: 118). Further, Schwartz 1998; van Henten (1997: 23–36) and (2003).

introduction of a foreign deity. This misdeed puts the very survival of the community in jeopardy – the author does not distinguish between the destruction of the identity of the community which the change of cult would automatically entail, and its physical destruction through killing the men and selling the women and children into slavery (5.24, 26). However, the disruption of the temple cult is not the only issue at stake, nor is it presented in abstract, 'theological', terms. Before his death, Antiochos IV acknowledges God's might, and sets out to 'confess' his past sins towards the Judaeans (9.14-16), ending up with his promise to become a *Ioudaios* (9.17). The detailed and concrete content of the list of the king's sins suggests that the selection of the misdeeds recorded in it is intended to delineate the dividing line between a 'good' and a 'wicked' king. The issues mentioned are military and economic:[40] Antiochos' pledge to grant Jerusalem the status of a 'free' city, i.e. free from its garrison (9.14), is meant to compensate for his earlier intention to destroy the city and the temple. His pledge to make gifts to the temple would constitute a return to the normal course of things (3.3), which had been disrupted by the king's robbery of the sacred vessels (4.32; 5.15-16) in the wake of the sacrilege of Lysimachos, the high priest's brother (4.29). The inclusion of these two economic issues in the list of Antiochos' repentances indicates that the defilement of the altar by Antiochos is seen, in the text, not only as a punishment for Israel's sins, in keeping with the so-called Deuteronomistic view of history, but as an inversion of a basic royal duty, the king's financial support for the sacrifices.

This list of Antiochos' sins must encapsulate a basic tenet in the world-view of the author of *2 Maccabees*. I suggest that the term *Ioudaismos* is used in *2 Maccabees* in a sense that corresponds to this worldview precisely. In other words, *Ioudaismos* denotes the religious system centred on the temple; that is, the religious system which the author saw as relevant. In this system, or worldview, the temple does not fulfil a merely symbolic role. As I argued above, the anthropological view of religion

---

40 A similar link between the royal acknowledgement of a god's might, and economic concessions to a temple, is documented in a letter by one king Antiochos to the sanctuary of Zeus Baitokaike, in Syria: 'A report having been brought to me about the power of the god Zeus of Baitokaike, I have decided to concede to him for all time the source of the god's power, (namely) the village of Baitokaike, formerly held by Demetrios, son of Demetrios [. . .], together with everything that appertains and belongs to it, according to the existing surveys, and including the revenues of the present year, so that the revenue from this village might be spent for the celebration of the monthly sacrifices and the other things that increase the prestige of the sanctuary by the priest designated by the god, as is the custom (*RC* 70 = *IGLS* VII, 4028, English transl. Austin 172, quoted in Kuhrt and Sherwin-White 2003: 65, spelling of Greek names modified). See also the royal correspondence about the appointment of one Nikanor as high priest, i.e. overseer, of the sanctuaries located in Mysia: *SEG* 37.1010 (= Ma 2000: 288–92), ll. 18-41.

posits that a religious system, especially one based on rites, is narrowly interconnected with the economic, social and political order of a community. This definition suits the religious world of *2 Maccabees* perfectly. Inasmuch as *2 Maccabees* sees the social order of the Judaean polity as centred on the temple, *Ioudaismos*, in this text, necessarily signifies all the things, processes and arrangements that contribute to the proper operation of the temple cult. This means, above all, the polity linked to the temple, in both its human and territorial dimensions. However, the religious system labelled *Ioudaismos* in *2 Maccabees* also includes, and organizes at a cognitive level, the political order of the community linked to the temple. Since Judaea was not an independent polity at the time of the events related in the work (the 160s BCE), the text takes the relations between the Judaean community and the external ruling power for granted, and makes sense of them at the cognitive level. Since the foreign king, through his economic support, made a vital contribution to the regular operation of the temple cult, the economic and financial arrangements which ordered the relations between king and temple, as well as between king and high priest, are an integral part of *2 Maccabees' Ioudaismos*. It follows from this definition that the author's theology coincides with what can be described as traditional royal ideology – providing the basic criteria for evaluating whether a king is 'good' or 'wicked' – in all that concerns the relations between king and temple.

As one would expect, *Ioudaismos* in *2 Maccabees* is conceived as the ideal version of this mutual contract between foreign king and local polity: *Ioudaismos* describes the proper order of things, in which a 'good' high priest and a 'good' foreign king guarantee the welfare of the community. It is, ideally, the situation that prevailed under the high priest Onias and Seleukos IV (3.1-3). Conversely, *Hellenismos* encapsulates all the forces of disruption which disturb the ideal order. *Hellenismos* is the disrupted socio-political order which follows from the combined misdemeanours of 'wicked' high priests and 'wicked' kings. Since, as we saw above, the word *Hellenismos* is, in all probability, derived from *Ioudaismos*, and not the contrary, we can surmise that *Hellenismos* in *2 Maccabees* must include all that hampers the smooth operation of the temple cult. Indeed, the problem stigmatized by the author in his denunciation of the gymnasium in 4.8-15 is not merely, or even primarily, the enthusiasm of the priests for physical exercise per se, but the resultant neglect of the temple cult (v. 14). Thus, although the term *Hellenismos* is associated with a gymnasium in *2 Maccabees*, its use in this text cannot support the old picture of the 'Hellenization' of the East as an 'acculturation' to Greek *paideia* through the medium of the gymnasium. If asked to detail what he meant by *Hellenismos*, I doubt whether the author of *2 Maccabees* would have listed, say, the Greek language. However, he would have listed all those misdeeds of Antiochos IV that make up the latter's portrait as a 'wicked' king; for example, the robbery of the temple vessels.

The meaning of *Ioudaismos* in *2 Maccabees*, encapsulating the ideal version of the socio-political order of Judaea in the time it is supposed to refer to, the 160s, is not an oddity for Hellenistic times. We only need to remember that the royal cult which was instituted in Greek cities as early as Alexander's time similarly aimed at defining and organizing, at a cognitive level, the status of the king vis à vis the civic communities, and vice versa.[41] More interestingly, the sense in which *Ioudaismos* is used in *2 Maccabees* reflects a conception of royal legitimacy which is also articulated in contemporary documents originating from other Near Eastern societies, such as the Borsippa cylinder in Babylonia, and the priestly decrees from Ptolemaic Egypt: in these epigraphic texts, the political relations between local polities and foreign kings are encapsulated in the material expressions of royal piety towards the local temples. In all cases, this is what defines the basis of the mutual contract between the two parts: the king's legitimacy is acknowledged as long as he displays piety and fulfils his religious duties towards the temple – either by carrying out the rites himself or financing the sacrifices – while the community's political loyalty towards the king is envisioned as a fair counterpart to the king's piety.

2 Maccabees' worldview in a diachronic perspective: adaptation in continuity

The similarities in the worldview underlying *2 Maccabees* and Hellenistic texts from Mesopotamia and Egypt, which all define, or, more accurately, posit, a place for the foreign king in their politico-religious systems, suggest that these features are adaptations to contemporary political conditions of an earlier common ideology. In effect, far from marking a break with the past, the worldview of *2 Maccabees* is best described as an updated version of a traditional worldview. Its central concern for the quality of the relationship between king and temple creates an interface between royal ideology and theology, which can be shown to derive from the ancient royal ideology which was indeed common to the whole ancient Near East, given some local adaptations related to time and place.

The version of this ideology found in *2 Maccabees* may be placed within a sequence of three or perhaps four stages within the Yahwistic/ Judaean tradition. The earliest known stage fits what may be called the

---

41   The imperial cult later fulfilled a similar function under Roman rule. See, in an inflated bibliography, Ma 2000; Price 1986.

'classical' model of ancient Near Eastern royal ideology.[42] In this model, it is the king alone who is entitled to build the temple of his tutelary deity or deities.[43] The building or re-building of the temple is the deed which establishes the king's legitimacy, especially if he is founding a new dynasty: the king who builds a house to the deity will have the deity build his house in turn, i.e. confirm his power and establish his dynasty. In the Judaean cultural scene, this ideology is first articulated in the covenant between YHWH and David (2 Sam. 7), and again with Solomon (I Kings 9.3-9), in a conditional form, which Arnaud Sérandour holds to be post-exilic.[44] Logically, this model of the king legitimizing his rule by building the temple of the deity was originally elaborated in political situations in which kings were local rulers. However, Cyrus the Great fitted himself into this model after his conquest of Babylon. In the well-known 'Cyrus cylinder', the conquering king claims that he was chosen by Marduk to restore order in Babylon and re-build the god's temple which had fallen into ruin.[45] Thus, while not concealing that Cyrus was ruling over many other peoples, the text presents Cyrus as the local king of Babylon.

While the model of the 'local' king found in II Sam and I Kings is well documented for the whole ancient Near East, the second stage of the Yahwistic/Judaean tradition is original, as Sérandour has pointed out,[46] at least among our extant sources: it consists in a dyarchy made up of a Davidic governor and high priest, alongside a foreign king. This world-view informs the editorial passages of Haggai and Zechariah on the one hand, and the editorial layer of redaction of Ezra–Nehemiah on the other.[47] The editor of the two prophetic texts acknowledges Darius throughout as the legitimate king: Darius is explicitly hailed as a king, and the narrative is dated according to his rule (Hag. 1.1 and *passim*).[48] Since the deity to whom the temple is (re-)built must be a victorious one, Sérandour suggests that the fall of the Neo-Babylonian empire to the Persians in 539 BCE was singled out as the victory which made the re-building of YHWH's temple possible.[49] Conversely, Zerubbabel, although of Davidic descent, is nowhere referred to as a king, but is consistently presented either as the

---

42   For this model, as well as that of the dyarchy, my summary closely follows Sérandour 1996. All references to the sources and most of the bibliography quoted are borrowed from this paper.

43   Lackenbacher 1982; Hurowitz 1992.

44   Sérandour (1996: 10).

45   Kuhrt (1983: 85–7); Sérandour (1996: 12).

46   Sérandour (1996: 11).

47   Sérandour 1996; Japhet 2006.

48   Sérandour (1996: 14).

49   Sérandour (1996: 14). Concomitantly, the building of this (second) temple is presented throughout as the re-building of the temple of Solomon.

'servant' (*'bd*) of YHWH (Hag. 2.23), or the governor (2.21), endowed with the ring (2.23).[50]

Thus, the 'dyarchy', i.e. the bicephalous organization of local power around Zerubbabel, the governor of Davidic descent (Hag. 1.1 and *passim* with 1 Chron. 3.1-19), and Joshua, the Zadokite high priest (Hag. 1.1 and *passim* with 1 Chron. 5.27-41), shows the remarkable adaptability of the 'classical' royal ideology to changing conditions of the political order.[51] The dyarchic model is best reflected in Zechariah's vision of the candelabrum framed by two olive trees (Zech. 4.1-6 and 10b-14). Moreover, the divine covenant is made with both men, with the implication that both of them are chosen by YHWH to re-build his temple,[52] and each of them is blessed with a dynastic pledge (Zerubbabel: Hag. 2.20-23; Joshua: Zech. 3.1-7). However, Joshua is the only one to be granted access to the divine assembly (Zech. 3.7), a prerogative reserved to the king in the 'classical' model. This introduction into the divine assembly endows the king in the classical model, and Joshua, the priest, in the dyarchic order, with knowledge of secrets of the cosmos. This cosmic knowledge is required for the leaders to rule justly, which means in conformity with the order of the macrocosm. It is no coincidence that Joshua is also the only one of the two co-rulers entitled to perform sacrifices.

As already noted, the structure of power is presented as reflecting the order of the macrocosm. This is precisely what makes it the legitimate order of society. In effect, the re-building of the temple is conceived, according to the traditional view, as a renewed cosmology, a deed of re-creation of the world. Given the bicephalous organization of local power, the re-vitalized world is described, in Haggai and Zechariah, as a twofold bi-polarity, as heaven above and earth below, and as dry land in the centre and sea around it (Hag. 2.6).[53]

---

50   Sérandour (1996: 17), *pace* the view prevailing in scholarship, which considers that Sheshbazzar and Zerubbabel were made kings. See, e.g., Niehr 1999, with earlier bibliography. Despite the fact that it seems isolated, Sérandour's contention is convincingly argued. Furthermore, the later modification of the original royal ideology, focusing on the figure of the high priest alone and a foreign king found in *2 Maccabees*, makes Sérandour's reading of the second stage as a dyarchy of a governor and high priest *alongside* a foreign king more than plausible.

51   Sérandour (1996: 31) suggests, on the basis of Zerubbabel and Joshua's genealogies, that the dyarchic model was inspired by the Zoroastrian worldview which was adopted by the Achaemenid dynasty as early as Darius I's reign. However, his description of the Persian support for the independence of the temples vis à vis the kings as a separation between sacred and secular spheres (1996: 31 and 13) sounds anachronistic. A more complex, and no doubt more accurate, picture is adumbrated by Dandamaev 1979.

52   The clearest statements are Haggai 1.1, 12, 14; 2.2; also, Zech. 6.9-14; Ezra 3.2-8. In Zech. 3.8-9, Joshua receives the founding stone, but Zerubbabel is referred to as the 'Branch' in v. 8. Zerubbabel is associated with the founding stone in Zech. 4.7, 9-10.

53   Sérandour (1996: 14-15).

In a careful reconstruction of the rationale underlying the editorial organization of the narrative in Ezra–Nehemiah, Sarah Japhet has, likewise, shown that its main purpose was to present the missions of Ezra and Nehemiah as coeval with each other. Since Ezra is described as a scribe and priest (Ezra 7.1-6, 12, 21; Neh. 8.1, 2, 4), while Nehemiah is emphatically presented as a secular, non-priestly, governor (Neh. 6.11; both figures together, Neh. 8.9), the editorial work on Ezra–Nehemiah reflects an ideology of power similar to that of the editorial layer of Haggai and Zechariah.[54]

One final issue needs to be addressed here: the time when the ideology of the bicephalous covenant, or dyarchy, crystallized. Sérandour has suggested that it was the priestly Zadokite dynasty who imposed this ideology upon the governors of the province of Judah after these officials ceased to belong to the Davidic dynasty, at some time around the end of the sixth century BCE. This implies that the editorial layer of Haggai and Zechariah should not be dated much earlier than 450 BCE.[55] If this view is accepted, it seems reasonable to date the similar political ideology underlying the editorial layer of Ezra–Nehemiah to the late Persian period too.

Texts from Hellenistic times, especially those written in Greek, illustrate either two further stages of adaptation of the 'classical' political model or, more plausibly, two variants of a third stage. One denominator common to both is the dismantling of the dyarchy. The figure of the governor has vanished, and the high priest now stands alone at the head of the local political organization. The substitution of a theocratic model centred on the high priest only instead of the dyarchy, naturally followed from the changes which the local political order had been undergoing.[56] In effect, the new model reflects the political reality which had probably been current in the local polity since the demotion of the Davidic dynasty at the end of the sixth century BCE, and the consequent increase in the high priest's prestige. It is less clear when this political reality was translated into a worldview.

One variant, illustrated in *2 Maccabees*, maintains the imperial dimension as part of its worldview, as a continuation of the dyarchic model sketched out in Haggai and Zechariah. In contrast, the other variant, first articulated in Hecataeus of Abdera (*ap.* Diodorus Siculus 40.3) and

---

54   Japhet 2006.

55   Sérandour (1996: 31–2). Sérandour further suggests (p. 31) that a post-Exilic date should be ascribed to all passages in the Hexateuch presenting a similar dyarchy: Moses and Aaron; Moses and Eliezer; Joshuah and Eliezer.

56   For a distinct, complementary, analysis of the development of the idea of democracy in Hellenistic Judaea, see Albertz (1994: 544–63).

less clearly in Ben Sirah 50,[57] focuses exclusively on the high priest, as though Judaea were an independent polity and not part of an empire. It is tempting, at first glance, to see these two representations of political power in Judaea as two genuinely distinct stages, reflecting the two successive phases of the political status of Judaea in the Hellenistic period – first as part of the Ptolemaic and Seleucid empires, and later as an independent polity under the Hasmonaean dynasty. However, the dating of the texts presenting these two reconstructions of the political order rules out such a conclusion. Hecataeus of Abdera's *floruit* is dated to ca. 300 BCE, long before the Hasmonaean era. Thus the vision of Judaea as an independent polity headed by a high priest is better seen as being due to the influence of contemporary Greek political thought. Since Greek intellectuals conceived of any polity, whether Greek or not, as a *politeia*, i.e. an autonomous political entity, they would only pay attention to the organization of power at the local level.

In view of this Greek intellectual tradition, it was only a matter of time before Jews acquainted with Greek political thought realized that the *politeia* of the Judaeans best paralleled a *monarchia*, with the important difference that the monarch was a priest, and not a king, so that they describe the *politeia* of Judaea as a *theokratia*. The term itself is first documented in Josephus' *Against Apion* 2.165, a text from the first century CE. However, there are grounds for thinking that it had been coined earlier. The description of Judaea in Hecataeus of Abdera already seems to call for it, as does the description of Jerusalem in the *Letter of Aristeas* (an Alexandrian work probably from the late second century BCE) 100–104 (together with 41).[58] A further question, unfortunately impossible to solve given the state of our evidence, is whether or not the term was first coined in Judaea. Judaea was not the only society forming part of the Hellenistic world which was centred on a temple and ruled by a high priest. Far from it. Temple communities are also documented in Syria and Asia Minor.[59] Thus the term could just as well have been coined in Syria or Asia Minor. It could also have resulted from the speculation of a particularly bold disciple of Theophrastos, who would have been open to conceptualize in new terms the descriptions of barbarian *politeiai* which he, or others before him, had collected. At all events, while the term *theokratia* is formally

57 On Ben Sirah's view of the high priest, see Aitken in this volume.
58 On Hecataeus, see Bar-Kochva 1996; on the description of Judaea in the *Letter of Aristeas*, Honigman (2004: 82–5).
59 On temple communities, or 'Temple-states', see Sherwin-White and Kuhrt (1993: 59–61). Known examples include Comana, Bambyke-Hierapolis, Baitokaike. Susan Sherwin-White and Amélie Kuhrt add Jerusalem, Uruk and Babylon.

a neologism in *Against Apion*, the socio-political reality it reflected was not – just like *Ioudaismos*.

As we saw above, while the 'classical' model of the politico-religious ideology found in the Bible (2 Sam. 7 and 1 Kings 9) strictly reproduced a model invented in Mesopotamia and documented elsewhere,[60] the dyarchic model seems to have been idiosyncratic to Judaea. It is far from certain that the theocratic model was also, in its turn, idiosyncratic. Like the term *theokratia* itself, it could easily have been inspired by neighbouring societies, apart from the political transformations which affected Judaea itself. One well-known case is Egypt. The ritual and theological problems raised by the fact that, under Persian rule, the Pharaoh neither was an Egyptian nor lived in Egypt, manifested themselves there in a particularly acute way. Since the absentee Pharaoh was unable to perform the daily ritual duties incumbent on his function, high priests, especially those officiating in the main religious centres at Memphis and Thebes, began to play a crucial role in the aftermath of the Persian conquest. Even though the establishment of a resident dynasty under the Ptolemies partly solved the problem, it has been suggested that an important factor for the secession of Upper Egypt in the second century BCE was the Ptolemies' failure to perform their religious duties in Thebes – needless to say, secessionist temptations were not a novelty in Thebes.[61]

Similarly, the attention paid to ethnic issues in *2 Maccabees* – the celebrated contrast between Judaism and Hellenism – may owe a lot to the *Zeitgeist*. Even though Antiochos IV is first and foremost described as a 'wicked' king, and not a Greek king, in terms that reflect an age-old perception of the foreign ruler in the political tradition of the ancient Near East,[62] some attention is undeniably paid to the ethnicity of the king, as the term *Hellenismos* beside the vaguer *allophylismos* shows. However, similar trends have been pointed out in other areas of the Hellenistic Near East. We have already mentioned the cylinder from Borsippa, near Babylon, which records the celebration of the rites of the New Year by Antiochos I at the local sanctuary of Nabû (Ezida). As Amélie Kuhrt and Susan Sherwin-White have argued, the wording of the cylinder itself, in cuneiform, is traditional, save for two details: the ethnic label of the king is noted, and the queen is referred to.[63] Further evidence comes from Egypt, although in this case it is iconographic. The relief engraved on the stele of Pithom, above the decree of Raphia (217 BCE) celebrating

---

60   Lackenbacher 1982; Hurowitz 1992.

61   Goyon 1988.

62   In his cylinder, Cyrus presents himself as the king of Babylon, with no regard to ethnicity. See Kuhrt 1983.

63   See Kuhrt and Sherwin-White 1991.

Ptolemy III's victory over Antiochos III, depicts the king killing an enemy with his spear. As Willy Clarysse has pointed out, the scene is typically Egyptian, save for two details: the king is shown riding on a horse (and not in a chariot), and he is wearing a Greek military garment, while holding a long Macedonian spear.[64] In view of this comparative material, it may be tentatively suggested that, although awareness of ethnic issues was new in *2 Maccabees* as compared with the earlier Judaean tradition, far from being specific to the encounter between Judaism and Hellenism, or between monotheism and polytheism, it merely kept in tune with intellectual transformations that were affecting the Hellenistic East at large.

The interrelated issues of the link between the social and the cosmic orders, on the one hand, and the link between local and imperial levels of power (i.e. the articulation of the relation between the king and the high priest) on the other, undoubtedly play a central part in the narrative of *2 Maccabees*. It is thus worth inquiring what is traditional and what is new in the specific perspective adopted in this text. The very fact that the political order of *2 Maccabees* is rooted in the cosmic order is clearly an element of continuity as compared with the 'classical' model of royal ideology and the subsequent dyarchy. However, the perspective is somewhat different in *2 Maccabees*, since authorial comments make both the king and the high priest accountable for social and cosmic harmony. In this text, the king who subsidizes sacrifices belongs to the proper world order (*2 Macc.* 3.3).[65] Conversely, a king who plunders sacred vessels instead of honouring the temple with new gifts not only loses his legitimacy, but actually overturns the natural order (5.21).[66] Antiochos' lack of respect towards the temple of Jerusalem and the Jews is a proof of his cosmic *hybris*, a notion further articulated in 9.8.[67] On the other hand, the literary

---

64   Clarysse (1999: 45).

65   Needless to say, the economic dimension of the temple as it is articulated in *2 Maccabees* represents a traditional element in this work: the role of the temple in the fiscal and economic configuration of Judah is a prominent feature of the book of Ezra–Nehemiah. See Schaper 1995 and 1997.

66   'Thinking in his arrogance that he had made the land navigable and the sea passable by foot, so high did his vain imagination soar.' Translation Goldstein 1983. It should be noted that a similar conception was held in the Greek political tradition, despite the latter's apparent 'secular' character as compared with the Near-Eastern one. The Corinthian Socles equals the Spartans' plan to overturn the Athenian democracy and bring the tyrant Hippias back to power with an attempt to reverse the cosmic order (Herodotos, 5.92.1).

67   'In his boastfulness', he 'had gone beyond what befits a human being (διὰ τὴν ὑπὲρ ἄνθρωπον ἀλαζονείαν), for he had been thinking of giving orders to the waves of the sea and had been planning to weigh the peaks of the mountains in a balance' (Translation Goldstein 1983). In the Greek cultural arena, Aeschylus ascribed a similar cosmic *hybris* to Xerxes who wished to conquer Europe instead of being content with his 'proper' lot, Asia. See also Herodotos, 7.24 (μεγαλοφροσύνης εἵνεκεν).

construction of *2 Maccabees* seems to endow the high priest with royal prerogatives.[68] In 3.1-3, the cosmic harmony appears to be dependent on the high priest. The devolution of this new role to the high priest seems to be a logical evolution within the traditional political ideology, once the dominant model had been re-conceived around the figure of the high priest. In effect, the editorial layer of Haggai and Zechariah already rooted the cosmic harmony in the figure of the two rulers chosen to form the dyarchy, and not in the imperial king. The reason why they fulfilled this role, and not Darius, is clear: although Darius I was the representative of the demiurge-god on earth, it was Zerubbabel and Joshua who were chosen to re-build YHWH's temple.

As for the relationship between local and imperial levels of power, some interesting nuances can be seen. In Haggai and Zechariah, the Persian king is an independent figure, whose role is relegated to the background. In particular, as just noted, the king is conspicuously *not* the figure chosen to re-build the temple. In other words, the imperial dimension of the political order is assimilated in an incomplete, and even awkward, manner in the worldview underlying these texts. In contrast, *2 Maccabees* reflects a stage of conceptual development in which the problem raised by the twofold – local and imperial – level of power, and their respective relationship to the temple, has been solved. The literary organization of the text creates an organic link between the high priest and the foreign king. Their pairing allows a reconciliation of the potential tension between the view that the order of society necessarily reflects the cosmic order, and the existence of two, uncoordinated, poles of power – especially if the local pole of power included royal prerogatives related to cosmology, apart from the king in title, and if both poles were related to the temple. The solution worked out in *2 Maccabees* has already been referred to above: the behaviour of the king is dependent on that of the high priest. This organic link has an important consequence on the definition of the ideal ruler. The concept of 'good' and 'wicked' kings went back to classical royal ideology: the statement that the former king was 'wicked' provided the main narrative medium through which usurpers legitimized overturning the former dynasty. In this context, 'wicked' had a very precise meaning, that of 'impious': the new contender had been chosen by the deity to rebuild his/her temple, because the impious king neglected his duties towards him/her.[69] From this point of view, the opposition between 'wicked' and 'good' king, which is spelled out with such conspicuous insistence in *2 Maccabees*, does not seem to

---

68   Compare *Ben Sira* 50.1-2.

69   See note 59 above. This motive is found in Mesopotamian inscriptions from an early date on. It is also found in the Cyrus cylinder (*ANET*: 315–16).

offer any innovative content per se in this text. The new point is that, here again, the high priest has acquired royal prerogatives: he is the one who can now be either 'good' or 'wicked', i.e. fulfil his duties towards the deity or not. By rushing to the gymnasium, the Hellenized high priest and priests became 'wicked' (4.14, 17). Moreover, the condition for receiving a 'good' king is a 'good' high priest, while the 'wicked' king is the inescapable consequence of the rule of a 'wicked' high priest.

Thus the specific inflection which the issue of the relations between the local and the imperial levels of power, between king and high priest, is given in *2 Maccabees* may be described as a mature stage of the adaptation of the traditional worldview centred on the temple to the political situation current in the region since Darius I. Even if the version of *2 Maccabees* shows 'changes' as compared to earlier texts, these changes are to be understood as reflecting a phase of *adaptation* of a traditional model, and not a break or new departure. This conclusion is all the more to be expected since Alexander the Great, and the various Hellenistic dynasties after him, basically took over the imperial structures designed by the Achaimenid dynasty. From this point of view, the substitution of Macedonian kings for the Persian dynasty did not entail any revolutionary change. Local priesthoods merely carried out some adaptations to suit the new dynasties.[70] These adaptations represent cosmetic rather than deep changes.

Thus, the very text that coined the word *Ioudaismos* and conceptualized the opposition between *Ioudaismos* and *Hellenismos*, at least for us, turns out to present many traits of continuity with pre-Hellenistic Near Eastern traditions. In the same way, it turns out to be much less original than is usually thought in comparison with contemporary surrounding societies. These aspects are all the more worth emphasizing since the establishment of the Hasmonaean dynasty in the wake of the 160s uprising is often considered by modern scholarship as representing a major break, not only with pre-Hellenistic, but even with early Hellenistic times. This view may be correct with hind-sight: many of the intellectual and religious trends which informed early Christianity and Rabbinic Judaism first emerged under the Hasmonaeans. It cannot be correct in an absolute way.[71]

---

70   Clarysse (1999: 50–52).

71   Inscribing the worldview of *2 Maccabees* back into an intellectual tradition deeply rooted in ancient Near Eastern political and religious tenets long before Hellenistic times raises a further question, which has been left aside in the discussion hitherto. The author of *2 Maccabees* purportedly summarises the work of one Jason of Cyrene, who, as the scholarly consensus holds, wrote in Greek, and was even not born in the cultural area in which the ancient royal ideology and its further adaptations evolved. It is beyond the scope of this paper to solve this conundrum – but it is worth noting.

Hierarchizing 'Judaisms'

The foregoing analysis of the worldview of *2 Maccabees* has defined it as one stage in the on-going adaptation of the royal ideology which had been a common denominator of virtually all societies in the ancient Near East for centuries – and as only one variant among the adaptations documented in Judaea (Hecataeus), Babylonia (the Borsippa cylinder) and Egypt (the Pithom stele), which all assimilated features specific to Hellenistic times, such as the new awareness of the ethnic stock of the king. This conclusion in turn poses a further question. It has become widely accepted that no form of Judaism in the Second Temple period, especially in Hellenistic times, should be regarded as 'normative', relegating all alternative forms to the status of 'marginal' and 'sectarian'. This view is certainly to be accepted in its broader lines. However, there is still a gap between rejecting the idea of a 'normative' form of Judaism and levelling out all forms of Judaisms in a fully relativistic way. Inasmuch as there can be no religion without a human group associated with it, religion is a social phenomenon, and society is never completely level. The successive worldviews derived from the 'classical' royal ideology fit the central socio-political organization of Judah/Judaea in Persian and Hellenistic times most accurately. The successive models all focus on both the temple and the ruler standing at the head of the polity, conceiving the former as the focus of the religious, political and economic life of the community, and the latter as the polity's representative vis à vis the temple, as well as vis à vis the imperial king from Persian times on. In its later phase, this worldview is not only illustrated in *2 Maccabees*, but appears already in earlier Hellenistic texts, such as Hecataeus and Ben Sirah 50. This worldview certainly deserves to be singled out in some way or another, precisely because it focuses on, and, at the cognitive level, makes sense of, the central organization of power in the local polity. This is not to imply that this form of Judaism is to be seen as 'normative'. It does, however, deserve a special designation, as either the 'central', or perhaps even the 'official' form of Judaism.

Since the very nature of the political and religious representation peculiar to this 'central' Judaism compelled it to undergo adaptations over time in order to keep in tune with the transformations affecting the central power in Judaea, it may reasonably be expected that the version found in Ben Sirah and *2 Maccabees* is not its latest stage of evolution. Indeed Philip Davies has contended that the elements singled out in *1* and *2 Maccabees* as key issues in what he calls the 'religious struggle' of the 160s – 'circumcision, diet, sabbath, holy books' – actually 'bec[a]me dominant characteristics of Judaism' much later.[72] Far from being age-old

---

72   Davies (1995: 174).

hallmarks, these items only gained importance in the years preceding the Maccabaean uprising. They were elements held as fundamental by 'those among the people of Judah who fought and won', and specifically by the Maccabees. In other words, they constitute the 'Judaism of the victors'.[73] While Davies' view that 'Judaism' as such did not emerge before the Hasmonaeans ultimately fails to convince, as argued above,[74] his proposition is tempting: circumcision could only draw attention and thus become a hallmark of Judaism at a time when people from outside the society began mocking it, driving some insiders to reject this rite in their turn.[75]

To summarize: On the one hand, if Davies' suggestion that circumcision, diet, sabbath and holy books became hallmarks of Judaism only in the wake of the Maccabaean uprising is accepted, this means that *2 Maccabees* devotes much attention to the newly emerging hallmarks of Judaism. On the other hand, the discussion of *2 Maccabees*' worldview offered above stressed that the narrative still accommodates the imperial dimension which was swept away with the establishment of the Hasmonaean royal dynasty. If these two analyses are accepted, *2 Maccabees* turns out to be a work typical of a transitional phase between one 'central' form of Judaism and the next. But if we can trace basic continuities, in the ever-evolving forms of 'central' Judaism, from the 'classical' model of ancient Near Eastern royal ideology echoed in 2 Sam. 7 and 1 Kings 9, through the Hasmonaean form of Judaism and, beyond this, following Davies,[76] down to the emergence of Rabbinic Judaism in the second century CE, we should perhaps be well advised to apply the reverse logic to the search for the origins of the branching out of Judaism into a variety of competing currents. The second century BCE is certainly too late a date. This will be our next step.

'Changes' in Hellenistic Judaea: 'Hellenization' in perspective

Judaean society: from an embedded structure to the emergence of individual options

Forms of Judaism whose worldview was *not* centred on the Temple developed well before Hasmonaean times. This is clearly demonstrated in Loren Stuckenbruck's analysis of the passages in the Book of Enoch

---

73 Davies (1995: 174). Incidentally, the phrase 'Judaism of the victors' can be seen as a further acceptable way of defining what I call 'central' Judaism.
74 See above, pp. 134–35.
75 Davies (1995: 174–76).
76 Davies (1995: 176–78).

datable to the third century BCE.[77] However, attempts at pinpointing the sociological milieu from which these texts stemmed are simply hopeless, given the poor state of our knowledge about Judaean society in late Persian and early Hellenistic times.[78] But the basic proposition that religious systems constitute the basis for group identity and group cohesion in pre-industrial societies may serve as a guiding principle. One can make an intelligent guess that the third-century sections of the Book of Enoch emanated from circles which did not identify, politically and/or socially, with the high priest in power. Next, since we have no grounds to think that Judaean society underwent major changes between the end of the Persian era and early Hellenistic times, there is no reason to think that the ideas expressed in these texts emerged all of a sudden in the third century BCE either.[79] Thus these texts may indirectly point to some form at least of continuity with earlier times.

In a 1990 paper aimed at clarifying the concept of 'Hellenization' in relation to 'acculturation' and 'culture', Jonathan Friedman suggested that more attention should be paid to the political, economic and military context of the circulation of cultural influences. As he argued, Near Eastern societies can be described as 'segmented' ones down to Hellenistic times. The notion of 'segmented' (or 'embedded') society refers to societies in which the place and role of each individual within the community is determined from the outset, according to his place and condition at birth. In contrast, modern individualistic societies are characterized by the possibility – in theory at least – that its members are free to make choices in all aspects of their life: place of living, profession, choice of marriage partner, political and religious affiliations.[80] Even though fully fledged expressions of individualism are an industrial – or even, perhaps, a post-industrial – phenomenon, processes that caused embedded societies to disintegrate into increasingly autonomous sectors, allowing groups and individuals some degree of free choice, have been observed in ancient societies. The end of the Roman Republic provides the most conspicuous example,[81] but the availability of social options has been pointed out in fourth century Athens too.[82]

---

77   Stuckenbruck, this volume.

78   Albertz 1994 provides useful overviews of the sociological developments in the Persian and Hellenistic periods.

79   See already Albertz (1994: 534–56) for similar remarks.

80   See Friedman 1990.

81   The classical analysis is Hopkins (1978: 74–96). From a different perspective, Wallace-Hadrill 1997 and 2005 has shown the crucial impact of 'Hellenization' in this evolution of the Late Roman Republic.

82   On structural differentiation in ancient Athens, see Humphreys (1978: 242–75). Josiah Ober's analysis of the control of the aristocrats under the democracy is also relevant to understand

While the Achaimenid empire had enjoyed remarkable political stability – despite occasional palace revolutions and some serious provincial revolts – the Hellenistic age was plagued from the outset with political and military instability. The latter was caused by never-ending rivalries, first between Alexander's generals, later between dynasties and finally between competitors for the same throne. Competition between dynasties for the control of various areas of the Hellenistic world (Athens in the late fourth century, Asia Minor and Coele-Syria in the third century) resulted in pervasive warfare.[83] This new geo-strategic situation meant that local discontents could easily translate into diverging loyalties and receive external backing of substantial political and military scope. In short, the new political and military instability triggered signs of disintegration of the close-knit societies into more open ones.[84] The well-known feud between the Tobiads and Oniads in Judaea illustrates the contemporary geo-political (dis)order.[85]

Jonathan Friedman's anthropological approach offers a new perspective on the emergence, at some time in the Hellenistic era, of the so-called religious 'sects'. The fact that the so-called sects quarrelled about sets of beliefs (e.g. in life after death), and not only about ritual issues (such as purity), has been taken as evidence for the impact of 'Hellenization'. However, it seems to me that the precise nature of these quarrels is to be seen as a secondary development in terms of chronological sequence – even though it represents, of course, the most important aspect in terms of cultural and religious implications. The emerging sects may be seen, in the first place, as a symptom of the break-up of society into distinct sectors clustering around conflicting interests. The very possibility of making free choices within the society, which resulted directly from political and social tensions, constitutes the indispensable preliminary step. Without it, one may doubt whether the 'sects' would have shown similar vitality, and, indeed, whether they would have appeared at all.

---

the emergence of free choice in Athenian society. See Ober (1989: 293–339). The concept of 'structural differentiation' is further illustrated in the evolution of portraits in fourth-century Athens. Whereas portraits of the fifth century distinguished between two main categories only, youthful athletes and bearded elder citizens, complex codes of visual differentiation were created in the fourth century to account for the now distinct public roles of poets, philosophers, generals, political orators and kings. See Smith 1993. The religious concept of Tyche, the Fortune by which low individuals are elevated and notables are debased overnight, certainly captured the amazement and anxiety which accompanied the new availability of social options for individuals. On Tyche, see Pollitt (1996: 1–4).

83   Austin 1986 offers an important analysis of the dynamics of warfare in the Hellenistic world.

84   Needless to say, this evolution was not specific to Judaea. See Friedman 1990.

85   On the multiple foci of (alternative) power in Judaea in early Hellenistic times, see further Grabbe in this volume.

However, the notion of 'free choices' needs further attention. Two distinct models may in fact be at work: one, aristocratic and the other, democratic – if I may be forgiven this inadequate borrowing of concepts from the Greek socio-political tradition. In the 'aristocratic' scheme, the emergence of differing and sometimes competing views, reflects social and political tensions within the élites. Inasmuch as their power has a territorial basis, whole segments of the population subjected to their economic and social control may have no choice other than to adopt the religious option of their local leader.[86] This process may therefore emerge within an embedded society; it may tentatively be described as a form of 'segmented choice'. The 'democratic' model fits a more atomized state of society, in which kinship groups and individuals can make their choices independently.[87] It seems more plausible that in Persian and early Hellenistic times, Judaean society met the aristocratic pattern only.

As I suggested above, the passages of the Book of Enoch datable to the third century BCE most probably display the religious side of the social and political tensions which divided the contemporary élite. If this is the case, then they also provide the missing link between our evidence for tensions within the élites in Persian and in Hellenistic times. In effect, while it is justified to describe the Persian empire as much more stable than the Hellenistic world on an international scale, this stability at the imperial level was accompanied by local tensions within the provinces. The Biblical sources of the Persian period disclose the extensive inner tensions which characterized post-exilic Judaean society.[88] Thus the book of Ezra–Nehemiah mentions both an impressive array of leaders of varying functions (priests, nobles, secular notables; Neh. 2.16), as well as several foci of opposition to Ezra and Nehemiah's missions. The latter include both leaders of neighbouring communities – Sanballat the Horonite, Tobiah the Ammonite and Geshem the Arab (Neh. 2.19) – and inner opposition. Furthermore, Lisbeth Fried has convincingly argued that the term '*am ha 'arets* denotes secular leaders in Ezra–Nehemiah as it does in all other Biblical books.[89] Notables from Jerusalem are presented as Tobiah's and Sanballat's allies (Neh. 6.10-12, 17-19), and prophets

86 This kind of situation seems to have prevailed in sixth-century BCE Athens. The primary goal of Solon, Peisistratos and Cleisthenes' reforms seems to have aimed at first weakening, and then dismantling the grip aristocrats had on the peasants subject to their economic influence in their territorial base. See Ober (1989: 53–75).

87 This situation may fit the society of Republican and early imperial Rome, beginning in the second century BCE. See North's (1979) remarks on the Bacchanalia affair of 186 BCE. A second-century CE example is found in Apuleius's *Golden Ass*. In Book 11, the narrator relates his conversion to the cult of Isis.

88 Albertz (1994: 493–522).

89 Fried 2006.

are further denounced (Neh. 6.14). Indeed, Tamara Cohn Eskenazi has contended that Ezra's reforms were aimed at broadening the religious and political authority at the expense of the priests, who previously enjoyed a monopoly. The levites, in particular, benefited from these reforms.[90] She further suggests that the attack on mixed marriages targeted either specific leaders, or a group of leaders.[91]

It is beyond the scope of the present discussion to ask why the book of Ezra–Nehemiah chose not only to mention, but even to provide such detailed information about the oppositions met by the two reformers. Whatever the case, the narrative, if reliable, provides evidence that the kind of rivalry which opposed the families of the Tobiads and the Oniads in early Hellenistic times existed much earlier – indeed, the feud between these very families may well date back to Persian times. Various explanations for the tensions between both secular and priestly élites in Persian Judah may be suggested. Recent studies have emphasized that the returnees formed a closed community in Judah, excluding other segments of the local population.[92] If this was the case, then each community would have needed its own leaders. Secondly, the socio-political order which was established in Judah in the early years of Darius I's reign (522–486 BCE)[93] was probably a novelty. Even though its supporters must have hastened to base it in continuity with past tradition,[94] such endeavours may not have persuaded every powerful leader who felt wronged by the new order into adhering to it. More tensions certainly arose after the demotion of the Davidic dynasty, with the increasing power of the high priest. In short, while the Hellenistic armies may have worsened the tensions within the élites, they did not create the problem.

The depiction of 'wicked' high priests in *2 Maccabees* may be contrasted with the prophet Malachi's assertion, in the Persian era, that 'the priest is God's "messenger" . . . and God's Torah is in his mouth' (Mal. 2.6-7).[95] In view of this conceptual gap between the two, it may be suggested that the presentation of the events of the 160s which is adopted in *2 Maccabees* captures the way the social consequences of regional instability were beginning to be translated into theological terms. In

---

90   Cohn Eskenazi (2006: 512).

91   Ibid., 513–17.

92   Becking 2006; Kessler 2006.

93   For recent scepticism about a mass return of exiles to Judah under Cyrus, see Becking 2006. Niehr (1999: 228–29). For the dating to Darius I, Sérandour (1996: 31 and 14).

94   It has been suggested that this was the main purpose of the lists of returnees included in Ezra–Nehemiah. See the studies recorded in the previous note.

95   Quoted by Schwartz (1992: 9).

this text, the high priest has clearly lost the exalted status he enjoyed in Malachi's time.

Individuals in 2 Maccabees

'Aristocratic individualism', or 'segmented choice', as I have called it, allows choices for the élites only, and may therefore appear within an embedded society, with the whole local population subjected to one leader being compelled to follow the latter's choice. It is not my purpose to check to what extent the sectarian texts of Hellenistic times offer evidence for individual adhesion to the sect, thereby reflecting genuinely individual choice. However, tokens of the further atomizing of the society into a 'democratic' pattern are found in *2 Maccabees*.

Martyrs are depicted in chs 6 (Eleazar), 7 (a mother and her seven sons) and 14 (Razis). It is beyond the scope of the present discussion to make a detailed study of martyrdom in *2 Maccabees*.[96] However, one aspect is relevant to our present discussion. In the traditional royal ideology, the only way to get rid of a 'wicked' king, so to speak, is to change one king for another. More accurately, the ruling king is, as a rule, 'good' – he becomes 'wicked' only in retrospect, as part of the legitimizing discourse of the usurper who succeeds him. *2 Maccabees*, as a work belonging to the literary genre of historiography, accommodates a more realistic perception of the rulers: one wicked high priest (Jason) evicts a good one (Onias), only to be replaced in his turn by an even more wicked one (Menelaos). More interestingly, the impious behaviour of the wicked high priests is not finally redeemed merely by their replacement by a pious leader – even though, of course, Judas Maccabaeus is this leader. Martyrs play an instrumental role in the scheme of sin-retribution-judgement and salvation which informs the narrative.[97] The martyrdom of the mother and her seven sons in ch. 7 is particularly worth attention, since the martyrs are simple citizens, not priests, and not even secular notables of the community like Razis. The crucial role ascribed to this modest family reflects a new emphasis on the individual.

I suggested above that aristocratic individualism constituted the indispensable social background to the emergence of forms of Judaism at variance with the 'central' tradition. If this is indeed the case, then it is quite remarkable that *2 Maccabees*, which continues the 'central' tradition and can therefore be identified as a text supporting the central, ruling power controlling the temple in Jerusalem, accommodates martyrdom in its worldview. If anything, this fact suggests that *democratic* individualism

96   On martyrdom in *2 Maccabees*, see further van Henten 1997.
97   See above, n. 38.

was already a well-rooted phenomenon in Judaea by the time the traditions followed by the author crystallized.

Was the emergence of democratic individualistic trends a product of the Hellenization of Judaea? Undeniably, there is some truth in the prevailing scholarly view that the encounter with the Hellenistic schools of philosophy triggered (democratic) individualistic trends in the most dynamic sectors of the society which had access to it. However, it is quite another matter to contend that individualism was the product of Hellenization alone. First of all, the encounter with Hellenistic armies must have been just as instrumental in precipitating the atomization of society as the intellectual and cultural influences. More decisively, the development of individualistic trends needs to be analysed within the grid of 'interculturation', and not 'acculturation'. Judaean élites were receptive to this specific aspect of Hellenistic Greek philosophy because it met pre-existing concerns. As suggested by the above discussion, these concerns themselves were rooted in social and political tensions which dated back to early Persian times, and cannot be seen as the consequence of the disruption entailed by the political and military instability that prevailed from the time of the Diadochi on.

From the point of view of the specific agents within Judaean society who were receptive to Greek cultural influences, Hellenization was a means, and not an end. It was a means to promote their own interests in their own society. Depending on their social position, the new intellectual tools offered by Greek culture could be used either to preserve a *status quo* in specific issues, or to take advantage of the transformations that were taking place in the broader political and military scene to introduce changes or reforms in local issues about which they had hitherto been dissatisfied. In other words, 'Hellenization' is not progressive in itself. It is not necessarily and deterministically bound towards reforms and the future. As a consequence of their vantage point of retrospective knowledge, historians tend to forget that social agents normally determine their action in relation with their immediate past, and not with the future. Revolutions are, more often than not, unintended consequences of the action of *reformers*, not to mention short-sighted competitors for power, whose goal was initially far more conservative.[98]

One episode may remind us that not all the cultural innovations of the Hellenistic age were harbingers of Rabbinic Judaism and Christianity in some sort of deterministic way. According to Josephus, after the Oniads

98   Jon L. Berquist's overview of the processes of identity formation in Judah addresses a related issue in a different perspective (Berquist 2006). Berquist emphasizes the ongoing tension, and reciprocal interaction, between 'identities imposed by imperialization' and 'identities of autonomy' (pp. 61–3).

were overturned in Jerusalem, Onias IV fled to Egypt with his followers, and founded a temple at Leontopolis.[99] We can only speculate as to
whether or not the so-called schism with the Samaritans, who stubbornly
clung to their own mountain as their main sacred site, had any influence
in luring Onias into believing that an overturned dynasty of high priests
could still remain high priests, provided they had a temple elsewhere.
Whatever the case, Onias' founding of a temple at Leontopolis is a clear
case of (aristocratic) individualism.

Even conversion, the practice that best encapsulates the idea of 'free
choice', turns out, on closer examination, to be a much less clear-cut
instance of a break with the past.

A complex evolution: the beginning of conversion
The process which eventually led to the revolutionary practice of
conversion probably best illustrates how old and new trends may be
interwoven.[100] At first glance, Hellenization is heavily involved in this
process. Conversion cannot appear, indeed cannot even be invented,
before the religious system of the community is reified; that is, becomes
a list of items concretely spelled out, one by one, in a finite enumeration.
Many scholars would be ready to add that conversion cannot be thought
of before beliefs (and not participation in rites) become the crucial criteria
of belonging. However, we certainly need to distinguish between the early
instances of mass conversion implemented by the Hasmonaeans, and
individual cases, for which the evidence is much more elusive, whether
in Judaea or in the diaspora communities.

Three phases may be distinguished in the attitude of the Hasmonaeans
towards the foreign populations of conquered regions. However, at no
point does their behaviour allow us to think that they had relinquished the
traditionally integrated conception of Judaism which organically linked
together people, temple and the territory which surrounded it. We know
that the conquered populations were first treated in a very traditional
way. After the conquest of Gezer/Gazara, Simon expelled the vanquished
inhabitants and replaced them with Judaean settlers, or, in *1 Maccabees*'
terms, 'men who observed the law'.[101] The second stage was the mass
conversion of the inhabitants of the Idumaean cities of Adora and Marisa,
in the 120s BCE, at Johanan Hyrkanos's initiative (*Ant.* 13.257-8), and the
Ituraeans, in 104–103 BCE, under Aristoboulos (*Ant.* 13.318). Despite the

---

99   Josephus, *BJ* 1.33 and 7.423 (referring to Onias III); *Ant.* 12.387 and 13.62ff. (referring to
Onias IV, his son). On Leontopolis, see Schürer (1987: 47–8); Gruen 1997.

100   On the novelty of conversion as compared with earlier practices, see Schwartz's analysis
of Esdras 9–10 (Schwartz 1992: 8–9), and Cohen (1990: 209–10 and 217–18).

101   *1 Macc.* 13.43-8. See Schürer (1973: 191) for further sources.

unquestionably innovative twist, from one step to the next, as far as the treatment of the defeated population is concerned, the mass conversions do not make any sense unless this proceeding is underlain by a conception of Judaism as an embedded whole: the conquered land, annexed to the territory from which the first-fruit offerings are brought to the temple, needs to be cleansed from foreign gods and their supporters.[102] There may also be a slightly different way to analyse Hyrkanos and Aristoboulos' initiative: their move, while assimilating the idea that a group may change its initial destiny during the course of its life, still exhibits a mentality typical of an embedded society, for which the various parts of the whole territory and its whole population need to be organically related to each other and to the cultic and ritual system. Thus the mechanism of mass conversion presents close affinities with the mechanism of 'aristocratic individualism', or 'segmented choice', which had already manifested itself at much earlier times, as seen above. Incidentally, the question of whether these mass conversions were imposed by force or 'voluntary' does not make any difference. Compulsion would mean that the aristocratic initiative came from outside, and not from within the group; being 'voluntary' would merely mean that local aristocrats, and not the Hasmonaean kings, took the lead.[103]

The third stage in the Hasmonaean attitude may be described as the logical consequence of their assuming the royal title. Beginning with Aristoboulos I Philhellenos,[104] the Hasmonaeans stopped resorting to conversion, and respected the local gods of each of the peoples who came under their control. This new shift shows that the Hasmonaeans had adopted the royal, or, more accurately, the imperial ideology which prevailed in the Near East long before the Achaimenid dynasty, together with the royal diadem. Like the Achaimenids, Alexander the Great, the Ptolemies and the Seleucids before them, the Hasmonaeans now presented themselves as 'good', and not as 'ethnic' (i.e. Persian, Greek or Judaean) kings.

Thus these three successive modes of action adopted by the Hasmonaeans vis à vis the alien populations living in conquered territories, provide additional evidence that the evolution from one conception of

---

102 Archaeological finds confirm the literary sources on this point. Finkielsztejn 1999 has shown that the importation of foreign wine abruptly stopped in Jerusalem after Jonathan, Judas Maccabaeus's brother, began besieging the Acra in 146 BCE.

103 On the question of whether these mass conversions were imposed by force or voluntary, see Cohen (1990: 211–16).

104 I follow Schwartz (1992: 12), quoting Jos. *Ant.* 13.318, for this sequential overview. However, I do not follow Schwartz's assertion that the now tolerant behaviour of the Hasmonaeans towards their non-Jewish subjects is predicated on an innovative conception of Judaism as a culture, after the model of the Greek *paideia*.

Judaism to another was anything but linear. Diverging conceptions clearly co-existed for a long time. In fact, it is questionable whether the territorial dimension of Judaism was ever totally abandoned by the Jews. In *Legatio*, 200–202, Philo (not exactly a conservative author!) basically reflects this conception, a few centuries later. The agricultural rules regarding the status of the 'Land of Israel' which were codified in *Mishnah Zera'im*, the careful definition of the geographical boundaries of the 'Land of Israel' illustrated, for example, in the Rehov inscription,[105] and, in fact, the very concept of the Holy Land as it was preserved and developed in Rabbinic Judaism well beyond the destruction of the Jerusalem temple, all include the territorial aspect.

The real change regarding conversion concerned the individual process. However, so far there is no evidence for individual conversions in Judaea.[106] We should perhaps accept that the phenomenon was more common, for obvious reasons, in diaspora communities, but indisputable evidence is unfortunately lacking for Hellenistic times.[107]

Conclusion

The 'democratic' individualism that gradually emerged in Judaean society in the Hellenistic era is often deemed to be the most conspicuous hallmark of 'Hellenization', in the sense of the influence of Greek culture and its way of thinking. Hellenistic philosophy certainly favoured individualistic trends. However, intellectual history has a social background. It is sometimes forgotten that Hellenistic philosophy, in Athens, Alexandria and elsewhere, developed in the social context of complex and partly atomized societies. I am, therefore, uncertain as to what was the strongest influence on the quarrels about beliefs that divided the various sects

---

105   Sussmann 1973–74; Lieberman 1975–76; Schwartz (2001: 260–61).

106   Cohen (1990: 210) suggests that Esther 9.27 and Judith 14.10 reflect the social practice of individual conversion in the age of the Maccabees. However, Esther 9.27 is vague, and therefore ambiguous. Moreover, the 'conversion' of leaders is better left out of the discussion of individual conversion to Judaism. Akhior's confession in Judith 14.10 recalls Antiochos IV's confession in *2 Maccabees* 9.17, but rulers acknowledging the mightiness of the local deity was a common literary means to dramatize the enemy's acknowledgement of his defeat. For an example of this in a Greek context, see the Lindian Chronicle (a text inscribed on a *stele* erected in 99 BCE in the sanctuary of Athena Lindia, at Lindos, on Rhodes). The text asserts that Datis, Darius's admiral in the invasion of Greece in 490 BCE, acknowledged the might of Athena Lindia after failing to take over the city. The motive of the 'conversion' of the leader in Jewish sources clearly derives from this widespread pattern, and thus cannot be taken as reflecting the social practice of the conversion of individuals other than kings and leaders. On the Lindian Chronicle, see Higbie (2003: 42–7, Section D, ll. 1–59).

107   On conversion in early times, see further Cohen 1983 and 1989; Goodman 1994: 60–90.

which flourished in Judaea – whether it was the encounter with Hellenistic philosophy, or with Hellenistic armies. Hellenistic armies were certainly indispensable (so to speak) to the process, since they created the social conditions which made Judaean individuals receptive to the messages of Hellenistic philosophy. Moreover, some of the social processes involved in the emergence of conversion continued processes which were initiated in Persian times, and would have continued evolving with any ruling power – always allowing for some possible nuances specifically ascribable to 'Hellenization'.

We tend to forget that new words, such as *Ioudaismos* and *theokratia*, and new mental tools, such as the propensity for abstract definitions, can be put to the service of a traditional social reality. This is what I have tried to show in my analysis of the concrete meaning of *Ioudaismos* in *2 Maccabees*, and it also holds true for the occurrence of the word *theokratia* in *Against Apion*. Continuity and change must necessarily co-exist during a transitional period. This much may readily be admitted by all. However, we also need to acknowledge some further premises. First, the pace of social and cultural evolution does not necessarily coincide with the phases of political history. Imperial dynasties change, but mentalities may only follow suit with a delay of several decades, as the successive transformations of the 'central' worldview of Judaism show. This means that a transitional period may stretch over several centuries. Secondly, innovations themselves may have diverging rhythms, which can make the picture in the transitional phase even more confused. Thirdly, innovations do not necessarily supersede the old order of things, they may just supplement it to meet new needs. Thus, beliefs never completely superseded genealogy in the definition of who is a Judaean/Jew, and genealogy never replaced all aspects of the territorial conception. The latter even survived the destruction of the Temple by the Romans. This is the only background against which we can begin to explain the presence of apparently contradictory trends in *2 Maccabees*.

5

FURTHER REVISED THOUGHTS ON JOSEPHUS' REPORT OF ALEXANDER'S CAMPAIGN TO PALESTINE (*ANT.* 11.304-347)

Aryeh Kasher[1]
Tel Aviv University

Modern scholarship has dedicated a great deal of attention to Josephus' account of the dramatic meeting between Alexander the Great and the High Priest of Jerusalem (*Ant.* 12.302-347). Scholars had often judged the story with scepticism and exhibited and had censured Josephus ardently by arguing against the historical likelihood of such a meeting. This point of view has apologetic connotations which discredit the story as a biased fiction of later generations destined to serve certain propagandist goals. Most prominent among the representatives of this view are those belonging to the so-called Classical School of Philology.[2] One of their main arguments is the fact that there are no traces of this story found in Graeco-Roman literature.[3] Other scholarly voices claimed that the author intended to exalt the Jerusalem Temple with the honour of the prestigious visit while showing the benevolence of Alexander the Great towards the Jewish people. Additionally, scholars pointed out that the Hellenistic Jewish diaspora would be interested in presenting Alexander as the first and ultimate source for the equal rights of the Jewish people. It is this notion that may have led some scholars to make a mistaken comparison between the struggle for 'Jewish rights' during the Second Temple period and Jewish 'emancipation' in modern history. There were still others who

---

1   This is an updated and revised version of a Hebrew article published first in 1974 and revised later in 1993; see bibliographic list below. Since the subject is still stimulating and can contribute to the authenticity of Josephus, we find it proper to offer an updated English and revised version for the benefit of non-Hebrew readers. This is the opportunity to thank Mrs Marian Gavish for her remarkable contribution to the translation.

2   See bibliographic selections: Schürer 1901: 180ff, 1973: 137ff.; Marcus 1937: Appendices B–C, 498ff.; Rappaport and Ronen 1993: 520. For a detailed bibliography and comprehensive review of the subject see: Mor 2003: 54–94.

3   See e.g. Goldstein 1993: 70–71, 74 (and note 44).

maintained that Josephus created this story, inventing a Jewish tradition to counterbalance Manetho's defamation of the Jewish people, a denigration that had caused a growing hatred of the Jewish religion and its people throughout the Graeco-Roman world. Josephus' version was intended to generate a positive image of the Jewish people and their religion and thus halt the growing antipathy. Each theory tried to uncover a 'true' event veiled behind an historic episode. But in fact, most of these attempts could not pass the basic test of historic criticism, since they all stripped the details of the plot from Josephus' story in order to force the literary adaptation to their speculative, artificial and allegorical theses.[4]

An accurate and realistic evaluation of the story must therefore, thoroughly examine the background of Alexander's campaign as well as his military activities in Palestine. This would be the only way of objectively analysing and balancing the criticism. Indeed, the studies offered by Spak, Torrey, Abel, Gutman, Schalit and Tcherikover aimed at this very direction.[5] However, they presented quite a wide spectrum of solutions based on historical reconstructions. These works remained deficient in character due to the fact that they did not as yet have the evidence of the archaeological discoveries from Wadi ed-Daliyeh and other finds.[6] Our intention is to follow every step made by Alexander in order to analyse the historic significance of his campaign with close reference to the geographic, political and military implications, and at the same time to pay attention to updated archaeological discoveries that we now have at our disposal to arrive at new interpretations.

Most of the ancient Greek–Roman authors, who reviewed the history of Alexander and his wars in the East, left relatively meagre information regarding his activity in Palestine. They actually focused on two main events: the campaign against Tyre and the battle for Gaza. Several modern scholars were under the impression that Alexander's personal military activity in the rest of Palestine was very limited, if any. It is almost commonly agreed that in the framework of his conquest of the interior territories of Syria, most of the fighting was carried out by Parmenion (son of Philotas), Alexander's commander-in-chief (Arrian 2.11, 10). Victor Tcherikover, for example, thought that Alexander did not linger in Palestine at all, and that after the conquest of Gaza he immediately turned towards Egypt (Arrian 3.1, 1). He even doubted the possibility that Palestine left any trace whatsoever on Alexander's historical recollection because he considered Alexander's main concern was only how to control

---

4 Just for example, see Willrich 1895: 9.

5 See Spak 1911; Torrey 1928: 380–89; Abel 1934/5: 42–61; Gutman 1939/40: 271–94; Schalit 1949: 252–72; Tcherikover 1963: 32ff., 1977: 41ff.

6 See Cross 1963: 110–21, 1966: 210–11, 1969: 45–69, 1974: 17–29.

the territories around Gaza and settling the Macedonian garrisons there. Tcherikover maintained that the Jewish people were those who could not afford to let such a poetic figure as 'the hero-king' to pass so close to their land without creating any significant contact with them. According to Tcherikover's understanding it was the Jewish wish that Alexander pay a visit to their capital, Jerusalem. For Tcherikover, 'legend filled the vacuum which history had left, and such legend we must scrutinize to discover whether or not it contains some germ of history'.[7] For him the 'legend' was of course the story narrated by Josephus in *Ant.* 11.304ff.

Quite a different and an almost conflicting approach was taken by Yehoshua Gutman. He considered that the conquest of Palestine could not be a trifling matter, nor a marginal issue in the history of Alexander, since in addition to the control of the eastern Mediterranean coasts it enabled him to create a bridgehead for his further expansion into the East.[8] In our humble opinion, Gutman's approach historically fits the actual situation far better.

We shall try to explore in sequence, not only Alexander's plans in the Palestinian arena, but the activities of his high commanders as well. This will offer a factually wider background of Alexander's activity in Palestine and help in understanding his aims. It appears that immediately after the victory of Issus (namely, in late October or early November 333 BCE), Alexander came to the conclusion that he needed to stop his pursuit of Darius III into the depths of Persia in order to go southward and conquer, first Syria, then Phoenicia, Coele-Syria and finally Egypt (Arrian 2.20). There were several objectives that led him to take this strategic decision: (1) The rich Persian treasure held in Damascus offered a tempting chance to solve his enormous financial difficulties in funding the war while at the same time providing a strong motivation for his troops to continue the war although so far away from home; (2) The bonus that capturing noble Persian families related to the supreme command would give him when negotiating terms with the Persian king; (3) The strategic consideration that dictated first conquering the western part of the Achemenide Empire in order to safeguard his military rear by preventing enemy contact with subversive elements in Greece.

When advancing towards the Phoenician cities of Marathus and Aradus, Alexander divided his army into two main parts: one assigned to Parmenion with the mission to conquer Damascus, while the other, under his personal command, was designated to subdue the renowned Phoenician cities in which the Persian fleet maintained their naval bases.

7   Tcherikover 1963: 32, 1977: 41–42.
8   See Gutman 1939/40: 171.

To ensure his hold in north Syria, he appointed his high commander Menon, son of Cardimmas, as governor of the region.[9] Simultaneously, he examined the possibility of political contact with Darius III, but as this move was doomed to failure, he successfully convened with Strato son of Gerostratus king of Aradus, who promised him the surrender of all cities under his and his father's rule.[10] Indeed, when the news about the fall of Damascus to Parmenion spread through Syria and Phoenicia, and when the siege of Tyre started in earnest, January 332 BCE (ibid., 18ff.), all the naval forces under the command of Gerostratus king of Aradus as well as those under the command of Enylus king of Byblus, changed sides in favour of Alexander (ibid., 13, 8; 20, 1). This development undoubtedly had a great impact also on the surrender of Cyprus and the city of Sidon (ibid., 20–21). Under those circumstances, judging from Josephus' evidence (*Ant.* 11.321) the Samaritans also changed sides. The Jewish people, by contrast, remained loyal to Darius III and thus enraged Alexander (*Ant.* 11.317-319).

The evidence related to Parmenion's activities imply that he was actually very busy in a variety of military tasks after the occupation of Damascus. According to Curtius Rufus (4.1, 4-5) he was not called by Alexander to assist him in the seven-month siege of Tyre, as he was appointed as governor of Coele-Syria and was engaged in fighting the 'Syrians' who showed staunch resistance (4.1, 5-6). Gutman was right in claiming that these 'Syrians' could not be identified with those of the Phoenician cities, since the latter were clearly designated by Curtius Rufus as 'Tyrians' and 'Sidonians'[11]. Furthermore, there is no geographical logic for such an identification since Parmenion's activities took place east of the Lebanese mountain range. Most of the Phoenician population there had already willingly surrendered to Alexander and even assisted him in his efforts to conquer Tyre. For similar reasons, it is also impossible to identify those 'Syrians' with the Arab tribes living in the Mount Lebanon region since they were explicitly designated as 'Arabs' and not as 'Syrians' and

---

9   According to Arrian (2.13, 7) Menon was appointed viceroy of 'Coele-Syria', but this is unacceptable, since that region was not yet in Alexander's possession. However, according Curtius Rufus (4.8, 9-10) his appointment occurred later, namely after the assassination of Andromachus, the governor of Samaria, by Samaritan rebels. It seems therefore that Arrian was just confused with the right chronological order; but it is not impossible that both testimonies should be evaluated as complementary to each other, so that each of them related to another appointment in different occasions. Probably 'Coele-Syria' that was mentioned by Arrian in that context was actually believed to be indicating the north of Syria. Gutman (1939/40: 273–77), however, had tried to complement the testimonies differently. Stalemate.

10   Arrian 2.13, 4ff.; cf. below.

11   Gutman 1939/40: 277ff.

Alexander acted against them in person.[12] Furthermore, the terminological use by Curtius Rufus did not leave room for the possibility that the region assigned to Parmenion, namely 'Syria called Coele-Syria', could be identified with what Curtius Rufus himself called 'the vicinity of Tyre' or 'the coastal strip along Phoenicia'.[13] It is therefore possible to assume, that the 'Syrians' against whom Parmenion acted, were actually the residents of the regions later known in the Hellenistic period as: Gaulanitis (Gaulan heights), Auranitis, Bathanaea, Galaditis, Scythopolis (Beth-She'an) Valley and Galilee.[14]

What was the great mission that Parmenion was in charge of while Alexander was fighting Tyre? In response, one should take into consideration that the siege on Tyre started in or around January BCE, that is, in the middle of winter. Regular food supplies for the Macedonian army during that season could not depend on the naval transportation from Greece for several reasons: (1) The winter storms of the Mediterranean sea; (2) The relatively limited power of the Macedonian naval force at that time;[15] (3) The need for seaworthy vessels to transport Greek reinforcements by sea;[16] (4) The emergent warfare missions imposed on any vessel, fitted or not, to carry out an efficient siege on Tyre.[17] In view of these facts, it is reasonable to presume that Alexander preferred to rely on a regular supply of local food. In this context Josephus offers a very significant piece of information that Alexander really asked the Jewish High-Priest to send him, inter alia, supplies for the army (ἀγορὰν τῷ στρατεύματι). This information supports, of course, the authenticity of Josephus as a source. Indeed, one of Arrian's remarks (3.6, 8) proves how important to Alexander a constant food supply for his army was. This issue actually became a 'no-compromise' element of Alexander's strategy in warfare. We are informed, for instance, that upon his return from Egypt he dismissed his viceroy in the north of Syria, Arimmas, because he 'seemed to have been remiss in collecting the supplies which he had been ordered to gather

12   Alexander's activities are described by Curtius Rufus (4.2, 18), Arrian (2.20, 4-5), and Plutarch (*Alexander*, 24, 3), indicating a limited scale of warfare by local raids. It appears, therefore, that there was no urgent need to bother Parmenion in such an activity, the more so as he had much more important tasks to take care of (see below).

13   Cf. Curtius Rufus 4.5, 9; 24. Arrian (3.1, 2) too had distinguished between Phoenicia, Syria and Arabia; cf. also to the terminological uses by Strabo, *Geographica* 16.2, 2; 21.

14   Cf. Gutman 1939/40: 278.

15   One should recall here the fact that shortly after the siege of Tyre had started, the Phoenician rulers of Aradus, Byblus, Sidon including the Island of Cyprus, joined Alexander with their fleets.

16   Arrian (2.20, 4) testified, for example, of the arrival of Cleander son of Polycrates with 4000 Greek mercenaries.

17   Arrian 2.20, 5ff. It is worth noting the battle assignments were given even to transporting vessels of horses (2.21, 3).

for the army and which he, the king (Alexander), was about to lead into the interior'. It appears, therefore, that one of the main tasks assigned to Parmenion concerned this very issue. For the sake of illustration, it is worth noting that when Antiochus III prepared himself for the 'Fourth Syrian War', he too paid great attention to a constant food supply for his army. This analogy is striking, as according to Polybius 5.70-71 it pertains to the same territories. Confiscating local agricultural crops to supply the Macedonian troops engaged in Alexander's siege of Tyre must have aggravated the population of those regions, namely the 'Syrians', as they are called by Arrian. It is therefore easy to assume that Parmenion's military expeditions were to suppress the incensed population that had rebelled. Indeed, Arrian (3.8, 11) testified at a later stage that there was even a special military unit serving under Darius III composed of 'Syrians from Coele-Syria and the men of Syria which lies between the rivers (Euphrates and Tigris)'. We know that this force was fully integrated to the Persian army and was trained and prepared for the battle of Gaugamela. We can learn, therefore, from the fragmental testimony of Arrian that Parmenion fulfilled a very important task; he was in charge of the logistical side of the war, both controlling the local population and acquiring their agricultural produce as supplies for the army.

Gutman tried to support his view about the Macedonian presence in Trans-Jordan by relying on the dim traditions preserved in the writings of Stephanus Byzantius (fifth century CE) on the cites of Pella and Dion whose foundation was ascribed to Alexander himself,[18] although this conclusion is open to scepticism due to the well-known desire in the ancient world to credit a city's primacy to Alexander. Plain logic however, tends towards the possibility that there was at least a kernel of historic truth in that tradition, which could be explained on the background of Parmenion's activity in that region.[19] In fact, the cities of Pella and Dion were established after Alexander's time, probably by Perdiccas, one of the Diadochs.[20] However, the fact that precisely these names were chosen for old oriental cities is significant and implies the purpose of commemorating

18   For quotations, see Schürer 1907: 175–76 and notes 334, 343; 1979: 146, 148 and notes, 332, 323.

19   One of Tcherikover's (1963: 79; 1977: 98ff.) main reservations is based on the argument that the eastern area of Trans-Jordan was not included in the military personal activity of Alexander as informed by late writers of his history. Their silence of such activity cannot, therefore, serve as an ultimate truth, the more so as their reports had almost totally focused on the heroic king and ignored the deeds of his subordinate officers.

20   See on this matter the suggestion by Schürer (1901: 175–76; 1979: 146, 148; cf. Tcherikover, ibid.; Jones 1937: 237).

the famous homeland cities when settling Macedonian garrisons in the newly obtained areas.[21]

It appears that Gerasa was also counted among cities that were re-established by Alexander. This case is quite illustrative, since a coin dated to the reign of Emperor Elagabalus (218–222 CE) stated the name of Alexander as the city's founder.[22] A second or third century Roman inscription – a dedicatory inscription in the memory of Perdiccas, one of the notable officers under Alexander, and later on of the Diadochs (i.e Alexander's heirs) – gives the impression that he could be associated with the establishment of the city.[23] To be more accurate, the inscription can demonstrate how a popular tradition connected the founding of a city to the days of Alexander.[24] Indeed, it is logical to assume that the city was actually founded by Perdiccas during his own reign (323–321 BCE), and that he acted according to the norms set by Alexander. Jones reasonably suggested that Perdiccas, the oppressor of the Samaritan revolt against Alexander also crushed a similar uprising in Trans-Jordan. As in the case of Samaria, Macedonian garrisons were settled in strategic locations, such as Dion, Pella and Gerasa to safeguard the Greek hold on the area.[25] Eventually, when the Macedonian garrisons grew, it became the basis of new Hellenistic *poleis* organized on Greek lines.

We cannot state with certainty when exactly Alexander called Parmenion to join him, since the sources at hand offer different timetables. According to Arrian (2.25), for example it was in the last days of the siege on Tyre. We are told that Parmenion even advised his master to accept a second peace agreement offered by Darius III. Plutarch by contrast stated (*Alexander*, 29, 7), that this happened in the second visit of Alexander to Tyre, namely after the conquest of Egypt. But apparently Plutarch's report is less reliable to that of Arrian's. Curtius Rufus (4.5, 9) noted that

---

21   See e.g. Tcherikover 1963: 71ff.; 1977: 90ff.). Indeed, the common explanation for choosing the name of Pella was based on an etymological association which connected this name with the oriental name of פהל or פהיל; see Jones 1937: 233. This, however, does not contradict the aforesaid view, since it could not apply to the name of Dion. An indirect argument in support of the antiquity of Pella (namely from the Diadochs' era) can be found in a statement by Stephanus Byzantius that during the Ptolemaic period the city was renamed as Berenice.

22   Tcherikover 1927, 76. On the coins see Seyrig 1965: 25–28.

23   The inscription indicates that during the second or third century CE there was still in the city an association of 'Macedonians'; see: Kraeling 1938: No. 78 (p. 410), 137 (p. 423); Jones 1937, 237; Seyrig 1965: 26ff.; Tcherikover 1963: 80, 356 [note 77]; 1977: 100, 448 [note 77]). It is worth recalling here also the existence of a Jewish 'tribe' of 'Macedonians' in Alexandria in the days of Josephus (*Apion* 2.36), a fact which have been verified by two papyri dated 14–13 BCE; see: Tcherikover 1960: nos. 142–43.

24   Illustrative in this context is also a certain coin mint from Capitolias (189 CE), in which Alexander was proclaimed Γενάρχης of the local people, see Seyrig 1959: 60, note 9.

25   Jones 1937: 237; Seyrig 1965: 26ff.

after the conquest of Tyre, Parmenion was assigned to carry out military missions. He further informs us that precisely then Alexander appointed Hephaestion as governor of 'the coast along Phoenicia' and Andromachus as governor of Coele-Syria (instead of Parmenion).[26] It appears that by this time a considerable portion of western Palestine was already occupied, possibly even most of it. Arrian (2.25, 4) reported in very certain terms, that when Alexander left Tyre 'all the other parts of what is called Palestine Syria had already yielded to him'.[27] Abel, in following the complementary evidence by Pliny the Elder (*Historia Naturalis*, 12.25, 117), claimed that Alexander used secondary forces for that mission which arrived at Jericho while Tyre was still under siege.[28] Gutman not only supported this line of events, but even linked them with the activity of Parmenion in Trans-Jordan.[29] Archaeological evidence from Wadi ed-Daliyeh supports the presence of Macedonian troops in the region of Jericho. It is from that data that we can learn that Macedonian troops slaughtered more than 200 Samaritan refugees who took shelter in a local cave (see below).

We have no information of Alexander's route from Tyre to Gaza in 332 BCE. Logically he must have turned south to Acre and marched along the shore to Dor and Strato's Tower.[30] Keeping to the coast was probably coordinated with his fleet (cf. Arrian 3.1, 1). From Strato's Tower, however, he must have deviated eastward to the mountain range to circumvent the sand dunes of the Sharon Coast, a difficult obstacle for any army to pass through. In addition, there were malaria-infected swamps in that region which needed to be avoided at all costs. In fact the paved road in use in those days turned eastward to straddle the mountain range of Samaria and from there the road led south to Lydda. On his way south Alexander apparently sent a secondary unit to Joppa (Jaffa) and Resheph (later Apollonia) in order to ensure their loyalty. From Lydda he

26   Cf. Eusebius, *Chronicon* (ed. Schoene), 2.114.

27   Apparently, his geographical terminology reflected the reality of his own days (i.e. the second century CE), namely when the term 'Palestine' returned officially to be used by emperor Hadrian, who borrowed it from the old terminology familiar in the writings of Herodotus (1.105; 2.104, 106; 3.5; 4.39; 7.89).

28   Abel 1935: 58.

29   Gutman 1939/40: 278–89, His argumentation for Alexander's motivation to lay hands on the treasures of Jericho, namely the Balsam plantations, are illustrative and very convincing indeed.

30   It is easy to guess that Acre was handed over to Alexander while Tyre was under siege, as did other Phoenician cities in the neighborhood. Acre was then politically independent and served the Persians as a naval base until the arrival of Alexander; see: Avi-Yonah 1962: 23–4. Apparently the city took advantage of the siege on Tyre to disinherit its functions in favour of Alexander. This can find an indirect proof by the fact that it became an official mint for Alexander. It is easy to guess that also the Sidonian cities south of Acre, namely Dor and Strato's Tower, also switched sides to be counted among Alexander's allies.

turned back westward to Yavneh (Iamnia), Ashdod (Azotus), Ascalon and arrived at Gaza. Part of this route passed through Samaritan territory, the Samaritans had become Alexander's allies during the siege of Tyre (*Ant.* 11.321). Following basic military logistics, he must have taken control of the hillside overlooking the road; otherwise he would have endangered his safe passage along this route on his return journey from Egypt. By securing the high ground above the road Alexander achieved predominance of this main artery, the *Via Maris*. This was also crucial in the event that the Samaritans would change their allegiance. Indeed, the formal loyalty of the Samaritans soon wavered and it was necessary to again subdue them. This was undertaken by Andromachus, Alexander's governor of Coele-Syria (Curtius Rufus, 4.5, 9), and it was against him that the Samaritans later revolted (4.8, 9-10), as will be shown below.

Among the coastal cities only Gaza offered firm resistance to Alexander. Apparently they resented him because of their special position in the Persian Empire. Under Persian rule they had had political independence from the big Phoenician cities, as well as excellent relations with their Arab neighbours. The ruler of Gaza, the eunuch Batis (or Babemesis), prepared himself diligently for a long siege. Batis remained loyal to the Persian monarch and was assisted in this by Arab mercenaries.[31] Arrian (2.26, 4) testified that the conquest of Gaza became a matter of special importance and personal prestige for Alexander. A statement like that might be too simplistic, unless we evaluate its military significance with regard to Alexander's future campaign to Egypt. The Gaza Harbour was actually the last in the chain of Palestinian harbours, since the minor anchorages of Raphia and Rhinocorura (now El-Arish) could by no means be compared with it. Gaza was actually the principal port for the exporting of oriental goods to Egypt, especially the so-called 'Arab merchandise' (see below). From a military point of view, the city was the most strategic location suited to being a barrier against invaders from the south, and, vice versa, invaders from the north on their way to Egypt. It was not by chance that the greatest battles of the Palestine Coastal Plain took place near Gaza. This location could in fact decide the fate of either Palestine

---

31   Arrian, 2.25, 4; Curtius Rufus, 4.6, 7; Josephus, *Ant.* 11.320. Those mercenaries must have come from territories which were not depending on Gaza, probably from the Arab tribes in the vicinity. Since the security needs of Gaza were closely connected to the caravan trade of the Sinai peninsula and the Negev, it is reasonable to maintain that the military skill of such mercenary forces was 'desert-warfare'. Apparently this skill was the major factor behind Antigonus Monophthalmus' failure to conquer Petra (312 BCE). Arab (or rather Nabatean) mercenaries were enlisted by the Ptolemies in Egypt, especially for safeguarding the fertile Nile Valley against nomadic raiders; see Kasher 1985: 55–6, 86, 116.

or Egypt.[32] This was probably the reason why Alexander insisted on the conquest of Gaza. Indeed, he invested enormous efforts to achieve this goal and this despite the difficulties of using heavy weaponry in the sand dunes of the area, and notwithstanding the stubborn resistance offered by the Gazaeans. Alexander was adamant he was determined to complete his goal, the conquest of Gaza, although he was badly wounded during the siege. A stone missile had penetrated through his armour into his shoulder.[33] After an arduous siege, which lasted at least during the hot months of August–September 332 BCE,[34] he was finally victorious and the city fell to him.

According to Josephus, after the conquest of Gaza, Alexander advanced towards Jerusalem, where he was supposed to meet Jaddus the Jewish High Priest. One of the main arguments for discrediting the story pointed out the statements by Arrian (3.1, 1) and Curtius Rufus (4.7, 2) that Alexander marched with his army from Gaza to Pelusium (the gate to Egypt), in just seven days.[35] Logically it was an impossible mission to reach Egypt in so short a time if he had first visited Jerusalem. Yet it has already been argued by I. Abrahams, as noted already above, that there was no indication whatsoever that he set forth to Egypt *immediately* after the fall of Gaza.[36] A meticulous examination of Josephus' report can verify this very well (below), the more so as Arrian (2.27, 2-3) informed us that Alexander '*was not easily cured*' of the aforementioned wound and indeed this injury occurred at the final stages of Gaza's siege. This would physically disqualify him from hurtling off on a fast march across the Sinai desert at the height of the summer and in the heat of the desert.[37] Diodorus Siculus hinted in general terms that Alexander had to solve several urgent

32   Take, for example, the battle of Gaza when Cambyses king of Persia invaded Egypt in 525 BCE. Another battle at this very location occurred in 312 BCE between Demetrius Poliorcetes and Ptolemy I Soter. The battle of Raphia (217 BCE) between the Seleucid king Antiochus III the Great and Ptolemy IV Philopator was one of the most famous in antiquity. Numerically speaking, it was the largest in scale that ever was fought in ancient Palestine; see the most comprehensive study on this battle: Galili 1999.

33   On the campaign against Gaza, see the description by Arrian 2.24, 5.

34   There is a remarkable parity between Arrian (*loc.cit*), Josephus (*Ant.* 11.325), Diodorus Siculus (17.48, 7) and Plutarch (*Alexander*, 24, 5) on this very point.

35   See: Tcherikover 1963, 33; 1977, 41; cf. also Büchler 1898, 1. As a matter of fact, there is no reason to marvel at that fact, since Ptolemy IV Philopator had done this way in 4–5 days; see the famous inscription commemorating the Raphia Battle (217 BCE), which was published by Gauthgier and Sottas 1925. The same is true with the campaign of Titus (69 CE), which lasted also five days, according to Josephus, *War* 4.661-662.

36   Abrahams 1927: 11.

37   This was somehow ignored by Mor (2003: 64–5), as well as other arguments, which will be specified below. No wonder, therefore, that Mor followed the common accepted error that Alexander set forth to Egypt immediately after the fall of Gaza.

problems in Gaza before his campaign to Egypt; unfortunately he did not specify them. However, as Arrian (2.27, 7) informs us that close to the surrender of Gaza Alexander sold the local population into slavery and settled in their place a population made up of local residents that were trustworthy. He also informs us that Alexander rebuilt the fortifications of the city in order to serve as an efficient stronghold for the future. From this we can deduce that these were the 'urgent problems' Diodorus Siculus referred to.[38] Logically these activities in Gaza would have lasted quite a long time. Apart from the time needed to rebuild the cities defences, the selection of a new and reliable group of settlers was a matter which could not be done without serious deliberation.[39] In brief, it appears that Alexander was very diligent with the military reorganization of the city and the future stability. This is understandable on the basis of his plans to return from Egypt via Gaza on his way to continue the war against Darius III. Plutarch's report (*Alexander*, 25, 5) also gives the impression that Alexander was held up for some time in Gaza due to another reason. A large quantity of perfume and spices had fallen into his hands as booty during the Gaza war, and he was eager to send it to Macedonia. This precious cargo was loaded on ten ships (triremes) under the command of Amyntas, and was delivered with an order of recruiting young soldiers to fill the ranks of his army (Diodorus Siculus 17.49, 1). This matter alone would have kept him busy in Gaza for quite some time. In addition, the unbearable heat of summer in the Sinai desert is a major consideration for delaying his departure and is in keeping with his care of the logistics of supplies; the lack of water for his army during the hot summer was likely to cause serious logistical problems. In any case, the crossing of the Sinai desert in day time was obviously an impossible mission and night marching could be very dangerous for an army inexperienced in desert warfare, as Alexander's Macedonian army was.[40] When Cambyses King of Persia, for instance, conquered Egypt (525 BCE) his meticulous preparations lasted several months, albeit he was assisted by experienced allies, the local Arabs.[41] It is not illogical, therefore, to assume that Alexander preferred to retain his army in the Gaza area and not march out till after

---

38 Strabo (*Geographica* 16.2, 30) was wrong in ascribing to Alexander the total destruction of the city, unless we accept that he just confused Alexander the Great with Alexander Jannaeus. The neighbours whom Alexander settled in Gaza were probably local Arabs like those who later cooperated with Antigonus Monophthalmus (306 BCE) when he prepared himself to invade Egypt. On Alexander's delay in Gaza see more: Kasher 1980, 23–6.

39 Cf. Stark 1852: 341–43.

40 Compare to Alexander's winter campaign to the Oasis of Siwah (in Libya), which almost ended with a catastrophe because of lack of water (Arrian 3.3).

41 Cf. also to the logistical preparations by King Herod when crossing the Sinai coast toward Pelusium when giving a splendid and luxury escort to Octavian on his way to Egypt (Josephus

the summer heat had abated. Certainly his wound, if nothing else, would not allow an immediate departure to Egypt. If the above points are correct then in fact Alexander probably remained quite a considerable period of time (possibly two or three months) in Gaza.[42] In our opinion this was also the time necessary for his preparations of the forthcoming Egyptian campaign. This may also have been an opportunity to re-examine his future strategy concerning his relationship with the rival ethnic groups: the Samaritan and Jewish peoples. Even Tcherikover, who was very sceptical of Josephus' evidence, admitted that it was impossible to refrain completely from some political contact with the Jewish people at that time.[43] We would remark, in addition, that it was illogical to think that Alexander avoided a meeting with the High Priest in Jerusalem, since this figure was after all the supreme political authority of the Jewish people. Such a policy dictated Alexander's relationships with other national leaders, and there are countless examples to verify this policy in the Graeco-Roman literature. We cannot deny that some legendary motifs found their way into Josephus' story, but this is not a reason to nullify or discredit the story in its entirety. In this aspect Josephus' narrative was not different from other historians like Arrian, Curtius Rufus, Plutarch, Diodorus, etc. that wrote about Alexander. Each of the abovementioned authors integrated legendary motifs in their writings but their credibility was not questioned at all, on the contrary they were observed as literary decorations and no more. Why should Josephus be considered differently and be maligned for concocting the whole event?

Let us now refer to another argument raised against the credibility of Josephus' story, the report that Alexander sacrificed in the Jerusalem Temple. In answer to those sceptics, it should be recalled that sacrificing in a temple was considered by Alexander a ceremonial act intended to exhibit a change in political reality, an amendment that entailed the population's recognition of his authority as the new ruler.[44] Furthermore, performing such an action should be evaluated on one hand as an attempt to placate the local god and on the other to conciliate the population. Once the

War 1.395; *AJ* 15.200). Although the conditions of this event were carried out without any military pressure, Herod invested a lot of exertions in the logistical arrangement of his escort.

42   When Marcus (1937: 525–26) weighed the possibilities of Alexander's case, he did not venture to question the general common view. He satisfied himself in raising some forced and mild doubts, in order to compromise himself with sceptic scholars of Josephus, but he did not support his reservation with any significant source. The same is to be said of Mor's (2003: 64–5) who postulated that Alexander could appoint one of his officers to carry out all the arrangements needed to be done in Gaza before his leaving to Egypt, but he has not supported this speculation with any solid source.

43   See Tcherikover 1963: 37–8; cf. 1977: 48–9.

44   Exactly this was the practice he took in different occasions; see e.g. Arrian 1.11; Plutarch, *Alexander* 23; Diodorus Siculus 17. 2 118; for further details see Golan 1982: 40.

sacrifice had been accepted it would be proof to Alexander that the local God had accepted him and that the population recognized the conqueror and his conquest. Alexander's ceremonial presence in the temple was thus tantamount to 'divine recognition' and understood as such by the subject peoples. This act would then facilitate the consolidation of a foreign ruler in a conquered land. This was as true regarding the Jerusalem Temple as to other temples where Alexander sacrificed. The example of Tyre is very illustrative, since the formal reason, or rather the pretext under which Alexander conquered the city, was the refusal by the Tyrians to allow Alexander to sacrifice in their temple, their denial reflected their political enmity.[45] Alexander's sacrifice symbolized therefore a reconciliatory act to the nation conquered and his acceptance by the local god. Significantly, his alleged wish to sacrifice in the Jerusalem Temple should be understood in a similar way to his wish to sacrifice in the Tyrian temple; that is, this act when taking place in Jerusalem was the equivalent of a symbolic reconciliation with the Jewish people, they as the Tyrians had overtly started their relations with him as enemies.[46]

Alexander's intellectual curiosity is also an important point well worth taking into consideration, intrigued as he was to visit all the temples he possibly could, even those in dangerous and remote locations. A remarkable example of this was his visit to the temple of Amon-Ra in the Oasis of Siwah; this endeavour nearly cost Alexander and his escort their lives as they almost died of thirst en route. Even Arrian (3.3, 1) could not find a reasonable cause for this visit, it was simply Alexander's strong personal motivation defined as, '*an ardent desire*[47] to visit the place'. Thus Alexander's intellectual curiosity probably played a certain role in his urge to visit the Jerusalem Temple. This 'desire' is even more understandable when taking into account the positive reaction of notable Greek personalities that had come into contact with Jewish people. Thus Alexander's association with such eminent philosophers as Theophrastus and Hecataeus from Abdera, who probably followed him on his eastern campaign, would have influenced his decisions concerning his actions towards the Jewish people and their Temple. Hecataeus is well known for his admiration of what he considered 'Jewish philosophy' and he had depicted the city of Jerusalem in extremely idealistic terms.[48] In addition Alexander, as the two aforementioned philosophers, were all disciples of Aristotle who seems to have had an admiration for the Jewish people. Certainly Clearchus of Soli, another disciple of Aristotle reports an

---

45   Cf. Curtius Rufus, 4:2, 2-5; Cohen 1982–83: 45–6.
46   Cf. Cohen 1982–83: 47–48, 55.
47   Cf. Golan 1982, 27.
48   See. e.g. Gutman 1958: 39ff.; Levy 1960: 3–59; M. Stern 1974: 8–17, 20–44.

encounter between Aristotle and a 'wise Jewish man' he met in Asia Minor and with whom he discussed the subject of 'Sleep'.[49] In our opinion, it is this favourable impression of the Jewish people that Alexander was aware of, possibly effecting a positive predisposition towards the Jewish religion and hence his desire to visit their temple. He was certainly exposed to the 'fashionable' intellectual interest of contemporary Greek philosophers in the mysteries of the East ascribed to particular nations, groups and sects. We therefore suggest that careful consideration be given to the fact that at that time the Jewish people and Judaism became subjects of great interest and admiration, to the degree that the Jewish people were considered to be 'a nation of philosophers'.[50]

As stated above, those scholars who doubted the authenticity of Josephus' story reasoned that as there were no traces of it in Graeco-Roman sources the story must be an enhancement added by Josephus. Methodically speaking, a claim such as that cannot be argued with, except by raising the counter-argument that there were many other instances in Josephus' writings that were not 'covered' by classical sources, and yet they were found to be factual and accurate rather than fabrications. In our humble opinion, a rejection of this incident should not be acceptable except on the basis of bona fide evidence. Conjectures supported by silence, and contradictions based on prejudices and 'general consensus' are unacceptable. Alexander's meeting with the Jewish High Priest at the gates of Jerusalem is no different from other visits to foreign temples as related by Arrian (2.15). In fact, those encounters, with the Phoenician rulers of Aradus and Byblus, were also held at the gates of their cities, namely the most important site for the reception of guests.

One of the main reasons for casting doubt on the credibility of Josephus' story was what seemed like the anachronistic mention of Sanballat in the description of the meeting between Alexander and the High Priest Jaddus. This story was narrated in the framework of a detailed review on the Jewish–Samaritan conflict and among the prominent persons involved was Sanballat noted as the satrap of Samaria. Scholars had considered that Josephus connected the name of Sanballat with Alexander the Great anachronistically, the more so as he had completely ignored him in his report covering the times of Ezra and Nehemiah. Furthermore, Josephus' description of the marriage of Manasseh (*Ant.* 11.302-303) brother of Jaddus the Jewish High Priest, to Nikaso the daughter of Sanballat is found in Nehemiah 13.28 – 'One of the sons of Joiada son of the high priest Eliashib was a son-in-law of Sanballat the Horonite; I drove him

---

49   See Levy 1960: 14–43; M. Stern 1974: 47–52.
50   See at length Levy 1960: 15–35; 39ff.; 74ff.; 89–90; 92ff.

away from me'. Scholars gave precedence to Nehemiah and credited the Book with reliability while rebuking Josephus for faulty dates. This situation supported the identification of Manasseh with the son of Joiada mentioned by Nehemiah.[51] Abraham Schalit tried to solve this difficulty by disqualifying Josephus' genealogy, but at the same time relying on one detail borrowed from Josephus with regard to Manasseh, when he tried to correct the biblical text Schalit claimed that Manasseh was the son of Johanan. Thus Joiada actually had three sons – Johanan, Jeshua and Manasseh. This new and revised genealogy, which has no factual basis in the book of Nehemiah, paved the way for a further claim by Schalit, that the split between Jaddus and Manasses reported by Josephus in *Ant.* 11.306ff. is just distorted; it was in truth a conflict between Johanan and Jeshua (*Ant.* 11.297-301). According to Schalit, they were the spokesmen of what he called the anti-Samaritan 'conservative party' (or the 'separatist party') on the one hand, and the pro-Samaritan 'liberal party' (or 'progressive party') on the other hand.[52]

Tcherikover accepted this thesis and even tried to strengthen it with additional scepticism when relying on literary arguments based on the disparity between Josephus' story and the biblical account of Nehemiah, this in particular follows in the footsteps of Abraham Büchler.[53] Further Tcherikover maintained that the plot of Josephus' story was composed of two different non-homogeneous parts. The first part concerned Sanballat and his alliance with Alexander and supposedly relied on a Samaritan source, while the second section was apparently dependent on a Jewish source. This supposition was based on a favourable account of the Samaritan cause in the first part, and the opposite hostile approach in the second part which is sympathetic to the Jewish cause. Tcherikover believed that the author (or the editor) of the story just patched together the two parts to create one story. Accordingly, the first part creates the impression that the temple on Mt Gerizim had not yet been built (*Ant.* 11.310; 322), whereas the second part gives the impression that it was already founded and stood in situ (ibid., 342). In quite a similar way, Tcherikover pointed out that in the first part Sanballat is depicted as the Samaritan representative that carried on negotiations with Alexander (ibid., 321ff.), whereas in the second part Sanballat disappeared without a trace and the Samaritans turned directly to Alexander without mediation (ibid., 340ff.). For Tcherikover this was a proof that the Manasseh–Sanballat story combined with the Jaddus–Alexander story was an artificial fabrication. This

---

51   Cf. Spak 1911: 12–13.
52   See Schalit 1949: 252–72.
53   Büchler 1898: 1–26; Tcherikover 1963: 32–3; 1977: 41ff.

had two odd results, first the sudden death of Sanballat, quite unjustified by the course of events (as though death needed to follow a time span), and second the amazing speed in which the Samaritan temple was constructed.[54] In his eyes, the contradiction between the two parts (of what he labelled 'the fable') is evident also from the description of the meeting between Alexander and the Samaritans after the visit to Jerusalem. To quote Tcherikover in this context: 'Alexander asks the Samaritans "who they are", as if he were seeing them for the first time, whereas he had already met Sanballat, who had brought him Samaritan auxiliary troops when he was at Tyre'.[55] In brief, these contradictions prove, according to Tcherikover, that Josephus did not succeed in patching the two stories to make one tale, and that he was satisfied with writing them one after the other, adding just a few linking words for the readers' convenience. However, this 'artificial' story complicated things further.

Although admittedly this prima facie method of literary criticism is very attractive, it is not founded on facts, and when the basic argument is weak it is easily repudiated. In reality, the first part of the story is in no way sympathetic to the Samaritans. On the contrary, Sanballat was depicted as a turncoat who deserted his Persian ally Darius III to lead his people into an alliance with Persia's enemy, Alexander. Moreover, he was portrayed as a conniving crook who tried to manipulate political intrigues and cunningly profit from his devious dealings. This can be seen clearly from his attempt to benefit from the conflict with the Jewish people by causing them treachery. His deceitful nature can be shown by his malicious advice to Alexander (*Ant.* 11.321–323). Neither could his loyalty to his new master warrant any merit as he actually had received favours from Darius III (*Ant.* 11.311) only to repay him by leaving him in the lurch with no consideration to his oath of fidelity. In complete contrast, Jaddus, the Jewish High Priest, was depicted in very positive terms as a reliable and faithful subject, who kept his oath of loyalty to Darius III. From both Jewish and Greek points of view alike, the violation of loyalty and the denial of an oath were forms of treason and considered a grave offence. As the Hellenistic world appreciated the integrity of political loyalty, Josephus proudly emphasized the faithful military service of the Jewish people in different kingdoms.[56]

The arguments offered by Tcherikover concerning the rapid establishment of the Samaritan temple are also not very convincing, for two

---

54 Tcherikover 1977: 44. Methodically, it is quite obvious that such an analysis is wrong, since it tried to hold poles asunder.

55 Tcherikover 1977: 44.

56 Cf. e.g. Ezek. 17.11-21; *Pseudo-Aristeas* 36; Josephus, *Apion* 2.42; *Ant.* 12.8, 150; Cf. also Schalit 1959/60: 289–318; Kasher 1985: *passim*.

main reasons: (1) Josephus patently wrote that 'Sanballat brought all his energy to bear to build the temple' (*Ant.* 11.324), which is an indication of its speedy construction; (2) and not less important, the archaeological finds at Tel er-Ras on the western slopes of Mt Gerizim above the city of Shechem justify Josephus' story. Beneath the ruins of the Roman temple built by Hadrian there were remnants of an older temple destroyed at the end of the second century BCE (in the reign of the Hasmonaean ruler John Hyrcanus I).[57]

However, the clinching argument comes with the archaeological discovery by Yitzhak Magen of an impressively large Samaritan temple, dated probably to the end of the third and beginning of the second century BCE. This has rightly captured the scholarly debate[58] and influenced a new line of thought that raised doubts on the traditional connection of the Samaritan temple with Tel er-Ras. The awkwardness of following the earlier ideas of the Samaritan cult has become even stronger with the recent acceptance of two Samaritan cult centres, a possibility which has gathered momentum with numismatic discoveries.[59] Prima facie the historic riddle seems to remain unresolved for the time being, the more so as it calls for further speculations and hypothetical suggestions.[60] We are inclined to think that the idea of two Samaritan holy sites for worship on Mt Gerizim as the correct solution, namely one temple in Tel er-Ras, and one on the summit of Mt Gerizim. The Tel er-Ras site was probably built during the transition from Persian to Greek rule (ca. 400–300 BCE) as Josephus informs us, whereas the second temple was built a century later at the transition from the Ptolemaic to the Seleucid rule (ca. 300–200 BCE), as proposed by Y. Magen. Although we concord with two sacred sites, *they were in fact connected* and created one religious centre. The first better suits the classification of a shrine, which is the equivalent of the Hebrew term במה or the Latin *sacellum*, whereas the second justified the title 'Temple' due to its location, size, magnificence and of course, the rich archaeological findings. The idea of having a complex composed of two components can find surprising and illustrative support in the archaeological evidence of Samaritan ceramic candles from the Roman period, decorated with a relief which very clearly shows the two sacred sites as being connected to each other by a long staircase: the greater one

---

57   A reliable report of the findings in this site is given by Bull and Wright 1965: 234–37; Bull 1968: 58–72 (= *BASOR* 190: 4–19). The wall which surrounded the main building was 60 metres long and 42 metres wide.

58   Magen 1986: 91–101.

59   Full details on these discoveries and the historic implications entailed, see Mor 2003: 74–5.

60   Take for example the notion by Eshel (1984: 141–55; 1996b, 359–65) that the first Samaritan temple was located in the city of Samaria; see Mor (2003: 76–8, 84) against this view.

on the summit of the mountain and the smaller one, which corresponds with Tel er-Ras,[61] on the slope.

Returning to our discussion of Tcherikover's apparent amazement at the question Alexander posed to the Samaritans in Josephus' story, 'who were they' (*Ant.* 11.343) – 'as if he was not familiar with their identity and saw them for the first time', although this seems to be perplexing it is not, once it is realized that this was a rhetorical question. When separated from its context we are led astray and assume that as proposed it was a bona fide question, whereas actually it was a remark in response to the Samaritan petition (*Ant.* 11.343) that hinted at something far more significant. This was not a query to ascertain their identity, but a sarcastic, if not provocative and challenging, statement of disdain. 'Who were they, the Samaritans, to make such a request?' Who were they to ask for benefits that were granted to the Jewish subjects?

Tcherikover's opposition of the second part of Josephus' story was strengthened by what he termed as errors:

1. Thus the request in Jerusalem to permit the Jewish residents of Babylon and Media to keep their own laws is anachronistic, since it may imply that these countries were already under Alexander's rule. By contrast, however, it could be argued that a Jewish request in this regard was formulated in conditional language, which meant that it was linked with Alexander's promise to do so in the future. After all, it was well known everywhere that he meant to conquer those countries, in accordance with his own official proclamations (see e.g. Arian 2.25, 2-3).

2. The anachronistic mention of the 'Chaldaeans' among those who cherished themselves with hope that Alexander would give them a permit to plunder Jerusalem upon his visit there (*Ant.* 11.338). In this case, in answer to Tcherikover, the term 'Chaldaeans' could be synonymous with 'astrologers' and 'soothsayers' in general, it need not necessarily mean the Babylonians as such. Furthermore, Tcherikover did not ignore the variant use for 'Chaldaeans' in the text, namely 'Chutaeans', which does make sense (historically speaking). (3) The anachronistic mention of prostration (προσκύνησις) in honour of Alexander (*Ant.* 11.332-333). Tcherikover, as others, was aware of the fact that the custom was a Persian one and was not accepted by Alexander prior to Darius' death, it therefore, according to Tcherikover, could not apply to Alexander while in Judaea. Indeed,

<hr>

61   The picture is taken from Meshorer 1984: 52. Indeed, the similarity of this candle to Roman coins from Neapolis (Shechem) is striking; see illustration, nos. 126, 135, 136, 147, 148, and catalogue, pp. 115–16.

this was true when speaking on the prostration of a Macedonian before Alexander,[62] but according to Josephus' story, it was Alexander who '*approached and prostrated himself* before the name of God' or rather 'before the High Priest of Jerusalem' (11.331). When amazed by this, Parmenion stated that all are accustomed to bow before Alexander (*Ant.* 11.333), but he meant it was true of oriental people who were traditionally accustomed to the norm of bowing in reverence, and this did not as yet apply to Macedonians. It is worth noting in this context Alexander's anger at the ruler of Gaza was the result of his refusal to kneel down before him as expected from an oriental subject. The fact that this incident that referred to the custom of prostration occurred in close proximity of time and was reported by a non-Jewish source (Curtius Rufus, 6.6, 26ff), reliable to Tcherikover, is very salient indeed. Admittedly, 'the prostration story' by Josephus is saturated with a typical Jewish outlook on the world, the main goal of which concerned the presentation of regal Alexander exalted by religious consciousness, admitting the superiority of King of Kings (Almighty God). This story was tantamount to God guiding Alexander through his impressive life and meteoric career. The story was edited according to the well-known pattern of Jewish–Hellenistic literature,[63] in the spirit of what was told by *Pseudo-Calisthenes*. Since it was just that, a literary ingredient of Jewish propaganda aimed to enhance the portrayal of Alexander's meeting with the Jewish high priest, it could not and should not serve as evidence for disqualifying the historicity of the entire story.

4. According to Tcherikover the anachronistic mention of the *Book of Daniel*, which predicted the fall of the Persian empire (*Ant.*11.357) and was allegedly shown to Alexander, was an error that demonstrates Josephus' story as fictitious as the *Book of Daniel* was written approximately 150 years after Alexander's time. Indeed, there is here a clear historiographic mistake, but we should assign it to a late literary tradition of popular origin, or even to the misinterpretation by Josephus himself, an interpolation which was probably borrowed from his commentary on *Daniel* (*Ant.* 10.266ff., esp. 273). Such a mistake however should not undermine the entire story especially as non-Jewish literary traditions on Alexander absorbed similar legendary motifs. Thus for example, Plutarch (*Alexander*, 17, 4) reported that while Alexander stayed in Lycia near the city of Xanthus, it happened that the waters of a local spring overflowed and a bronze tablet with

---

62 See Tcherikover 1963: 33–34; 1977: 43–45.
63 Cf. Gutman 1939/40: 286 and see also below.

ancient writing was heaved up from the depths, the inscription on the tablet was a prophecy predicting the destruction of the Persian kingdom by the Greeks. The literary motif of the revelation of the Jewish High Priest to Alexander in his dream, is principally not different from the 'epiphany' of Heracles which occurred during the siege of Tyre.[64] Not in vain, Gutman came to the reasonable conclusion that non-Jewish legends were a source of inspiration for legendary Jewish traditions about Alexander. These were picked up by Josephus and the Talmudic literature alike.[65] Indeed, Alexander was depicted as a messenger of God and not as one who was motivated by himself. This very approach was already to be found in biblical parallels such as the traditions surrounding Cyrus King of Persia which depict his mission as messenger and agent of God.[66] Cyrus opens the Persian chapter in Jewish history, and Alexander launches the Hellenistic chapter while ending the Persian one. This is very significant as this demonstrated the supervision of Almighty God on Jewish people and general history of the world alike. In other words, Josephus' story was edited according to typical Jewish values rooted in the Bible and were aimed to observe the historical vicissitudes as part of a heavenly plan foreseen and foretold and thus praising the prophetic ability of Judaism. An evaluation of that kind should not therefore be an obstacle on the historiographic path of our study.[67]

At this point we shall skip over the implications of the archaeological and papyrological discoveries from Wadi ed-Daliyeh to deal with Josephus' story regarding the Samaritan leader Sanballat. It will suffice the reader

64   Arrian 2.18, 1; Plutarch, *Alexander* 24, 5.
65   See the excellent article by Gutman 1939/40: 289–90.
66   See Isa. 44.28; 45.17; cf. also Ezra 1.1-2; 2 Chron. 37.22-23.
67   See the excellent article offered by Gnuse (1993: 349–68), in which he has argued that the question whether or not the event reported by Josephus about Jaddus and his dream took place historically is irrelevant. He has rightly maintained that 'Josephus wished to describe the response of the Jewish community to Alexander the Great and the fall of Persia, and he desired to demonstrate that their actions were divinely directed at this dramatic juncture in human history . . . It was important for Josephus to describe the theophany of Jaddus in a fashion more dignified than those found in Hellenistic shrine inscriptions . . . The ambiguity in the text is by design, and the resultant presentation resembles dream reports in the Hebrew Bible . . . Like the biblical authors before him, Josephus would not let his narratives violate his beliefs . . . Here the craft of historian, literary artist, and theologian is woven together in delicate fashion by Josephus' (367–68); cf. 1996: 225–45; 1998: 457–72. Although Cohen (1982-3, 55) has denied the historicity of Alexander's visit to Jerusalem, he has been aware of the popular genres of Hellenistic Jewish literature which 'forced Alexander to an epiphany to acknowledge the God of the Jews' (57). According to Gnuse, this is exactly the reason why the historicity of Alexander's visit to Jerusalem is irrelevant, since nobody can deny or verify it in decisiveness.

wishing to obtain a reliable summary on that issue to refer to the work of Menachem Mor, despite his contention that Alexander's visit to Jerusalem was 'a legend'. One of Mor's main arguments for its legendary character was based on the story (see below) that perpetrates Alexander's favourable attitude towards the Jewish people. The story in itself is problematic and seems to have occurred together with Alexander's denigrated regard for the Samaritans. In *Ant.* 11.327-328, Josephus relates that Jaddus, the Jewish High Priest, had a dream (or a vision) in which God stipulates that his meeting with Alexander at the gates of Jerusalem would be successful if he took with him a priestly escort wearing fine white linen garments. Josephus goes on to describe 'how Jaddus rose from his sleep, greatly rejoicing, and announced to all his oracular revelation'. It is exactly this sudden elation that indicates the former tension Jaddus was under and intimates that relations with Alexander had until then not been good. This revelation was undoubtedly inserted by Josephus as a literary motif to enhance the story, dramatize the meeting and give it an essence of sanctity.

For Josephus this would be another way of claiming that providence and God's protection formed the history of the Jewish people, whose fate was thus predestinated. This, of course, reflected a very typical Jewish–Hellenistic trend perceptible in the literature of that period and is not intended as historical fact but as an enhancement of the story, elevating, even sanctifying, the encounter.

Historically, Alexander's radical twist in Palestinian politics occurred just after his conquest of Gaza, and thus is quite reasonable. In fact it would be impossible to explain the outbreak of the Samaritan rebellion against Alexander without taking into account Jewish Samaritan rivalry (*Ant.* 11.338-339, 342-344). Josephus, although saying nothing specific about the reasons behind Alexander's change of mind, leaves several hints to the situation. Apart from which, logically, Jewish politics were astute enough not to stay idle while the world around them was rocked by changes. During the fatal year of 332 BCE the world witnessed the rapid collapse of the powerful Persian kingdom, and the spectacular emergence of a new kingdom that replaced it. As 'West took over from East' essential political changes meant that no power involved could remain untouched. The anecdotal tradition in *Pseudo-Callisthenes* (11, 24),[68] can indirectly illustrate the Jewish awareness of political changes. Following the information of this source, messengers were sent to Alexander with the intention of discovering his real strength and this in order to estimate the chances of Jewish resistance. The resulting significant decision was, surrender to the Macedonian conqueror as there was no chance of success

---

68   See: Pfister 1914: 1–32; Marcus 1937: 512 ff.

against his troops. Alexander's forces were so devoted to him they would readily sacrifice their lives for him and his cause. In my opinion, this anecdote can indirectly complete, even by intimation, what Josephus had missed. In other words, upon witnessing Alexander's victory over the Persians, Jewish leaders could not remain indifferent to what was happening around them, and therefore attempted to settle their relationship with Alexander. This in turn would explain Jaddus' apprehension before the aforementioned meeting, as portrayed by Josephus. Especially as we have learned from Josephus (*Ant.* 11.318) that Jaddus the High Priest had declared loyalty to Darius III King of Persia and declined Alexander's application for troops and supplies in his siege of Tyre. Although that occurred before the conquest of Palestine, when the legal rule was still Persian, Alexander could now take revenge. In all probability the Jewish people, as almost all other nations' people in the region, would have had difficulties in adapting to the swift decisive defeat of Darius III at the battle of Issus, since everybody was 'convinced that the Macedonians would not even come to grips with the Persians because of their great number. But the events proved other than they expected' (*Ant.* 11.315).[69]

It is reasonable to maintain that Jewish people were cautious enough to enquire carefully what their future position would be before making the necessary alliance. Nor was the Jewish nation alone in this; the Phoenician kings in the vicinity of Tyre only surrendered to Alexander after recognizing his success and realizing his power. Thus the Jewish decisions were similarly delayed. The Jewish decision was formerly affected by an unwanted political entanglement and an even less desirous military engagement with Darius III. Sheer numerical weight was considered advantageous enough to ensure victory – after such a triumph the ensuing punitive measures by Darius against those unfaithful to him were bound to be severe. Tension between the Persian kingdom and the Jewish people had, however, already begun to appear. It seems the Jewish people had suffered some harsh calamities that had unsettled the formerly well-balanced relations.[70]

Sanballat, on the other hand, was quick to realize the Greek potential; he moved swiftly allying himself to them and planting intrigues that

---

69   Cf. Marcus 1937: 466, note b.

70   Under the reign of Artaxerxes II (359–338 BCE), heavy clouds darkened the Jewish–Persian relations; cf. Josephus *Ant.* XI, 297–301. A dim memory of other calamities can be found in the writings of the Fathers of the Church; see Schürer 1904: 7 & note 11; 1986: 6 & note 12; Klausner 1949, vol. 2: 11–18, as well as in the Book of Judith; see Grintz 1957: 18ff. Clear traces of destruction were evident in archaeological findings at cities in Palestine, as shown e.g. by Barag 1966: 6–12 and E. Stern 1973: 250–55. Perhaps the memory of at least some of those calamities are mentioned by *Pseudo-Aristeas*, 36; Josephus, *Apion* 2: 191, 194.

complicated the Jewish situation. Alexander however, seems to have carefully reflected the situation of allies. After staying in the country for almost a year he became aware of the potential advantage of the Jewish numerical superiority over the Samaritans, to the degree that he considered a change in his political orientation. Apparently, he also began to realize that Sanballat's scheming stemmed from his conflict with the Jewish people and therefore Alexander conducted a realistic and flexible policy that reflected his astute understanding of the leaders and the politics involved. Alexander came to the conclusion that an ally like Sanballat was volatile and could easily betray him, as he did his previous master Darius III but while engaged in the sieges of Tyre and Gaza, he was not free to 'change horses'. After the fall of Gaza, he was able to consider such a move. Unluckily for the Samaritans, Sanballat died exactly at that time (*Ant.* 11.325), a coincidence that eased the political shift and released Alexander from his prior commitments. It is possible to assume that while consolidating his relationship with the Jewish people, Alexander became aware of the large demographic concentrations of Jewish communities in the countries he was about to conquer (*Ant.* 11.338). The implications of this are vital to understanding Alexander's Judaean policy; his alliance with the Jewish people in Judaea would be of value in his future military efforts. It is the political aspects that we believe should be considered carefully before dismissing Josephus' story as 'legend'. As presented above, Alexander's policy towards friendly nations would entail a visit and possible sacrifice at the temple of that nation, in this case the Jerusalem Temple of the Judaean people.

Political preference for the Jewish people above the Samaritans placed the Samaritan community in an awkward position but this, together with the sudden death of Sanballat, and the lack of a designated heir,[71] had an immense impact on their political position. Such a conclusion can be clearly derived from Josephus when he states that, 'the Shechemites approached him (Alexander), bringing along the soldiers whom Sanballat had sent to him, and invited him to come to their city and honor their temple there' (*Ant.* 11.342). Alexander's response was to assign Andromachus as direct ruler of Samaria, in addition to being ruler of Syria and Palestine[72] and this despite his awareness of a possibly violent reaction on their part. Alexander had little to fear from a Samaritan uprising. Thus soon after his visit to Jerusalem and just before his departure to Egypt 'Alexander marched off against the neighboring cities' (*Ant.* 11.340) in order to assure their loyalty to him. Nevertheless, when all their efforts to obtain privileges

---

71 There are no sources that can give any indication of a nominee to replace Sanballat.
72 Curtius Rufus, 4.9, 9-11; Stern 1974: 447–49; Mor 2003: 60.

failed, the embittered Samaritans revolted against Andromachus and burnt him alive. Alexander was away in Egypt when the uprising erupted and upon hearing the news rushed back in a fury to take his revenge and impose harsh punitive measures. His anger should be explained by also taking into consideration the great importance he had attributed to the region of Palestine as an essential passageway for his future campaigns. Spak considered Alexander's visit to Jerusalem to date to that time.[73]

Indeed, this conclusion, although reasonable, is problematic as there are indications that the Samaritan's rebellion was subjugated by Perdiccas, and not Alexander himself.[74] Macedonian troops were however most probably settled in Samaria by Alexander himself, while Perdiccas was probably the one who founded the polis of Samaria but at a later stage (323–321 BCE).[75] Gutman, although aware of the deficiency of the Talmudic traditions, sought to rely on *bYoma* 59a; *Scholion to the Fasting Scroll*, 9. In this tractate, the meeting between Alexander and the Jewish people is located at Antipatris and not in Jerusalem.[76] Worse, this tradition connected the figures of Alexander the Great with the Jewish High Priest Simon the Just; thus the dim legendary echoes here relate to the days of John Hyrcanus I.[77]

Tcherikover both rightly and quite reasonably had reservations about Antipatris as the location of the meeting,[78] and rejected the possibility on several grounds; firstly Josephus' version was earlier, secondly its presentation was superior providing a more convincing set of details related to the events concerned. Furthermore, According to Arrian (3:6, 1), Alexander was not delayed in Palestine, but went straight to Tyre. A total denial of any visit would be negligent of the due consideration necessary towards Alexander's policy of visiting the holy places of other nations, as well as disregarding his well-known religious curiosity. Alexander's policy of visiting temples is worth emphasizing and his eagerness in paying visits to eastern temples in particular[79] needs consideration due to

73   Spak 1911: 35.

74   These indications are based on fragmental evidences from the Church Fathers' writings; see for details: Schürer 1907: 195–96; Willrich 1895: 16–18; cf. also above including notes 22–23.

75   See for example Schürer 1907: 195; 1979: 169; cf. also Willrich, *loc.cit.*; Marcus 1937: 524; Tcherikover 1930: 148; 1963: 37, 39, 83–85; 1977: 103–105; Hengel 1974: I, 14; Goldstein 1993: 76 (& note 51).

76   Gutman 1939/40: 294; cf. also Schalit 1966: 654–55. Goldstein (1993: 73–74) concurred with this view, but did not offer in support any substantive proof. His hypothesis that the 'pharisees could easily have come to substitute the name of the famous Simeon (the Just) for that of the lesser known Jaddus' is unrealistic and not convincing.

77   Gutman 1939/40: 280, 285. See in detail Noam 2003: 100–101, 151–53, 262.

78   Tcherikover 1963: 37; 1977: 45f.

79   On his attitude to Egyptian gods and their temples, including visits there, see e.g. Arrian, 3.1, 3-4; VI, 19; 7.14, 6; Diodorus, 17.40, 2. On his attitude to Babylonian holy sites see e.g. Arrian,

the 'goodwill' it would bring about, and in this context it may be worth noting the Samaritan animosity caused due to the lack of any such visit. It is also possible that the Samaritan revolt enhanced the alliance between Alexander and the Jewish people; it is also feasible that Jewish soldiers participated in the suppressive measures taken against the Samaritan rebels.[80]

Unfortunately the geographic details of the extent and the course of revolt are unknown. Apart from a slim shred of evidences in Curtius Rufus and even smaller fragments from the Church Fathers, it is possible to indirectly 'rescue' some gloomy echoes from the archaeological finds of Shechem and Samaria,[81] in particular from the cave of Wadi ed-Daliyeh, 13 kilometres north of Jericho. Here large amounts of pottery, clothing, food, and remnants of papyri were found among the gruesome vestiges. Hundreds of skeletons, of men, women and children, all had been slaughtered in a moment of disaster by a common enemy. Apparently this group of people had taken refuge in the cave when the revolt against Andromachus failed, possibly on hearing of the close arrival of Alexander from his Egyptian campaign.[82] They had brought with them their private archives, their papers; these papyri are the documentation of their lives and the testimony of their distress. Seeking refuge in the cave the community found instead, a common grave. These discoveries shed light on the last stages of the revolt, the final suppression. The papyri were mostly judicial documents, pertaining mainly to slave transactions (trade, ownership or manumission bills), real estate, loans, disputes on violating contracts and divorce agreements. The dates of the documents, bullae and seals belong to the 40 years between 375 BCE until 335 BCE and witness the period when the Samaritans flourished. The coins establish the time of Alexander the Great as a *terminus ad quem* for hiding in the cave. Of the many seals found, one of which was gold, it seems that some of the group, if not all of them, were related to an aristocratic Samaritan family. Since the archaeological finds in the cave testify to the diverse population of Samaria, from the ethnical point of view,[83] it has been supposed that the group was denounced by an informer.

3.16, 7ff.; 7.17. On his severe approach against violating the sanctities of eastern people at large, see e.g. Arrian, 6.27–30; 7.19.

80   Even Tcherikover (1963: 37; 1977: 47) thought of this possibility; see also below.

81   The findings from Samaria can testify the destruction dated to the beginning of the Hellenistic era. Probably the vast dimensions of Herod's construction projects 'contributed' also to the erasure of remnants from the Persian period; see details in E. Stern 1973: 31ff. The findings in Shechem reviewed by Bull and Wright 1965: 234–37; Bull 1968: 58–72.

82   Similarly at the end of the Bar-Kochba revolt (132–135 CE) the survivors hid in caves.

83   The seals imply that apart from names with a *Jehovah* component which were common among Samaritans, there were also pagan typical names with the components of *Cos* (Idumaean),

Indirectly it may be possible to discern the participation of Jewish soldiers in the suppression of the Samaritan revolt from Josephus. Relying on Hecataeus of Abdera, Josephus states that Alexander, 'in recognition of the consideration and loyalty shown to him by the Jews, added to their territory the district of Samaria free of tribute (*Apion* II, 43).[84] Scholars evaluated this information as anachronistic, even an exaggerated forgery, pointing out that *1 Macc.* 11.34, indicates that during the rule of the Seleucid king Demetrius II in 145 BCE there were just three Samaritan regions or administrative districts (νόμοι) annexed to Judaea.[85]

Any attempt to assess from this information proof that Alexander created a temporary political-administrative area joining Samaria to Judaea[86] is insubstantial, since during both the Persian and the Ptolemaic periods the segregation between the two regions was total. It is furthermore unacceptable that Alexander even considered such an act, therefore we recommend judging this as a simple exaggeration or a *lapsus calami* and nothing more.[87] Despite that, it may be conceivable that Alexander annexed minor parts of Samaritan territory on the border of Judaea.[88] Possibly the three districts mentioned in *1 Maccabees* are to be identified with the toparchies of Apherema, Lydda and Ramathaim, which were alternatively dependent on Samaria or Judaea, as a result of changes in the circumstantial politics of their time. From a demographic point of view, their population was a mixed one, but with quite a strong, if not a major, Jewish element.[89]

No doubt such a situation caused constant conflicts between both sides. Thus if Josephus' quotation from Hecataeus (*Apion* 2:43) is reliable, and the three toparchies rather than the whole region of Samaria was assigned to Judaea, then these areas must have been lost some time after Alexander and regained in the time of Demetrius II in 145 BCE.[90] Considering the historic developments in the region, it is reasonable that the Jewish loss of the aforesaid toparchies occurred at the end of the Ptolemaic period when

---

Sa'har (Arabic), *Kemosh* (Moabite), and *Ba'al* (Phoenician). It is worth noting here that Phoenicians were familiar also to Josephus, who even sorted out a community of 'Sidonians in Shechem' (*Ant.* 11.344; 12.259, 262).

84   In our opinion, Goldstein (1993: 75 and note 49) just misunderstood Josephus' testimony in *Apion* 2.43.

85   Cf. also *1 Macc.* 10.30; 38. Among scholars who discredited Josephus for forgery, Willrich (*Judaica*: 94) was the most prominent one to be followed; cf. also Schürer 1901: I. 184.

86   See Levy 1960: 48.

87   Cf. Thackeray 1926: 309, note d.

88   Compare to the somewhat hesitant view by Tcherikover (1962: 36–37, 333 [note 23]) on this matter, which did not utterly reject that possibility.

89   See: Alt 1953, vol.2: 346ff.; Kallai 1960: 99ff.

90   Graetz 1857: 51–52 was the first to raise this idea.

relations between the Jewish people and the Ptolemaic authorities had deteriorated. This seems to be in effect what Josephus is saying: 'Now at this time the Samaritans were flourishing, and much distressed the Jews, cutting off parts of their land (τὴν τε χώραν αὐτῶν τεμόντες),[91] and carrying off slaves'(*Ant.* 12: 156): (trans. by Whiston).[92]

Obviously, the act of cutting off parts of Judaea and annexing it to Samaria could not be done without the permission of the central Ptolemaic ruling authorities. Thus it appears that the Greek masters of Palestine, when guided by certain interests, navigated their rule through the turbulent waters of local politics by appropriating problematic border territories from one side and annexing them to their rivals. In brief, the evidence of *Apion* 2.43 can shed light on the Jewish–Samaritan conflict, and at the same time offer a good example for the involvement of the Greek authorities in local politics.

Summing up it seems more prudent to tender Josephus' testimony on Alexander's conquest of Palestine, 'the benefit of the doubt', if not for his oft proven reliability as an important source of Jewish history, then at least due to his contribution of enhancing our understanding of that history.

91   The meaning of the Greek verb τέμνω is mostly 'to cut', 'to cut off', etc.; see Liddell and Scott 1968: 1774–5.

92   Possibly on this background the harsh words of *Ben Sira* (50:26) against the Samaritans; cf. M. Stern 1954: 119 (note 53).

6

THE INTRODUCTION OF THE GREEK LANGUAGE AND
CULTURE IN THE THIRD CENTURY BCE, ACCORDING TO
THE ARCHAEOLOGICAL EVIDENCE IN IDUMAEA

Amos Kloner

It is quite clear that during the fourth century BCE Aramaic was the *lingua franca* and language of daily life in Idumaea, based on ostraca, the vast majority from 'unknown provenances' (most probably, Kh. el Kom, identified with Maqqeda), as well as provenanced ostraca from Beersheba and other sites in Idumaea, including Maresha.

During the past two decades, over 1,600 Aramaic ostraca identified as having a provenance somewhere in Idumaea have appeared on the antiquities market (Porten and Yardeni 2004: 161). Recent estimates raise the possibility that more than 2,000 ostraca exist in many private and public collections. Of these, 1,380 are considered legible; approximately 800 of these have been published in the last 15 years.

The vast majority of the ostraca can be dated to the fourth century BCE. Eph'al and Naveh (1996) date their material in a range from 10 Sivan in Artaxerxes II's 42nd year (14.6.363 BCE) to 20 Shevat of Alexander IV's fifth year (22.2.311 BCE) and slightly later. Lemaire's materials (1996; see also 2002; 2006: 413–56 and 2007: 53–74) are within the same chronological range, even though he does not accept some readings and datings. To this corpus must be added ostraca from Maresha: several fifth century BCE ostraca as well as approximately 60 ostraca mainly from the fourth century BCE, and some from the third and even the beginning of the second century BCE (Kloner, Eshel, Korzakova and Finkielsztejn 2010). The importance of ostraca from a known provenance, albeit a small percentage of the total number, cannot be overstated.

The 1,300 names represented in the Idumaean onomasticon based on these ostraca are more than a representative sampling of the onomasticon of late Persian period Idumaea. As Porten and Yardeni correctly point out (2004: 168; Porten and Yardeni 2006: 457–88), the format of these ostraca are variegated, presenting quite a few patterns. They generally include a regnal date, the name of the individual(s) paying, the person(s) who receives the payment, and the amount of payment in goods. Occasionally a toponym is included as well as patronyms and/or familial/clan/tribal associations.

The ethnic breakdown reflected by the ostraca reveals a mixed population within Late Persian period Idumaea. The published names mentioned above were used for a statistical analysis (Kloner and Stern 2007: 141–43) that yielded the following percentages: approximately 32 per cent Arab names, 27 per cent Idumaean names, 25 per cent Western Semitic names, 10 per cent Judahite names, and 5 per cent Phoenician names were identified (the remaining 1 per cent represents smaller ethnicities). The ethnic breakdown of the names from ostraca found at Maresha is similar to the above general breakdown; even though the present author believes that Idumaeans formed the largest ethnic group at Maresha, because at least some Idumaeans also used Arabic and Western Semitic names (for the findings at Maresha, see also Eshel 2007, 145–56). It is clear that the Idumaeans used Aramaic as the language of daily life in the fifth and fourth centuries BCE. We have clear evidence and findings for the continuing use of Aramaic among the Idumaeans residing at Maresha in the third and second centuries BCE as well (Eshel and Kloner 1996; Eshel, Puech and Kloner 2007: 39–62).

Beginning at the very start of the third century BCE, possibly even the end of the fourth century BCE, we see evidence for the use of the Greek language (alongside Aramaic) and Greek art (as well as local Idumaean art) by the local population of Idumaea.

During the third century BCE Maresha (Marissa) was under Ptolemaic rule and became the main city of Idumaea. Coins and tombs provide clear evidence for Greek and Ptolemaic influences at Maresha and Kh. Za'aquqa from the end of the fourth century and beginning of the third century BCE. These two sites will represent the appearance of Greek language, customs and art in Idumaea.

Of the 950 coins found at Maresha, 135 are Ptolemaic (only two were pre-Ptolemaic). Of these, 116 coins were dated from Ptolemy I (305–283 BCE) to Ptolemy VIII (170–117 BCE). Of these, 12 were from Ptolemy I Soter (10.35 per cent of the total) and 78 were from Ptolemy II Philadelphus (67.25 per cent of the total). These coins are clear evidence that in the third century BCE the local population of Maresha used Ptolemaic coins and may also indicate that almost all of their trade was conducted with Egypt and Egyptian-dominated lands.

The burial caves of Hellenistic Maresha form a ring around and outside the city limits of the Lower City (Kloner 2003b: 21–30 and extensive bibliography there). The tombs (especially Painted Tomb I [T551]) contain two types of inscriptions: the first are single words identifying painted animals and other objects, as well as names of the deceased, a typical Hellenistic practice; and the second are longer inscriptions referring to the deceased in the tomb. All the inscriptions in the burial chambers were written in Greek, none in Aramaic. This is one of the first questions the author would like to explore: why did the local population (including Idumaeans) choose to use Greek rather than Aramaic for their burial inscriptions? The general assumption until now has been that the population of Maresha included Phoenicians, and for this reason Greek was used, but this does not answer the question of why no Aramaic inscription has yet been found in the burial tombs.

Two of the burial caves (Tomb I [T551] and Tomb II (T552]), published at the beginning of the twentieth century by Peters and Thiersch (1905), and discussed by Kloner (2003b: 21–27 and bibliography there) contained clear evidence of Greek sepulchral art, including gabled *loculi* and other architectural details and murals.

The dates mentioned in the tombs are from the Seleucid period (196–110 BCE) and years one to five in a regnal era. The suggestion put forward by Peters and Thiersch (1905: 76–80) that the years one to five refer to a local era at Maresha is unacceptable. According to Rappaport, the dating would seem rather to be Ptolemaic, in which regnal years are counted (Oren and Rappaport 1984: 148). Ptolemy V Epiphanes ruled in Egypt between 204 BCE and 180 BCE, but his control over Palestine ended with the fifth Syrian war in ca. 200 BCE. The years would cover his rule in Palestine, and no later dates are to be expected. The year Z (=7) was discovered in an inscription in another tomb (T500) and should be attributed to an earlier Ptolemaic king. The dates of Ptolemy V's reign are followed in the Maresha inscriptions by dates according to the Seleucid era, of which the earliest is year IZP, i.e. 196 BCE. Thus a sequence of dates from the Ptolemaic to the Seleucid periods are found at Maresha. According to Oren and Rappaport it becomes clear that Tomb I began to be used in the first half of the third century BCE, since the latest internments were from the year B (203/2 BCE) and year E (200/199 BCE).

The burial caves at Maresha are similar to ones at Alexandria from the time of the Ptolemaic dynasty of the early Hellenistic period. The closest parallel to Tomb I and Tomb II is found at Shatby, Alexandria. The gabled *kokh*, characteristic of almost all the Maresha tombs appears in Hypogeum A at Shatby, dated to 280–250 BCE. It has been suggested (Tal 2003, 288–307) that the gabled *kokh* originated in local customs or in Phoenicia, but this suggestion is not accepted by the author, who believes that these gabled *kokhim* arranged in rectangular halls are another example of Alexandrian influence on Maresha in particular and Idumaea in general. The wall paintings in the Maresha tombs are mainly characterized by Greek sepulchral elements: eagles, the flute and harp players, *Kerberos*, the cock and the amphorae and possibly the rider. The animal frieze in Tomb I is influenced by Ptolemaic menagerie drawings such as those known from Hellenistic Alexandria and is a unique document of its kind in the Hellenistic world (Erlich 2009: 61–85; Kloner 2010).

Another burial cave (T561) was discovered intact and undisturbed. The gabled *kokhim* were sealed with masonry and contained primary burials; only *Kokh* 3 contained collected bones (Kloner 2003b: 26–7). Ten pieces of pottery were found in the tomb, which allowed us to date it to the first half of the third century BCE.

More evidence of a completely Hellenized population, from a village or farmhouse and not a main economical centre, is found in a burial tomb at Khirbet Za'aquqa, about 6 km east of Marissa (Kloner, Regev and Rappaport 1992). Approximately 20 separate graffiti were found in this large *loculus* cave, of which 16 were read and published. These contained 33 personal Greek names and indications of kinship, as well as one date (the twelfth regnal year of Ptolemy II Philadelphus, corresponding to 272/1 BCE), all of them written in Greek. The *loculi*, larger than those in the contemporary cemetery at Marissa, appear to have been intended to accommodate wooden coffins. Numerous inscriptions and graffiti were incised on the cave walls, including human portraits, architectural representations and a boat. The reading of the better preserved inscriptions follows:

1.   Year 12. Of Boutas son of Demophilos.
2a. Year 12. Of B . . . / . . . / son of . . .
3.   Diodotos son of Demophilos.
4a. And of Rhodion, daughter of Demophilos.
4b. Of Bryon son of B . . .
5a. Of Demophilos son of Bryon.
5b. And of Rhodion daughter of Demophilos.
6.   Of Botrichos and of Dorotheos his father.
7a. Of Athenion daughter of Demophilos.
8.   Of Athenion.
9a. Of Athenion daughter of Demophilos.
9b. Of the father of everyone.
9c. Of Demophilos, the father of everyone.
10   Of Nikobos son of Lys[imachos].
11   Of Botrichos son of Botrichos.
12   And the son of Dorotheos.
13a. Baukis.
14. Of Philoklea wife of Dorotheos.
15a. Of Demophilos son of Dorotheos.
15b. Of Hegesias and/Byron (his/the) son/ of Hermias' wife.
16. Of Byron Geonios (?)/ of Hedylion.

The onomasticon is purely Greek with no identifiable regional character-istics like Idumaeans, Arabs or Judahite names, and may be ascribed to Greek settlers who arrived in the early Hellenistic period – a date sup-ported by the material culture remains found in the tomb. During the three or four generations the tomb was in use, there is no sign of intermingling with local Idumaeans or other Semitic groups.

At the beginning of the third century BCE the Greek language had become widely used among the local populations of Idumaea, as testified by the names inscribed in the tombs of Marissa and Za'aquqa. Greek presumably reached Marissa directly from Alexandria, and it is amazing how quickly it became used in the daily life of Idumaea.

7

JERUSALEM BETWEEN TWO PERIODS OF GREATNESS:
THE SIZE AND STATUS OF THE CITY IN THE BABYLONIAN,
PERSIAN AND EARLY HELLENISTIC PERIODS

Oded Lipschits[1]
Institute of Archaeology
Tel Aviv University

The history of Jerusalem between 586 and 167 BCE is an 'interlude' between two periods of greatness and political independence: the end of the first temple period on the one hand and the period of the Hasmoneans on the other. Between these two periods Jerusalem was a very small city and Judah was a small province under the rule of great empires.

According to both biblical and archaeological evidence, Jerusalem was destroyed in 586 BCE and left deserted by the Babylonians for a period of nearly 50 years (Lipschits 2005: 210–18, with further literature). Biblical accounts assert that the temple in Jerusalem was rebuilt at the beginning of the Persian period. During this period, the city once again became the centre of the Judahite cult. According to an account in Nehemiah, the fortifications of Jerusalem were rebuilt in the middle of the fifth century BCE. As a result, Jerusalem became a *Bîrāh*, replacing Mizpah, which had served as the capital of the newly established province of Yehud for 141 years, from 586 BCE (Lipschits 2001a), through the Neo-Babylonian period (Lemaire 2003: 292), until the time of Nehemiah (445 BCE, Blenkinsopp 1998: 42, n. 48; *cf.* Lemaire 1990: 39–40; 2003: 292).[2] The available archaeological data for the Persian period that might

---

1   *Author Note*: This paper is a summary of ten years of research on Jerusalem between the seventh and fourth centuries BCE (Lipschits 1999a; 2001a; 2001b; 2003; 2005: 206–71; 2006; 2009; Lipschits and Vanderhooft 2007a; 2007b). A comprehensive methodological discussion and a detailed archaeological survey concerning Persian period finds in Jerusalem were published in Lipschits 2009.

2   On the word *Bîrāh* and its optional interpretations, see: Grabbe 2009: 133–34, who suggested the option (p. 135) that Jerusalem became the central city of the province later than the time of Nehemiah.

corroborate this biblical evidence is minimal, and scholars have assumed that the city did not become a large and important urban and administrative centre before the middle of the second century BCE.

The aim of this paper is to present the archaeological material from Jerusalem, dating between these two periods of greatness, and to consider its size and status in the sixth century BCE ('the period of the Babylonian Exile'), in the fifth to fourth centuries BCE ('the period of the return' and the time when Judah was a Persian province), and to add some observations regarding the history of the city in the Early Hellenistic period (third century BCE).

Jerusalem in the Babylonian, Persian and early Hellenistic periods – Some Methodological Notes[3]

During the late eighth and seventh, as well as during the second century BCE, the built-up area of Jerusalem expanded to the Western Hill of Jerusalem (the area of the modern-day Jewish and Armenian Quarters and the so-called Mount Zion) and was enclosed by strong fortifications. The Southeastern Hill (the 'City of David') was rebuilt and fortified as well. These two periods, together with the later Herodian period, became the most defined and easily recognizable in the historical and archaeological research of Jerusalem in the First and Second Temple Periods. In contrast, not many building remains from the intervening period, i.e. the Babylonian, Persian and early Hellenistic periods, have been uncovered in Jerusalem. It is not a unique phenomenon to Jerusalem, but a well-known phenomenon in Judah and Samaria. Under the Assyrian, Babylonian and Persian rule, there was a marked process of attenuation in urban life in Judah (Lipschits 2006: 26–30, with further literature). No new cities were built, and the administrative and urban centres that survived the catastrophes of those periods were small and weak compared to their late eighth to seventh century or second century BCE counterparts. However, this scarcity of building remains from the Persian and Early Hellenistic periods does not fully reflect the actual, admittedly poor, situation at that time. Rather, it is the outcome of incomplete archaeological data (Stern 2001: 461–62), especially in the case of Jerusalem (Lipschits 2009).

Contrary to views that take the negative finds, especially in Jerusalem, as reflecting the actual situation in the city ('the negative is as important as the positive', Finkelstein 2008: 505), I have suggested that the Persian

---

3 For a detailed discussion on the methodological subject of the finds in Jerusalem from the Persian and Early Hellenistic periods see: Lipschits 2009.

and early Hellenistic period occupation levels, which were not as strong, imposing and big as in the glorious periods of independence before and after them, were severely damaged by intensive building activities conducted in the late Hellenistic, Roman, Byzantine and even later periods (Lipschits 2009). The situation in Jerusalem is not unique or exceptional, especially when dealing with hilltop sites, but it is much more dramatic because of the scope and grandeur of the subsequent building efforts, as well as the frequent destruction of the site. The religious, cultic and political status of Jerusalem probably motivated not only frequent political upheavals and destruction, but also a desire to remove previous political and religious structures, and to reshape the city. It seems that the main destructive force in Jerusalem is the efforts of people in later periods to build new buildings and leave their own impression in the city. Additionally, the topographical nature of the Southeastern Hill, which is very steep and narrow at the top, requires that buildings, especially the more prominent ones, be built on bedrock. This may explain why the remains from the intervening sixth to third centuries BCE were discovered mainly in 'pockets' between the late complexes, or in the dumps down in the valleys to the east and to the west of the hill. When discussing the meaning of the archaeological remains dated to the Babylonian, Persian and early Hellenistic periods discovered in the city, one should be very careful about concluding that the city was empty or nearly empty throughout these periods. In this case, it is more difficult to assert that the absence of finds means that there was nothing there; explanations regarding the negative finds must be taken seriously.

Jerusalem in the 'Exilic' Period – Between Destruction and Restoration

The Assyrian's conquest of the Levant during the last third of the eighth century BCE caused heavy destructions upon most of the urban centres and a deportation of large parts of the population. We may assume that the Assyrian policy was to retain fortifications only in provincial capitals (Stern 2001: 50) and to build forts and Assyrian economic and military centres in strategic places all over the country (Lipschits 2006: 19–21). Most of the major towns were abandoned or only poorly rebuilt and most of the population in the Assyrian provinces, especially in the interior areas, used to live in farms and villages; there was a marked decline in the urban life.

The geopolitical and administrative character of the Levant did not change under Egyptian rule, during the last third of the seventh century BCE (Lipschits 2005: 31–5; 2006: 21–2), nor during the beginning of Babylonian rule which started with the military campaign conducted by

Nebuchadrezzar in ïattu-Land between June 604 and January/February 603 BCE (Lipschits 2005: 37–42). Besides Ekron and Ashkelon, there is no reason to ascribe any other destruction to the Babylonian army during the first years of the Babylonian rule in Palestine: most of the country was arranged in a line of provinces that dated back to the Assyrian period. It seems that the Egyptian retreat left the country unopposed to the rule of Nebuchadrezzar.

The Babylonian policy in the region did not change even following Nebuchadrezzar's failed attempt to conquer Egypt, and the subsequent temporary weakening of Babylonian rule in the region (Lipschits 1999: 472–80; 2005: 49–52). However, the continued instability during the days of Psammetichus II (595–589 BCE), even more during the first years of Hophra (589–570 BCE), and the increasing threat by Egypt over the Babylonian rule in this region, caused Nebuchadrezzar to modify his policy (589 BCE): during the next years he conquered the small vassal kingdoms that remained close to the border with Egypt, annexed them and turned them into provinces (Lipschits 1998: 482–87; 2005: 62–8).[4]

The 586 BCE destruction of Jerusalem is one of the prominent archaeological finds to appear in the many years of excavations in the different parts of it. The excavations led by Avigad in the Jewish Quarter from 1969 to 1978 disclosed, adjacent to the late Iron age tower, the remains of a fire, and Scythian bronze triple-winged arrowheads (Avigad 1980: 52–4). In the excavations conducted by Kenyon on the eastern slope of the City of David in the 1960s, evidence was found of destruction of the wall from the end of the Iron age (phase 9) (Kenyon 1974: 170–71; Franken and Steiner 1990: 57). Excavations led by Yigal Shiloh in the City of David between 1978 and 1982 produced evidence of the destruction of all the buildings (including the wall) and of a fierce fire that sealed stratum X in areas D, E, and G (Shiloh 1984: 14, 18–19, 29). Remains of the Babylonian destruction were also found in excavations in the Citadel (Johns 1950: 130, Fig. 7, No. 1; Geva 1983: 56–8), and in part of the structures excavated by Eilat Mazar in the Ophel (Mazar 1993: 25–32).

The finds of the archaeological survey within the confines of the city of Jerusalem and its environs indicate the force of the destruction and the

---

4 Judah was the first goal of the Babylonians. Afterwards, apparently in 585 BCE, they attacked Tyre and Sidon, putting a closure on Tyre that lasted for 13 years (until 572 BCE) (Katzenstein 1973: 330; 1994: 186; Weisman 1991: 235; Redford 1992: 465–66; Vanderhooft 1999: 100–102). Apparently during the years of siege against Tyre, the Babylonians also attacked Ammon and Moab (Lipschits 2004), and established their rule also over Gaza, Arwad and Ashdod. One may accept the idea, that the successful takeover of north Arabia by Nabunidus and his move to Tema (553–543 BCE) caused the disappearance of the kingdom of Edom and probably the integration of its territory within greater Arabia (Lemaire 2003: 290, and see also Briant 2002: 45).

degree of demographic decline in and around the city (Lipschits 2003: 326–34; 2005: 210–18). Even at the zenith of the Persian period the settlement in Jerusalem was limited to a narrow extension of the historic City of David; settlement in the city and its surroundings amounted to about 15 per cent of what it had been on the eve of the destruction. The slight continuity reflected in the settlement patterns in this area calls for the assumption that previously, during the sixth century BCE, the condition of settlement and demography had been even worse (Lipschits 2003: 330–32; 2005: 215–18). The conclusion is that Jerusalem and its environs took a heavy blow from the Babylonians at the beginning of the sixth century BCE, and they were almost entirely depleted of their inhabitants.

The city remained desolate and deserted throughout the next 50 years (Lipschits 1999: 2001a: 129–42; 2005: 215–18). The laments that 'the roads to Zion mourn, for none come to the appointed feasts' (Lam. 1.4) and 'all who pass along the way clap their hands at you; they hiss and wag their heads at the daughter of Jerusalem: "Is this the city which was called the perfection of beauty, the joy of all the earth?"' (Lam. 2.15) faithfully reflect this historical reality. Nor is Jerusalem mentioned in the account of the rule of Gedaliah at Mizpah (2 Kings 25.22-26; Jer. 40.7–41.18) (Lipschits 2005: 304–47), and the events described encircle the city to the north (Mizpah and Gibeon) and to the south (around Bethlehem). In light of this, and in light of the archaeological data, it may be assumed that the systematic acts of destruction by Nebuzaradan, about four weeks after the conquest of the city, were accompanied by political instructions that created this situation and made it permanent (Cogan and Tadmor 1988: 319). This was the sight that met the earliest Returners to Zion (compare Zech. 1.12; 2.5-9), as well as the later (compare Neh. 2. 13-17; 7.6).

No information exists on events in Jerusalem between the time immediately after the destruction and the restoration period. Nevertheless, the perception that the status of ritual in Jerusalem was a result of Babylonian policy requires the assumption that any change in this status would have to be connected with a change in policy.

The fate of Jerusalem was not exceptional. Unlike the fate of the political entities along the Phoenician coast, the consequence of the new Babylonian policy was destructive of the southern part of Palestine as well as of the Transjordanian kingdoms.[5] In all this area, Nebuchadrezzar

---

5   The Babylonians evinced a different attitude towards the kingdoms of Philistia and those on the Phoenician coast. The former were conquered and turned into Babylonian provinces. Although the fate of the latter is unclear, it appears that during most years of Babylonian rule, certainly during the Persian period, they were ruled by kings (Katzenstein 1994: 46–8). For an explanation for this different attitude, see Oppenheim 1967; Brown 1969: 101; Katzenstein 1994: 48; Lipschits 2006: 26–9.

created a buffer zone between Babylon and Egypt that consisted of devastated, diminished provinces (Lipschits 2006: 22–4). There is no evidence that the Babylonians invested any kind of effort in economic development in this region, and it seems that Nebuchadrezzar used the destruction of the region as a lever for rebuilding those parts of Babylonia that had been damaged during the long years of war, devastation and deportation caused by the Assyrians.[6]

Jerusalem in the Persian Period: The Geopolitical Background

During the long years of the Persian rule in Palestine many geopolitical changes and administrative reorganizations were made, especially along the coast, but also in the hill country and in the southern areas of Cis- and Transjordan. The main evidence for this can be found in the rich and big urban and commercial centres that were established at the very beginning of the Achaemenid period along the Mediterranean coast, most of them well built and planned, some according to the Hippodamian plan (Kenyon 1960: 311–12; Stern 1990; 2001: 380–401; 461–64; Lipschits 2003: 347; 2006: 34).[7] In contrast with the rich and well-developed cities along the coast, not many Persian period building-remains have been uncovered within the borders of the province of Yehud, as well as within the borders of the province of Samaria (Lipschits 2001b; 2005: 214–16; 2006: 29–34). This settlement pattern is a continuation of the process that began during the Babylonian period, after the harsh blow the Babylonians dealt to the small kingdoms in the hill country west and east of the Jordan. Neither the Babylonians, nor the Persians had any interest in encouraging and developing urban centres in the rural hilly regions on both sides of the Jordan. The Achaemenids, like the Babylonians, were interested in the continued

6 Total devastation of the southern part of Palestine was, however, against Babylonian interests, and the rural settlements all over the land continued to exist, even if on a much smaller scale (Lipschits 2004: 42–3; 2005: 212–61; 2006: 29–30). Since the Babylonians did not have any direct policy of developing and protecting such areas, especially in the peripheral regions of the south, many changes occurred there, apparently as a side effect of the collapse of the central systems and the infiltration of semi-nomadic groups (Lipschits 2005: 140–47; 227–40).

7 The Achaemenid regime had governmental, military and economic interests in basing its rule along the Mediterranean coast, stabilizing the political situation in this area and encouraging the maritime and continental trade. One of the major goals of the Persians was to secure the Via-Maris, as well as the roads in southern Palestine, as part of the military, administrative and economic effort to keep the way to Egypt open (Eph'al 1998: 117; Stern 2001: 371). Another interest was to establish a strong political, military and economic coalition against the Greeks. From the economic point of view, the Persian regime tried to develop and encourage the maritime trade, dominated by the Phoenicians (Briant 2002: 383, 489–90).

existence of the rural settlement in the hill country. It was an important source for agricultural supply, which was probably collected as tax. They had no interest in establishing urban centres in the hill country and in creating new social, political and economical local power structures.

Persian Period and Early Hellenistic Finds in the Western Hill of Jerusalem

Only a few pottery sherds and other small finds from the Persian Period have been found in the many excavations conducted in the Western Hill of Jerusalem. In most cases, these finds were excavated in landfills from the Late Hellenistic and especially from the Roman period and with no clear stratigraphic context.[8] The unavoidable conclusion is that throughout the Persian and early Hellenistic periods, the Western Hill was entirely abandoned, and the area was only first resettled in the second century BCE.[9] This fact stands in agreement with the finds of *Yehud* stamp impressions, since according to the new typology developed by Vanderhooft and Lipschits (2007), no stamp impressions belonging to the early (late sixth and fifth century BCE) or middle types (fourth and third centuries BCE) were discovered in any of the excavated areas outside the limits of the City of David (Lipschits and Vanderhooft 2007a: 108–12). All the stamp impressions discovered on the Western Hill belong to the two late types (dated to the second century BCE, maybe even to the middle or second half of this century), and some of them came from clear Hasmonaean archaeological contexts, in some cases together with *yršlm* stamp impressions and other material dated to this period (Geva 2007a; Lipschits and Vanderhooft, 2007a: 111–12).[10]

---

8   For a detailed discussion of all Persian period archaeological finds from the Western Hill, see: Lipschits 2009.

9   This is the common view among scholars, and see, e.g., Kenyon 1974: 188–255; Tsafrir 1977: 36; Avigad 1983: 61–3; Geva 1983; 1994; 2000a: 24; 2000b: 158; 2003a: 113–14; 2003b: 524–26; Geva and Reich 2000: 42; Geva and Avigad 2000b: 218; Shiloh 1984: 23; Tushingham 1985: 85; Broshi and Gibson 1994; Chen, Margalit and Pixner 1994; Sivan and Solar 1994; Finkielstejn 1999: 28*; Lipschits 2005: 212–13; Lipschits and Vanderhooft 2007a: 108–12.

10   See, for example, the six stamp impressions discovered in the Kenyon–Tushingham excavations in the Armenian Garden; all were excavated in a fill connected to the podium of Herod's palace, which includes a mixture of pottery from the First and Second Temple periods (Tushingham 1985: 37, Fig. 17: 18–23). Also in Amiran and Eitan's excavations in the Citadel a stamp impression was discovered in the fill of the podium of Herod's palace (Amiran and Eitan 1970: 13).

Persian Period Finds in the City of David

The northern part of the City of David, just below the Ophel, contains a significant number of Persian period finds. The fills in which these finds were found seem to have originated from the Ophel, just above this area to the north, and were laid before the late Hellenistic and Roman periods (Lipschits 2009).

The most important area where finds from the Persian period were discovered is the one excavated by Macalister and Duncan (1923–25), at the northern area of the City of David and just below the Ophel (Macalister and Duncan 1926: 49–51; Duncan 1931: 143).[11] Persian period finds were discovered a bit to the north of the Macalister and Duncan's Persian tower where Kenyon excavated her square AXVIII, and identified there part of 'Nehemiah's wall'.[12] Shiloh continued the excavations in this area as part of his Area G,[13] and Eilat Mazar renewed the excavations in the same area in 2005.[14] In 2007, as part of the conservation project of the Hasmonaean northern tower, Mazar excavated the landfill under the tower, and discovered the same Persian period material previously exposed by Kenyon and Shiloh.[15] The fill in this spot contains finds only from the sixth–fifth centuries BCE, which seems to indicate that it was part of the cleaning of the area above it (in the northern edge of the city of David, just under the Ophel), which in turn indicates that that area was populated in the Persian period. E. Mazar suggested dating the tower and the wall attached to it (wall 27) to the fifth century BCE and identified it as a part of Nehemiah's wall (2007a: 49–60; 2007b: 17–21; 2008: 31–37).[16]

---

11   The Persian period finds from this area include a lot of Persian period pottery sherds, as well as 54 *Yehud* and 6 lion stamp impressions.

12   Kenyon (1963: 15; 1974: 183–84, 191–92, Pl. 77; *cf.* 1966: 83–4; 1967a: 69) observed that the tower was attached to an earlier wall that was built of large stones on a rock scarp about 7–8 metres high, dated the wall to the Persian period, and assigned its construction to Nehemiah. She dated the tower as part of the Hasmonaean fortification.

13   Shiloh (1984: 20–21, and figs. 27, 28; *cf.* the photo in Mazar 2007a: 64) connected the northern tower to the first century BCE glacis that was already excavated by Kenyon. Its connection to Macalister's northern tower was well demonstrated.

14   Mazar (2007a: 49–60; 2007b: 17–21) identified Kenyon's Persian wall as part of the northern Iron Age IIA fortification of what she called 'David's Palace'.

15   According to Kenyon, this fill was connected to the tower that was built on the bedrock, and this is why she attempted to date it to the Persian period. Franken (Franken and Steiner 1990), however, presented the drawing of the cut of Kenyon's Square XVIII and demonstrated that this fill was not connected to the wall, as Macalister and Duncan had earlier presumed.

16   The date of the landfill, where there are no indications for a late Persian material (including *yehud* stamp impressions) may indicate that it was laid before the landfill above it, discovered by Macalister and Duncan, but it is certainly not sufficient grounds to date the northern tower to the fifth century BCE or identify it as part of Nehemiah's wall.

On the same line of the upper part of the City of David, but on its western slopes towards the Tyropoeon, some more Persian period finds, including one *Yehud* stamp impression, were discovered in Crowfoot and Fitzgerald's excavations (1927–28) at the 'western gate' of the City of David (Crowfoot and Fitzgerald 1929: 67). Pottery sherds dated to the Persian period, as well as another stamp impression, were excavated by Shukron and Reich, just a few metres to the north, in the Givati parking place (Shukron and Reich 2005: 8). These finds provide further evidence that the hill above this area – the Ophel and the northern part of the City of David – were settled during the Persian period.

Beside the upper part of the City of David, most of the Persian period pottery sherds and stamp impressions from the central and southern parts of the City of David were discovered in Shiloh's excavations along the eastern slope of the ridge, where three Strata were observed and dated to the period between the late sixth or early fifth and the second century BCE: Stratum 9 was dated to the Persian period, Stratum 8 to the early Hellenistic period, and Stratum 7 to the second century BCE (Hasmonaean Period). Stratum 9, however, does not appear in all the excavated areas (Shiloh 1984: 4, Table 2). Finds attributed to this Stratum appeared in Area D1 (Ariel, Hirschfeld and Savir 2000: 59–62; De Groot 2001: 77), Area D2 (Shiloh 1984: 8–9),[17] and in Area G (Shiloh 1984: 20).[18] Shiloh's finds from the Persian period were also partially represented in Area E1 (Shiloh 1984: 14; De Groot 2001: 77), and included some chalk vessels (Cahill 1992: 191–98, fig. 14). Sherds dated to the Persian period were discovered in the fills in Area H, to the east of the Siloam Pool, on the eastern slopes of Mount Zion (De Groot and Michaeli 1992: 50–51; De Groot 2001: 78).[19] Persian period sherds and seal impressions were discovered in Reich and Shukron's Areas A and B, above the Kidron Valley, ca. 200–250 m south of the Gihon spring (Reich and Shukron 1998: 2007). The finds from these areas probably come from the settlement on the ridge above.

The most significant finds from the Persian period were excavated in Area E, where three different stages from the Persian period Stratum 9 were distinguished (De Groot 2001: 77, and *cf.* Cahill 1992: 191–98, fig. 14). The early stage (9C) is a reuse of a large Iron Age building that was destroyed along with the rest of the city in 586 BCE, and should be dated to

17   The finds assigned to Stratum 9 at Area D2 include a Lycian coin dated to 500–440 BCE (Ariel 1990: C1) and an ostracon (Naveh 2000: IN 16).

18   In this area Kenyon also discovered Persian period finds (dated by her to the fifth–third centuries BCE) in the fill adjacent to the Northern tower, and this is the reason why she assigned this wall to Nehemiah's fortifications. See, however, the critique of De Groot 2001: 78.

19   De Groot assumed that the finds from the Persian period are a proof that the Siloam pool was fortified during the Persian period.

the end of the sixth and first half of the fifth century BCE (De Groot 2001: 77–8). A sloping level of quarrying refuse (composed of limestone chips with very little interspersed earth or pottery) was ascribed to the second stage (9b), and can be dated to the reconstruction of the city undertaken by Nehemiah in the middle of the fifth century BCE (De Groot 2001: 78; 2005: 82).[20] The Persian period date, the location of the works, and the long line along the eastern slope of the ridge, are all indications of the 'missing' wall of the Persian period.[21] A few terrace walls and some floors with ovens were attributed to the third stage (9C) of the late Persian period (Ariel, Hirschfeld and Savir 2000: 59).

These Persian period finds may be combined with the observations of Ariel and Shoham (2000: 138) and Reich and Shukron (2007: 64) concerning the location of the *Yehud* stamp impressions,[22] and the conclusion that Persian and early Hellenistic settlement was restricted to the top of the ridge, to the south of Area G (*cf.* Finkelstein 2008: 506). The problem with this assumption is that it relates to the area down the slopes of the settled area on the ridge, where above the Gihon spring and Area G of Shiloh's excavations, there were many more Persian period sherds and *Yehud* stamp impressions that were excavated by Macalister and Duncan (1926: 49–51; *cf.* Cook 1925). The actual significance of the distribution of the Persian period finds in this area is that the Gihon spring was not in use since the water flow in Hezekiah tunnel to the southern part of the City of David, and the spring itself, was blocked and covered, far below the limits of the city. The finds on the ridge of the City of David, as well as on the slopes

20   The same level of quarrying refuse appeared also in Area D1, 500 m to the south, and was dated to Stratum 9 (Ariel, Hirschfeld and Savir 2000: 59, and *cf.* Shiloh 1984: 7; De Groot 2001: 78). In some cases the levels of those chips were separated by thin layers of earth, without any coherent pattern. The quarrying activities above the eastern slope were documented in the excavations by Bliss and Dickie (1898), Weill (1920) and in Area K of the City of David excavations (Ariel and Magness 1992). It should be emphasized that the existence of such levels of quarrying refuse is an indication that the areas where it was discovered were outside the limits of the city (Ariel, Hirschfeld and Savir 2000: 59), but it also indicates that immediately above this area significant construction activity was undertaken.

21   It can be assumed that the heavy destruction of the city in 586 BCE forced the late sixth and fifth century BCE settlers to move the wall to the upper part of the ridge, where there was a need for preparation-quarrying activity.

22   Most of the *Yehud* stamp impressions from Shiloh's excavations originated in Areas B, D and E. Of the eight stamp impressions discovered by Reich and Shukron on the eastern slope of the Southeastern Hill of Jerusalem, five originated in Area A, located in the Kidron Valley, some 200–250 metres south of the Gihon spring, two in Area B, at the mid-slope of the hill, above Area A, and next to Shiloh's Areas B and D1. Only one *Yehud* stamp impression was retrieved in the areas excavated around the Gihon spring, where vast amounts of late Second Temple debris were excavated above a huge fill containing late Iron Age II pottery.

of the hill are indications for a poor but existing settlement all along the narrow ridge of the City of David (Lipschits 2009).

Early Hellenistic Finds in the City of David, Yehud *Stamp Impressions, and Settlement Processes in Jerusalem During the Fourth–Third Centuries* BCE

The Early Hellenistic Stratum 8 is fully represented in the City of David only in Area E2 (Shiloh 1984: 4, Table 2 and *cf.* to p. 10; De Groot 2004: 67–9). This Stratum is also partially represented in Areas E1 (Shiloh 1984: 14–15) and E3 (*cf.* to pp. 10–11), and scarcely represented in Areas D1 (*cf.* to pp. 7–8) and D2 (*cf.* to pp. 8–9). In this case, too, the finds that can safely be attributed to this Stratum are meagre, and mainly consist of three *columbaria* (De Groot 2004: 67–8; 2005: 84) and a structure (in Area E1) that yielded a rich corpus of pottery dating to the third century BCE.[23] The excavators did not find *Yehud* stamp impressions of the late types, dated to the second century BCE, in either of these strata (Stratum 9 and 8). Most of the late types were discovered in Stratum 7 (Ariel and Shoham 2000, Table 1, and see also Reich 2003: 258–59 and Tables 7.1–7.2).

The 27 *Yehud* stamp impressions discovered in different areas of the Western Hill are more than 30 per cent of the total finds of the late group of *Yehud* stamp impressions discovered in Jerusalem (59 more stamp impressions from the late group were discovered in the City of David). This proportion is much higher than the Rhodian stamp impressions, of which only 5 per cent of the finds were discovered on the Western Hill, and most of the rest were discovered in the City of David. The difference in the proportion of the two types of stamp impressions discovered on the Western Hill and in the City of David probably does not point to different population groups in these areas before the destruction of the Akra in 141 BCE by Simeon (*1 Macc.* 13.49-51), as assumed by Finkielsztejn (1999: 28*–31* with further literature, and see against this idea Ariel 1990: 25; 2000: 269, 276–80). Instead, this fact likely indicates that the settlement on the Western Hill did not start before the beginning of the second half of the second century BCE (Geva 1985: 30; Lipschits and Vanderhooft 2007a: 112), a period in which there was a sharp decline in the importation of wine from Rhodes (Ariel 1990: 21–5; 2000: 267–69). We can also assume that the settlement process of the Western Hill was a much slower and

---

23   This is the only pottery assemblage of a pre-Hasmonaean phase in the City of David (Shiloh 1984: 15).

gradual process than described by some scholars (see, e.g., Finkielsztejn 1999: 28*).

Archaeological Finds, Demographical Processes and the History of Jerusalem between the Sixth and Second Centuries BCE

The archaeological finds from Jerusalem can only be interpreted as evidence of a meagre settlement, confined to the City of David, between the late Iron Age and the Hasmonaean period (early sixth to second centuries BCE).[24] The settlement in the Persian and early Hellenistic periods concentrated on the upper part of the ridge, in a very narrow north to south strip, with an average width of no more than 80–100 metres, and along the edge of the ridge, about 350 metres from north to south (Lipschits 2009). The settlement on the ridge included a settled area of about 28–30 dunams. However, since the area in the northern part of the ridge of the City of David is the richest with Persian period finds (with more than 75 per cent of the finds from this period), and the finds in this area were mostly discovered in earth fills that probably originated from the area above it; namely, the Ophel hill, this area should be considered as an important settled area during this period (Lipschits 2009). The importance of the 20 dunams of the Ophel hill, between the ascension of the hill towards the Temple Mount and the northern part of the City of David, as the main built-up area in the Persian period, was never discussed in the archaeological and historical research. However, this is the only flat, easy to settle area in the Persian and Early Hellenistic Jerusalem. Its closeness to the Temple Mount on the one hand and the easy option to fortify it on the other, made it the preferable option for settlement in the Persian and Early Hellenistic periods.

The settled area of Jerusalem during the Persian and Early Hellenistic periods included an area of about 50 dunams. The population of Jerusalem did not include more than between 1,000 and 1,250 people.[25] In light of this clear archaeological evidence, we should interpret the 'Return to

---

24   This is an observation shared by all scholars dealing with Persian period finds in Jerusalem (Kenyon 1963: 15; Carter 1999: 285; Eshel 2000: 341; Lipschits 2003: 330–31; 2005: 212; 2006: 32; Lipschits and Vanderhooft 2007a; Schniedewind 2003; 2004: 165–78; Grabbe 2004: 25; Geva 2007b: 56–7; Finkelstein 2008: 501–04).

25   This population estimate is very close to the accepted estimations in research in the last years – these of Carter (1999: 288) and Lipschits (2005: 271; 2006: 32) – of about 60 dunams and 1250–1500 people respectively, or that of Geva (2007b: 56–7) of a settled area of 60 dunams and population estimate of about 1000 people.

Zion' as a slow and gradual process, that did not leave its imprint on the archaeological data. Even if a real change in the history of Jerusalem occurred in the middle of the fifth century BCE, with the rebuild of the fortifications of Jerusalem, with all its dramatic implication on its status, it did not change the actual demographic situation of the city. Jerusalem did not become a real urban centre until the Hellenistic period.

8

THE SAMARITANS IN TRANSITION FROM THE PERSIAN TO THE GREEK PERIOD

Menachem Mor
University of Haifa

The conquest of the Land of Israel by Alexander the Great in 332 BCE constitutes on one hand the termination of a period in which the country was ruled by Eastern kingdoms such as Aram, Assyria, Babylon and Persia, and on the other hand the beginning of a new period in which the conquerors were from the West, such as the Macedonians with whom the Hellenistic period was to begin and extend its influence over the whole area under conquest for hundreds of years.

I shall examine and summarize how the Samaritans managed to cope with the changes that occurred in the region during the years of transition from Persian to Hellenistic rule. The discussion will cover the years from the beginning of the twilight period of Persian rule over the Land of Israel (350 BCE) up to the Seleucid conquest in 200 BCE by Antiochus III, known as Antiochus the Great.

The discussion will focus upon four areas in which the Samaritans were influenced during the transition period, and will examine how the Samaritans dealt with the effects of this transition period between Persian rule and Greek–Hellenistic rule:
1. The building of the Samaritan temple
2. The Samaritan leadership
3. From Samaria to Shechem
4. Land disputes between Jews and Samaritans

The discussion on these four subjects will be based mainly on the testimony of Josephus Flavius, principally on his descriptions in *Jewish Antiquities*, Book XI, 302–407 which is almost the sole source for describing what occurred in the Land of Israel in the final years of Persian rule and the period of the Macedonian conquest of the East, including the provinces of Judaea and Samaria.

Questions have usually been raised as to the authenticity and credibility of Josephus as a historian in general and his descriptions in *Antiquities*, Book XI in particular. For many long years historians have doubted the credibility and historical value of his descriptions, especially those in Book XI. Their arguments were based mainly on two central claims. The first was to discredit Josephus' knowledge about Persian rule in general and his ignorance of the Persian kings in particular.[1] The second was to claims that Josephus conducted a backward projection of Jewish–Samaritan relations as they stood in his own time, such as for example the event that occurred during the days of the procurator Coponius when the Samaritans scattered human bones in the Temple precincts during the Passover festival in order to defile it (*Antiquities* XVIII, 29–30).[2]

However problematic the descriptions of Josephus for this period might be, the archaeological sources covering these years are surprisingly rich in quantity and value. For the period in question one can consult a rich variety of finds such as the papyri from Yeb (Elephantine)[3] and from Wadi ed-Daliyeh;[4] inscriptions from Delos;[5] and coins in the province of Yehud[6] and Samarin.[7] There are archaeological finds from digs in cities such as Samaria[8] and Shechem;[9] a wealthy find from Wadi Daliyeh,[10] and especially the rich finds from the excavations on Mount Gerizim.[11]

In spite of the relative wealth of archaeological finds, without the narrative of Josephus we would not know much about the period under discussion. For our purposes, the only thing in common between Josephus' account and the archaeological finds is the name of Sanballat, which is mentioned in both of them and in a biblical source. But even this fact raises difficulties. The Sanballat that is mentioned in Josephus and in the papyri is described as a governor of a province of the mid fourth century BCE, while the biblical Sanballat is of the fifth century BCE. If so, what would

---

1   See for example, Mor 2005: 48 and for a collection of articles on the general issue, see: Rodgers (ed.), 2007.

2   See Smith 1999: 244.

3   For the papyri see: Cowley 1967 [1923]; Porten and Yardeni 1986–1989; Porten, with Farber et al., 1996.

4   Gropp 2001; See the more recent publication of: Dušek 2007.

5   Bruneau 1982: 465–504; Kraabel 1984: 44. For more recent discussions on the inscription, see: White 1987: 133–60; Llewelyn 1998: 148–51, No. 12: An Association of Samaritans in Delos.

6   See the recent publication by Betlyon 2005: 47–50.

7   Meshorer and Qedar, 1991 and 1999.

8   Reisner, Fischer and Lyon 1924; Crowfoot 1957; and a review by Tal 2006: 97–9, 324.

9   Wright 1965; Campbell 1991; 2002.

10   Lapp and Lapp 1974; Leith 1997.

11   Magen, Misgav and Tsfania 2004.

we have known at all about the Samaritans in the period under discussion without the problematic descriptions of Josephus?

I have dealt with the question of the historical reliability of Josephus in my book (Mor, 2003). My main supposition on this issue is that the descriptions in *Antiquities* XI of Josephus, with all the accompanying difficulties, maintains a trustworthy historical resonance in the parts that concern the Samaritans.[12] This assumption will be implicit in dealing with the four subjects mentioned above.

1. *The Building of the Samaritan Temple*

The question regarding the building of the Samaritan temple on Mount Gerizim once again stands at the centre of a research dispute.[13] As I have already noted, the question of the temple is a complicated enigma. Researchers are in agreement that the temple was destroyed in 111 BCE during the territorial expansion of John Hyrcanus I. But agreement disappears when it comes to the question of the building date for the temple, or that it was ever built as was once suggested.

Josephus mentions the Samaritan temple a number of times. I shall focus on three of his testimonies:

Jewish Antiquities, XI, 322–325
'As Alexander received him in friendly fashion, Sanballat now felt confident about his plan and addressed him on that subject, explaining that he had a son-in-law Manasseh, who was the brother of Jaddua, the high priest of the Jews, and that there were many others of his countrymen with him who now wished to build a temple in the territory subject to him. It was also an advantage to the king, he said, that the power of the Jews should be divided in two, in order that the nation might not, in the event of revolution, be of one mind and stand together and so give trouble to the kings as formerly given to the Assyrian rulers. When therefore, Alexander gave his consent, Sanballat brought all his energy to bear and built the temple and appointed Manasseh high priest, considering this to be the greatest distinction which his daughter's descendants could have. But Sanballat died after seven months had been spent on the siege of Tyre and two on that of Gaza.'[14]

---

12   See Kasher's article in the current volume, 131–157, in which he added more credibility to *Antiquities* XI.

13   See, for example, the discussion in the Introduction, pp. 27–29.

14   All the translations of Josephus were taken from the *Loeb Classical Literature series.*

The Samaritan temple according to Josephus' description was erected with the permission and agreement of Alexander after Sanballat persuaded him of the benefits that would accrue to him by its construction.[15] Josephus dated the building of the temple to the time of Alexander's visit in the region, and the impression the reader receives from what he writes is that the building process lasted for nine months.

> *Jewish Antiquities, XIII, 255–256*:
> 'And he (John Hyrcanus) captured . . . in addition to these, Shechem and Gerizim and the Cuthaean nation, which lives near the temple built after the model of the sanctuary at Jerusalem, which Alexander permitted their governor Sanballat to built for the sake of his son-in-law Manasseh, the brother of the high priest Jaddua, as we have related before. Now it was two hundred years later that this temple was laid waste.'[16]

Josephus describes the destruction of the temple by John Hyrcanus I, and makes two chronological references. The first asserts that the temple was built with the agreement and in the time of Alexander the Great. The second notes that the temple stood for two hundred years.

> *Jewish Antiquities, XIII, 74–79*:
> 'Now there arose a quarrel between the Jews in Alexandria and the Samaritans who worshipped at the temple on Mount Gerizim, which had been built in the time of Alexander, and they disputed about their respective temples in the presence of Ptolemy (Philometer) himself, the Jews asserting that it was the temple in Jerusalem which had been built according with the laws of Moses, and the Samaritans that it was the temple on Gerizim . . .'

Josephus describes the dispute that took place in the second century BCE in Alexandria between the Jews and the Samaritans, and which was held

---

See also: Pummer 2002: 404, no. 175: George Syncellus, *Ecloga chronographica* 306. 5-6 – Mosshammer: 'Manasses the brother of Jaddus the high priest built the sanctuary of Samaria on Gerizim.'

15 See: Goldstein, 2002: 61–3. The story refers to the erection of the Temple as the story of a schism and the opposite of a story about the founding of a cult.

16 Hieronymus, *Chronicle GCS* 47.143. 14–18 (143ᵈ) – Helm, PL 27, 473–74, 158th Olympiad (148 BCE) 'With Ptolemy as judge, the Samaritans and the Jews in Alexandria argue about the honours that are to be paid to their temple by both parties, and the Jews win' (Pummer 2002: 196, No. 83).

in the presence of King Ptolemy Philometor on the question: Which of the two temples is holier?[17]

The description of the Samaritan temple by Josephus is one of the criteria for researchers dealing with the question of the reliability or unreliability of Josephus in *Antiquities* XI. Researchers rejecting the historical description of the erection of the temple as being unreliable extend their assertion to cover the whole text of *Antiquities* XI. However, anyone who rejects the temple's existence on the basis of Josephus' words cannot ignore the two pieces of evidence indicating the existence of the Samaritan temple that are independent of Josephus. The first is the two dedication inscriptions in the synagogue in Delos, and the second is the *Prayer of Joseph* from Qumran.

2.1 *The Delos Inscriptions*:
The Israelite on Delos who makes offerings to hallowed[18] Argarzein[19] (Αργαριζείν) crown with a gold crown Sarapion, son of Jason, of Knossos, for his benefactions towards the

(the) Israelites (of Delos) who make offerings to Hallowed, consecrated Argarzein

The inscriptions according to palaeographical standards were dated by Philip Bruno, the first one during the years 150–50 BCE, and the second one to the years 250–175 BCE. The earliest date for the second inscription, the mid-third century BCE, testifies to the existence of a sacred sanctuary or even a temple at this date, to which the Samaritans in Delos who called themselves 'Israelites' sent offerings.[20]

Prayer of Joseph from Qumran
10. . . . And in all this, Joseph was cast into lands he did not k[now]
11. among a foreign nation and dispersed in all the world. All their mountains were desolate of them . . . [*fools* were dwelling in their land]

---

17   Pummer 2009: 179–81; 187–96.

18   McLean 1996: 193–94. They translated this line as: The Israelite on Delos who contribute their offerings to the holy temple (of) Argarizin.

19   On the significance of the name 'Har Gerizim' as one word, see: Pummer 1987: 18–25. See also: Eshel 1991:129–34; Talmon 1997: 220–32.

20   For the translation, see: Kraabel 1984: 44; For further discussions on the inscription, see: Bruneau 1982: 465–504; White 1987: 133–60; Llewelyn, 1998: 148–51, No. 12.

12. and making for themselves a high place upon a high mountain to provoke Israel to jealousy; . . .[21]

We have here a section of a prayer dated to the second century BCE, which is directed against the Samaritans and against their temple on Mount Gerizim.

The two sources mentioned above are additional evidence that the Samaritan temple was standing at least during the second half of the third century or the second century BCE.

More than 30 years ago, long before the archaeological finds from Mount Gerizim, I had already claimed that the description of Josephus should be adopted, including the circumstances and the period in which the temple was erected. This means that the construction of the temple should be ascribed to the end of the Persian period, more precisely to the year 332 BCE, the transitional year between Persian rule and the conquest of the Land of Israel by the Macedonians. The temple stood on its site until the year 111 BCE, when it was destroyed by John Hyrcanus I during his expedition of conquest to extend the boundaries of Judaea (see above for the source).[22]

It may be assumed that, during the course of the Persian period, the requests of the Samaritans to erect a temple were rejected by the central Persian government. The involvement of the central government in the granting of permits to erect various temples in their kingdom is obvious in all the stages of constructing the Temple in Jerusalem (Ezra 1.2-6; 5.3–6.12). This also appears to be evident in the Cyrus Cylinder.

Another proof of the link between the erection of the Temple and the central government in the period under discussion can also be seen in the Letter of Yedania written in 407 BCE from which we learn about the destruction of the Jewish temple in Yeb, Egypt. The letter is a request for the restoration of the temple, and it is addressed by the leaders of Yeb to the leaders of Judaea and Samaria to intercede with the authorities for the restoration of the temple.[23]

Further evidence for the part played by the government in granting a permit for the erection of the temple is associated with the Samaritan

---

21   Translation by Schuller and Bernstein 2001: 169, 171–72; Bernstein 2003: 19–33; Knibb 1992: 164–77; Schuller 1990: 349–76; Eshel 1991: 125–29; Schuller 1992: 67–79.

22   We shall not deal here with the causes for the destruction of the temple on Mount Gerizim and of the city of Shechem. See: Schwartz 1993.

23   Cowley 1967: 30–32; Porten, with Faber et al. 1996: 90–99. 'If it please our lord, take thought of that Temple to rebuild (it) since they do not let us rebuild it . . . Let a letter be sent from you to them about the Temple of YHW the God to rebuild it in Elephantine the fortress as it was formerly built.' Reinhard Kratz has recently dealt with the temple in Yeb. See: Kratz 2006.

temple itself. Josephus knew that it was not possible to erect a temple without the consent of the king and therefore he notes: 'When, therefore, Alexander gave his consent, Sanballat brought all of his energy to bear and built the temple' (*Antiquities* XI, 324). As for the Samaritans, the opposition of the Persian government was probably due to the fact that they did not want to have another temple within the area of the Land of Israel, especially since for them there was apparently no difference between the Samaritans and the Jews.

From the description of the erection of the Samaritan temple as given by Josephus, I accept the date but reject the circumstances. The temple, in my estimation, was built without the consent of Alexander. Sanballat III took advantage of the void created in the region. This void was caused, on one hand, by the weakness of Darius III, the last Persian king, as a result of his defeat by Alexander, mainly in the Battle of Issus. On the other hand, the difficulties that Alexander was compelled to face in Tyre and Gaza disrupted his plans to reach Egypt and forced him to invest enormous efforts in besieging the city of Tyre that lasted for seven months, with another two months besieging Gaza.

The political uncertainty that prevailed in the region also found expression in the different policies conducted by the local leaders towards Darius III and Alexander. Some of the cities such as Sidon, for example, transferred their allegiance from the Persian government to Alexander and the city surrendered without a fight. Jaddua the high priest in Jerusalem continued to maintain his loyalty towards the Persian king, while for Sanballat III, the fluid situation in the region allowed him to take advantage of the political realities that prevailed there in order to erect the temple on Mount Gerizim. In my view, the construction took place in the period between the start of the siege on Tyre and the murder of Andromachus by the Samaritans, a period that lasted for less than a year. Sanballat built the temple, making it a fait accompli, in the hope that the victor in the region would accept the existence of the Samaritan temple.[24]

In 2004, Yitzhak Magen, the staff officer of archaeology of Judaea and Samaria, together with Haggai Misgav and Levana Tsfania, published a glossy edition that included all the Aramaic, Hebrew and Samaritan inscriptions from Mount Gerizim. In the introduction, Magen devoted a few pages to discount the historical value of *Antiquities* XI. I mention below three of his inferences and conclusions to demonstrate this.

An anomalous situation was thus created where the people of Judah

---

24   See the recent article by Yassif 2006. In note 10, Yassif makes reference to two comprehensive bibliographies on Alexander, one of the University of Calgary in Canada, and the other of the University of Leiden in Holland.

and Benjamin had a temple in Jerusalem and the people in Samaria had nowhere to pray because the cultic sites that Jeroboam the son of Nebat had built in Dan and Bethel were outside the territory under control of the province of Samaria, and seem to have fallen into disuse. This situation was not overlooked by Sanballat the Horonite, probably a descendant of an old Samaritan–Israelite family of ancient Israelite lineage. It is also possible that his origins were in the Hawara settlement at the foot of Mount Gerizim.

In any case, most of the ancient inscriptions should probably be ascribed to the Samaritan sanctuary of the Hellenistic period during the third and second centuries BCE. But it is also possible that some of them were from a more ancient sanctuary dating back to the fifth and fourth centuries BCE.

1. 'The many coins and pottery vessels discovered in the sacred precinct attest to the construction of the temple in the Persian period, during the 5th century BCE. The finds include pottery, as well as 68 coins from the fifth and fourth centuries BCE (preceding the arrival of Alexander the Great to the Land of Israel). The earliest coin dates from 480 BCE.'
2. 'The temple on Mt. Gerizim was thus built in the days of Sanballat the Horonite (Sanballat I) governor of Samaria in the days of Nehemiah, who arrived in the Land of Israel in 444 BCE (Neh. 2:1-10). The temple remained in use during the Ptolemaic and Seleucid periods as well, and also withstood the destruction of the city of Samaria and the construction of a Macedonian city on its ruins. If anything, these changes bolstered its status, and Mt. Gerizim became the capital of the Samaritans.'
3. 'The construction of the temple on the mount by Sanballat indicates that it was not the result of a hasty decision. The sanctity of Mt. Gerizim and the city of Shechem were deeply entrenched in the religious tradition of the north, just as Mt. Moriah was the sacred mountain of Jerusalem and Judea. According to the Samaritan tradition, Joshua built the first altar on Mt. Gerizim where he also constructed the Tabernacle . . . thus when Sanballat the Horonite decided to construct a temple for the inhabitants of the province of Samaria and thus sever ties with Judea, the choice of place was obvious: Mt. Gerizim was the sole appropriate site.'[25]

The main conclusions of Magen were that, in view of the archaeological finds, the Samaritan temple was built in the mid-fifth century BCE, in 444 BCE, when Nehemiah arrived in Jerusalem. The builder of this temple was Sanballat I, mentioned in the memoirs of Nehemiah as Sanballat the

---

25 Magen, Misgav and Tsfania 2004: 10.

Horonite.[26] The fact that it was he who had built the temple shows that the construction was not done impetuously, but with deliberate intent. The choice of Mt Gerizim and Shechem derives from the sanctity of the mountain, and in fact Mt Gerizim and Shechem are an indivisible pair just as Mt Moriah and Jerusalem.

The new date for the erection of the temple according to the estimation of Magen has raised a few questions that should be discussed in depth, which I shall do below:

1. What motivated Sanballat I to build the Samaritan temple precisely in the year 445 BCE? The reliance of Magen on the words of Nehemiah to his adversaries, to Sanballat the Horonite, Geshem the Arabian and Tobias the Ammonite, are not convincing. Nehemiah certainly rejected them and told them during his construction of the wall around Jerusalem: '. . . but you have no share or right or memorial in Jerusalem' (Neh. 2.20). But Magen's statement afterwards, that Nehemiah's reply left them without any cultic site, does not conform to the critical facts. Is this the first time they were rejected? Already in 538 BCE, when the first group of people returned to Zion, those who were called the 'opponents of Judah and Benjamin' and 'the people of the land' (Ezra 4.1-4) were rejected by the Jewish leadership with the words: 'You do not have the same purpose as we do in building a house for our God, for we alone shall build [a house] for Yahweh God of Israel' (Ezra 4.3). Moreover, where was the cultic centre for the Samaritans from 538 to 445 BCE, the year in which the temple was constructed by Sanballat I according to Magen's proposal? One can even go further and ask where they worshipped God between the year 720 when Samaria was conquered by the Assyrians and the year 445 BCE? But the main question regarding Magen's dating is whether it was at this date that the historical opportunity was created to erect the Samaritan temple.

2. Was it Artaxerxes I who granted Sanballat the permission to erect the temple on Mount Gerizim? Nehemiah needed the agreement and permit of that same king in order to go to Jerusalem and rebuild it: 'As I answered the king and if your servant has found favor in your sight, then send me to Judah, to the City of the graves of my fathers, that I may rebuild it' (Neh. 2.5).[27] The rebuilding of the Temple following the Edict of Cyrus (Ezra 1.1-4; 6.3-5) and the permit granted during

---

26   The year in which Nehemiah arrived in Jerusalem was 445 and not 444 BCE. In parenthesis, I should like to note that already in 1921, without having recourse to the archaeological findings that were made later on, Edward Meyer claimed that it was Sanballat the Horonite who had built the temple. See: Meyer 1921: 9, note 2.

27   All the translations from the books of Ezra and Nehemiah are from: Myers 1965.

the reign of Darius I (Ezra 6.6-12) clearly demonstrate that without permission of the central government it would not have been possible to erect the Temple in Jerusalem. Furthermore, there are several scholars who claim that not only would the construction of the Temple in Jerusalem have been impossible without Persian consent, but that the main reason for its erection was to satisfy the administrative requirements of the Persians.[28]

3. Why was the temple erected on Mount Gerizim? Magen was right in saying: 'Sanballat did, indeed, possess a site whose sanctity was confirmed by the Pentateuch itself, and to which not even the Judeans could object'[29]. But his claim that: 'The sanctity of Mt. Gerizim and the city of Shechem were deeply entrenched in the religious tradition of the north, just as Mt. Moriah was the sacred mountain of Jerusalem in Judea'[30] is unfounded. In the year 445 BCE it was not yet possible to pair Mount Gerizim with the city of Shechem because at that time the urban centre of the Samaritan population was in the city of Samaria and not in Shechem.

4. We shall not resume here the continuing discussion on the lists of Samaritan leaders during the Persian period, but will only note that in a review of these lists, ever since the articles by Cross and others that followed, the conclusion was that there were at least three Sanballats during the Persian period.[31] Josephus mentions at least two Sanballats. Can we assume that he confused the Sanballat of Nehemiah's time with the Sanballat of the period of Darius III and Alexander the Great?[32]

5. How and why would the extensive pottery and coins from Mount Gerizim dating to the fifth and fourth centuries BCE prior to the expedition of Alexander the Great to the Land of Israel, with the date of earliest coin being 480 BCE, constitute proof that the temple was erected during Nehemiah's time? The most that can be learnt from this is that Mount Gerizim, the 'mountain of blessing', continued to be considered for centuries as a sacred site.[33]

---

28 See Bedford 2001: 183–299. Chapter 4 is devoted to the various factors behind the erection of the Temple in Jerusalem during the reign of Darius I, and pages 185–230 are devoted to 'Temple Rebuilding as a Judean Initiative'. For the main studies of this approach, see: Meyers and Meyers, 1987 and 1993; Weinberg 1992. Following the publication of Bedford's book, see: Trotter 2000: 276–93. See also: Edelman 2005: 344–49. However, Edelman dates the building of the Samaritan temple to the days of Nehemiah.

29 Magen et al. 2004: 13*. See also: Na'aman 1993.

30 Magen et al. 2004: 10*.

31 See: Wright 1965: 257–69.

32 For latest review of these issues see: Grabbe 2004: 155–59; Dušek 2007.

33 For a detailed discussion of this issue, see: Mor, 2003: 93–4.

6. The main argument against Magen's dating of the temple to the days of Nehemiah and Sanballat I is an *argumentum e silentio*. The silence regarding the Samaritan temple in the Book of Nehemiah is a resounding example! Sanballat, Tobias and Geshem, the three adversaries of Nehemiah, are given a central place in the memoirs of Nehemiah, and the political and ideological differences between them and Nehemiah are extensively described (Neh. 2. 10, 19-20; 3.32-35; 4.1-2; 6.1-19; 13.4-9), including the marriage of Sanballat's daughter to the son of the high priest in Jerusalem and their expulsion from the city as a result of this (Neh. 13.28). Can it be assumed that the author of Nehemiah's memoirs would have ignored the existence of the Samaritan temple built by the enemy of Nehemiah? Would he have passed over in complete silence the construction of a temple that would be considered by Nehemiah to be an illegal temple?!

One of the interesting questions that Magen asks is: 'Furthermore, why is there no archaeological evidence of the existence of a cultic site on Mt. Gerizim prior to the Persian period?'[34] The answer to this question is very simple: just keep digging! For over 20 years Magen has been asking the same question about the various archaeological strata on Mount Gerizim. According to the report of 1987, a fortress city of the Hellenistic period was exposed on Mount Gerizim.[35] In 1991 they reported on the mountain as a sanctuary,[36] and in the report of 2001, after 18 years of excavation, Mount Gerizim became a temple city.[37] In effect, from the summary of the excavations and the historical introduction, two outstanding contributions are made to the history of the temple. The important one is that on Mount Gerizim there was a sacred sanctuary in the centre of which stood a temple, and the other is that the temple was built during the Persian period. Beyond this, the archaeological finds do not support any exact date for the erection of the temple.

In order to strengthen our supposition regarding the erection of the Samaritan temple in the later stages of Persian rule over the Land of Israel, I shall find support once again in the Yedania letter from the Yeb papyri that was mentioned above. As I noted there, the letter of 407 BCE was a plea made by the leaders of Yeb after the destruction of their temple to Bagohi, the governor of Yehud and to Delaiah and Shelamiah the sons of Sanballat governor of Samaria. In this letter they request assistance in restoring their ruined temple, and note the fact that three years earlier, in

34 Magen et al. 2004: 10.
35 Magen 1986.
36 Magen 1991–2; 1993.
37 Magen 2000.

410 BCE, they had addressed their request to Johanan the high priest in Jerusalem, but he had not answered them at all. Therefore, if in the year 410 BCE there had been a temple on Mount Gerizim, would not the leaders of Yeb have addressed their request to the high priest on Mount Gerizim, just as they did to the high priest in Jerusalem? Does not the application to Delaiah and Shelamiah indirectly indicate that the Samaritan temple had not yet been built?

Another difficulty is seen in the Aramaic and neo-Hebraic inscriptions that were brought together in an impressive collection, regarding whether they can serve as evidence for the construction of a temple on Mount Gerizim during the days of Sanballat I. As Magen himself notes with regard to these inscriptions: 'In addition, since the Mt. Gerizim inscriptions were not found in situ, no time frame could be determined for the use of the various scripts. All the inscriptions date from the Hellenistic period (3rd–2nd centuries BCE), a time in which, with a few exceptions, the lapidary style is not known to have been in use'.[38] If so, how can evidence from the third and second centuries serve as proof for the early existence of the temple?

The Samaritan temple existed for over two hundred years and was used by the Samaritans as their religious centre. Its destruction in the year 111 BCE caused an ideological–religious transformation among the Samaritans. Not only did they never try to rebuild their temple but even denied the existence of the temple in the past. Instead, they turned the whole of Mount Gerizim into a 'sacred sanctuary'.[39]

2. *The Samaritan Leadership*

Since 1962, with the discovery of the findings in Wadi ed-Daliyeh, and in the wake of the first attempts by Cross to reconstruct the Samaritan leadership during the Persian period,[40] many research studies have been published in which scholars reconstructed the list of the provincial governors in Samaria and the order of their rule. We shall not deal here with this complicated issue, except that in view of the consensus in research with regard to the use of eponymous names among the Samaritan leadership, it is possible to reconstruct the order of rule for the Samaritan provincial governors at least for the years between 445 BCE, the year in which

---

38   Magen et al. 2004: 12, 41.

39   Zedaka 2001: 16–17.

40   Cross 1969: 41–62; 1974: 17–29; 1988: 17–26; For a summary of Cross work on this topics see in Hebrew, Cross 2002.

Nehemiah arrived in Jerusalem, and 332 BCE, when the Land of Israel was conquered by Alexander the Great.

During this century, the governance of the province of Samaria was held by the members of one family, the Sanballat family. Sanballat I was a contemporary of Nehemiah and his actions are described in detail in Nehemiah's memoirs. The last governor of this family was Sanballat III, who was appointed to this position by Darius III, the last Persian king (338–331 BCE), and as we have seen above, it was he who built the Samaritan temple on Mount Gerizim.[41]

Josephus, in one of his versions for the erection of the Samaritan temple, describes with relative amplitude, and in a sarcastic manner, the background for the construction of the Samaritan temple. In this description, Josephus notes that Sanballat III persuaded his son-in-law Manasseh not to leave Nikaso, Sanballat's daughter and Manasseh's wife, and in exchange he promised to build a temple for him on Mount Gerizim, and to appoint him as high priest and the next governor of Samaria.[42]

The victories of Alexander and his military successes in the region upset their plans and did not enable Sanballat III to keep his promises to his son-in-law Manasseh. However, the temple on Mount Gerizim was built and Manasseh was the first high priest in it, and was apparently the founder of a dynasty of priests that served in the Samaritan temple (*Antiquities* XI, 324).

Josephus gives chronological indications for the construction of the Samaritan temple: '**After seven months had passed in the siege of Tyre and two months in siege of Gaza, Sanballat died**' (*Antiquities* XI, 325). The death of Sanballat III led to far-reaching changes in the Samaritan leadership. As we saw above, Sanballat III had put his trust in Alexander, and even supported his army during the siege on Tyre. But all of this was of no avail in the future.

In the organization of governance over the areas conquered by Alexander and his generals, neither Sanballat nor his heirs were included in their

41   For a summary of the research on this issue, see: VanderKam 1991: 67–91; Crown 1995: 133–55. For the view that rejects the existence of three Sanballats, see: Schwartz 1990: 175–99.

42   See also *Antiquities* XI, 309–312: 'Manasseh went to his father-in-law Sanballat and said that while he loved his daughter Nikaso, nevertheless the priestly office was the highest in the nation and has always belonged to his family, and that therefore he did not wish to be deprived of it on her account. But **Sanballat promised not only to preserve the priesthood for him but also to procure for him the power and office of high priest and to appoint him governor of all the places over which he ruled**, if he were willing to live with his daughter; And he said that he would build a temple similar to that in Jerusalem on Mount Gerizim – this is the highest of the mountains near Samaria – and undertook to do these things with the consent of king Darius. Elated by these promises, Manasseh stayed with Sanballat believing that he would obtain the high priesthood as the gift of Darius, for Sanballat, as it happened was now an old man.'

plans. In fact the Macedonian conquest eliminated the Persian division into provinces together with the position of governor. According to the testimony of Quintus Curtius Rufus, Parmenion appointed Andromachus to be the governor of Coele-Syria that included the previous province of Samaria. The main losers in the administrative changes that occurred in the region were Manasseh the high priest in the new temple that had just been built, and the Samaritan aristocracy that had enjoyed the greatest benefit from the ruling Sanballat family during the Persian period. Curtius also describes the violent reaction of the Samaritan aristocracy in burning Andromachus alive.[43] The administrative changes that occurred in the region are not described at all by Josephus. On the other hand, he describes at length Alexander's change of attitude towards the Samaritans. The change as described by Josephus arouses doubts as to the credibility of his words. But if to these changes in the Jewish–Samaritan–Macedonian system of relationships we add the information from Curtius Rufus about the burning of Andromachus, this clarifies the matter.

According to Curtius, Alexander had injured the Samaritan aristocracy, which then rebelled against him, and he punished them harshly after those chiefly responsible were handed over to him. Indeed, the evidence from the many finds in Wadi ed-Daliyeh testify to the bitter fate of the Samaritan aristocracy.[44] Following these events, the Samaritans lost the political autonomy they had enjoyed throughout the Persian period. However, it may be assumed that this would have occurred in any case even had they not rebelled, since the Macedonians preferred to appoint their generals to administrative positions in the conquered areas. Later on the Sanballat family disappears from descriptions in which the Samaritans are

---

43 See: Curtius Rufus, *Historiae Alexanderi Magni*, IV, 8:34:9-11: '(9) The sorrow was made greater by news of the death of Andromachus, to whom he had given the charge of Syria; the Samaritans had burned him alive (10) To avenge his murders, he hastened to the spot with all possible speed, and on his arrival those who had been guilty of so great a crime were delivered to him. (11) Then he put Menon in place of Andromachus and executed those who had slain his general'. Translation: J.C. Rolfe, LCL, For later sources see: Hieronymus, *Chronicle* GCS 47.123.16-24 (123ᵈ)- Helm, PL 27, 473-474: '112th Olympiad (332 B.C.E) Alexander, after capturing Tyre, invades Judaea, When he is favourably received by it, he offers sacrifices to God and greatly honours the priest of the temple; Andromachus, whom later the Samaritans kill, was sent as governor of the area. Therefore, when Alexander returns from Egypt, he punished them severely and gives their captured city to Macedonians to live in it.' Pummer 2002: 194, No. 79. George Syncellus, *Ecloga chronographica* 314.8-13 – Mosshammer: '(Alexander) besieged Tyrus, appropriated Judaea, and honoured the high priest Jaddus, offering a sacrifice to God, as if to say that he has received the region from him; he appointed Andromachus governor of it together with the other regions; the inhabitants of the (city) of the Samaritans having killed him, paid a just price when Alexander returned from Egypt. Seizing the Samarian city Alexander settled in it Macedonians' (Pummer 2002: 406, No. 177).

44 See: Pummer 2009: 144.

mentioned. In fact, there are very few sources that describe the history of the Samaritans in later periods. The government over the areas in Samaria was in the hands of representatives of the foreign power. For example, Antiochus IV appointed an officer called Andronicus to be the governor of Mount Gerizim (*2 Macc.* 5.23) and the Seleucid king subsequently appointed Apollonius, the conqueror of Jerusalem, as the governor of the district of Samaria (*Antiquities* XII, 261).[45]

3. *From Samaria to Shechem*

Curtius Rufus notes that the additional punishment imposed by Alexander on the Samaritans was their expulsion from their urban centre in the city of Samaria and its conversion into a military settlement for veteran Macedonian soldiers.[46] Some of the Samaritan population remained living in the Hura (χωρα) around the city of Samaria, but most of the Samaritan refugees went to Shechem that later on became their urban centre. The city stood beside the place sacred to them in Mount Gerizim, and according to Bickerman this was a standard phenomenon that after the establishment of a military settlement, the earlier population leaves and converges around a place with an ancient and sacred tradition.[47]

Shechem during the Persian period was an open, unwalled city that was very sparsely inhabited, and its florescence began with the exile of the Samaritan population from the city of Samaria. Archaeological finds in the city of Shechem confirm that the city and the entire region flourished during the Hellenistic period.[48] There is no dispute regarding the position of Shechem as a strategic crossroads in the Central Mountain. However, it is far fetched to conclude that the Persian rulers stationed a military outpost there. Therefore, the attempt to reject the processes of settlement as described above on the basis of sporadic archaeological data is inconsistent with the realities of the period under discussion.

The unclear evidence of a number of tombs that were discovered in Shechem, cannot be evidence for the population there. It is not clear whether they are the tombs of the family members of Iranian soldiers

---

45   On the identity between the Apollonius who conquered Jerusalem, mentioned in *1 Macc.* 1.29 and *2 Macc.* 5.24, and the Apollonius mentioned in *Antiquities* XII, 261 see: M. Stern 1965: 63.

46   On the archaeological excavations of the city of Samaria testifying to the Macedonian character of the city, see: Reisner, Fisher and Lyon 1924; Crowfoot 1957: 24–7. See also Tal, 2006: 20–22 who asks a number of questions regarding the dating of the round towers in the city of Samaria.

47   See: Bickerman 1962: 43–4; Bickerman 1988: 10–11.

48   On the archaeological excavations in Shechem, see: Wright 1965: 179. Na'aman 1993: 28 rejects Wright's conclusions.

stationed in Shechem during the Persian period, or of the family members of the exiles brought here from various regions in Mesopotamia (Babylon), Elam, or the mountains of Iran who observed the burial customs of their country of origin.[49]

It is possible that throughout the Persian period Shechem was the settlement site of a Persian army unit as suggested by a number of scholars, although this suggestion does not add anything to the discussion here.

As I noted before, most of the archaeological evidence from Shechem and its surroundings indicate that it was sparsely inhabited. Campbell, who reviewed Shechem and its surroundings in the Persian period, reached unequivocal conclusions that the scanty population in the region during the Persian period contrasts sharply with renewed florescence in the fourth century BCE.[50] Similar evidence can be derived from the coins found in Shechem dating to the Ptolemaic and Seleucid periods.[51]

In view of all these testimonies it appears that Shechem, during the Persian period, was an unwalled and sparsely populated city, and that only during the Hellenistic period, after the Samaritan population settled there, did Shechem begin to flourish.

4. *Land disputes between Jews and Samaritans*

One of the subjects characteristic of the history of the Samaritans in this period of transition is associated with land disputes between them and the Jewish population. Josephus, in *Against Apion*, quotes Hecataeus of Abdera in saying that Alexander distributed the land of the Samaritans to the Jews and exempted them from taxation.

> *Against Apion, II, 43*:
> 'For he [Alexander the Great] held our nation in honor, as Hecataeus also says concerning us: because of the kindness and loyalty that the Judeans showed to him, he added the Samaritan territory to theirs, free of tribute.'[52]

---

49   See: Stern 1980: 108.
50   Campbell 1991: 22.
51   Sellers 1962: 87–96.
52   I used the latest translation to English, See: Barclay 2007: 192. For other translations see: Bar-Kochva 1996: 52–3: '(Alexander) honored our people. As Hecataeus states about us, in return for the loyal regard which the Jews had shown to him, he granted to them to hold the region of Samaria free of tribute'. Doran 1985: 913–14: 'The honour in which he [Alexander] held our nation may be illustrated by the statement of Hecataeus that, in recognition of the consideration and loyalty shown to him by the Jews, he added to their territory the district of Samaria free of tribute'. Translation: H. St. J. Thackeray *LCL*.

This single paragraph became the subject of a prolonged dispute among the many scholars that dealt with it. For example, Willrich and other scholars in his wake claimed that the testimony of Hecataeus was anachronistic, and that in fact it attributes to Alexander's time the events that took place in 145 BCE when Demetrius II, fulfilling a promise to Jonathan, annexed three districts to Judaea: Aphrema, Lydda and Ramathaim.[53] Even scholars who accept the words of Hecataeus as reliable disagree among themselves. For example, Robert Doran transfers the events described to Egypt. In his view, Hecataeus is describing an event that occurred in Egypt in the village of Σαμαρειτις in the region of Fayum, and therefore there is no connection with the Samaritan community.[54] Sterling, however, claims that the testimony is possible but cannot be proved.[55]

Following the rebellion of the Samaritans, as described above, Alexander changed his attitude towards the Jews and the Samaritans. In addition to the punishments decreed on the Samaritans one should probably add the loss of the three border districts between Judaea and Samaria. Curtius Rufus, in his description of the Samaritan rebellion, notes that: '. . . on his arrival those who had been guilty of so great a crime **were delivered to him**'. Was it the Jews who had delivered the Samaritan rebels? And did Alexander reward them by the annexation of the districts? If the three districts were indeed transferred to the Jews in 331 BCE, then a review of certain testimonies in *1 Maccabees* that describe events during the days of Jonathan the Hasmonaean are surprising and raise serious difficulties.

In *1 Macc.* 10.25b-45, in the letter of Demetrius I dated 152 BCE, among other promises made to Jonathan, Demetrius promises that:

> '. . . so that I will not take (them) from the land of Judaea, and from the three governments which are added thereunto from the country of Samaria and Galilee, from this day forth and for all time" (*1 Macc.* 10.30).

These promises were not realized since Jonathan preferred to support Alexander Balas, the rival of Demetrius I. Therefore, before Demetrius II came to power, Jonathan demanded the following in exchange for supporting him:

> 'And Jonathan requested of the king, that he would make Judaea and

53   See *1 Macc.* 11.34; Willrich 1900: 97.
54   Doran, 1985: 913–14. See: Kuhs 1996.
55   Sterling 1992: 85–6, and note 120.

the three provinces of the country of Samaria free from tribute . . .'
(*1 Macc.* 11.28).[56]

This demand was answered with the letter sent by Demetrius II to Jonathan
in 145/4 BCE. Among the exemptions and benefits that he granted him
was the annexation to Judaea of the three districts severed from Samaria:

1 Macc. 11.30-36: The letter of Demetrius II to Jonathan
'King Demetrius to his brother Jonathan and to the nation of the Jews,
greeting . . .

We have determined to do good to the nation of the Jews, who
are our friends, and observe what is just toward us, because of their
good will toward us.

We have confirmed to them, therefore, the districts of Judea, and
the three districts (regions) of Aphaerema, and Lydda, and Ramathaim
– (these) were added unto Judaea from the country of Samaria –
and all things appertaining to them, for all such as do sacrifice in
Jerusalem, instead of the King's dues which the king received of them
yearly aforetime from the produce of the land and the fruit of the trees.

And as for the other things which appertain unto us, from henceforth, of the tenths and tolls that appertain to us, and the salt pits, and
the crowns that appertain to us.'

If these three districts were actually annexed to Judaea in 145 BCE, the
question arises as to when they were lost to Judaea.

Josephus, Jewish Antiquities XII, 156:
'At this time the Samaritans (Σαμαρείς) who were flourishing, did
much mischief to the Jews by laying waste their land and carrying off
slaves; and this happened in the high-priesthood of Onias'.[57]

Again, a number of objects arise in connection with this paragraph. The
first is on the question of the identity of the Samaritans (Σαμαρείς) mentioned in the paragraph. The second, without any reference to the identity
of the Samaritans, is the question of the dating of the event.

With regard to the problem of the Samaritans' identity, does Josephus
in his description of the Samaritan community use the terms Σαμαρεύς

---

56   Rappaport, *The First Book of Maccabees:* 254–55; 273–75. He notes that this should be
read as 'the three districts from/of Samaria'.

57   Translation Ralph Marcus 1943.

and Σαμαρειτις indiscriminately, or does he distinguish between the two and use them differently?

Rappaport and others, for example, claimed that by using the term Σαμαρείς in this paragraph, Josephus did not mean the community but the inhabitants of the Hellenistic city Samaria. As an example of this he notes his use of Σαμαρείς in *Antiquities* IX, 61, when describing the siege that the King of Aram placed upon the city of Samaria.[58] Therefore, in his opinion, one cannot learn from this source anything about the system of relationships between the Jews and the Samaritans.

One of the reasons that underlie the assumption of Rappaport is linked with the issue of the loan that Josephus received 'from his friends in Samaria' (τοὺς φίλους εἰς Σαμάρειαν (XII, 168). In his opinion 'there is no reason to suppose that sources of ready funds were specifically in the hands of members of the Samaritan sect. In a city that had a strong money economy and perhaps had already received the status of a Hellenistic *polis*, it would have been much easier to have found such funding rather than from an agricultural society, whether the one in Judaea or in the hills of Ephraim'.[59] However, we have other examples, such as in *Antiquities* XIII, 74 in the argument between the Samaritans and the Jews in Alexandria, where he uses the word Σαμαρείς for 'Samaritans'. Rita Egger, in her research studies, rightly claims that Josephus does not always use a different Greek word in order to distinguish between the inhabitants of the city of Samaria and the Samaritan sect.[60]

As for the economic reason, the basic supposition of Rappaport is perhaps correct with regard to the city of Samaria, and it may be that the people of the city lent Josephus money. However, this supposition is not precise, mainly regarding the distinction that the reference made was supposedly to the Samaritans in that period, who were merely an agricultural society. But in that same period the Samaritans had gathered in two urban centres – in Shechem and in the city that was being developed on Mount Gerizim. Moreover, the very combination of words 'his friends from Samaria' can be interpreted as members of the Samaritan community. Since the days of Nehemiah we hear of the friendly ties between the Tobiad family and the Samarian Sanballat family.[61]

Support for our claim that the paragraph refers to the Samaritan community is found in two research studies that have recently been published:

Oded Lipshits suggests that the name Samarians was usually used to describe the inhabitants of the Samaria region, before the erection of the

58 Rappaport 1990: 382.
59 Rappaport 1990: 382.
60 Egger, 1986: 82–4; Egger, 1991: 109–14.
61 S. Schwartz 2007: 224–36. See mainly: 'Interethnic Friendship' pp. 224–26.

Samaritan temple. The reference is to those whom Bickerman called the 'proto-Samaritans', but after the erection of their temple they could be called Samaritans.[62]

Pierre Briant, in his reference to the first half of the fifth century BCE, the days of Nehemiah and Sanballat I, notes that the term 'Samaritans' does not yet indicate the Samaritan community, and that the change and sectarian use of the word began only after the erection of the rival temple on Mount Gerizim.[63]

As for the question of the date of the event, one should examine the context in which Josephus integrated the paragraph. In *Antiquities* XII, 1-118, Josephus describes the Ptolemaic period, including the story of the *Septuagint* during the reign of Ptolemy II Philadelphus. Later on, in paragraphs 119–55, Josephus describes a few events that occurred at the beginning of Seleucid rule over the Land of Israel:

> 119–28: Seleucus I Nicator, founder of the Seleucid dynasty, granted citizenship to the Jews in Antioch and in the cities of Asia and Lower Syria.[64] He then goes on to describe events that occurred during the reign of Antiochus III the Great:
> 129–37: Events from the time of the fourth and fifth Syrian wars that led to the conquest of the Land of Israel by Antiochus III.
> 138–46: Rights granted by Antiochus III to the Jews.
> 147–53: The letter of Antiochus III to Zeuxis, Governor of Lydia, concerning the transfer of thousands of Jewish families from Mesopotamia and Babylon to Phrygia.[65]
> 154–55: The marriage of Cleopatra, daughter of Antiochus III, to Ptolemy V Epiphanes in 193 BCE. As dowry, he was given territories in Coele-Syria, Samaria, Judaea and Phoenicia, and the collection of custom dues in these areas was granted to local dignitaries.[66]
> Paragraph 156 ends the description of the continuous events from the beginning of the Seleucid period and immediately afterwards, in paragraph 158 and onwards, Josephus once again describes the events of the Ptolemaic period associated with the Tobias family:
> 158–85: The story of Joseph the Tobiad.
> 186–222: The story of Hyrcanus the son of Joseph the Tobiad.

---

62 Lipschits 2006: 31, note 38.

63 Briant 2002: 587.

64 Josephus describes an event that is dated to the years 16–13 BCE, clashes between Greeks and the Jews, See: Pucci Ben Zeev 1998: 269, 279, 289, 422.

65 Gauger 1993: 63–9. On the credibility of the letter, see: Ma 2000: 267.

66 Huß 2001, 489–92; Gera 1998: 20–135; and recently, Cotton and Wörrle 2007: 193, note 5.

A review of the order of events described by Josephus makes it clear that the story of the Tobias family is placed chronologically in the wrong place. The story of the Tobias family took place during the Ptolemaic period, during the reign of Ptolemy III Euergetes I.[67]

In paragraph 156, in which descriptions of the Seleucid period are linked up with events of the Ptolemaic period, there are two chronological indications that will help us to fix the date of the event mentioned in the paragraph.

The first indication is: 'at that same time' (ἐν τούτῳ χρόνῳ); the second one is: 'such (deeds) occurred in the days of Onias the High Priest'.

Onias the High Priest is Onias II who was the high priest during the years 240–218 BCE. Josephus accuses him of pettiness and love of lucre that led to his refusal to pay taxes to the Ptolemaic king:

> 'This Onias was small-minded and passionately fond of money and since for this reason he did not render on behalf of the people the tribute of twenty talents of silver which his father had paid to the kings of their own revenues, he roused the anger of Ptolemy. And the king sent an envoy to Jerusalem to denounce Onias for not rendering the tribute, and threatened that, if he did not receive it, he would parcel out their land and send his soldiers to settle on it. Accordingly, when the Jews heard the king's message they were dismayed, but Onias was not put out of countenance by any of these threats, so great was his avarice' (*Antiquities*, XII, 158–159).

The background to the refusal of Onias II to raise the tribute money for the Ptolemies is connected with the third Syrian war, the 'Laodicean War' in the years 246–241 BCE. The initial victories of Seleucus II Kallinikos inspired some of the Judaeans led by Onias with hope for the end of Ptolemaic rule, and they apparently transferred their support to the Seleucids. However, the final defeat of Seleucus II, the continuation of Ptolemaic rule in the region and the visit of Ptolemy III to Jerusalem,[68] caused changes in the status of Onias II. The high priest lost his position as a tax collector, and it was transferred to Joseph the Tobiad, who had apparently remained loyal to Ptolemaic rule during the third Syrian war.[69]

---

67   See: Ji 1998: 417–40; pls. 19–20; Gera 1990: 21–38; Rosenberg 2006: 85–92.

68   On the visit to Jerusalem see: *Against Apion*, II, 48, and Hengel 1974, I: 268–69.

69   The date for the appointment of Joseph to the position of tax collector is in dispute. Recently, Daniel Schwartz postponed the activities of the Tobias family to the second century BCE, to the years 204–175 BCE. See: Schwartz 1998: 47–61. In opposition to the suggestion of Schwartz, see: Fuks 2001b: 35456. Fuks remained loyal to a third century BCE date. Schwartz, in his reply to Fuks, continued to claim a later date. See: D. Schwartz 2002: 146–51.

Josephus colourfully describes the situation of the population in Coele-Syria:

> '. . . It was the lot of the Jews to undergo great hardships through the devastation of their land, as did also the inhabitants of Coele-Syria . . . they had to suffer, and whether he was victorious or defeated, to experience the same fate; so they were in no way different from a storm-tossed ship which is beset on either side by heavy seas, finding themselves crushed between the successes of Antiochus and the adverse turn of his fortune' (*Antiquities*, XII, 128–130).

Similar events occurred during the fourth Syrian war (221–217 BCE). Ever since the year 219/218 BCE, Antiochus III had controlled most of the Land of Israel. His enormous successes at this stage of the war apparently caused Joseph the Tobiad for political considerations to transfer his support to Antiochus III. But the final outcome of the war was unexpected, and Ptolemy IV defeated Antiochus II at the Battle of Raphia in 217 BCE,[70] and the Land of Israel remained under Ptolemaic rule. Joseph the Tobiad was probably discharged from his position as tax collector, and it was then transferred to the son of Hyrcanus who had remained loyal to the Ptolemies.[71]

As we have seen above, Josephus describes the years of the Syrian wars in the region as years of uncertainty and political insecurity. The region passed from hand to hand and resembled 'a storm-tossed ship which is beset on either side by heavy seas' (XII, 129).[72] This political reality caused the population in the region to split up and divide into groups whose different political considerations dictated their support for one of the two kingdoms struggling over control of the Land of Israel. The schism did not only occur among the Jewish population, but the Samaritans also were undecided as to which kingdom they should give support, and these indecisions and contradictions led each side to profit from the failure of the other side.

In my opinion, the event mentioned in *Antiquities* XII in which the Samaritans were 'laying waste' the land of the Jews, took place in the period that preceded the conquest of the Land of Israel by the Seleucids

---

70   On the Battle of Raphia, see: Galili 1999.

71   On his loyalty to the Ptolemies, see: *Antiquities*, XII, 236. He committed suicide in 175 BCE when Antiochus IV became king.

72   See the Hefzibah inscription. Although it presents the realities in the region during the first years after the Seleucid conquest, one can learn from it about the situation in the region even before this. See the recent discussion of the inscription: Piejko 1991: 245–59 (SEG 41, 1574). See also: H. Müller 2000: 521.

in the fifth Syrian war. The event should be dated to the period of the third Syrian war, more specifically in the year 242 BCE when for a short while complete areas passed from the hands of the Ptolemies to the Seleucids and back again. For a short while the victorious Seleucids aroused hope among their supporters who wished to bring the Ptolemaic conquest to an end and that the Land of Israel would be transferred to Seleucid rule. This is the background for the refusal of Onias to pay tribute to Ptolemy III who was the temporary loser, and it may be that he transferred his support to the Seleucids. However, the subsequent victories of Ptolemy III changed the internal balance of power among the Jews. Ptolemy III renewed his control over the region and while threatening to turn Jerusalem into a military settlement, he changed the status of Onias II who lost his position as a collector of taxes and transferred it to Joseph the Tobiad. The latter won this position since he remained loyal to the Ptolemies and seems to have headed the pro-Ptolemy party in Jerusalem.

There is no doubt that the Samaritans also faced similar problems of loyalty. In my opinion, the Samaritans remained loyal to the Ptolemies throughout the course of the fourth Syrian war, and Ptolemy III rewarded them for this loyalty and punished Judaea for the lack of loyalty by their leader Onias II. The three border districts: Aphrema, Lydda and Ramathaim, that had been severed from the territory of the Samaritans during the time of Alexander the Great, were restored to Samaritan control who held these areas until 145 BCE, when they were returned to Jonathan the Hasmonaean by the Seleucid king Demetrius II.

9

THE ALPHABET THAT NEVER WAS: A POSSIBLE EGYPTIAN INFLUENCE ON THE NEAR EAST

John Ray
University of Cambridge

The question of Egyptian influence on the literature of the Hebrew Bible is an old one, and one which will be familiar to anyone who has studied the field. He or she will know about the relationship between Psalm 104 and the Great Hymn to the Aten, the resemblances which link Proverbs 22–24 and the Wisdom of Amenemope, and the motifs and echoes which connect the Song of Songs and some of the Egyptian love poetry of the Ramesside period. These have been long debated, and do not need to be rehearsed again (for a necessarily arbitrary selection see Rodd 2001, Aitken 2001, Currid 1997, Fox 1985, Ray 1995 and Williams 1961).

Nevertheless, though it is well known that Egyptian literature could, and did, influence Hebrew thinking and has surfaced from time to time in biblical writings, surprisingly little influence has been found in biblical Hebrew of the Egyptian language itself. There is the occasional proper name, such as Phineas (*P3- n□sy*, 'the Nubian'), possibly Miriam (from *mri* 'to love'), and perhaps even Moses (from *msi* 'to bear'). There are some loan words, no doubt, though some of these may be explained by the fact that the two languages shared many roots derived ultimately from a common ancestor. But the combined weight of all this is not that great. This is even more surprising if we take into account the tradition of a 400-year sojourn in Egypt which culminated in the Exodus. One would have expected more trace of Egyptian words and idioms to appear in the language. But this is a controversial theme, and (perhaps fortunately) one that is too large for a paper such as this.

Nevertheless, one more Egyptianism may have gone unrecognized until quite recently. In Job 38.36 the text reads, 'Who placed wisdom in the □u□ôt, or who gave the *sekwî* understanding?' Most translations suggest that these words mean something like 'inner parts', or the seat of intelligence, but a *sekwî* in modern Hebrew, I am told, is a cock or hen, and the Latin Vulgate translation agrees with this. Could the ☐u☐ôt be a bird as well? Could it be an ibis, the sacred bird in Egypt of the god of wisdom, whose name was pronounced something very like ☐u☐ôt? Is this an Egyptian loan word, in the heart of the Book of Job? Whatever the truth of this, let us keep ibises in mind for a while, because we will need to meet them again in another context.

The origins of our alphabet are an intriguing topic, and many studies have been devoted to it. Its origins seem to lie in the so-called Proto-Canaanite or Proto-Sinaitic script found mainly in Egypt, the Sinai peninsula, and southern Palestine, but the exact nature of this script is still not completely understood (Driver 1976: 94–103; 140–44). The first undeniable example of our alphabet appears to be on a well-known tablet found at Ugarit, on the north Syrian coast, and this dates to the fourteenth or thirteenth century BC. It was discovered in 1948, and is now in the Damascus museum. This tablet is written, not in the letters with which we are familiar, but in a system derived from Mesopotamian cuneiform. However, although the signs are unfamiliar, the order of these letters is the one we know from Hebrew and Greek: ', *b, g, d*, etc., a scheme which corresponds to *'aleph beth gimel daleth* and *alpha beta gamma delta*. With the occasional exception, such as the ostracon from Izbet Sarte, this alphabet disappears from view for a few centuries, but it then reappears, no longer in cuneiform, but in the form of the 22 Phoenician letters that are the ancestors of the Hebrew, Aramaic, Greek and Arabic alphabets. In the latter it is known, mnemonically, as *'abjad*, a name which has recently been adopted by linguistics experts who are apparently tired of the term 'alphabet' (Rogers 2005, 115–44 and passim). This *'abjad*, or alphabet, has gone on to conquer the world, with the exception of China, Korea and Japan. Even the writing systems of India and South-East Asia, which look so exotic to Western eyes, may be derived from a form or forms of the Aramaic alphabet. The ABC, or ABG as it started its life, has been one of the great success stories of history.

But there is also a second alphabet, which is far less well known, and which raises some difficult problems. The story of this second alphabet, at least as far as recent scholarship is concerned, may as well begin in Egypt. In the mid-1960s the Egypt Exploration Society began its excavations at a site known as the Sacred Animal Necropolis at North Saqqâra, on the edge of the western desert some 15 miles south of Cairo. As its somewhat abstruse name suggests, this site was the burial place of the million or more mummified animals who were revered as the embodiment of various Egyptian gods. However, the site turned out to contain far more than pickled birds and baboons. It produced a series of temples, several thousand statues in stone and bronze, inscriptions written in an undeciphered language (Carian from Asia Minor), underground galleries lined with graffiti, and several hundred papyri. Among these papyri was one which so far is without parallel in Egyptian literature. It was published more than 20 years ago by H. S. Smith and W. J. Tait, in their magnificent volume *Saqqâra Demotic Papyri I*, where it is listed as Papyrus Saqqâra 27. It is believed to date from the fourth or third century BC (Smith and Tait 1983: 198–213 with Pl. 17).

In this text, there is a series of lines, which are damaged, as is so often the case with papyri. However, as the editors soon realized, each line originally contained the name of a bird, which perches on a particular bush. Later in the text, the same birds fly off to a particular place. In each case, the bird, the bush and the place begin with the same letter. It is as if we were to recite, 'The crow perched on the chrysanthemum and flew away to Croydon', etc. The arrangement of this text was clearly far from random', and the editors went on to suggest that Papyrus Saqqâra 27 contained nothing less than the order of the ancient Egyptian alphabet. The jingles in the lines of this text were either an attempt to make the order easier to remember, or an exotic exercise to help apprentice scribes in their training, and perhaps to improve their knowledge of natural history in the process.

Egyptian hieroglyphs are not an alphabetic script in the usual sense of the word. Like Mesopotamian cuneiform, they are a complex system which employs ideograms and phonetic elements in a variety of ways. However, unlike cuneiform, they also contain a series of some 25 to 30 signs which are used to write single sounds such as *f*, *h*, *m* or *r*. In other words, there is an alphabet of sorts embedded within the several hundred signs which make up the complete writing system, and it is natural to suppose that the Egyptians were aware of this. It is also natural to think that they must have had a method of organising the sounds of this alphabet if they were to record things in anything like a systematic way. There are, in fact, good reasons to believe that this was the case.

We can begin with the Greek writer Plutarch, in the second century AD. Plutarch, if he had lived, might have gone on to write the London telephone directory and give public recitals from it, but he was an observant man, and the range of his knowledge was truly wide. In his *Quaestiones Conviviae* (9.3.2 [738E]), he records that the Egyptians had an alphabet, and the first of its letters was an ibis. At first sight this is puzzling, because there is no ibis among the alphabetic hieroglyphs that we have, although there are several other birds. However, the ibis was the sacred emblem of Thoth, the god of learning and calculation, and the choice would certainly be an appropriate one. The Egyptian name for this bird was *hb* (pronounced *hib* or *hibi*, a term which has come down into modern languages via Greek), and the first letter of this word is *h*. *H* is the letter which begins the bird, the bush, and the place-name of the first line of the Saqqâra papyrus. Plutarch was right after all.

Other Egyptian texts are known which list words, and a noticeable
number of these similarly contain names beginning with the sound *h*.
The site of Saqqâra, where the bird and bush text was discovered, has
also given us several examples of personal names carefully spelt out, and
these regularly start with *h*. A fair number of these lists are now attested,
and it is clear that ancient Egyptian schoolboys had works of this sort
regularly inflicted upon them in an attempt to improve their literacy. The
second letter of the Saqqâra papyrus is *r* or *l* (these sounds are not always
differentiated in Egyptian writing), and the third is *ḥ*, the more emphatic
h-sound which is also found in most of the Semitic languages. The fourth
letter is equally unpredictable: *k*. The contrast with our familiar ABCD
could hardly be greater. The notion that is often heard, that the ancient
Egyptians were different from other men, seems to be true, at least when
it comes to their writing system.

Something very similar occurs in an illustrated papyrus found at Tanis,
a site made notorious by Indiana Jones and his search for the lost Ark.
However, the Tanis text is far from being fictional, and it turns out to be
very informative. It was found by Flinders Petrie, the father of Egyptian
and Palestinian archaeology, in a private house (number 35) on that site
in 1884 (Griffith and Petrie 1889: 1–19 with Pls I–VIII; most recent
treatment in Quirke 2004: 20–21). This text is divided into columns, and
the first five of these were found to contain a list of hieroglyphic signs,
followed by brief descriptions, also in hieroglyphic. This is the ancient
predecessor of the sign-lists which are found at the back of modern gram-
mars of Egyptian, and it is impossible not to feel sympathy with the scribe
who copied it. In Column 6 of this text, it is time for the alphabetic signs
themselves to make their appearance. The first one is missing (it may have
been at the bottom of column 5, where fire has got to it). But *r*, *ḥ*, and *k*
are there, and so are most of the rest. The order of the signs in the Tanis
list is the same as in the alliterations and jingles of Papyrus Saqqâra 27.
The date of the Tanis papyrus is probably early in the Roman period; this
too is late by Pharaonic standards, but the point to emphasize is that the
same alphabet is at work in both these texts.

There is also a hieroglyphic dictionary in Copenhagen, which gives ety-
mologies for a variety of words, some of them mythological and distinctly
fanciful to modern eyes. This is Papyrus Carlsberg 7 (Iversen 1958). Here
too the first section is devoted to the letter *h*, and the order of the rest of
the letters, as far as can be reconstructed, corresponds to the order of the
birds and bushes of the Saqqâra papyrus. In fact, the very first entry to
be featured in this dictionary is the word for 'ibis'. Other word-lists in
Copenhagen turn out to contain the same sequence of letters. There are
a few references in classical writers which have been taken to mean that
the Egyptians had an alphabet of 24 or 25 signs. (The principal references

are Plato, *Philebus* 18b, which has been taken to imply an alphabet of 24 letters, and Plutarch, *De Iside et Osiride* 374, which opts for 25. There is a useful discussion in Griffiths 1970: 509–10.) Here then, we seem to have the order of the ancient Egyptian alphabet, at least as it was recognized in the last few centuries BC and the first century AD, which is the period from which these dictionary texts survive.

But is this alphabet really Egyptian, or does it come from somewhere else? After all, its appearance in Egypt is late by the standards of the 30 dynasties into which its 3000-year history is divided. The Egyptians borrowed astrology, cylinder seals and glass-making from the Near East, and coinage from the Greeks, so they no doubt borrowed other things as well. The first attempt to shed light on this question came over a decade ago, from the German Egyptologist Joachim Quack (Quack 1993). This still young scholar is a master of ancient philology, and he had no difficulty in showing that the alphabet scheme used in the late papyri from Egypt was the same as the order of the South Arabian script. The HLḤ scheme, or *halaḥam* as it is sometimes called, was clearly used at the far end of the Arabian peninsula.

The South Arabian writing-system was developed around the seventh or eighth century BC, and it lasted more than a thousand years (Kitchen 1994: 132–36). At its best, it is a magnificent script, used to write the records and monuments of the kings of Saba (the Biblical Sheba) and Mina (convenient account in Driver 1976: 144–48). It went on to influence the writing of the early Ethiopians, where the HLḤ order is also observed, and where it is still used today. The South Arabian script is older than any of the alphabetic documents that have been found in Egypt, and this gives strength to the idea that it was the Arabians who got there first. In addition, Joachim Quack was able to point to the strange fact that, in the Saqqâra papyrus, there is no separate entry for the sound *f*. This phoneme is characteristic of Egyptian, where it has important uses, including the suffix for the elementary pronouns 'he' and 'his'. On the other hand, the sound is absent from many Semitic dialects. According to Quack, its omission in a Semitic context would make sense, whereas for the Egyptians to have left it out would have been unthinkable. The argument, then, is that the 'other' alphabet, with its HLḤ arrangement, went from Arabia to Egypt, probably as part of the trade along the coasts of the Red Sea which developed in the fourth century BC and the early Hellenistic period.

So far so good. But the archaeology of the Near East is still developing, and it has not lost the habit of surprise. It turns out that our mysterious alternative alphabet had been known all along, in a find from an unexpected place. In 1933 the excavator Elihu Grant found a small tablet at the site of Beth Shemesh, which lies some distance east of Ashdod. (This is otherwise known as the place where the Ark of the Covenant first rested after the Philistines returned it to the Israelites.) The inscription is said to have been found at the base of a wall which the excavators dated to the Late Bronze Age (Grant 1933; most recent discussion in Sanders 2006. The text is now numbered as KTU 5.24 = 8.1, and it is kept in the Rockefeller Museum, Jerusalem). At first the text was taken to be some kind of amulet. It had a series of signs on it, which resembled those used at the site of Ugarit, far away to the north, but it was otherwise unique. In the 1960s no less a scholar than W. F. Albright attempted a decipherment, in which he thought he could detect a reference to birth goddesses, apparently known as *kosharôt* (Albright 1964; it is some consolation when looking at one's own mistakes to think that someone as distinguished as Albright could come unstuck too). In spite of the efforts of Albright, the Beth Shemesh text was keeping its secret.

The breakthrough in the case of the Beth Shemesh tablet did not come until 1987, when A. G. Loundine suggested that this too could be an alphabet of the South Arabian type (Loundine 1987). Dramatic confirmation of this came the following year, when yet another tablet from the site of Ugarit was published (treatment in Bordreuil and Pardee 1995 and 2001. The text in question is formally known as KTU 9.426, and it is now in Damascus). This tablet was also an alphabet, but it was not the familiar ABG one which was otherwise used at that place. Instead, it was the ugly sister, the HLḤ alphabet of South Arabia. As we have seen, the texts from Ugarit come from the fourteenth century BC or the one following, and there is only one conclusion we can reach: the alphabet which was used in South Arabia had been in circulation in the Near East for more than half a millennium before it found its way into print in the Yemen. The Ugarit text threw immediate light on the small tablet that had been found 50 years earlier at Beth Shemesh. This too was an HLḤ alphabet. This second alphabet therefore stretches back into the second millennium BC, and it was known on the coast of Syria and on the edges of Philistia before it ever appeared in Arabia.

There is a tendency in the literature to be coy about the date of the Beth Shemesh tablet. This is understandable, since the text is a one-off, and such things are by their nature difficult to define. But the similarity of the signs on this tablet to the ones which are used in Ugarit make it unlikely that it can be much later than these. As far as we know, knowledge of the Ugaritic script was lost when that city was destroyed by the Sea Peoples, somewhere around 1200 BC. Whatever its exact date, the Beth Shemesh tablet must also go to show that the HLḤ alphabet was no newcomer to the Near East. It is every bit as old as the ABG alphabet which we use.

So where did this second alphabet originate? One possibility is that we stay with the suggestion of Joachim Quack, and say that the HLḤ alphabet is Arabian after all. But in that case, how do we explain the fact that the

Arabians waited six or seven centuries before sharing their invention with the world? And if they were keeping their alphabet such a close secret all this while, how did it come to be leaked twice, once to the merchants of Ugarit and a second time to the good people of Beth Shemesh? Intellectual property is intellectual property, whether we are in the first millennium BC or the third millennium AD. It is clear that an Arabian origin is not the best explanation for the facts as we have them.

Could our alternative alphabet have originated in the Near East? The ABG alphabet was almost certainly born there, and there could easily have been several attempts at the same idea. This is always a possibility, and future discoveries may add weight to this explanation. Nevertheless, it is clear that the HLḤ alphabet was only ever a minority interest in the region: a mere two examples compared with the multitude of ABG arrangements that have been found. Is there a chance that its true home lies elsewhere?

As an Egyptologist I can be expected to favour my own, but I cannot help thinking that Smith and Tait, the editors of the Saqqâra papyrus, have been right all along. In that case, the HLH version of the alphabet is the creation of the ancient Egyptians. There are several reasons for believing that this is the most likely explanation. The first reason is admittedly an argument from silence, but it is a silence which is close to being deafening. The alphabetic order which appears in the late papyri from Egypt is known only from the fourth century BC or thereabouts. What were the Egyptians doing before this? Did they have no means of ordering lists of names or places or people's occupations in ways that a particular entry could be found quickly, when it was needed? Were they prepared to read through 30 columns of a closely written text before they could find the thing they wanted? We do not have so much in the way of earlier lists from Egypt, apart from some topographical texts which are arranged, sensibly enough, by geography, and several lists of titles which are presumably compiled by hierarchy. These work well if we happen to know where a particular place is, or the rank of a particular title, but what if we do not? There has to be some way of steering through the maze of information. If we are fortunate enough to find the earlier Egyptian equivalents of the Saqqâra bird-list or the Copenhagen dictionaries, my suspicion is that they too will turn out to begin with *h*, *r* or *l*, and *ḥ*, just like their demotic descendants.

If the Egyptians were really content to wait 2500 years before coming up with an order for the sounds in their language, why, when the equivalent of the penny finally dropped, did they bother to go all the way to Yemen to find their inspiration? By the fifth century BC they were surrounded by alphabetic scripts, all of them of the ABG type. They had known Phoenician traders for centuries, and Phoenician inscriptions have been found in Egypt in plenty, on amphorae, in dedications and in graffiti. The Greeks were settled at Naucratis in the Delta, and the Greek script was to become familiar to the Egyptians of the Late Period. The same, to a lesser extent, is true of the Carian script. Above all, by the end of the sixth century BC, Egypt was a province of the cosmopolitan empire of the Medes and the Persians. The Persians adopted as their *lingua franca* Aramaic, and by the time of our Saqqâra papyrus the Aramaic script had long been familiar along the Nile. As every student of the period knows, Egypt is a major source for Aramaic documents. What would have been simpler for a fifth-century Egyptian than to have picked up an ABG in a quiet moment from a Semitic trader in a caravanserai, or in the office of a Persian official?

It is worth recalling the impact that the Persian conquest must have had on Egypt. The north of the country had been occupied long before, when the Hyksos ruled from Avaris in the Delta. There had been incursions by the Assyrians and Babylonians in the seventh and sixth centuries, but these were short-lived. The invasion of Cambyses in 525 BC had a very different consequence. For the first time, Egypt found itself part of a superstate, something resembling a world empire. The reaction of the Egyptians to this change of fortune was complex, a mixture of denial that anything would be different, and defiance in the face of a superior military power (Ray 1987: 275–80). One way of protecting oneself against an upheaval of this sort is to fall back on tradition and concentrate upon the superiority and longevity of one's own culture. History was rewritten to make Cambyses a relative of the previous royal house (hence not an alien usurper), and Egyptian doctors secured lucrative posts at the court of Darius. Things which were typically Egyptian, such as sacred animals and the elaborate cult of the dead, received a new emphasis. They were ways of keeping contact with a past, real or imagined, where Egypt was faithful to its own identity. One of the most characteristic parts of this identity was the hieroglyphic script, which was both unique in the Near East and highly decorative at the same time. It would not be surprising if the Egyptians under Achaemenid occupation went back into their scholarly traditions to revive an alphabetic scheme which was known to be their own. The ABG alphabets of Aramaic, Phoenician and Greek were widely used in the country, but they were essentially interlopers. The HLḤ arrangement, on the other hand, may well have been part of the Egyptians' sense of their own belonging, and this sense of belonging is unlikely to have been rooted anywhere outside Egypt.

There is also the fact which was noted by Plutarch, that the letters of the Egyptian alphabet began with an ibis, the sacred bird of the god of writing. As we have seen, this is the equivalent of the sound *h* which stands first in the HLḤ alphabet. Is this a coincidence, as it would presumably have to be if this alphabet were a borrowing? I suspect that this is not a coincidence, and that the HLḤ (or HRḤ scheme as it appears in Egypt) began life as the opening sounds of the lines of a hymn, or song of praise addressed to the god Thoth. This was the god whose head was an ibis, or a ⸢u⸣ ōt as we might have in the Book of Job. If this seems fanciful, it is worth recalling that the familiar *Sound of Music* sequence *do, re, mi* originates in the opening syllables of a Latin hymn, penned by a mediaeval monk, Guido of Arezzo. Here *do*, which replaced an earlier (and less euphonic) *ut*, is simply the beginning of the word *Domine* 'Lord'. *Do* is for *Domine*; *h* is for ibis. What would the letter *h* have to stand for in Semitic, to make it so important?

We are still left with the points made by Joachim Quack when he argued for the Arabian origin of the HLḤ scheme. There are small differences in the order of the signs in the two localities, and there are more noticeable divergences in the phonetic structures of the two versions, the Egyptian and the Yemeni. But the languages of the two places were not closely related, and such discrepancies are only to be expected. In fact, this sort of thing is standard when an alphabet migrates from one area to another or one culture to another, and there are even variants between the known abecedaries from South Arabia. The biggest problem from the Egyptian point of view is the absence of the letter *f* from the Saqqâra papyrus, since, as we have seen, this was an important component of the Egyptian language. The Saqqâra text was, however, meant to be an amusing composition, with birds, botany and holiday bookings mingling together. If there was no bird in the demotic language whose name began with *f*, there would simply be no call for that line to appear. So far, I have to state that I have been unable to find any such bird, and we can say this with the authority of the on-line Chicago Demotic Dictionary, where the entry for *f* happens to be one of the shortest in the volume. The explanation may be as mundane as this. Even if the Egyptians had borrowed their alphabet from elsewhere, sooner or later they would have had to invent an entry for the sound *f*, since they could not have managed without it. The letter does appear in the Tanis list, though in a different column. The fact that it is absent in one demotic text does not mean that we have to borrow the entire scheme from somewhere far away in the Semitic-speaking world.

Trade ran along the Red Sea, but it ran in two directions, not one. Rather than having the Egyptians floating down to Yemen to borrow an alphabet, it would have been just as easy for South Arabian traders to have come to Egypt and copied one that they found there. Such traders certainly came to Egypt, since they have left inscriptions in that country. Surely this is the simpler explanation?

How then are we to account for the earlier occurrences of the HLḤ alphabet, at Ugarit and Beth Shemesh? A point to note is that Ugarit lay on the coast of Syria, and Beth Shemesh, though not on the sea, was not far from the territory of the Philistines. The presence of Egypt was always strongest along the coast, in places like Byblos, Beirut or Jaffa, but it tended to evaporate as one went further inland, where the influence of Mesopotamia began to make itself felt. Much of Egyptian trade was maritime, as texts such as the *Shipwrecked Sailor* and the *Voyage of Wenamun* make clear, and this trade hugged the coast of the eastern Mediterranean. An alphabet could easily have been carried as part of that trade, as it almost certainly did when it passed from Phoenicia to the Greeks. Perhaps it changed hands in a tavern, over a jug or two of wine, or perhaps it squeezed itself into the curriculum of a Near-Eastern school that had particular links with its homeland. As was the case with the maharajahs' sons who were sent to Eton or Harrow, the Egyptians were in the habit of bringing back the heirs of Near-Eastern princes to be educated alongside the Crown Prince, their future overlord. As a result the princes became assimilated to Egyptian culture, while also serving as a bargaining-point if their fathers back in Asia were thinking of starting any trouble. This too could be a way that an Egyptian alphabet found its way into foreign courts. This is of course the most romantic possibility, but being romantic is not an automatic barrier to being true.

A final point to consider is the orientation of the HLḤ alphabet in its earliest appearances. Ugaritic cuneiform, in agreement with Mesopotamian writing in general, normally runs from left to right. However, the example which was found at Beth Shemesh is written in the contrary direction. (The Beth Shemesh tablet is essentially two lines written in boustrophedon, but the first, and noticeably longer, line, clearly runs from right to left. The forms of the individual letters show beyond doubt which side of the tablet is uppermost.) At the time when this text was inscribed, such an orientation would be extremely rare in the Near East. To the best of my knowledge, cuneiform is never written from right to left in Mesopotamia, and the practice is no more than sporadic even at Ugarit (Dietrich and Loretz 1988: 285–86, 306). A small number of right-to-left texts are also known from other sites, but overall the arrangement is an unusual one (Driver 1976: 252 ref. p. 152 n. 1). On the other hand, Egyptian writing regularly runs in this direction. This is invariably true of hieratic and its later replacement, demotic, and it is the preferred arrangement for hieroglyphic texts. Examples of hieroglyphs running from left to right do occur, but there is normally a reason for this, for example in a text which is designed to mirror a right-to-left counterpart, or one which is orientated to face the figure of a king or god. The right-to-left preference may have been encouraged by the use of papyrus rolls, where it would be easier for a right-handed person to arrange his text in such a way; but, whatever the reason, the orientation is typical of Egypt. The fact that is also characteristic of the Beth Shemesh tablet is therefore unlikely to be a coincidence. If the HLḤ alphabet originates in Egypt, it too will have been written in the prevailing direction. The right-to-left habit later left its mark on the Phoenician writing-system, possibly because papyrus was used as a medium at sites such as Byblos. The clearest evidence for this is the well-known reference in *Wenamun* 2, 8, where the ruler of Byblos proceeds to consult the day-books of his forefathers (cf. the discussions in Redford 1986: 100 and Redford 1992: 330, together with the remarks of Emerton 2005).

In the same *Voyage of Wenamun* there is an episode where the hero is brought into the presence of the ruler of Byblos, one of the principal ports on the Lebanese coast. 'I was ushered into his presence, and the shadow of his lotus-shaped fan fell upon me. But Penamun, an (Egyptian) cupbearer who was employed by him, took me to one side and said, "The shadow of Pharaoh your master has fallen upon you". The ruler was angry with him, saying, "Leave him alone".' (*Wenamun* 2, 44–7.) This is presumably meant to be satirical, or a prophecy of some ill omen, but it is an episode we may choose to remember. The shadow of Pharaoh, the sun-king of Egypt, stretched over the Near East, and there are reasons to think that this shadow was visible in more places than we know.

Acknowledgements

I owe information on cuneiform, and much more, to the kindness of Professor Alan Millard of the University of Liverpool. I am also grateful to the Academic Study Group on Israel and the Middle East, and especially to Professor Lester Grabbe, for their invitation to attend a most stimulating and hospitable conference.

10

EMPIRES AND FARMERS

Eveline van der Steen

Introduction

This paper explores the impact that power changes within a region, or a country, have on the local population. How do empires, or external governments, generally deal with the people in the lands they conquer? How does the local population respond to the changes in power? What happens to the local power structures, the social organization?

I shall look at various power changes that took place within, or were imposed on, Palestine, in subrecent periods, starting with the Islamic conquest. The information that is available to us from these periods, especially from the eighteenth to early twentieth centuries, is more extensive and varied than that from earlier periods, such as the Iron Ages and the Persian and even Hellenistic periods. As a consequence we may be able to say something about these earlier changes in power, and how they affected the local population.

It is not my intention to draw conclusions from this relatively basic comparison between two societies that are over 2000 years apart. My aim is to point out similarities in the relationship between conquerors and conquered in different circumstances, and suggest that there may be other similarities that would not show up in the sources, particularly in the history of Judah and Palestine.

Power Changes in the Persian and Hellenistic Periods

During the Persian and Hellenistic periods, there have been various changes of power on an international level. The first one was not strictly an international power change, but it nevertheless had a major impact on the power relations within Judah. This was the return of the exiles from Babylon, under Nehemia and Ezra as narrated in the Bible.

The second change was the conquest of Palestine by Alexander, and the third was the take-over by the Ptolemies after Alexander's death. The next change was the conquest by the Seleucids, the final outcome of the Syro-Palestinian wars, and the last change was the Hasmonaean conquest, again not strictly an international change of power, but certainly a national one.

The impact of these changes was different in every case, but all had, in one sense or another, an impact on the shaping of a national identity in Judah.

The first change, the return of the exiles with the support of the Persian king, created a new demographic and ideological situation in Judah. In spite of the fact that the archaeological record does not reflect a major population increase or demographic change (Tal, this vol.), it is often assumed that the philosophical and religious concepts that eventually shaped the books of the old testament (and eventually the new testament as well) started here.

Honigman (this vol.) points towards the focus on descent as a major shaping factor in the self-identification of the Jews. This, according to her, to a certain extent replaced the focus on territory, although the territorial issue did not disappear.

The necessity for a focus on descent as an ethnic factor for the returnees was self-evident. If they wanted to claim the region as its rightful possessors, the returnees had to make a claim to it that was stronger than that of the people who lived there already, so territorial claims were not good enough. Descent, however, as a claim for belonging to the place, could overrule the territorial claims of the inhabitants, who had themselves been moved from elsewhere into the country, a point that the returnees were eager to stress.

This 'claim to the land of the fathers' based on descent rather than residency, is a tribal concept. The returnees adapted it for pragmatic reasons, but that does not mean that it was new to them. The narratives of the Patriarchs, of the exodus and the conquest of the land were revived, and adapted to the needs of the present, but they were rooted in old oral traditions that had been kept alive over the centuries. It has generally been taken for granted that early Israel was a tribally organized society. While these assumptions are based on the picture painted in the biblical narrative, which is itself largely constructed in the post-exilic period, archaeological and external textual evidence support it. The relationship between ancestry and territory is a complex one, and while it is rare to find texts that flesh out this relationship in pre-exilic contexts, there are references to ancestry in texts such as the Amarna letters (which refer to ruling 'houses' in the meaning of family) and the Mesha stela. Modern parallels show that narratives of origin, or genealogies were generally part of the oral tradition of a tribe, and were rarely written down (Oppenheim 1943 *passim*, Shryock 1997).

A famous example is that of the *sirat Beni Hilal*, the epic of the journey of the Beni Hilal, under their legendary leader Abu Zaid, from Arabia to northwest Africa. The extensive corpus of versions, both oral and written, of this epic contain episodes that are reminiscent of the narrative of the exodus of Israel. They are rooted in the historic events of the tenth and eleventh centuries when the Beni Hilal were driven out of the Arabian peninsula by the consequences of a severe drought, and later used by the Fatimid government of Egypt, to quell the insurrections of the Berbers in the Maghreb (Connelly 1986; Norris 1988; Wansbrough 1968: 645–46). Likewise, Andrew Shryock has shown the importance of preserving, manipulating and constructing genealogies as a means to claim territory or positions of power, even in modern society (Shryock 1997: 241, 246–48). Modern parallels also show the connection between ancestry and geneal-ogy, and territorial claims. Shryock (1997: 57–9) describes how parts of the old territory of the Adwan, sold, and resold, and now occupied by a Palestinian refugee camp, nevertheless was considered Adwan territory – inalienable, in spite of the tribe itself giving up the land.[1]

This relationship between ancestry and territorial claims was further strengthened by the presence of ancestral burials. The tombs of patriarchal saints, welis, were a common phenomenon in Palestine and Jordan in the Islamic period, and generally represented a claim to the land in which they lie. Some nomadic tribes would have cemeteries in their territory, and whenever someone died, he would be carried back to the territory to be buried. Gravestones would often have the mark of the tribe to which the deceased belonged, scratched on it (Schumacher 1888: 66; 189; Musil 1928: 419; Golding 1938: 268). The importance of the return of Joseph's bones into Canaan lies in this tradition, as it strengthened the claim of his descendants to the land.

This may all seem self-evident, but it shows that the basically tribal concepts of ancestry and territory as used by the returnees in the Persian period, to claim the land, were not new, but a pragmatic use of a tradition-ally tribal society.

In an address at the conference, Yuval Shahar discussed the silence in the biblical narrative about the Samaritan temple on Mount Gerizim. The archaeological record supports a construction in the fifth century, the same period as the return of the Jews to Jerusalem under Nehemia.

---

1   The same can be said of modern Israel. The claim of the returnee Israelis to the land was based on ancestry, and still is for those who want to become an Israeli citizen. Little has changed in 2500 years.

According to Shahar, the Jews were simply not aware of the presence of the temple on Mount Gerizim. I find this hard to believe. The story of the returnees as told in Ezra, suggests that the 'adversaries' of Benjamin and Judah offered to help rebuild the temple in Jerusalem, and take part in the rituals, because that is what they were doing already – presumably elsewhere. But the returnees rejected them, claiming not only the land, but also its God for themselves exclusively. This episode suggests first, that there was already a temple somewhere, dedicated to the god of the land, and secondly, that the various groups of people were aware of what was going on in the region. It is unimaginable that the returnees were not aware of the existence of a temple to Jahweh elsewhere. It is more likely that they chose to ignore it, and the whole cult surrounding it, as the most effective way of rendering it non-existent. The Jahweh cult was the exclusive cult of the returnees, and by pretending there were no adherents elsewhere, they made it part of their exclusive claim to the land, together with their ancestral claims. That way, the religion became an argument in the returnees' claim to the territory.

All this changes after the Samarian rebellion, when the focus of government moves to Shechem, where most of the surviving population resettled. It is possible, as Shahar suggests, that the temple on Mount Gerizim became involved in the government, and from then on it was impossible for the Jews in Jerusalem to ignore it.

It seems that most of the re-editing of the existing traditions about pre-exilic Israel was geared towards this three-tiered claim to the land: territorial, ancestral and religious, and the three concepts were strongly interwoven in the resulting narratives as we know them (Aitken, this vol.).

This way of creating a national identity is not very different from what we know of later, nineteenth and twentieth century forms of tribal identification, as shown above. The religious pillar in this identity construction is more difficult to detect in later sources, as the religion of Islam was all-pervading, and united the different groups rather than separating them. Nevertheless, the presence of tribal sanctuaries, and particularly the fanatical destruction of them by the Wahabis in the beginning of the nineteenth century, may throw light on it. Ostentatiously the saints' tombs were seen by the Wahabis as paganism, a corruption of the faith, involving the veneration of saints, in violation of the exclusive veneration of Allah. At the same time, however, this reformation was aimed at unifying the whole of the Islamic world, overruling the separate tribal identities, and the destruction of tribal sanctuaries may well have been part of that.

The administration of the town was centred in Jerusalem, and in the hands of the high priest and the priests, who functioned as rulers and bureaucracy, closely marrying religion to administration, and thus creating a theocracy. This is Ioudaismos (Honigman, this vol.), a practical theocracy, with the high priest as king, and the oral traditions about pre-exilic Israel were adapted to reflect this concept as much as possible.

According to Nehemia 11, nine-tenths of every returning clan or tribe lived outside Jerusalem, in the towns and villages of the land, and only one-tenth would live in the city, and obviously be part of the administration.

This situation is comparable to the situation on the Kerak Plateau in the sixteenth to twentieth centuries (Gubser 1973: 49, 75, 178–79, map 6); van der Steen 2007). The Kerak Plateau was controlled by one family, the Majali, who had their headquarters in Kerak. On the plateau there lived a number of tribes, who were pastoralists, or farmers, and all of which had representatives, families that lived in the town of Kerak. In fact, the map of Kerak, even in the 1960s, reflected on a smaller scale the territorial map of the plateau, with representatives of the various tribes living in separate quarters, while the two main confederations each had its own sector in the town. This facilitated interaction between the rural tribes and the town-based government of the Majali sheikhs – although they would occasionally travel to the more remote parts of their territory to administer justice in camps and villages and solve conflicts. So the biblical narrative reflects a situation that was not uncommon in a society that was basically tribally organized, but veered towards a more centralized administration.

It also explains why Jerusalem could remain relatively small and still be the focus of government. Lipschitz (this vol.) points out a discrepancy in the archaeological record of Jerusalem, with a difference in the architectural remains and the small artifacts such as pottery, seals and coins. Perhaps the interaction between the rural population of the land, and its representatives in the town can account for some of this discrepancy.

Persian to Hellenistic Rule

The transition from Persian to Hellenistic rule, according to most sources, and as stressed by the participants of this conference, did not affect the province of Judah much; Alexander's conquest of the region largely seems to have passed the area unnoticed, with the exception of the coastal area and the revolt in Samaria. The conquest of Jerusalem by Ptolemy I was probably disruptive for the town itself, but may have had more consequences for the Jewish community outside Palestine, as it is seen as the effective beginning of the large Jewish community in Alexandria.

In the province itself, Alexander, and the Ptolemies after him, did not interfere with the existing administration. The heavy-handed and swift response to the Samarian rebellion proves that rebellion was not tolerated in the centres of government; however, in general, the conquered regions were treated more like vassals than anything else. Jerusalem, capital of the province, maintained its own rulers, the high priests and the priesthood.

The same thing happened after the Islamic conquest of Palestine in the seventh century. The archaeological record suggests that the Islamic 'invasions' may have been relatively peaceful. There is little evidence of destruction. Textual material shows that the Byzantine administration and methods of tax-collecting were largely adopted by the Islamic conquerors, and adjusted to their own needs. Even the language was only gradually changed from Greek to Arabic when Khalif Abd el-Malik decided that the administrative documents should be translated into Arabic, and henceforward written in Arabic (sources in Nahlieli 2007).

Likewise, the administration in the Ptolemaic period was probably largely left intact in most of the conquered provinces, and there was a strong participation of the local population in government. Administrative documents were often written in the local language. This seems to have been the most efficient way of maintaining peace in the area, as well as collecting the optimum revenue (Grabbe, this vol.). The population in the countryside would hardly notice the difference, as long as the amount of taxes remained more or less stable.

Grabbe suggests that there was a 'formal' and an 'informal' system of governance, the 'informal' one largely independent of the official government. He compares it to the Sicilian *mafia* and gives two examples that underline this independence, from the Zenon letters.

The first one is that of a man Jeddous, a Jew, who was a local leader, possibly a *komarches* of an unnamed village, and who owed money to Zenon, or perhaps to Apollonius. When Zenon sent messengers to collect it, they were thrown out of the village by Jeddous.

The second story is that of two brothers in Idumea, named Kollochoutos and Zaidelos, who had sold slaves to Zenon. However, when transported to Egypt, the slaves escaped and returned to their former master, who then returned them only after payment of a considerable sum on top of the sale price. The correspondence shows Zenon's efforts to involve the local authorities in the case. These cases demonstrate the independence of the region from the empire, and the power of local elites and local rulers. This situation is reminiscent of the southern part of the Ottoman empire in the eighteenth and nineteenth centuries, where the effectual authority of the empire was limited to the coastal area and the larger cities such as Damascus and Jerusalem; outside these areas the local population was virtually independent and controlled by local sheikhs and leaders such as the Majali family in Kerak, or the sheikhs of the local villages and tribes. These chiefs were often 'appointed' by the Ottoman empire, and paid, in the hopes of keeping their loyalty, so that they could act as middlemen and buffers between the local population and the government. Often they were also responsible for tax-collecting. Although these chiefs readily accepted the payment, their loyalty to the government always remained doubtful, and there were frequent skirmishes and battles, in which the empire's soldiers more often than not lost. When in Salt, at the end of the eighteenth century Ibrahim Pasha of Damascus tried to install a local ruler, the people of Salt cut off his head, and sent it back to Ibrahim (Oliphant 1880: 199; although Seetzen [1854–59/I:397] gives a different version of this event).

Towns like Salt and Kerak were notorious as sanctuaries for people who were persecuted by the government.

So it is possible that during the Ptolemaic period, as in the later Ottoman empire, the authority of the absentee ruler outside his core area in Egypt was limited to the towns and perhaps the coastal area (the story concerning the attempted smuggle of slaves through the Tyre harbour suggests that perhaps the authorities had more control in the harbours) whereas further inland, and outside the cities that were of direct interest to them, the Ptolemies had little control. Collection of taxes, the main raison d'etre of these provinces, would be done through tax farmers, who negotiated with the local authorities, the *komarches*, the sheikhs and rulers of the villages and tribes. These local rulers had to keep on the right side of both their own villages and tribes, and of the authorities, a situation that created a buffer against clashes between the rural population and the government, and at the same time could be lucrative for the leaders themselves, if they played their cards properly. As Grabbe puts it: there seemed to be two levels of governance: the formal and the informal, and the informal was as important as, perhaps even more so than, the formal system. He compares it to the Sicilian *mafia*, but it may equally well be equated to the local systems of government in the southern Levant and the Arabian peninsula in the nineteenth century.

At the same time, material culture in towns such as the harbour of Yavne-Yam, or Marisa, show that Greeks and others within the Hellenistic empire made considerable marks on both culture and economy, particularly, it seems, in the international trade. Yavne-Yam had a cosmopolitan population probably mostly involved in trade. The archaeological record shows a rich complex of imported and local materials, suggesting a small but wealthy foreign merchant class mixing with a larger local population. The records of Marisa likewise show a mixed population, identified by their names rather than their material culture, which seems to have been heavily Ptolemized (Kloner, this vol). The vast majority were Arabs, Idumaeans and west Semites, suggesting an involvement in the Arabian trade, which is also borne out by the location of the site. Cooperation between the Hellenistic occupiers, whether Ptolemaic or Seleucid, and the various local groups, seems to have been quite smooth in these cases, although Fischer (this vol.) suggests, based on later events, that the local population of Yavne-Yam must have been hostile to the foreign merchant class.

Ptolemaeans to Seleucids

The change to Seleucid rule may have been more disruptive for the population of Yehud. In the various wars preceding the final takeover it seems that Antiochus was already supported by a large section of the population of the region, including the Arab tribes in Transjordan (Hengel 1974: 15,17f). Jerusalem also supported the take-over by Antiochus, and was richly rewarded. Whether the rural population also supported the new rulers is not clear entirely – however, the ease with which Antioch overran the country, as well as the edicts he proclaimed for their protection and well-being, suggest he must have had considerable support from them.

We can perhaps compare this situation with that of the government change in the tenth century AD, from the Abbasid to the Fatimid dynasty, with its seat in Cairo. The Fatimids originated in the religious sect of the Isma'ilites. Towards the end of the Abbasid period various religious sects were opposing what they saw as a decadent government. Carmatians were a religious sect from the Peninsula who fought first against the Abbasids, but when the Fatimids gained power in Egypt, they turned against them. Internal strife among the tribes of Palestine was the result. The tribes were divided, either supporting the Carmathians, or the Fatimids. The majority of the Tay tribes, who had by then established themselves firmly in Palestine, originally supported the Carmathians, but changed their support to the Fatimids after the take-over of Cairo. After the Fatimid conquest of Palestine this move increased their status and power even further. They were granted land, status and political power by the new government. They actually tried to establish an independent kingdom in the Negev, but then the Fatimid rulers stepped in, as a result of which the power of the southern Tay tribes was broken up, and the Sinbis, one of the major tribes, was exiled to Egypt. The Tay, however, remained powerful in Palestine.

In the case of the Seleucids it is clear that Antiochus wanted to stay on the right side of the people, both in the cities and in the countryside. The decrees referring to local rule seem to have been a continuation of the previous period. The fact that they were issued anew may suggest that actual implementation had eroded, although it may also have been a formality from the side of the new ruler.

Subrecent Changes of Power and their
Impact on the Local Population

Information about the early Islamic periods, up to and including the
Crusaders and Mamluks, is still relatively scant, where the impact on the
local population is concerned. From their own accounts it is clear that the
Crusaders saw the locals as infidels and barbarians, and had no qualms
about raping, robbing and murdering them wherever they came across
them. However, as strangers in a strange land, they eventually had to
cooperate, and they did, as can be judged from the material remains found
in Crusader sites: locally influenced architecture, local artifacts (notably
pottery, although it may be significant that one, very common, type of pottery, known as Arab-Geometric, seems to be missing from Crusader sites
altogether (van der Steen 1998)). Written sources confirm this, although
the contacts must have been largely limited to the settled population.
Usama ibn Munqidh's account (Hitti 1929) suggests that tribes were sometimes recruited by local rulers either in their internal wars, or against the
Crusaders. It is likely that Saladin's army at the battle of Hittin consisted
largely of tribesmen. After he had beaten the Franks by the Horns of Hittin,
Saladin saw fit to redistribute the land. Oppenheim (1943: 8–9) suggests
that this meant a complete redivision of tribal territories. This is possible,
Saladin may have used this division as a means to reward his supporters
in battle, but it is also to be expected that the new divisions reflected at
least partly the status quo, the existing territorial divisions, after the defeat
of the Crusaders. Either way, the new division shows that the major tribal
groups were broken up into smaller tribes or clans, each with their own,
rather limited territory. These small, almost feudal units spent much time
fighting each other, which suited the government well. Only the Djarm
in the south, descendants of the legendary Tay confederation, still had
some of their former power left, and were a force to be reckoned with for
the Mamluk government. It is likely that the Mamluks cultivated their
relationship with the Djarm and vied for their support. One argument for
this is the fact that the Djarm lost all power after the fall of the Mamluks
and the rise of the Ottomans. The Djarm may well have backed the wrong
horse. Local power shifted to the Beni Hareta (like the Djarm, a Tay tribe),
who had supported the Ottomans, and now reaped the benefits. They were
given hereditary rulership over their territory, the Sanjak Lejjun (near
Jenin in the Highlands), with the right of taxing.

The importance of the support of the tribes (the 'Arabs' of the third
century) should not be underestimated. Throughout recent history, the
support or lack of it of the tribes has been decisive for the outcome of
battles and wars, including World War I in the region.

Power Changes in the Ottoman Period

The Ottomans, after they had taken control, did not substantially change the local administration. The provinces that had been designated by the Mamluk government after the defeat of the Crusaders were maintained in most of the empire, only the head rulers being replaced by Ottoman pashas.

Daftars from the period (Hütteroth and Abdulfattah 1977) show that in the middle of the 16th century the empire was at its political and economic zenith. Settlement was dense and agricultural productivity had reached a height that it never reached afterwards (Hütteroth and Abdulfattah 1977: 8), with both the settled population in the villages, and the groups classified as tribes (jama'a) paying taxes (Hütteroth and Abdulfattah 1977: 28).

After the reign of Suleiman, the central government began to weaken considerably, the result both of internal corruption and nepotism, and of military losses. Warfare and misgovernment induced tax increases, which were extracted from the local population. The result was a depletion of villages, and a decline in agriculture, a vicious circle, that led, towards the beginning of the 18th century, to a serious decline (Cohen 1973: 1–5).

One of the consequences of this situation was that there were various attempts, both from inside and from outside, to seize power in (parts of) Palestine.

One attempt was made by Zaher al-Umar, a local Bedouin sheikh in the Galilee. He was allowed to pursue his aims until he allied himself with the rebelling Egyptian Ali Pasha and conquered Saida. The governors of Lebanon and Damascus with a Turkish contingent routed Zaher out, and killed him.

His successor was a man named Ahmed al-Jezzar (the butcher), who was governor of Saida. He, like Zaher, was allowed to extend his power both north and south, and eventually he also conquered Acco. He maintained the favour of the Ottoman government, and was eventually appointed Wali of Lebanon, and for several terms, also of Damascus. He managed to maintain order and remained useful to the Ottoman government in that he squeezed the countryside for taxes. The result on the longer term was that under Jezzar's rule the country was definitely declining. According to Ulrich Seetzen, who travelled the country in 1807 (but was not published until 1854–59) the plain around Haifa and Acco was full of villages, and the whole area was cultivated. In the Marj ibn Amr (the plain of Beth Shean), however, Bedouin were roaming, and demanding tax from both villages and travellers. Local warlords, such as Abu Gosh in the Jerusalem area, remained unchecked. In the south and east, control of the government was limited to a small area around Gaza, and attempts to keep the pilgrims' route safe by paying off the Bedouin, in order to keep the stretches that went through their territory, safe from attack (also Browne 1806).

It is well possible that the decline at the end of the Ptolemaic rule of Palestine came with comparable tensions, which would explain the support of the local population for the Seleucid conquerors.

Muhammad Ali Pasha

When the Wahabi movement swept over the empire at the turn of the nineteenth century, the government was utterly powerless to stop it, and eventually called in the help of Muhammed Ali Pasha of Egypt.

Muhammad Ali checked the Wahabis, but he did not stop when he had fulfilled his task. Instead he made a bid for power himself. With his son Ibrahim Pasha he conquered Palestine, and marched into Anatolia.

Western witnesses of Ibrahim's conquest of Arabia have recounted many of the atrocities the Egyptians committed in the region, and the consequent clashes with, and animosity of, the local Bedouin tribes (Sadleir 1866/1977, Burckhardt 1830).

The ruthless suppression of the Bedouin tribes by the Egyptian pashas was also reflected in their rule in Palestine. Palestine at the beginning of the nineteenth century was largely controlled by the Bedouin tribes (see above) and the effect of Ibrahim's rule was that their power was curbed. They were even forced to pay taxes. Some of the 'independent' cities, such as Nablus and Hebron, were integrated into the new centrally controlled government, and forced to pay taxes, and to provide soldiers for the army. Agriculture flourished, and peasants and villages were secure.

Ibrahim also brought Egyptian farmers, and settled them in the Jordan Valley to cultivate it, and soldiers, belonging to various Egyptian tribes, such as the Henadi, who eventually also settled in the region. After the defeat of Muhammad Ali, the Henadi remained, and grew into one of the major tribes of the Galilee.

The End of the Ottoman Empire

The end of the Ottoman empire in the region came with the onset of World War I. British forces had already been active in the area, particularly in the Arabian Peninsula, in the decades before the war. They were interested in the region partly because of the trade with India, and partly for strategic reasons, and they supported the Ibn Sa'ud of Riadh and their allies the Ibn Sabah family of Kuwayt, against the Ibn Rashid emirate of Hayil, who were likewise supported by the Turks. This 'support' consisted largely of lavish gifts of money and arms, and as a result the whole region was crammed with arms and ammunition (Musil 1928: 250), something that greatly contributed to the general chaos on the Peninsula just before the war.

During the course of World War I, and particularly towards the end, this form of politics was expanded to Jordan largely due to the efforts of T. E. Lawrence, who recruited the support of the other large tribes in the area, the Howeitat and the Rwala. The way the tribes saw these efforts is perhaps best reflected in a story told by Gertrude Bell, who was also heavily involved in these politics. One day a sheikh of a tribe came to a British officer, to offer the support of his tribe to the British, in exchange for payment of 100,000 pounds. The officer refused, and the sheikh commented: 'Pity. I think the British will win the war, and I would have liked to be on the winning side.'

Being on the winning side was lucrative for the tribes, as history had already proven. Not only were there pecuniary advantages, but tribes that had sided with the winning side, rose in power, and gained governing positions in the newly formed governments. In general it can be stated that this sort of involvement in politics in times of power changes almost invariably led to a change in the local power relationships, with the tribes that had supported the winning side profiting, and the losing tribes often paying heavily.

Discussion and Conclusions

Very generally it can be said that there are two forms of conquest, or change in power: those that ignore the power structures of the local population, and suppress the population, and those that try to use the local power structures to their own ends. At the same time, there are power changes from 'within', contrived by local leaders, and fuelled by internal troubles, and changes from 'without', conquerers that came from elsewhere, with no previous bond to the local situation. Sometimes, as was the case in the British–Ottoman struggle, the external power, although a stranger to the region, could and would use the local situation, and try to win over the local tribes. The same tactics seem to have been used by the Babylonians in the seventh century (Eph'al 1982: 143, 225). Antiochus III employed the same tactics.

The Crusaders, equally strangers to the area, made no efforts to recruit the local tribes, but, on the contrary, suppressed, even massacred them, creating a situation wherein they were opposing the whole of the local population, instead of – as was the case in World War I – only part of it. Eventually the Crusaders, being strangers in a strange land, had to cooperate with the local population. Sources are particularly silent about this local interaction. However, the ease with which Saladin regained the land once he set out to do so, suggests an almost undivided support for his cause, something that is perhaps reflected in Antiochus' conquest.

On the other hand, local, internal changes of power could likewise either use and depend on local power structures, or ignore and suppress them. Daher al-Umar was a local sheikh, who rose to power with the support of his own tribe. On the other hand, Jezzar Pasha, an Ottoman officer, had no immediate need for the support of the local tribes, and suppressed them, as well as the settled population, as well as he could. Muhammad Ali supported the settled population but suppressed the nomadic tribes in the region. In this, as in other cases, the immediate result of suppressing the Bedouin tribes, and supporting agriculture for tax purposes, was an increase in settlement and agrarian productivity. In the long run, however, because the new forces were not very sensitive of, and interested in, the local power structures, and mainly tried to extract as much revenue out of it as possible, the decline would become general.

Judah had, at least according to Nehemia and in its ideology, reorganized itself as a tribal confederation, with extensive genealogies, and a leading tribe which provided the leader, namely the high priest, who was the political as well as the religious leader, and as such guarded the tribal ideology. A practical manifestation of this 'tribal ideology' was that every tribe had its representatives in Jerusalem. The sources all suggest that Jerusalem remained the religious focus of the Jews uninterrupted until the Maccabaean revolt. At the same time, the archaeological record shows that it did not expand physically, although small finds suggest intensive activity. This suggests that the political and ideological structure of the society did not change, at least not with regard to Jerusalem: representatives of the largely rural population resided in the town as middlemen, but it never became a metropolis in any sense. The attitude of Judah towards the Ptolemaic and Seleucid rulers was one of vassalage while retaining their tribal independence, expressed in the religion and the religion-based government. They could withdraw their loyalty when they felt wronged, and did so when they supported Antiochus. Antiochus appreciated the value of the Jewish support as he had earlier the Arab support in the east, and rewarded the town and the people handsomely, respecting their political/religious independence.

Conquests and changes of power in the past have been described and analysed in various sources and with various aims and agendas.

The Fatimids were supported by several of the Tay tribes who as a consequence rose to power when the Fatimids ruled the land. The Djarm, who had become powerful under the Mamluks and supported them in the take-over, completely lost their power after the Mamluks were defeated by the Ottomans. The use of existing power structures is most clear in World War I and the period that preceded it, when both the Ottomans and the British tried to rally the support of powerful tribes and confederations, first of the Arabian peninsula, but later also of Syria. The result on the local level was a change of local power structures to the advantage of the 'winning' tribes.

There is a clear conceptual difference here with the next approach, that of suppression and total control. For the Fatimids, the British and also the Ottomans, the land they were taking over was a community of people that they would have to deal with. The land WAS the people in it and to control the people was to control the land. It was therefore important to have the support of the people even before the take-over.

For the Crusaders, or Jezzar, or the Egyptian Pashas, the land and the people were two different things. The land was important, as holy territory, or a source of potential wealth, and the people were merely the tools to get to that wealth (for the Crusaders the population of the Holy Land were the infidels, that had soiled the sacred earth and should ideally be rooted out, only that was not practical).

The result, in terms of changes in the local organization of the land, was an increase in production centres: farmsteads, agricultural units, small villages and a growth and perhaps new creation of the 'control centres', towns, but also fortresses, and administrative centres. The new rulers also tended to bring in their own 'workforce': soldiers, administrators, in the case of Ibrahim Pasha, Egyptian farmers which he settled in the Jordan Valley (and which were immediately chased out by the local Bedouin once the Egyptians were gone), which brought with them aspects of their foreign culture, particularly visible in the control centres. The Crusader period provides a ready example.

However, if and when the demands of the rulers were increasing, and life for the local inhabitants became more difficult, they were inclined to revolt, or simply move away and the initial signs of prosperity (which was prosperity of the rulers, rather than of the local population) would disappear. In the case of the Crusaders, the local power structures seem to have been disassembled to a large extent, judging from the new territorial divisions after Hittin.

The archaeological record of the Persian and Hellenistic periods show no clear increase in farmsteads or fortresses, nor a decline, that can suggest this approach of 'total control' of any political power in the region. But then, there is much that still needs to be discovered.

At the same time, there is no clear rule that connects the background of the conqueror or the nature of the conquest to the effect it has on the conquered land. There are only tendencies that can be highlighted. Our recent sources, particularly those of the Ottoman period and its aftermath, are more informative about the effects on the local population than earlier sources, which tended to focus more on the élites and the rulers. However, by comparing the nature of the conquest, and the effect on the local population in subrecent times, we can perhaps say something about the local population in the Persian and Hellenistic periods, the interaction with the local and foreign governments that they had to deal with and the effects of conquest on the land itself.

11

EARLY ENOCHIC TRADITION AND THE RESTORATION OF
HUMANITY: THE FUNCTION AND SIGNIFICANCE OF *1 ENOCH* 10

Loren T. Stuckenbruck
Durham University

Introduction

The purpose of this article is to explore a passage from the *Book of
Watchers* (*1 En.* 1–36) which refers to what is frequently referred to as a
'conversion' of all nations to be anticipated among eschatological blessings once the earth has been 'cleansed'. The text comes at the climax of a
literary unit in *1 Enoch* chs 6–11, and falls within 10.17–11.2. At verses
20-22, the text reads:[1]

> (20) But as for you, cleanse the earth from all uncleanness,
>   and from all injustice,
>   and from all sin and godlessness.
>   And eliminate all the unclean things that have been done on the
>   earth.
> (21) And all the children of men will become righteous,[2]
>   and all the peoples will serve (λατρεύοντες)
>   and bless (ε῾υλογου῀ντες) me,
>   and they will all worship (προσκυνου῀ντες) me.
> (22) And the entire earth will be cleansed
>   from all defilement and all uncleanness.
>   And no wrath or torment

---

1   The translation below is my own, based on the Ethiopic I recension, with insertions of
corresponding Greek terms from the Codex Panopolitanus. For a recent discussion on the relative
value of the Ethiopic recensions, see Stuckenbruck 2007: 19–26. For the Greek text, I rely on the
edition by Black (1970).

2   The text 'and all . . . righteous' is original, though probably omitted in Grk. Cod. Pan. by
homoioarcton, perhaps at the stage of its Semitic *Vorlage* (וכל< . . . וכל>).

> will I ever again send upon them,
> for all the generations of eternity.

Commentators on this text have mostly treated its vision of the future in passing, noting either its coherence with received biblical traditions regarding the fate of the nations or its influence on the later Enochic (and perhaps other) texts.[3] Over a century ago, R. H. Charles, in an overview of apocalyptic ideas that flourished during the second century BCE, comments tersely that, '[a]ccording to I Enoch x. 21, all the Gentiles are to become righteous and worship God'.[4] Charles's general view of the passage has been largely retained, with the exception that there is now wide agreement among scholars that the date of the *Book of Watchers* – all the more, the non-Enochic chs 6–11 within that work – goes back at least to the third century BCE.[5]

Thus, while we have to do with a tradition that circulated during this period, we may ask and address several questions that move the discussion forward. How has the passage appropriated received tradition? How widespread were the sentiments of this text during the third century BCE? To what extent is the passage shaped by a function within its literary context? To what extent are its particular features retained by later Enochic traditions that came under its influence?

The framework for addressing these questions is determined by three factors: (1) its relation to passages in the Hebrew Bible which refer to the eventual recognition of Israel's God among the nations (Isa. 2.3; 18.7; 19.22; 45.14-15; 60; 66.18-23; Jer. 16.19; Zech. 8.20-23; 14.16-21; Ps. 22.27-28; 47.8; 63.2-4; 86.9; 102.15; 117.1); (2) its role and function within the *Book of Watchers*, especially the originally independent unit of chs 6–11; and (3) its conceptual relation to late Second Temple traditions which either signal the recognition by the nations of Israel's God (Pss. Sol. 17.29-32, 34; *Similitudes* in *1 En.* 48.5; 50.2; Dan. 7.14) or similarly anticipate among the nations some kind of 'conversion'[6] or worship of God (Tob. 14.6; *Animal Apocalypse* at *1 En.* 90.37; *Apocalypse of Weeks* at *1 En.* 91.14; *Epistle of Enoch* at *1 En.* 100.6; 105.1; Dan. 7.14). It is along

---

3   See especially Black 1985: 140; Nickelsburg, 1977: 224, 228; Uhlig 1984: 531–32; and Olson 2004: 40.

4   R. H. Charles, 1963 [1913]: 246. Charles offers no comment on the text in his commentary, *The Book of Enoch or 1 Enoch*, (1912: 26) but rather reserves his discussion on 'the conversion of Gentiles' under *Animal Apocalypse* at *1 En.* 90.30 (ibid., pp. 214–15).

5   Cf. Milik 1976: 24; Nickelsburg 2001: 169–71.

6   Though this term is frequently applied by scholars to the *1 Enoch* passages under consideration, it is important to note that my use of it in this article is non-technical; failing more specific indications in the texts, it does not denote a formal turning of Gentiles to Judaism that inter alia is carried out through circumcision, though at the same time the possibility of this cannot be excluded.

each of these lines that the present discussion shall proceed, beginning with a brief discussion of (1) while focusing more weight of analysis on (2), and then on (3), which will focus on the interpretive trajectories of *1 En.* 10.21 reflected within the early Enoch traditions.

The Nations in the Hebrew Bible

A number of texts in the Jewish scriptures express the belief that the nations of the earth will worship Israel's God. Such texts are primarily motivated by the conviction that what happens to Israel – whether it be exile or restoration – forms part of God's grand design of things for the rest of the world.[7] In the texts the response of the nations to the God of Israel is expressed in a number of ways:

they will come to Jerusalem to be instructed and 'walk in his paths' (Isa. 2.3; Mic. 4.2)

they will bring gifts and wealth to Jerusalem (Isa. 18.7; 45.14; 60.5, 11)

they will supplicate God (Isa. 19.22; Zech. 8:21-22)

they will be subservient to Israel (Isa. 45.14; 60.10, 12)

they will recognize that the God of Israel is unique (Isa. 45.14-15; 66.18; Ps. 102.15)

they will recognize the special status of Israel amongst the nations (Zech. 8.23; cf. Isa. 60.3)

they will worship God in Jerusalem (Isa. 66.23; Zech. 14.16-19; Ps. 22.27; 86.9)

they are exhorted to praise God for his justice and mercy (Ps. 67.3-4; 117.1)

they will 'turn' to God (Ps. 22.27).

---

7   N. T. Wright aptly states that 'the fate of the nations was inexorably and irreversibly bound up with that of Israel' (1992: 268).

Why, we may ask, is the motif of the nations' eventual worship or recognition of God so important in these texts? First, and fundamentally, it
is a way of re-enforcing the supremacy of Israel's faith. This motif thus
reflects an outcome that emerges logically from a fundamental conviction
that Israel is the elect people of a God who, at the same time, is Creator
of the cosmos. However nationalistic or ethnic the expressions of Israel's
faith may be, God is held to be at work throughout the world in a way
that affects the other nations which, though not elect, nevertheless are in
principle subject to God's rule (e.g. Ps. 22.28; 47.8; 86.9). Second, the
motif of the nations' worship of God expresses hope for a reversal of the
conditions of subjugation which in many of the texts Israel presently suffers. Despite Israel's present lowly state, the nations' acknowledgement
of God will demonstrate that they should be the ones who are subservient
(see esp. Isaiah 60). Third, Jerusalem (and the Temple) is the unmatched
place of the divine presence. In the proper order of things, when Israel is
restored from her dispersion among the other nations to worship in the
place where God is actually present, the nations will recognize the futility
of their gods and follow in tow (e.g. Jer. 16.19).

It is not clear, however, that any of these passages refer to a 'conversion'
of the nations, especially if we define the term 'conversion' as the *complete*
transfer from one religion to another. To be sure, the nations can receive
instruction, be governed by God's justice and mercy, and even 'walk in
his paths' (Isa. 2.4; Mic. 4.2). However, in the passages we have noted
they remain without a special covenant, do not enjoy the status of being
'elect' or 'chosen', 'righteousness' is never associated with them and they
only indirectly participate in the Temple cult (through the offering of their
wealth, submission or compliance).

The Role and Function of 10.21 in the Book of Watchers

Here, we look especially at the more original setting in which the passage
appears: *1 Enoch* chs 6–11, which elaborate and expand on the story
about 'the sons of God' and 'the daughters of men' and their gargantuan
progeny in Gen. 6.1-4 and its aftermath in the Great Flood (6.5–9.17). As
is well known, these chapters, which in turn are a fusion of distinguishable
traditions about rebellious angels,[8] form a distinct unit within the *Book of
Watchers*. Unlike the rest of the book, the patriarch Enoch is neither named
nor receives any, even implicit, attention. Both this oddity and the address

---

8   See Hanson, 1977: 195–233; Nickelsburg 1977: 383–405; Collins 1978: 315–22; Dimant
1978: 323–39; Newsom 1980: 313; Nickelsburg 2001: 171–72.

to 'the son of Lamech' at the beginning of chapter 10 (vv. 1-3), has rightly suggested that the acquired form of chs 6–11 was Noahic.[9]

That the figure of Noah should be connected with the story about the rebellious angels is not surprising. In the biblical tradition, the mating of 'the sons of God' with women on earth serves as a prelude to the Great Flood narrative and its aftermath in which Noah is the main protagonist (Gen. 6.5–9.17), while the few verses mentioning Enoch (Gen. 5.21-24) have been left behind. Moreover, the figure of Noah circulated as a constituent part of several sources that date back to at least the second century BCE. Two of these works are concerned with the birth of Noah (*Genesis Apocryphon* = 1Q20 ii 1 – v 26; *Birth of Noah* in *1 En.* 106.1–107.3), while another, the *Book of Giants*, is preserved in fragments which – as *1 En.* 10.1-3 – focus on the theme of Noah's escape from the flood (cf. 6Q8 2).[10] In a Euhemeristic tradition such as the so-called *Pseudo-Eupolemos* (fragments preserved, respectively, in Eusebius, *Praeparatio Evangelica* 9.17.1-9 and 18.2), a genetic link is even drawn between Noah (and Abraham) and the giants, a connection which the Jewish apocalyptic traditions just mentioned categorically refute.[11] Finally, and analogous to *1 Enoch* 10, the *Book of Giants* picks up the tradition which describes future bliss in terms of unprecedented fertility in the created order (cf. 1Q23 1+6+22 with *1 En.* 10.17-19).

As far as chs 6–11 are concerned, the Noahic framework makes sense not only because of the reference to Noah as 'the son of Lamech' in 10.1-3 but also because of motifs and imagery in ch. 10 that reflect the Great Flood story. In the present shape of the text, the introduction of the Noahic storyline occurs as a divine response to the complaints of murdered humans against the injustices which the giants have carried out against them (8.4–9.11). Here God's message, mediated through the angel Sariel, comes to Noah and declares three things: (1) that a destruction of 'the whole earth' through a deluge is imminent (10.2); (2) that Noah is to be instructed on how to survive this cataclysm (10.1, 3); and (3) that from him a 'plant' (Eth.; Grk. 'seed') will be established 'for all generations of eternity'.

---

9   So especially Charles 1912: 13–14, who regarded chs 6–11 as a 'fragment' from a now lost 'Apocalypse' or 'Book of Noah'.

10   Interestingly, the work refers to Enoch as the authoritative interpreter of the giants' ominous dreams, although it was copied in a ms. (4Q203) which Milik identified as the same ms. (4Q204) which contains several parts of *1 Enoch* (*Book of Watchers, Animal Apocalypse, Apocalypse of Weeks, Epistle of Enoch*, and *Birth of Noah*). However, the *Book of Giants* is *not*, as *1 Enoch* 6–11, an Enochic pseudepigraphon.

11   See further Stuckenbruck 2000: 354–77; see further idem, 2007 under the Notes to *1 En.* 106.4-7 and 106.9-12.

Readers familiar with the biblical narrative might at this point have expected a retelling of the Flood story (Gen. 6.5–8.22). The writer or compiler of tradition, however, is doing more than recounting events from the antediluvian period. The narrative plays up an analogy between the Noahic period, on the one hand, and the present and imminent future, on the other. But the extent of this analogy is not immediately clear. While the Noahic storyline is not entirely lost – indeed, motifs related to the Noah account intermittently recur later in the chapter (esp. from v. 14) – what follows in 10.4-13 focuses instead on the punishments meted out to Asa'el (10.4-6 – bound, thrown into darkness, and burn with fire at the Great Judgement), the giants (10.9-10 – condemned to annihilate one another) and 'Shemihazah and his companions' (10.11-13 – bound for 70 generations until eternally confined in a prison to undergo fiery torment). These acts of divine judgement, carried out, respectively, by the angels Raphael, Gabriel and Michael, come up directly against the demonic world against which the human souls have complained. By having the same quartet of angels carry out divine commands in ch 10 (vv. 1, 4, 9, 11) that has conveyed the human souls' appeals for justice to heaven (9.1, 4), the narrative in its received form has inseparably woven the story of Noah into the fabric of the fallen angels tradition.

Both the 'plant' to come from Noah 'for eternity' (10.3) and the final judgement against the rebellious Watchers (10.5-6, 12-13) demonstrate that the story correlates Noah's time with eschatological time. *Urzeit* and *Endzeit* converge, so that what happens in the one time has its counterpart in the other. Thus the story about fallen angels at the beginning of ch. 6 is relevant to how the writer(s) conceived of the future, and vice versa. Significantly, *the scope of this correlation involves all humanity*. The story begins with the mass of humanity – 'the sons of men' and 'the daughters of men' (6.1-2) – with whom the rebellious angels intermingle and who are overwhelmed by oppression. Through Noah this humanity's survival until the end is assured. It is not surprising, then, that in the end, at 10.20-22, all humanity will be found to worship God.

The path to this end is not, however, straightforward. The condemnation of the Watchers and slaughter of their offspring (10.14-15) – events inaugurated with the announcement of the Flood[12] and brought to an inevitable conclusion at the end – is in force during an intervening time characterized by the appearance of 'the plant of truth and righteousness'

---

12 However, the Flood does not itself constitute the punishment of either the Watchers or giants. Instead, deluge imagery relates to the theme of Noah's escape (10.3), the destruction and elimination of iniquity and impurity from the earth (10.16, 20, 22), and the escape of the righteous in the eschaton (10.17).

(10.16). This second 'plant' alludes to the 'plant' associated with Noah's progeny in 10.3, but does so in a narrower sense.

Who or what is this 'plant of truth and righteousness' in the text? Here the narrative is not concerned with post-Noahic humanity as a whole, but rather with those who are obedient to the covenant; that is, a community with whom the writer(s) would have identified. Significantly, this community is characterized by 'works of righteousness' (Eth.; omitted in the Grk. through homoioteleuton[13]). As such, they are the ones who, presumably as Noah during the Flood, will 'escape' when 'all iniquity' and 'every evil work' is destroyed (10.16; cf. also *Birth of Noah* at *1 En.* 107.1). Read in relation to the story about the Watchers story, the text offers an analogy between the destruction and eternal punishment of the Watchers and giants (cf. 10.9-14) with the destruction of iniquitous *activities*. Given the demonic origin of evil, punishment is not anticipated for human beings as much as the reprehensible *deeds* and *knowledge* they have learned from the angels (7.3-5; 8.1-3).[14]

I am therefore hesitant to regard the 'fallen angels' and 'giants' simply as decipherable metaphors for the late fourth century BCE diadochi (so Nickelsburg[15]) or wayward priests (so Suter[16]). While the former explanation provides a setting which would make it plausible to place the tradition within the background of Jewish resistance to unwelcome incursions of Hellenistic culture, chs 6–11 operate on a more profound level: demonic forces are at work behind those who have not only engaged in and adopted reprehensible activity and teaching, but even *behind* those who have introduced them. For all its rejection of aberrant forms of culture and the oppression associated with them, the story's *essentially mythic character* lends it a remarkable openness that holds the existence of a community of obedient Jews in tension with the existence of a humanity who, though largely aligned with the demonic world, are created by God and, as such, *in themselves*[17] have not set the world down the wrong path. By contrast, the angels have breached the boundaries that distinguish the heavenly from the earthly sphere (implied here and explicated in 15.7-10), while the giants are *mala mixta*.[18] The fundamental distinction between human

---

13 See Nickelsburg 2001: 218, who notes with Milik (1976: 189) that the longer reading is supported by the Aramaic text in 4QEn[c] 1 v 1.

14 In this way, the tradition's focus on the culpability of the Watchers and giants is nuanced: it does not imply that humans who have been taught by them are not held responsible.

15 1977: 383–405 and 2001: 170.

16 Suter 1979: 115–35, taking 10.9 as his point of departure.

17 Because the text emphasizes the destruction of 'works' and deeds (10.16, 20).

18 See Stuckenbruck 2003: 318–38.

nature, on the one hand, and the demonic, on the other, keeps humanity as a whole within the purview of divine purpose of redemption.

This does not do away with a distinction between 'the plant of truth and righteousness' (10.16) and 'all the children of men' (10.21). The former – that is, 'the righteous ones' who will 'escape' the punishment of the Watchers – are promised a limitless period of reproductive and agricultural activity (10.17-19) that reverses the annihilation and oppression suffered in the time before the Flood (7.3-5). The extant Ethiopic and Greek texts do not spell out that this bliss will include all humanity, nor do any of the recensions specify precisely how the special 'plant' is related to the rest of humanity. However, the arena of what 'the righteous' will enjoy is 'all the earth'. While the idea of a new beginning evokes the Noahic covenant following the deluge (Gen. 9.1-17; see the allusion to Gen. 9.11 in 10.22), the passage draws conceptually on the language of Isa. 65.17-25 and 66.22-23. Both these Isaianic texts refer to God's creation of a 'new heaven and earth', the former passage associating it with images of fertility (cf. 10.17-19; 11.1) and the latter anticipating a world order in which 'all flesh' (כל בשר; LXX πάσα σάρξ) will 'worship God' (cf. 10.21).

In two respects, however, the text in *1 Enoch* 10 differs from the antecedent traditions in Isaiah. First, it places eschatological expectation within a Noahic framework. This narrative setting is reformulated through a reading of Genesis 6 that addresses the cosmic dimension of evil. Following from this, it also projects the activity of divine redemption onto the world stage. Thus, whatever its precise status, 'the plant of truth and righteousness' must be linked up with the entire human race, which has been subjected to demonic powers. Second, unlike Isaiah, the text nowhere specifies that the worship of God will happen in Jerusalem. To be sure, the Greek Codex Panopolitanus may imply participation in the cult when it declares that all humanity will 'serve' God (λατρεύουσιν), and there is no attempt to reject Jerusalem as the centre of worship. However, the complete lack of emphasis on Jerusalem is conspicuous and contrasts with the biblical traditions which anticipate that this is where the Gentiles' worship of Israel's God will take place.[19]

How is it that the worship of God by all humanity will come about? The text in 10.14–11.2 does not draw a direct line of continuity between 'the plant of truth and righteousness' and the deliverance of humanity from destruction; 'the righteous' of the former do not testify or bear witness to anything in order to bring the conversion of the nations about. Instead, to the extent that the Isaianic paradigm is operative here, the eschatological

---

19 Interestingly, the Eth. mss. traditions all read here the vb. *yāmelleku* (lit. 'to be subject to'), which has no obvious cultic connotation.

activity of the nations will take place as part of the establishment of a new world order after divine eradication of all 'uncleanness' and godless activities from the earth. For this 'new beginning' of humanity in the coming era (10.22), the period after the Flood (Gen. 9.1-17) serves as an archetype.

To summarize thus far: the conversion of the nations in a world cleansed from 'uncleanness' and 'defilement' builds on a setting constructed out of the biblical Noah narrative. The narrative, which takes primordial history as its point of departure, begins and ends with a concern for the situation of humanity as a whole, while providing crucial signposts for divine redemptive activity along the way (the deliverance of Noah, the escape of 'the plant of truth and righteousness' from destruction, and the definitive punishment of evil). Even more profoundly, the motif of the nations' worship of God moves beyond biblical antecedents in its fundamental distinction between the essentially integrated nature of humanity as God's creation and the breach of cosmological order brought about by the rebellious angels and embodied by the giants. The destruction of evil *activity* by the Flood, a type that anticipates eschatological salvation and judgement, could therefore be carried through without doing away with the human race itself. Given the Noahic setting and with conditions for a new, eschatological start in place, the conclusion to chs 6–11 comes as no surprise.

Significantly, if we read the tradition within the context of the third century BCE, the text was not simply placing blame for cultural, military and social upheavals on Alexander the Great's successors and those who spread and supported their influence. The 'demonic' could not, and should not, be reduced in this way. Instead, while linking cultural and religious incursions with angelic powers that have fallen from heaven, the author(s) of chs 6–11 held out for the restoration of humanity. The stage occupied by these chapters was also that of a growing historiographical consciousness which euhemeristically attempted to place local traditions within a larger framework that forged connections with and between other cultures (cf. Berossus' *History of Babylonia*; the *Pseudo-Eupolemos* fragments), and to it they contributed a fragment taking ancient Jewish tradition (from Genesis 6–9) as the essential point of departure.

1 Enoch *10.21: Its Enochic Reception and Place in Second Temple Literature*

The absorption of *1 Enoch* 6–11 into the growing Enochic pseudepigraphical tradition secured its influence in the midst of considerable adjustment.

1 Enoch 12–16. The attachment of the unit with *1 Enoch* chs 12–16 juxtaposed the Noahic framework with a parallel storyline in which Enoch

plays the central role as he is commissioned to mediate divine pronounce-
ments against the Watchers. Here, the aberrations of the fallen angels and
their progeny are reflected upon cosmologically (15.3–16.4). In addition,
attention is given to the ongoing activities of the demonic through the
disembodied evil spirits that had come from the giants when they were
destroyed. The implied distinction between the angels and giants, on the
one hand, and human nature, on the other, is consistent with what we have
inferred from chapter 10. However, the temporal horizon of this section
does not extend into the eschatological future.

1 Enoch 17–36: The remaining chapters from the *Book of Watchers* take
the eschatological discourse in a very different direction. In chs 17–19 and
20–22, the Enochic seer's journeys through the cosmos take him to the
places of fiery punishment for the wayward stars and fallen angels (cf.
18.11-16; 19.1-2; 21.1-10). During the course of the second journey, he
sees four chambers inhabited by four classes of souls: (1) the righteous,
(2) sinners of the first rank, (3) victims of sinners, and (4) a lesser rank
of sinners (22.8-14). Unlike chs 6–11, the text begins to focus on the
consequences of human participation in sin, while the significance of the
fallen angels' tradition is relegated to a position of lesser prominence. This
posture is retained through the remaining chapters of the book.

1 En. 5.4-9: A parallel tradition to the eschatological events described
in ch. 10 re-enters the *Book of Watchers* as it was supplied by an introduction in chs 1–5. At this point, remnants of the Watcher tradition have
all but disappeared, while the spotlight is almost exclusively cast on the
sinners and the righteous among humanity. Thus, the wicked, who are
without prospect for salvation, are cursed (5.4–6a, 7b). By contrast, at the
conclusion of the section, the destiny of the righteous, who are described
as 'chosen ones', is described in several ways: they will be given 'light
and grace' and 'wisdom', they will no longer 'sin', and they, 'the wise
ones', shall

> 'complete the full number of the days of their lives. Their lives will
> grow in peace. The years of their joy will increase in gladness and
> eternal peace throughout the days of their lives'. (5.9)

Thus precisely the bliss associated with *all humanity* when they worship
God in ch. 10 is here delimited to the righteous. There is no hint that 'sinners' will be transformed, not least any wider group of humanity (if the
writer is applying the label 'sinners' to other Jews). Indeed, if there is any
eschatological metamorphosis at all, it is 'the chosen ones' who undergo
it and who will be alone to enjoy eschatological blessings.

The second century BCE traditions that that would accrue to the Enochic corpus – the *Apocalypse of Weeks* (91.14), *Epistle of Enoch* (100.6 and 105.1) and *Animal Apocalypse* (90.37) – largely wanted to have it both ways; they refer to a turning or recognition of Gentiles by drawing on ideas from both *1 Enoch* 10 and 5. Here, we consider these texts briefly in turn.[20]

1 En. 91.14 *(Apocalypse of Weeks)*. The *Apocalypse of Weeks*, composed during the early part of the second century BCE (i.e. just before the Maccabaean revolt), schematizes history into ten parts called 'weeks'. The period described as 'the seventh week' is that of the author, who refers to a community of 'chosen ones from the eternal plant of righteousness' who will be given special 'sevenfold instruction' (93.10). To the rest of week seven and in week eight, the *Apocalypse* ascribes a punishment of 'the wicked' in which 'the righteous' will be given a part to play (91.11-12). Week eight concludes with the righteous being rewarded and with the rebuilding of the Temple for eternity (91.13). Then, for week nine, the text reads as follows:

> 'And after this, in the ninth week, the righteous judgement will be revealed to all the world, and all the works of the wicked will depart from the whole earth. And the world will be written down for destruction, and all people will look to the way of uprightness.' (91.14)

Whereas the eighth week is concerned with the elect of Israel and the establishment of the Temple cult, the ninth week takes up eschatological events on a broader stage that in week ten will be extended even further to encompass the cosmos as a whole. This broader focus suggests that the 'wicked' whose deeds are expunged from the earth are not the same group as the oppressors mentioned in week eight. Whereas in week eight 'the wicked' themselves are destroyed (i.e. the author and his community's inimical opponents or oppressors), in week nine it is 'the works' (Eth.; Aram. text from 4QEn^g is lost at this point) of the wicked which will be removed. If this is the correct reading of the text, then the *Apocalypse* may be picking up on a distinction implicit in *1 En.* 10.16; that is, one between iniquitous activity and the human beings who engage in them (cf. *Birth of Noah* 107.1; *Exhortation* 91.6-8).[21]

---

20 For a more detailed treatment of these texts, including preliminary issues of date and setting, see Stuckenbruck 2007: 91–108. The translations of the texts cited below are my own.

21 Within a more sectarian framework that does not envision a conversion of humanity, the similar distinction is operative in the *Treatise on the Two Spirits* in 1QS iii 13–iv 26. According to the last section of this text (iv 15-16), God's final visitation will bring an end to evil by removing 'the innermost framework of human flesh' and replacing it with purity and 'the spirit of truth' (iv 18-21). In the end, the 'flesh' emerges purified.

This, in turn, makes it possible for the text to anticipate that all humans 'will look to the way of uprightness'.[22] Thus their conversion or turning towards uprightness is not so much surprising as it denotes a proper conclusion (cf. Isa. 49.6) to a narrative in which God, the Creator of the world and the one who has fixed each of the weeks from the beginning, renews and realigns the created order to its original purpose. While sharing with ch. 10 the emphasis on the destruction of wicked deeds and the subsequent righteousness of humanity, the *Apocalypse* places much less emphasis on the wickedness of the Watchers who, until a possible allusion to them in the tenth week (91.15),[23] have disappeared from the scene. The *Apocalypse* also picks up on biblical tradition by having the transformation of humanity follow restorative events associated with the Temple (here, its building "in glory" 91.13); with the eschatological Temple in place, God's rule manifests itself in a new way.[24] This introduces a logical tension into the narrative that is less apparent in chs 6–11: on the one hand, the wicked are destroyed by the sword (91.11-12) while, on the other, in the wake of the justice and judgement brought about by God's kingly rule, 'all people will look to the way of uprightness' (91.14). The writer's more immediate concern for justice against contemporary apostates involved in oppression (93.9, 11) is resolved by the slaughter of humans, whereas the punishment of the fallen angels and their offspring in ch. 10 leaves the destiny of humanity more open. The pattern *within 91.14 itself*, however, retains the influence of its Enochic predecessor.

1 En. 100.6 and 105.1-2 (Epistle of Enoch). The texts mentioned here are found, respectively, in the main body and the conclusion of the *Epistle*. Though the passages in which they occur probably do not stem from the same author, they share an emphasis that juxtaposes a coming to understanding of Gentiles and the vilification of 'sinners' for whom eschatological punishment is deemed irretrievable.[25] The texts, extant in Ethiopic (with only 100.6 extant in Grk), may be translated as follows:

> 'In those days, says the Lord, they will summon and give testimony
> to the children of the earth from their wisdom. Show (it) to them, for
> you are their leaders and the rewards upon the whole earth. (2) For
> I and my son will join ourselves with them forever on the ways of
> righteousness during their lives. And you will have peace.' (105.1-2)

---

22 Though Isa. 2.3 and Mic. 4.2 may lie in the background, there is no mention here of any instruction through which this is to happen; see, by contrast, 105.1-2 (discussion below).

23 On the textual problem, see Olson 2004: 222.

24 According to 91.13 in 4QEn[g] 1 iv 17-18, the Temple is described as being 'of the kingdom of the Great One'.

25 This juxtaposition is analogous to the tension attributed to the *Apocalypse of Weeks* above.

> 'And men among the wise will see what is true, and the children of
> the earth will understand the entire discourse of this book, and
> they will know that their wealth cannot save them during the
> collapse of their sin.' (100.6)

These texts share the hope that 'the children of the earth' will eventually
comprehend the wisdom that has been disclosed to the author and his
community. Moreover, the writer of 105.2 expects that humanity will
embark 'on the ways of righteousness' (cf. 91.14). Even more than what
we observed in the *Apocalypse of Weeks*, however, the field of vision
has narrowed. The message of the *Epistle* is overwhelmed by a conflict
between the author's community and 'the sinners' who are repeatedly
denounced through a series of invectives (mostly woe-oracles and oaths).
This is especially true of 100.6, in which 'the children of the earth' are,
in effect, treated as 'the sinners' who can attain little more than the recognition that the Enochic revelation is true. The function of this acquired
understanding, then, is the validation of Enochic revelation rather than
any turn-around among the nations as such. This is much in contrast to
the derivation of evil in the *Book of Watchers* from rebellious angels (esp.
chs 6–36). In the body of the *Epistle* the blame for oppression and false
teaching is laid so completely at the feet of 'the sinners' that the writer
claims that 'sin was not sent to the earth, but the people have created it
by themselves, and those who commit it will subject to a great curse'.
Clearly, the human dimension of sin in *1 En.* 5.4–6a, 7b lies more in the
background than *1 Enoch* 6–11, and, unlike *1 Enoch* 10 (and the *Animal
Apocalypse*), there is no real distinction between deeds and human beings
who commit them.

What, then, of 105.1-2? Within what framework is the coming to
wisdom of humanity to be understood? Unlike the earlier Enochic counterparts, the writer of 105.1-2 draws a direct line of development between
the righteous community and 'the ways of righteousness' to be shared by
'the children of the earth'. The text assumes that the righteous themselves
will play an active role in the dissemination of their revealed knowledge
in the world.[26] While in the other Enochic texts the role of the pious is
either non-existent (chs 10; 91.14[27]; cf. on *Animal Apocalypse* in ch. 90
below), here it is expected that the righteous will dispense their wisdom
to others, and even do so with success. If we take the preceding verses
(104.12-13) into account, the means by which the divine revelation would

---

26 Though the references to instruction and paths of righteousness is influenced by the language of Isa. 2.3 and Mic. 4.2, the Enochic writer is giving the Enochic community a more explicit
role in the dissemination of the instruction.

27 The phrase 'will be revealed' denotes divine activity more than any human meditation.

be brought to the world is conceived as the faithful copying and transla-tion of the Enochic tradition. To this extent, it is possible that the writer himself probably thought he was participating in passing on the testimony to which he refers in 105.1.

1 Enoch 90.30, 37 (Animal Apocalypse). Composed in the mid-to-late 160s BCE, the *Animal Apocalypse* adopts a position comparable to the ones we have outlined for the *Apocalypse of Weeks* and, especially, the Epistle. The work, which is a much more elaborate recounting of human history than the *Apocalypse of Weeks*, draws on zoomorphic symbols to represent human characters from the time of Adam all the way to the Maccabaean revolt under Judas Maccabaeus.

In 90.16-38, which occurs near the conclusion to the document, the Enochic author sketches eschatological scenes of judgement and reward which build on the symbolism that has already featured in the narrative.[28] Here Gentile nations, which have usually been symbolized as oppressive 'wild animals' and 'birds' (and an assortment of other such animals) in the previous part of the vision (cf. esp. 89.10, 42-44, 49, 55-56, 66; 90.2-4, 8-9, 11-12, 13), come to feature in an increasingly positive manner (cf. 90.16, 18, 19, 30, 33, 37-38). The negative presentation of the Gentiles reaches its climax in the battle of Beth-Zur in 90.13-15 (cf. *2 Macc.* 11.6-12). The description of this battle merges with initial stages of what the writer presents as an imminent eschatological future (90.16-19) in which the righteous 'sheep' are given a 'big sword' with which to kill 'all the wild beasts' as an act of retribution (v. 19; cf. *Apocalypse of Weeks* at 91.11-12).

Whether these slaughtered animals specifically represent the Seleucid armies or Gentiles more generally,[29] what follows in the vision takes a different turn. The consistency of the document's "anti-Gentile" attitude in the allegory gives way to scenes that involve some measured acceptance of Gentiles. This happens in three stages, in 90.28-30, 90.33 and 90.37-38. The first stage describes the Gentiles as 'falling down and worshipping those sheep, and entreating them and obeying them in every command'. This is an image of subjugation along lines familiar through biblical tradition (Isa. 45.14; 60.10, 12); the Gentiles submit to the authority of the sheep after the re-establishment of a 'new house' – which probably refers to the restoration of Jerusalem as the place of eschatological blessing

---

28   The present discussion is indebted at several points to the recent treatment of the place of Gentiles in the *Animal Apocalypse* by Herms, *An Apocalypse for the Church and for the World*, pp. 120–36.

29   Nickelsburg (2001: 401) maintains that 'the present text appears to envision the participa-tion of the righteous in militant judgmental action against a broader contingent of the Gentiles than those with whom they had been in immediate conflict'.

and rest. Thus, as in the *Animal Apocalypse* (91.13-14) and the Book of Tobit (13.11-17; 14.5-6), the re-establishment of Jerusalem (and Temple) in all its intended glory provides the essential prelude to the inclusion of Gentiles in the vision of the future. While it is tempting to think that the subjugated Gentiles are those who did not oppress Israel and thus have escaped judgement,[30] the textual evidence does not support such a precise reading.[31] While this submission of the nations to the righteous – expressed through prostration, petition (for mercy) and obedience – takes the narrative in a decidedly new direction, it is not yet activity that has God as the immediate object of their worship.

The second stage gets under way when 'all those who had been destroyed and dispersed, along with all the beasts of the field and all the birds of heaven, gathered together in that house, and the Lord of the sheep rejoiced with great joy because they had all become good, and they had returned to his house' (90.33).[32] Those who were destroyed and scattered could refer to either the Gentiles slaughtered by the sword in verse 19 or to the 'blinded sheep' (apostate Jews) who were judged by fire in verses 26-27 (hence, the verb 'returned' here), or to both groups (as seems most likely). The inclusion of Gentiles with the statement 'they had all become good' ensures that, alongside Jews to be restored, Gentiles will be the object of divine joy.

The third and final stage of Gentile inclusion in the eschatological vision occurs with the appearance in 90.37 of 'a white bull' with big horns (an image based on the presentation of Adam in 85.1-3). Initially, the author emphasizes the Gentiles' subservience as in verse 30, though this time they fear the white bull 'and made continual petition before it'.[33] This activity leads to the climax. In 90.38 the text states, 'As I watched, all of their species were transformed: they all [i.e. the beasts and birds mentioned in v. 37] became white bulls. . . . The Lord of the sheep rejoiced over these and over all of the cattle'. This conversion of the Gentiles takes place through a divine act of recreating the human race, which is treated as the proper conclusion to the reconstitution of Israel.

The *Animal Apocalypse* does not entertain the possibility that the

---

30   This is the view of Tiller 1993: 377.

31   In 90.19, the slaughter by the righteous of 'wild beasts' is supplemented by a statement that 'all the animals and birds of heaven fled before them'. The text in 90.30 makes no attempt to identify precisely which Gentiles are being subjugated to the sheep.

32   For the *Animal Apocalypse* I follow the translation by Olson 2004: 211.

33   The second and third stages outlined here have their closest contemporary parallel in Dan. 7.14, which does not necessarily demand that one decide whether or not the 'one like a son of man' (7.13) is an angelic divine agent (cf. *1 En.* 90.37) or a corporate figure that represents Israel (cf. 90.33).

righteous might play a role in the salvation of humankind (in contrast to the *Epistle* at 105.1-2). Instead, it picks up the new creation motif implied in the *Apocalypse of Weeks* (91.14 implies such for the earth, while the tenth week in 91.16 mentions the appearance of 'a new heaven') and, more fundamentally, set forth in the *Book of Watchers* (10.17–11.2). The *Animal Apocalypse* also shares the predominant concern behind chs 6–11 in the association of Gentiles with oppressive conditions for Israel, albeit in a different way. We have noted that in chs 6–11, the bearers of Hellenistic culture – perhaps those who held power and had sway over the cultural ethos of Jerusalem and the Land – are not referred to in any way other than by allusion through the fallen angels. The *Animal Apocalypse*, by contrast, adopts a discourse that distinguishes both the demonic and the bearers of socio-political power. The vision describes the demonic or wayward angelic world as 'stars' and 'shepherds' while, as we have seen, the Gentiles are symbolized as wild animals and birds. In this way, the *Animal Apocalypse* explicates what the earliest tradition in the *Book of Watchers* implies: though heinous deeds have been carried out against God's people, those who have committed them are not entirely demonized. The ultimate establishment of God's rule in creation demands that human beings who are part of this creation be restored. *Endzeit* reflects Adamic *Urzeit*. However, the *Animal Apocalypse* moves away from ch. 10's focus on the destruction and punishment of the fallen angels and the giants. The author of the vision wanted to have it both ways: not only have the demonic beings made a mess of the world; humans too (both Gentiles and unfaithful Jews) are held responsible and punished for their wrongdoing. The crucial distinction between humans and their deeds in the *Book of Watchers* – which is picked up in the *Animal Apocalypse* and *Exhortation* – is lost, replaced by a more contradictory image of total punishment (90.16-19, 26-27) and total restoration and conversion (90.33, 37-38).

Conclusion

In this discussion, I have argued that the worship of God by all humanity as described in *1 Enoch* 10 is remarkable in several respects. First, it is shaped by and integral to the literary unit in which it appears, the *Book of Watchers* 6–11. This narrative, which is at once Noahic and steeped in mythological discourse, is in turn inspired by the biblical tradition in Genesis 6–9. Second, this eschatological inclusion of humanity is presented as a contrast to the complete eradication of evil, inaugurated by the Flood and to be concluded at the time of eschatological judgement. Third, this categorical distinction between humanity and the demonic world has its corollary in the author's theological anthropology. The angelic rebellion runs counter to the way God has arranged and organized the cosmos, and the race of giants, who are the very embodiment of this breach, have no place in the created order. Though some among them are complicit to the instructions of the angels, human beings, on the other hand, are essentially victims. Whatever part they have had in the promulgation of violence, oppression and reprehensible practices, they as a whole remain a constituent part of creation. Thus the motif of Noah's rescue and escape from the deluge not only serves as a type for a community of the righteous called 'the plant of truth and righteousness', but also – and ultimately – makes it possible for the document to conclude with the full restoration of humanity.

The writer (or compiler) of *1 Enoch* 6–11 reflects a worldview not entirely absorbed by intramural conflicts with other Jewish groups. The message was rooted in a Jewish appropriation of sacred history that attempted, during the course of the third century BCE, to address directly the wider challenges that Hellenization was beginning to pose for Jewish self-definition.[34] As such, its themes provided a language around which the subsequent Enochic traditions surveyed here would be oriented, though in very different ways. With respect to the motif of Gentile conversion in the eschaton, *1 Enoch* 10 was not alone during the third century; the Book of Tobit, which presupposes a diaspora setting, similarly attempts to reconcile the strict preservation of Jewish piety with an outlook that ultimately embraces the Gentiles (cf. 14.5-6). The earliest tradition of *1 Enoch*, however, has done so in a remarkably open way; its combination of myth and sacred tradition and its concern with contemporary manifestations of the socio-cultural and political fallout from the wave of Hellenization brought by the ascendancy of Greek culture in the Eastern Mediterranean world had implications for political critique and theological anthropology that would wield a surprising degree of influence on later Jewish and early Christian thought.

---

34   The focus on the destruction of deeds does not mean a wholesale rejection of Gentiles within the divine economy per se; as much as the *Book of Watchers* rejects the promulgation of Hellenizing culture, the room it leaves for the restoration of humanity implies a theological coming to terms with the non-Jewish world.

12

'HELLENISTIC FOUNDATIONS' IN PALESTINE

Oren Tal[1]

Abstract

This paper reviews royal Ptolemaic and Seleucid policy concerning the 'foundation' of Palestinian urban centres against the background of their archaeological, social and political history. Consequently, it makes a distinction between founding as the establishment of a settlement where none previously existed, and founding as a formal step in which an existing settlement is accorded with recognized administrative status.

Given the historical and epigraphic sources at hand we lack direct evidence on Ptolemaic and Seleucid foundations in Palestine and the common view relates to a change in the city name (and sometimes its administrative structure, that is, to a *polis* as evidencing foundation or refoundation. Although this idea is common in Hellenistic historiography, it dates back to Flavius Josephus, who was defending the antiquity of the nations of Palestine.[2]

---

1   I am indebted to Catharine Lorber for her valuable comments on numismatic-related issues; the responsibility for the ideas expressed below, however, is mine alone. Greek names, terms and places appear in Latin forms.

2   Cf. *Antiquities* I, 121: 'Of the nations some still preserve the names which were given them by their founders, some have changed them, while yet others have modified them to make them more intelligible to their neighbours. It is the Greeks who are responsible for this change of nomenclature; for when in after ages they rose to power, they appropriated even the glories of the past, embellishing the nations with names which they could understand and imposing on them forms of government, as though they were descended from themselves.' [trans. by H. St. J. Thackeray; edition Loeb]. In this respect cf. e.g. listings of refoundations, new foundations and foundations at or near major religious centres in Cohen 2006: 424–26 which on the one hand admits that in many of the listed settlements there is no extant evidence bearing on this question yet on the other gives no lucid interpretation on the meaning of the term in its Near Eastern context. Notwithstanding the above, Cohen defines 'new' as foundation built at a previously uninhabited site and confesses on relatively few firm attestations for new foundations. Moreover, Cohen adds that these sites were

Thus, for example, the fact that, in some of the Zenon Papyri of the year 259 BCE and of the year 258 BCE, the mention of the city as Ptolemaïs,[3] and not Acco/*ʿkh*, is taken by many historians as evidencing foundation. This epigraphic source accords with the royal coins of the city of Ptolemaïs that bear a ligatured monogram of the Greek letters ΠΤ,[4] as an abbreviation of the new name, and date from Ptolemy II's 25th regnal year,[5] that is 261/60 BCE (Svoronos 1904–08: No. 765).[6] Another example that relates to the same period of time is the site of Beth-Shean, which was renamed Scythopolis. A hoard of 20 silver *tetradrachms* of Ptolemy II (FitzGerald 1931: 51–56, Nos. 1–20), in which 11 coins are dated to Ptolemy II's 27th through 37th regnal years, i.e. 259/58–249/48

often near or adjacent to an older town. Hence, he concludes, that the relatively few firm attestations for new foundations undoubtedly reflect the fact that most of the Hellenistic colonies resulted from the refounding or renaming of older settlements for economic reasons (1995: 428).

3   Durand 1997; i.e. P. Cairo Zen. 1, 59004 – February–May 259 BCE; P. Cairo Zen. 1, 59008 (recto) – September–November 259 BCE (?); P. L. Bat. 20, 32 – 9 February 258 BCE; PSI 5, 495 – 30 November 258 BCE. The remainder mention the city of Ptolemaïs, i.e. PSI 4, 406; PSI 6, 616; P. Lond. 7, 2022; P. Lond. 7, 2141 (a customary completion), bears no dating.

4   The term royal coins refer to issues that bear the portrait of the king, usually together with the name of the city (the mint), either abbreviated (the beginning of the name) or by monogram (control mark) of the mint (often a combination of the letters that make up the name of the city) and sometimes also the name of the king.

5   For the sake of our argument his first regnal year started in 285/84 BCE, although it is known that he inherited the throne only in 282 BCE but later backdated his regnal count to 285/84 BCE while he was co-regent with his father Ptolemy I. R. A. Hazzard attempted to demonstrate that the backdating occurred as early as 282 BCE in documents dated according to the Macedonian calendar, and in 267 BCE in documents dated according to the Egyptian calendar (1987).

6   The city of Ptolemaïs minted 'monogrammed' royal coins even earlier, but these coins are undated, and customarily assigned to Ptolemy II's first series which dates to 273–268 BCE (Svoronos 1904–08: Col. 108, No. 764, Pl. 25, 1). A. Davesne demonstrated however that Svoronos' No. 764 is an obverse die-linked of Svoronos' No. 365, i.e. a *tetradrachm* that shares the same upper monogram but has the letter -Α- below, instead of the circled ligatured ΠΤ monogram. Davesne thus argued that in the context of this die link, this circled ligatured ΠΤ does not seem to be a mintmark for Ptolemaïs. It probably reflects the personal name of a moneyer (by the name of Ptolemaios). Davesne included these two varieties in a larger series that he attributed to Cyprus, perhaps Citium. He dated Svoronos' Nos. 365 and 764 between 265/64 and 260/59 BCE and his whole system of dating was based on the assumption that circulating *tetradrachms* lost weight at a regular rate, and that the dated *tetradrachms* of the Syro-Phoenician mints could provide a benchmark for dating the coin age of other mints (Davesne and Le Rider 1989: 213 [at Nos. 5081–85], 283). This is an ambitious but obviously speculative theory, and it can produce some problematic results. Consequently, it is difficult to rely on Davesne's chronology; even if Svoronos' No.764 is justifiably removed from the output of the mint of the city of Ptolemaïs, we can safely assume that under Ptolemy II it was operated from his 25th year, i.e. 261/60 BCE, based on the dated series of silver *tetradrachms* with the reverse legend ΠΤΟΛΕΜΑΙΟΥ ΣΩΤΗΡΟΣ (Svoronos 1904–08: Nos. 765–84), rather than ΠΤΟΛΕΜΑΙΟΥ ΒΑΣΙΛΕΩΣ (ibid.: No. 764). In fact, the city of Ptolemaïs continued to mint 'monogrammed' royal coins under Ptolemy III, IV and V (?). For a historical coverage of Hellenistic Ptolemaïs cf. Cohen 2006: 213–21.

BCE, may provide evidence that intense Hellenistic re-occupation of the site, namely Tell el-Ḥutzen, began under Ptolemy II's third regnal decade (as suggested by Fuks 1983: 44–53).[7] The recently published Rhodian amphorae stamped handles recovered from A. Mazar's excavations of Tell el-Ḥutzen (mostly from Area P), lend support to such a conclusion (Ariel 2006: 596–97). Two other examples that may relate to the same period of time are the site of Beth Yeraḥ, located on the southern shore of the sea of Galilee, which was renamed Philoteria, apparently after Ptolemy II's sister,[8] and the site of Rabat-Ammon, which was renamed Philadephia, after Ptolemy II's pseudonym, which may have occurred during his life or after his death. Interestingly, in the case of Rabat-Ammon, both the Zenon papyri (Durand 1997),[9] and Polybius (V, 71, 4), that is in the contexts of the Fourth Syrian War (221–217 BCE), relate to the site as Rabat-Ammon. In the same manner, one may assume that Joppa/*ypy* was 'founded' anew, under Ptolemy II's 25th regnal year, in 261/60 BCE, when the city struck gold *octodrachms*, silver *tetradrachms* and bronze coins with a ligatured monogram of the Greek letters ΙΟΠ, that denotes the city's new name, Iopé (Svoronos 1904–08: No. 795, Nos. 818–20 [undated bronze coins]). We may even further suggest that other minting cities under the Ptolemies were 'founded' anew. These are Gaza/'*zh* like Iopé, under Ptolemy II's 25th regnal year onwards, in 261/60 BCE, when the city struck gold *octodrachms*, silver *tetradrachms* and bronze coins which differ from those of Iopé by the ligatured monogram of the Greek letters ΓΑ – for Gaza (Svoronos 1904–08: No. 822 [silver *tetradrachm*], Nos. 834–38 [undated bronze coins]).[10] Ashkelon/Ascalon, under Ptolemy IV's

---

7   It should be noted however that Fuks relates the foundation of Scythopolis, Ptolemaïs, Philoteria and Philadelphia to the contexts of the Second Syria War (260–253 BCE). In the case of Scythopolis, Fuks sees Flavius Josephus' account on the refusal of the people of Scythopolis to pay their taxes to the tax collector Joseph the son of Tobias (*Antiquities* XII, 182–83), in the 240s BCE, as evidencing a *terminus ad quem* for the site foundation (1983: 47–51). Be that as it may, Josephus' diachronic use of 'Scythopolis' cannot be taken as evidencing the site name in the time of Joseph the son of Tobias.

8   Indeed, it is only in Polybius V, 70, 3–5, and in the contexts of Antiochus III's invasion of Coele Syria during the Fourth Syrian War (218 BCE), that the city is referred to as 'Philoteria', where 'Scythopolis' is mentioned as well; see in this respect the discussion of Cohen 2006: 273–74, 290–99.

9   I.e. PSI 6, 616, which is not dated but generally fixed to the years 261–252 BCE, mentions ἐν Ραββαταμμάνοις, that is Rabbatammana (see also Cohen 2006: 268–72).

10   In fact, the cities of Iopé and Gaza minted 'monogrammed' royal coins under Ptolemy II and III, while Iopé has also minted under Ptolemy V. It should be noted that Svoronos' Nos. 794 and 821 refer to coins of Iopé and Gaza of Ptolemy II's 23rd regnal year; however Otto Mørkholm reattributed these coins to Ptolemy III (1980). One should bear in mind that Iopé and Gaza are not proper new names but 'Greek-sounded' modifications of the original Semitic names; the mere fact that these cities served as royal Ptolemaic mints does not necessarily imply that they were refounded

third regnal year onwards, in 219/18 BCE, when the city struck silver *tetradrachms* with an abbreviation of the Greek letters AΣ – for Ascalon (Svoronos 1904–08: No. 1188; see also Seyrig 1950a: 5–6, No. 105), and similarly Dor was 'founded' anew, under Ptolemy V, for the city struck silver *tetradrachms*, with an abbreviation of the Greek letters Δω – for Dora (Svoronos 1904–08: No. 1262; see also Mørkholm 1981: 6). The fact that Jerusalem was virtually the only mint of the Ptolemaic kingdom to strike (royal) silver fractions on the Attic weight standard under Ptolemy I and Ptolemy II (Ronen 2003–06),[11] while the Lagid kings were promoting the use of bronze coinage with a similar range of values is of special interest.[12] Can we understand the numismatic evidence as a proof for the city's 'refoundation' in about 301 BCE? More interesting is the fact that Jerusalem was apparently deprived of minting rights once the coastal cities of Ptolemaïs, Iopé and Gaza were granted ones and reasons can only be speculated.[13]

Can the true meaning of 'foundation' in Ptolemaic Palestine be illuminated by the aid of other epigraphic evidence of royal nature? The problem is the scarcity of such finds and apart from an inscription from Iopé, dated to the time of Ptolemy IV, we do not have information. This

---

by Ptolemy II, as new foundations (and re-foundations) normally distinguished by new names, deriving from the ruling royal family: e.g. Ptolemaïs, Philadelphia, Arsinoë, Berenice and Philoteris/a under the Ptolemies; and Seleucia, Antiochia, Apamea and Laodicea under the Seleucids. However, given the case of Scythopolis whose name remains enigmatic, or Apollonia(-Arsuf) (which was probably originally named Arshoph after the Phoenician god Reshef) the idea that foundations and especially refoundations should not necessarily be defined by entirely new royal names cannot be rejected altogether. For a historical coverage of Hellenistic Gaza cf. Cohen 2006: 282–88.

11   After the Graeco-Macedonian conquest the weight standard of the provincial coinage of Judah changed, when the gra (*gerah*) and half-*gra* were replaced by fractions of the *obol* on the Attic weight standard with a modal weight of 0.19 g for the quarter-*obol*.

12   These issues show a clear Ptolemaic iconographic influence (e.g. Meshorer 2001: Nos. 29–35; Gitler and Lorber 2006: Group 5) and are dated from circa 301–261/60 BCE (Gitler and Lorber 2006). Recently it was suggested that the coins bearing the personal name *yḥzqyh hpḥh* (Meshorer 2001: Nos. 22–23), should be attributed to the period of the Diadochi (after 312 BCE) because of the use of an Attic weight standard apparent from these coins (Ronen 1998: 125); the considerably small number of specimens (31 coins) and consequently the unreliable statistic results, as well as the use of Achaemenid title provide doubts for this suggestion. Following Mildenberg (1979) who was of the opinion that *yḥzqyh*-type coins (without the Achaemenid title *pḥh* should date to the 'Macedonian period'; that is, to the period between 332 and 301 (namely Macedonian-Diadochi), Gitler and Lorber (2008) examined the weights of *yḥzqyh*-type coins (Meshorer 2001: Nos. 24–26). They found that, except for Meshorer's 2001: No. 25a, these coins are on the Judahite *šql/grh* standard. Gitler and Lorber dated however Meshorer's 2001: Nos. 14, 20–23, 25a, 27–28 to the 'Macedonian period' based on either statistically assumed Attic weight standards (Nos. 22–23, 25a, my reservations above) or stylistic, epigraphic considerations (Nos. 14, 21–22, 27–28) (2008: Table 1).

13   This seems to be the case only if one accepts Gitler and Lorber's (2006) revised chronology.

dedicatory inscription was rightfully attributed to a temple that was not discovered (or correctly identified) during the excavations. The inscription is conventionally dated by some scholars to the summer of 217 BCE (*SEG* 20, No. 467; Lupo 2003: 193–95; Tal 2008: 174), that is after the Battle of Raphia at which time Ptolemy IV may have visited the site. The fact that the inscription is carved on a marble slab, rock that is foreign to the Palestinian geological environment, may suggest that it bears a somewhat fixed formula that did not necessarily have religious or social meaning for the inhabitants of Iopé. In other words it does not contribute significantly to our understanding of the administrative status of Iopé under the Ptolemies.

But before elaborating on the true meaning of foundation in the context of Hellenistic Palestine, let us first review the different views on Ptolemaic and Seleucid state policy towards urban settlements, since the founding of cities was one of the hallmarks of intentional imperial policy. However a distinction must be drawn between founding as the establishment of a settlement where none previously existed, and founding as a formal step in which an existing settlement is accorded with recognized administrative status. It was V. Tcherikover who defined the term *polis* in relation to Hellenistic Palestine as an autonomic city, which took upon itself Greek law and usually also a new name, and underwent a process of social/administrative Hellenization; that is, it established urban institutions, a *boule* and officials (of Greek/Athenian bureaucratic titles) appointed by the people (1963: 26, 86, 90). This definition was also adopted by many other scholars. In Tcherikover's opinion, the coastal cities became *poleis* under the Ptolemies. M. Avi-Yonah, who did not devote extensive discussion to the essence of the *poleis* in Palestine, saw Phoenician Hellenization as impacting both geographical and social spheres, and Phoenicia (a term that includes the Palestinian coast) as a bastion of Hellenization due to the independent past of its urban agglomerations as city-states (1978: 182–88 passim). This argument holds, of course, internal contradiction. According to M. Stern, the process continued for a number of generations, since clear information about the regime in those cities derives only from the second and first centuries BCE, namely under the Seleucids. Stern was also cautious about a link between the giving of a new name to a city and the establishment of a *polis* regime, at least in the case of Ptolemaïs (1991: 8). G. Fuks, in contrast, argues that the Ptolemies, whose rule was centralized, did not give the rights of the *polis* (that is, autonomy) to new and veteran cities, and that the change in their status in fact began only at the time of Seleucus IV, 187–175 BCE. This is because the government wanted the cities to have full control of their surrounding villages, and to make things easier for the central government. The cities however bought the rights of *polis* at full price, which was essential to the Seleucids, whose economic situation was difficult (1983: 26–27, 36–39; 2001a: 25–26). F. Millar expressed a different opinion, rejecting the existence of *poleis* during the Ptolemaic and Seleucid periods. Although he only discussed Phoenician urban centres, including those on the coast of Palestine, his arguments reflect his opinion regarding the rest of the country (1987: 129–33). Millar discerned clear evidence of the existence of cities with the status of *polis* only during the Roman period (1983: 63). He also adopted the approach of Kreissig, which saw an essential difference between the Greek *polis* and the Eastern, Asian *polis* and its modes of production, which devoted a central place to its economic aspect, that is private commerce and industry (1974: 1082–83). Millar's contention, that historical and epigraphic evidence do not clarify the status of Phoenician cities, contradicts, in Fuks' opinion, the numismatic finds. The minting of autonomous silver and bronze coins attest, according to Fuks that these cities were awarded the status of *polis* as early as the first half of the second century BCE (in Ptolemaïs) (1983: 36–39; 2001a: 26–27). There is, of course, a clear distinction between royal coins of the Ptolemaic and Seleucid periods and municipal (or civic) coins known as semi-autonomous and autonomous coins that were struck only under the Seleucids (on terminology, see above note 3). The term semi-autonomous coins normally refers to those of Ptolemaïs from the time of Antiochus IV, bearing his portrait on the obverse and a goddess holding a sceptre or a torch, on the reverse, alongside the inscription ANTIOXEΩN TΩN EN ΠTOΛEMAIΔI – 'Of the Antiochs of Ptolemaïs' (Houghton and Spaer 1998: Nos. 1156–60). These coins' reflection of autonomy is not well-founded, since this formula does not necessarily imply autonomy. Autonomous coins on the other hand do not bear the portrait of the king or his name. Their iconographic motifs are often taken from coins of the period by adopting known motifs or are sometimes a reflection of the material, religious and artistic culture of the population group that minted them. Thus such municipal issues frequently attest to the cities' central political status. In fact, it is only in late second and early first centuries BCE that such Hellenistic coins are known to have existed; in Gaza and in Ascalon. Those of Gaza that bear the formula ΓAZAIΩN ΔHNOY (i.e. ΔHMOY) or ΔHMO[Y ΓA]ZAIΩN – 'Of the People of Gaza' or ΔHMOY ΣEΛ[EYKEΩN] TΩN EN ΓAZH – 'Of the People of Seleucia in Gaza' (Hill 1965: lxix–lxx, Pl. 15, 1–3) were dated by a few scholars to the time of Seleucus IV (e.g. Le Rider 1965: 410, note 1), based on the reasoning that sites named after Seleucus were 'founded' or 're-founded' in his days. In the case of Palestine where only one example of such a site is documented, that is Seleucia in the Golan heights (known in present-day as Khirbet Seleukie), Seleucus IV is preferred over Seleucus V who ruled for less than one year (cf. e.g. Tcherikover 1927: 70). In any case dating these coins to the time of Seleucus IV seems arbitrary.[14] The coin-types of both Gaza and Ascalon who bear the formula ΓΑΖΗΣ ΙΕΡΑΣ ΑΣΥ[ΛΟΥ] – 'Of Holy Asylum Gaza' (Hill 1965: lxix–lxx, Pl. 15, 4–5) or ΑΣΚΑΛΩΝΙΤΩΝ ΔΗΜΟΥ ΙΕΡ[ΑΣ] ΑΣ[ΥΛΟΥ] – 'Of the People of Holy Asylum Ascalon' (Rosenberger 1984–85: No. 1) or ΙΕΡ ΑΣΥ (i.e. [τῆς] ἱερ(ᾶς) [καὶ] ἀσύ(λου) 'Of Holy Asylum' (Houghton 1983: Nos. 825–26), are evidence that both cities gained partial autonomy in the time of Antiochus VIII (see in this respect Rigsby 1996: 519–23). Some of the autonomous coins of Gaza bear a new urban calendar, which denotes the year the city received its autonomic standing (Kushnir-Stein 1995a; Hoover 2006; 2007a: 63–70).

If we are to accept Fuks' theory, that the right to strike autonomous coins is evidence that the transformation of a city to a *polis* was an intentional policy of the centralized Seleucid rule, then only very few of the urban settlements were formal or recognized as city-states (*poleis*), namely the coastal settlements of Ptolemaïs, Ascalon and Gaza.[15] The status of the other minting cities under the Seleucids remains unclear, as they minted royal coins intermittently, and under different Seleucid kings; for example, silver and bronze coins of Demetrias-by-the-Sea (probably Strato's Tower, i.e. present-day Caesarea) under Demetrius II (Hoover 2007b),[16] bronze coins of Samaria possibly under Antiochus IV (see below, note 17) and silver coins of Samaria possibly under Antiochus IX

14　It is worth noting that no extant coin can definitely be attributed to Seleucia in the Golan; see in this respect Imhoof-Blumer 1901–02: 140; and also Cohen 2006: 288–89.

15　In fact, only a few genuinely municipal coinages were struck by cities that were subject to the Seleucids. In the time of Seleucus I, Seleucia in Pieria produced a municipal bronze coinage alongside a royal bronze coinage in the name of the king (Newell 1941: 86–88) Antioch-on-the-Orontes began to strike its municipal bronze coinage while it was still under the rule of the Seleucids immediately after the death of Antiochus XI, during the second reign of Antiochus X, and this probably came to replace the royal Seleucid bronze series at Antioch (Hoover 2007c).

16　It was Henri Seyrig who after restoring the reading as ΔΗΜΗΤΡΙΑΔΟΣ ΤΗΣ ΠΡΟΣ ΤΑΛΑΣΣΗΙ 'Of Demetrias-by-the-Sea' on an inscribed lead weight of half-*mna* at the museum of Beirut that bore the date ΘΝΡ (i.e. 154/53 BCE), consequently associated bronze coinage marked with the letters ΔΗ and civic era dates with a foundation in Phoenicia, based on the idea that the sign -L- which preceded the dates on the coins, was used only in those parts of the Seleucid realm which had formerly belonged to the Ptolemies (1950b: Fig. 4 for facsimile; cf. *Syria* 67 [1990], p. 511, Fig. 30B for photograph). More recently Kushnir-Stein (1995b; see also Lampinen 1999) endorsed Seyrig's reading and conclusions and suggested two periods for these coins, in the later second century BCE (undated bevel-edged municipal bronze issues of head of Zeus/cornucopia type, flanked by the letters Δ-Η on the reverse) and in the first century BCE under the Romans. She has also suggested that the site of Demetrias-by-the-Sea should be identified as a refoundation of Strato's Tower based on similarities in neighbouring Dora's and Demetrias' Roman issues (see Cohen 2006: 203 for other supporting evidence). Accordingly, Hoover (2007a) attributed dated silver *drachms* struck under Demetrius II's first reign (146–138 BCE) of uncertain 'southern mint' that bear the ligatured letters ΔΗ on their reverse (as well as die-linked obverse type) with Demetrias-by-the-Sea.

(Houghton 2000),[17] bronze coins of Jerusalem under Antiochus VII
(Houghton and Spaer 1998: Nos. 2133–50),[18] and possibly bronze coins
of Marisē under Antiochus VI and VII.[19] These autonomous coins were
in almost exclusive use of the cities or their region and not outside them,
and served to meet the needs of the local market only. It can therefore be
assumed that municipal autonomous coins from the Hellenistic period do
reflect a change in the status of a city – giving it the right to mint coins
that are representing the urban authority, even perhaps a certain amount of
judicial autonomy as well. However, they do not prove that the city adopted
Greek laws and social order and, therefore, they do not reflect a city's
foundation or refoundation, if we follow the line of reasoning stressed so
far of a city's foundation or refoundation as a reflection of a *polis*.

17   That is undated *hemidrachms* and *obols* Antiochus portrait/Athena royal silver coin-type,
flanked by the inscription ΒΑΣΙΛΕ ΑΝΤΙ ΦΙΛ. The attribution to Antiochus IX is secure, as it rests
on the portrait and a reverse type specific to this king. Based on the provenance of these coins in
the region of Samaria, and in keeping with the Persian-period tradition of low denomination silver
coin minting in Samaria, it was suggested that they were minted during the reign of Antiochus IX
(Houghton 2000). Such an attribution seems however too tentative.

18   Dan Barag has recently suggested that a certain Antiochus portrait/seated goddess undated
royal bronze coin-type, flanked by the inscription ΒΑΣΙΛΕΩΣ ΑΝΤΙΟΧΟΥ is dated to the days
of Antiochus IV, and evidencing a royal issue of the city of Jerusalem at the beginning of the
Maccabaean revolt before the city was taken by Judas Maccabaeus (circa 167–164 BCE), representing its transformation into a *polis* (2002), following *1 Macc.* 1.14; *2 Macc.* 4.9. Barag's argument
is based on the distribution of the coins in Palestine and the attribution of the flan, fabric and
iconographic content to a 'southern mint'. However, too few coins were actually found in Jerusalem
and its close environs (see Barag's distribution list, 2002: 61–63), thus such an argument is highly
theoretical. Many of the coins came from the region of Samaria and may point to a mint north of
Jerusalem, possibly the city of Samaria itself (see in this respect Houghton, Lorber and Hoover
2008: 94–95; and Cohen 2006: 255–63 for Jerusalem Seleucid history).
     Jerusalem's lily/anchor royal bronze coin-type, flanked by the inscription ΒΑΣΙΛΕΩΣ
ΑΝΤΙΟΧΟΥ ΕΥΕΡΓΕΤΟΥ, and a Seleucid date (basically 132/31–131/30 BCE), were minted
under Antiochus VII, and although attributed by some scholars to Ascalon (e.g. Meshorer 1981:
11), their current attribution to Jerusalem seems to be more accepted (Syon 2006; Houghton, Lorber
and Hoover 2008: 391–92). This can also be strengthened historically from *1 Macc.* 15.6 which
explicitly says that Antiochus VII gave Simon, the high priest in Jerusalem, the right to coin money
for local use.

19   Cf. Houghton, Lorber and Hoover 2008: 333, No. 2028 (Antiochus VI), head of Apollo/
Tyche type, flanked by the inscription ΒΑΣΙΛΕΩΣ ΑΝΤΙΟΧΟΥ, with vertically set controls marked
ΗΔΛΜ or ΗΔ, that are attributed to Marisē based on 20 coins found during the excavations, and
ibid.: 392–93, No. 2125 (Antiochus VII), diademed head/splayed double cornucopiae type, with the
inscription ΒΑΣΙΛΕΩΣ ΑΝΤΙΟΧΟΥ, based on provenance in Israel and similarity in style and fabric
to the previous type. Such attributions seems however too tentative, since the idea that considerable
numbers of the same coin-type found in a site during excavations is evidencing products of a local
mint is not necessarily true. It should be noted, however, that these coins were previously attributed
to Gaza (e.g. Houghton and Spaer 1998: Nos. 2105–12), but this attribution is now questioned
because of their provenance and due to the fact that they not bear a mintmark of Gaza or the sign
of Marnas (cf. e.g. Houghton, Lorber and Hoover 2008: 333).

Therefore, we ought to ask, can the true meaning of 'foundation' in Seleucid Palestine be illuminated by the aid of other epigraphic evidence of royal nature? Although the material at hand is richer than Ptolemaic epigraphic evidence; we are still left with more questions than answers. Urban Greek titles may come to our aid; the most common found on epigraphic material is the title *agoranomos*, that is 'Who is in Charge of the *Agora*', and appears on lead weight, inscriptions and amphora handles (Tal 2006: 45–46, 311–14). Its earliest appearance is dated to the days of Antiochus IV, and comes from Marisē (Finkielsztejn 2004: 248). Like municipal autonomous coins, the production of local lead weights attest to the partial autonomy in a city's commercial life, and to date only weights that were found at Scythopolis and Marisē can be securely defined as products of these sites given their defined motifs (Tal 2006: 311–12). The several royal inscriptions do not contribute significantly to our understanding of the administrative status given their contents. The royal edicts refer to hierarchical structure and taxation system rather than to the status of the cities; for example the Hefzibah inscription documents nine letters exchanged between Antiochus III, Ptolemy the governor of Syria and Phoenicia and high priest, and other Seleucid officials, and reveals the hierarchic structure of the royal administration and the fact that the governor owned private lands that were leased to villages owned by the king, apparently in the eastern Jezreel valley (*SEG* 29, No. 1613). The recently published Heliodorus inscription (that came from Marisē) documents royal correspondence in three letters exchanged between Seleucus IV, Heliodorus and other Seleucid officials and contains an order by the king to appoint Olympiodorus in charge on the sanctuaries (namely high priest) of *Koilē Syria and Phoinikē* (Cotton and Wörrle 2007; Gera 2009). The Yavneh-Yam inscription documents an exchange of letters between Antiochus V and the Sidonian inhabitants of Yavneh-Yam who sought an exemption from taxes (*SEG* 41, No. 1556). Other royal inscriptions such as the one from Scythopolis (*SEG* 8, 33; Rowe 1930: 44, Fig. 9), Samaria (*SEG* 8, 96; Reisner, Fisher and Lyon 1924: 165–66, Plan 12) and Ptolemaïs (*SEG* 19, No. 904) are basically cultic and most probably belonged to temples; the one from Scythopolis lists priests of Olympian Zeus; the one from Samaria too lists priests of Olympian Zeus and a secretary (*grammateus*) apparently of a garrison stationed at the site; and the one from Ptolemaïs is a dedicatory inscription to either Antiochus VII or IX, made by the chief-secretary (*archi-grammateus*) of the military forces (Van't Dack et al. 1989: 124–27).[20] With this survey of

---

20 Cf. in this respect, Cohen's list of civic institutions and offices, 2006: 428–29 (under Phoenicia and Southern Syria).

epigraphic evidence in mind, we turn now to the silent material culture of both the Ptolemaic and Seleucid rule in Palestine.

Archaeologically, in most of the urban settlements we are witness to the continuity of urban traditions from periods preceding the Hellenistic period. In some of them, new fortification systems were built during the Hellenistic period (Ptolemaïs, Iodefat/Iotapata, Dora, Samaria, Mt Gerizim, Iopé and Mareshah/Marisē), while in others (Shechem, Gezer/Gazera, Gaza[?] and Tel 'Ira) fortifications from periods preceding the Hellenistic period continued to exist after refurbishing. The construction techniques are not new to the period discussed, reflecting in the main earlier local building traditions, though some scholars tend to see their origin in Phoenicia (e.g. Stern 1992), and to a lesser extent in Greece (e.g. Sharon 1987). The preference for ashlar constructions in some of the urban settlements can be seen as socio-economic rather than cultural. The few extant city gates are divided between types of earlier (biblical period) tradition (as in Mt Gerizim and Gezer) and simple types with an entrance in a straight axis protected by a buttress (as in Dora), which are also known from periods preceding the Hellenistic period, but in military architecture. The dates of the fortification systems given by the excavators are divided between the fourth, third and second centuries BCE and thus cannot be interpreted as a sudden royal initiative (Macedonian, Diadochi, Ptolemaic or Seleucid). The few public and administrative buildings discovered show local building traditions. In some urban settlements public and administrative buildings have similar plans to those of domestic buildings (as in Iopé[?], Mt Gerizim and Marisē), that is a central court-yard surrounded by rows of rooms. A similar conclusion also arises from methodological analysis of the cult buildings in the period discussed. The few extant sites with a clear plan (Tel Dan, Mt Miṣpe Yamim, Ptolemaïs, Makhmish, Tel Mikhal, Lachish and Beersheba – some urban and some not) demonstrate the dominance of local building traditions, whether they are longitudinal or latitudinal in plan. A number of these were founded prior to the Hellenistic period (Tel Dan, Mt Miṣpe Yamim, Makhmish and Lachish[?]), and their core plan remained as it had been in the foundation phase; there was presumably no change either in the deity worshipped (Tal 2008). There are fewer extant examples of large residential buildings. The best example of the latter is the one found at Tel Anafa. This building, even though there are clear Greek influences mainly limited to the architectural decoration, is nevertheless similar in ground plan to the smaller domestic buildings. One can distinguish two types of domestic buildings: the first is the commonest type of the period, that is the central courtyard house; the second, which is much rarer, is termed the frontal courtyard house. Both originate from local Palestinian architecture, and they differ from their so-called 'Greek' counterparts for they lack the most characteristic components of Greek houses, the *prostas* and the *pastas*. Each urban component found in the urban settlements of Hellenistic Palestine turns out to be an integral part of the environment, culture, and social and political background of the period discussed and those preceding it. A study of the archaeological remains in most of these urban sites reveals that the settlements – whether they continued in existence from the Persian period or were resettled in the Hellenistic period – were built according to local architectural principles.[21]

This is the place to note that the archaeological record from Hellenistic Palestine supports Millar's conclusions, since these urban settlements revealed no buildings in the Greek tradition for the use of the public (an agora, a basilical structure, etc.), for administration (*bouleuterion*),[22] for education (*gymnasium*),[23] or even for entertainment (theatre).[24] The status of all urban settlements in Palestine in the Ptolemaic and Seleucid periods was certainly not equal; only a few of them had mints (or the right to strike royal and municipal autonomous coins) and received more authority and greater room to manoeuvre than the others. Their conduct as *poleis* (in the light of modern historiographic research) is to be found in the Palestinian content of the term, which does not overlap the Classical, Greek term (Kreissig 1974; 1977). Since the urban settlements were subservient to

---

21   All the above was amply analysed and summarized by Tal 2006: 15–115, 323–35.

22   It was recently suggested that one of the structures excavated by B. Maisler and M. Stekelis in Beth Yeraḥ/Philoteria changed its nature from commercial (under the Ptolemies) to public (under the Seleucids), based on the idea that the newly established eight equidistant pilasters built in two rows served the city's *basilica* (Tepper 1999). However, given its considerable small internal dimensions (8.7 × 11.9 m), the irregularity of the width of its naves, and the hypothetical assumption that the structure was located in the city's centre, its 'basilical' characteristics are purely theoretical.

23   With two exceptions; the one is Jerusalem, where a *gymnasium* was operated as of 175 BCE (under Antiochus IV) according to *1 Macc.* 1.14; *2 Macc.* 4.9 and probably was dismantled in the contexts of Judas Maccabaeus' Temple purifications in 164 BCE; the other is an undated epigraphic evidence for a *gymnasiarch* (and, hence, a *gymnasium*) at Philadelpheia (cf. Gatier 1986: 2, 29). The short-lived *gymnasium* building in Jerusalem was taken by numerous scholars as evidencing Jerusalem's status as a proper *polis* – 'Antioch in Jerusalem', whose Greek institutions include also an *ephebeum*, i.e. an educational military-oriented union who qualifies youngsters, and allows them to become citizens (*demoi*) in a *polis* (cf. e.g. Tcherikover 1974: 146–55; Hengel 1974: 70–78; 2001: 16–28; see however Feldman 2006: 26–27, 77 for counter-arguments). This so-called Hellenized Jerusalemites (*2 Macc.* 4.13) were obviously confined to parts of the city's élites, by necessity or by choice (which I dare to say was mostly economical rather than cultural/social), yet vigorously invalidated by the majority of the Jerusalemites and Jews. The fact that we hear of no other *gymnasia* in historical and epigraphic writings on Hellenistic Palestine lend support to such a conclusion.

24   Notwithstanding the above conclusion one should note, however, that Gadara (Transjordan) was the birthplace of renowned Greek intellectuals of the Late Hellenistic (Hasmonaean) and especially Early Roman period (see, e.g. Strabo, *Geography* XVI, 2, 29; cf. also Hengel 1974: 83–87; Geiger 1985). In addition, Josephus described Gadara, Gaza and Hippos as 'Hellenic *poleis*' (*Antiquities* XVII, 320, *War* II, 97) although in Early Roman period context.

the central government, the extent of their independence was certainly limited and subordinate to various procedures that did not allow city states complete autonomy. It should also be added that the roots of the Greek *poleis* and the reasons it came into being are fundamentally different from the roots of the major urban settlements that developed in the ancient Near East (de Polignac 1995).

In summary 'Hellenistic Foundations' in Palestine seem to have been in most cases a formal procedure in which an existing settlement is accorded with recognized administrative status and role or in other words 'refounded'. The fact that the minting authorities under the Ptolemies (Ptolemaïs, Dora, Iopé, Jerusalem, Ascalon and Gaza), were harboured in coastal centres (with the exception of Jerusalem, above), with an affluent Achaemenid past, most probably garrisoned with military forces,[25] may suggest that economically, royal Ptolemaic coins were in a sense auxiliary coins that met the immediate economic needs of its Ptolemaic rulers, and thus minted at a royal municipal minting authority (Jenkins 1967). In other words they formed part of a monetary inter-urban economy at its various levels; first and foremost the state/provincial level, i.e. a response to the needs of the government and the army, and second, at the level of the individual – the municipal/urban economy.

A similar conclusion may be drawn with regard to the royal Seleucid issues. Here, too, the minting authorities (Ptolemaïs, Demetrias-by-the-Sea, Samaria, Jerusalem, Asaclon and Gaza), were in most cases harboured coastal centres (with the exception of Jerusalem and Samaria, above), with affluent Achaemenid past, most probably garrisoned with military forces. However, the municipal (or civic) autonomous issues of Ascalon and the royal-municipal or semi-autonomous issues of Ptolemaïs during the reign of Antiochus IV, and their production continuance in Ptolemaïs, Ascalon and Gaza under later Seleucids kings in the second half of the second century BCE, highlights political and social aspects in the status of these cities, which received (or even purchased) a certain level of autonomy at various times in the later Seleucid period. The fact that the cities of Ptolemaïs, Ascalon and Gaza, are the only minting authorities to mint royal coins under both the Ptolemies and the Seleucids, suggest that the imperial administration of both the dynasts choose to invest in existing urban centres (founded in much earlier times) rather than in proper new foundations.

Only a few cases in Hellenistic Palestine can be defined as true

---

25   For Persian–Achaemenid archaeological remains cf. *NEAEHL* 1–5 passim, s.v. Akko, Ascalon, Dor, Gaza, Jaffa and Jerusalem. Evidence on military forces may also come from nearby fortresses as discovered in Ashdod (near Ascalon) Tel Michal (near Jaffa) and Shiqmona (near Dora) (cf. e.g. Tal 2005: 80, note 13).

Hellenistic 'foundation' that is the establishment of an urban settlement where none previously existed; surprisingly, all the Palestinian minting cities of either Ptolemaic or Seleucid rule, have had Achaemenid past, and urban foundations basically refer to military strongholds that in cases grew to become urban settlements per se already under the Seleucids; the sites of Scythopolis and Philoteria may provide an illustration to such a process, although both of these sites do not lack Achaemenid material culture alto-gether, their Hellenistic remains are archaeologically better documented than their Persian ones, and both probably did not mint coins under their Hellenistic rulers.[26] In the case of Demetrias-by-the-Sea (if identification with Strato's Tower is truly the case), Samaria and Jerusalem, not only did these sites have an Achaemenid past,[27] but coin minting was episodic, thus serving a certain economic (and to some extent political and social) need.

26 Other such examples may include other inland sites such as, Iotapata, Hippos and Gam(a) la, the latter became urban settlement rather under the Romans, cf. *NEAEHL* 5, s.v. Gamala, Hippos (Sussita), Yodfat.

27 With the possible exception of the site of Strato's Tower (Στράτονος Πύργος P. Cairo Zen. 1, 59004 – February–May 259 BCE; Durand 1997: 61–62), as there is a debate over the identifica-tion of the founder – Straton, namely one of the Straton/'Abdaštart kings of the Sidonian dynast (under the Achaemenids) (cf. e.g. Levine 1973; Roller 1992) or rather a general of one of the royal Ptolemies (cf. e.g. Raban 1992; Stieglitz 1996). Although hardly published or recorded in the site excavations, Persian-period pottery was found in a number of surveys in the central and northern parts of Roman Caesarea.

13

WILL THE PROPHETIC TEXTS FROM THE
HELLENISTIC PERIOD STAND UP, PLEASE!

Lena-Sofia Tiemeyer[1]
University of Aberdeen

Introduction

This article provides an overview of a selection of prophetic texts that are
normally viewed as stemming from the late Persian and early Hellenistic
period (400–200 BCE). My primary aim is to elucidate what criteria are
used for dating these texts, and to evaluate to what extent these criteria
are sound. Accepting a gradual composition of prophetic texts, where
subsequent generations have added interpretative layers to an original
core (*Fortschreibung*), few scholars date an entire prophetic book to the
Hellenistic period. Instead, they often distinguish between earlier non-
Hellenistic textual units and the final Hellenistic composition.

This article falls into two parts. We shall first explore the three chief
criteria for dating a text to the Hellenistic period, namely linguistic features, eschatological/apocalyptic features, and references to recognizable
historical events. Thereafter, we shall look at a selection of texts in more
detail: Isaiah 18–25; 24–27; 56–66; Ezekiel 7; 28 and Zechariah 9–14.
In each case, we shall investigate the scholarly theories that suggest a
Hellenistic dating. This article does not aim to date the various prophetic
books in any exact way – that belongs in the realm of several monographs
– but only to uncover *why* some texts are dated to the Hellenistic period
and to determine whether the arguments in favour of such a dating are
convincing.

It should at this point be acknowledged that there are scholars who
date the Hebrew Bible as a whole to the Hellenistic period. Lemche, for

---

1   I am indebted to Prof. Andreas Lindemann who let me have access to the library of the
Kirchl. Hochschule Bethel, Bielefeld. I am also indebted to Ms Helena Wilson who weeded out as
many infelicities in my treatment of the English language as she could find.

example, argues that given that the LXX is the oldest textual evidence that we have of the Hebrew Bible, we have to start from there and work backwards. 'We do not know that the books of Samuel existed around 1000 BCE but we are certain that they did in 350 CE!' (the date of codex *Vaticanus*, the oldest manuscript of the LXX). Accordingly, our task is to provide reasons for an earlier date. In Lemche's view, we get a glimpse of a society in which great literature may have been composed only after the conquest of Alexander the Great.[2] Lemche's four arguments in favour of a Hellenistic date of the Hebrew Bible do not, however, convince. Rather than providing extensive arguments *for* a Hellenistic dating, they merely aim to cast doubt upon earlier dates. Thus, the present writer agrees with Albertz's exclamation that the Hebrew Bible, at its core, is definitely not a Hellenistic book![3]

Criteria for determining the date of a text

Are there no Greek texts in the Hebrew Bible then? There are several criteria for dating a text, such as language, subject, form and style. In the specific case of whether or not a biblical text was composed during the Hellenistic period, scholars tend to look at its linguistic features. In the specific case of prophetic texts, scholars explore their use of eschatological/apocalyptic motifs and their allusions to historically datable events.

Linguistic features as indicative of a Hellenistic dating
The decisive tool for determining the Hellenistic origin of a biblical text is that of *language*, although it is used less with prophetic texts than with other texts. This method takes a diachronic approach to linguistics, assuming that typology in many respects equals chronology. As languages develop, certain types of orthography, vocabulary and syntax become connected with certain *time* periods. Accordingly, by recognizing the types, we can identify the time.

Avi Hurvitz is the chief advocate of this method in the case of Biblical Hebrew.[4] In our particular case of looking for signs that betray a Hellenistic

---

2   Lemche 2001: 287–318. See also Carroll (2001: 91–107) who argues that we should begin backwards with the material from Qumran in our attempts to date the Hebrew Bible. Along similar lines, although accepting the possibility of some material from the Persian period, Thompson (2001: 274–86) sees the Hellenistic and Graeco-Roman periods as the earliest date for the Hebrew Bible.

3   Albertz 2001: 30–46.

4   See, e.g. Hurvitz (1997: 307–15) who distinguishes between pre-exilic and post-exilic Hebrew on the basis of extra-biblical inscriptional materials. See also Hurvitz 2000: 143–60. A comprehensive list of his articles can be found in Young 2003a: 338–40. See also Polzin (1976),

date, we are first of all looking for orthographical, lexical or syntactic signs that are normally associated with Late Biblical Hebrew (henceforth LBH, as opposed to EBH – Early Biblical Hebrew). Secondly, we have to determine whether we can distinguish between LBH of the Persian period and that of the Hellenistic period. In particular, does the language of a particular text contain elements of Qumranic (QH) or Mishanic Hebrew (MH), and if so, do these elements confirm the Hellenistic origin of the book?

The situation with regard to the development of languages is, however, seldom this clear-cut. To create a chronology out of linguistic typology, two provisions are essential. First, a number of individual samples of Biblical Hebrew need to be independently datable. Secondly, Biblical Hebrew must represent a *single* linguistic tradition. Beginning with the latter, there may be a difference between the spoken versus the written language. What thus exists in one book may be formalized written style while another book may preserve more colloquial forms. Furthermore, what we may think is typical of the language of an *era* may instead be typical of a *region*. We know too little about the dialects of Ancient Judah to be able to make certain claims.[5] Moreover, a later author may, for various reasons, write in a style reminiscent of older writings. Thus, unless that person makes an obvious mistake, it is difficult for us, with our limited knowledge of Biblical Hebrew, to distinguish between, for example, authentic pre-exilic Hebrew and a post-exilic text containing archaisms.

Greek loanwords

In rare cases, a biblical text contains words that appear to be of Greek rather than of Semitic origin or idiomatic constructions that are semantically similar to Greek expressions. As Attic Greek became the *lingua franca* after the conquests of Alexander the Great, it is reasonable to assume that only then would Hebrew have incorporated Greek loan words into its vocabulary. Nonetheless, it is questionable whether the study of loan words is such an exact science that the mere presence of a few loanwords can settle the question of the date of a book in the Hebrew Bible. As Young points out, although we can easily detect a non-Semitic word in a Hebrew text, it is much harder to determine its exact origin and the process

---

who, although he differs from Hurvitz in his methodology, advocates a chronological study of Biblical Hebrew. For a good overview of the diachronic study of Biblical Hebrew, see Rooker 1988: 199–214.

5   See, e.g. the issue of the relative article אשר versus -ש. Morag (1988: 160–61) suggests that rather than relating to this issue as a *chronological* issue, it is more likely that both conjunctions belong to different *dialectal* areas. See also Young 1993, as well as the critique by Davies (2003: 150–63).

of its arrival in Hebrew. The word in question could be a loanword in the language where it is identified, for example, and/or it could have reached Hebrew via an intermediary language. That an acceptable etymology can be found in a certain language does not dictate that the word must be a loanword from that language into Hebrew.[6] Furthermore, in the cases where expressions are reminiscent of Greek phrases and idioms, we have to investigate whether this expression is peculiar to Greek or whether a similar expression is attested in another earlier textual source.[7] Finally, similar idioms may exist in several languages with no evidence of direct influence.[8]

Looking at specific examples, Ecclesiastes and Song of Songs alone contain loanwords of possible Indo-European origin (פרדס – Eccl. 2.5; Cant. 4.13 = 'park, grove', equivalent to the Avestan *pairidaeza* = 'circular enclosure' and פתגם – Eccl. 8.11 = 'message'). Yet the Persian origin of פרדס has recently been doubted as it is not attested in Old Persian of which we have only scant remains. Instead, we find cognates in, e.g. Akkadian, Greek, Arabic and Aramaic.[9] It has also been argued that Song of Songs contains two Greek loan-words: the *Hapax legomenon* אפריון (Cant. 3.9, suggested Greek parallel *phoreion* = 'sedan chair' as in the LXX [φορεῖου]) and the *Hapax legomenon* תלפיות (Cant. 4.4, suggested Greek parallel *telopia* = 'looking into the distance').[10] The Greek origin of אפריון is contested, however, as there are other, more likely derivations such as the Iranian *upari-yāna*.[11] Likewise, the alleged Greek origin of תלפיות does not stand closer scrutiny. In particular, the fact that the LXX *transliterates* the word (εἰς θαλπιωθ), understanding it as a proper name, speaks against it being a Greek loanword. Instead, a Semitic etymology (Arabic root *lpy* = 'to be arranged in courses'), referring to necklaces hanging around the neck, is more likely.[12]

Even if we were to accept the Greek origin of a loanword, this does not

---

6   Young 1993: 67–68.

7   See, for example, Geyer (1970: 87–90) who argues that while the expression קצות הארץ in Isa. 41.5 is reminiscent of the Greek phrase ἔσχατα γαίης and therefore indicative of a Hellenistic or even Maccabaean dating of the chapter, it is also reminiscent of the Akkadian *šar kibrati irbitim*. Accordingly, there is no reason to date Isa. 41.5 to the Hellenistic period.

8   A good example is that of the relationship between 'to narrate' and 'to count', found in various languages (German: *zählen/erzählen*, Hebrew: *Qal* versus *Piel* of the root ספר. Even in English, a person counting money in a bank is a 'teller', and a person 'recounts' a story.

9   Young 1993: 161–62.

10   See, e.g. Sáenz-Badillos (1993: 123–25) for a pithy and representative discussion of the lateness of the language of Song of Songs and Ecclesiastes.

11   See, e.g. Pope 1985: 441–42 and Young 1993: 162.

12   See Honeyman 1949: 51–52. This etymology is accepted by most recent commentaries, e.g. Pope 1985: 465–67, Murphy 1990: 155, Snaith 1993: 61–62, Exum 2005: 153, note h.

necessarily imply that it was incorporated into Hebrew in the fourth century. There were ties between the Semites and the Greek-speaking world long before Alexander the Great conquest of the Near East. The inhabitants of the Syro-Phoenician coast made systematic sea-voyages across the Mediterranean, introducing Asian inventions to the Minoans. The Mycenaean vocabulary provided by Linear B (thirteenth century BCE), for example, contains several borrowings from the Semitic languages,[13] and we cannot reject the opposite possibility out of hand. Furthermore, as attested by a Mycenaean tomb found at Tell Dan, Mycenaeans were present in pre-Israelite Canaan (fourteenth–thirteenth century BCE).[14] Along the same lines, the Philistines, an Indo-European people lived in close proximity to the Israelites and were even, according to the book of Judges, their overlords at times. It is not unlikely that some Aegean influences could have crept into Hebrew during the period of Philistine domination of Israel.[15] Finally, as the Arad ostraca (e.g. Arad 1, 2, 4, 7) refer to the 'Kittim', probably referring to people from the Cypriot town Kition, we can conclude that there were Greek mercenaries in Judah in the seventh and sixth century BCE.[16] Hence, although it is clear that the contact between Hebrew and Greek increased drastically after the conquest of Alexander the Great, it is hard to sustain the equation that Greek word equals Hellenistic Age text. A Greek word in Biblical Hebrew thus renders a Hellenistic dating *likely*[17] but *not necessary.*[18]

The language of the prophetic writings
There are remarkably few linguistic features in the prophetic books that suggest a Hellenistic dating. In fact, there are also virtually no indicators of Aramaic influence. This aspect can naturally be understood in several ways. First, we can contend that given the uniformity of the language, together with its often clear classical style, the idea of much later additions to the prophetic books must be discarded. Alternatively, we can argue that, given the existence of later additions as suggested by literary criticism, we must conclude that the post-exilic scribes continued to write good classical Hebrew long into the Hellenistic period.[19]

13   Astour 1965: 323–61. For the dating of Mycenaean Greek, see Palmer 1980: 53–56.
14   Biran 1974: 34.
15   Young 1993: 65–66.
16   See Pardee 2003: 82–83, including note 4. Yadin 1974: 30–32.
17   See further Eskhult (2003: 8–23) whose study of loanwords in BH suggests that their presence follows a pattern that by and large fits into the political history of Ancient Israel.
18   Young 1993: 69.
19   Davies 2003: 155. See also Young (1993: 84–5) who stresses that the language of Ezekiel, Haggai, Zechariah and Malachi is very close to Classical Hebrew. He argues that even if the exile

Ehrensvärd's and Young's contributions are significant. Noting the similarity between the language of Isa. 40–66, Ezekiel, Haggai, Zechariah and Malachi to what is normally called Classical Biblical Hebrew (CBH), Ehrensvärd proposes using these books, with their certain exilic/post-exilic date, as the starting point of the discussion. Even though there are similarities between CBH and pre-exilic inscriptions, there is no complete correspondence. Furthermore, CBH is closer to the language of Haggai and Zechariah than to the pre-exilic inscriptions. Accordingly, giving precedence to linguistic considerations, a post-exilic date for the final linguistic form of the texts written in CBH seems preferable. This further means that CBH and Late Biblical Hebrew (LBH) co-existed in the post-exilic period.[20] Also stressing the similarity between the language of Haggai and Zechariah and CBH, Talshir argues that the linguistic shift from CBH to LBH happened during the fifth century with Ezra and Nehemiah. He further contends that LBH is connected with the exiles, with Ezekiel as its first example, followed by Esther, Daniel, Ezra-Nehemiah and Chronicles. Hence, two different types of Hebrew in Judah existed side-by-side from the fifth century and onwards.[21] Looking at the issue from the opposite spectrum, Young demonstrates that there is epigraphic material that reveals that at least some LBH elements were used before the exile. Therefore, we may be dealing with dialects in pre-exilic Israel that contain 'proto-LBH' linguistic features. At the same time, he points out that we have virtually no extra-biblical evidence of the Hebrew of the Persian period. It follows that we cannot exclude the possibility that the sort of Hebrew used in the inscriptions from the monarchic period continued to be used at least for a while after the exile, at least until Nehemiah.[22]

To sum up, there are few distinguishable linguistic features within the prophetic material that enable us to determine the date of a section. First, there are only minor differences between the prophetic books that claim to pre-exilic and those claiming to be post-exilic.[23] Secondly, within a prophetic book, it is virtually impossible to distinguish between the different textual layers on the basis of language alone. Consequently, in order to date a particular textual strand or section, we need to turn to other criteria.

was the decisive event that changed Biblical Hebrew, the effects did not appear to a significant extent in the literary language for about a century.

20   Ehrensvärd 2003: 164–88.

21   Talshir 2003: 251–75. See also Young (2003c: 314–17) who argues that texts from the Persian period before the middle of the fifth century reflect CBH while later works reflect LBH.

22   Young 2003b: 276–311.

23   One characteristic feature of post-exilic prophetic texts is the frequent use of the shorter form of the 1sg. pronoun אֲנִי (rather than אָנֹכִי) throughout Zech. 1–8, Haggai and Malachi. For an extensive discussion of these features, see Seow 1996: 661–64.

The language of the prophetic writings

Finally, orthography is only of limited help. There are no differences in spelling between the various parts of the prophetic books that enable us to distinguish between a Persian and a Hellenistic date. While there is a general chronological development from defective to full spelling, these variations neither reveal the absolute nor even the relative time of the *composition* of the biblical books. Instead, we learn only about the time of its copying, as a book or a section of a book composed at an early period could be represented in the MT by a late copy. In case of parallel texts, it is also possible that the younger text copied a version of the older text that we no longer have access to. In those cases, the younger text may attest to a defective spelling while the older text, preserved to us in updated version, has the full spelling. Nonetheless, the biblical books that are written with full orthography are generally the books that were composed at a later period (e.g. Ezra–Nehemiah, Chronicles).[24] We must thus assume that the orthography of a prophetic book, although containing material from various time periods, would have been streamlined by its scribes. In fact, no part of a prophetic book, not even those of early post-exilic origin such as Haggai, Zechariah 1–8 and Malachi, contains the full orthography attested in Ezra–Nehemiah and Chronicles. In addition, there is a clear orthographic difference between the inscriptional pre-exilic material and the spelling of all known biblical manuscripts. It is accordingly unlikely that any manuscript tradition is earlier than the Persian period. Either the texts were originally composed at that time period or they underwent scribal revision then.[25]

Eschatological and apocalyptic features as indicative of a Hellenistic dating

Turning from matters of language to those of content, the question arises as to whether it can be determined that certain sets of ideas and motifs – in this particular case that of 'prophetic eschatology' and/or 'proto-apocalyptic eschatology' – stem from certain historical time periods. As with linguistic topological methods of dating, there is an assumption that typology equals chronology: certain sets of ideas and motifs came into existence in a certain time period, and, accordingly, any text displaying these ideas and motifs cannot have been composed prior to that date. Moreover, we assume a linear development, beginning with 'prophetic eschatology', via 'proto-apocalyptic eschatology' to full-blown 'apocalyptic eschatology'. These terms denote the *sets of ideas* and the *motifs*

---

24 See further Tov 1992: 220–29, and Barr 1989: 168–85.
25 Young 2003b: 310.

displayed within a given text rather than the literary genre (such as apocalypse) in which they are found.[26] The term 'prophetic eschatology' is here defined as referring to events taking place *within* the course of history: the destruction of the kingdoms of the world, redemption of Israel assembled in Jerusalem, paradise for the community, a new ruler (YHWH or the Messiah) and the conversion of the nations. This term is contrasted with the (chronologically later) term 'apocalyptic eschatology', characterized by periodisation of history, dualism or fluctuating pessimistic/optimistic world view, immediate divine intervention, strong tendency to universalism, interest in angels and demons and communicated with the help of a celestial mediator. Moreover, apocalyptic writing tends to have certain literary features: the presence of an interpreting angel, pseudonymity, coded secretive speech, symbols taken from myth, number symbolism, etc.[27] Finally, I use the term 'proto-apocalyptic eschatology' for texts falling in between 'prophetic eschatology' and 'apocalyptic eschatology'. As several scholars note, much of post-exilic prophetic eschatology (e.g. Isa. 24–27; 65) contains some, although not all, of the characteristics of the later apocalyptic eschatology. It is thus preferable to use the term 'proto-apocalyptic' for the later prophetic eschatological texts in order to distinguish them from the full-blown apocalyptic material (e.g. Daniel).[28] The texts that are normally considered to be proto-apocalyptic are Isaiah 34–35, Ezekiel 38–39, Isaiah 24–27, Isaiah 56–66, Joel 3–4, Zechariah 9, Zechariah 12–14 and Malachi 3–4. Petersen has created, for our purposes, a useful table displaying the ten main ideas of the eschatological scenario that these biblical prophetic texts all, to a various extent, display: Return of prophecy, Theophany, Conflict on a cosmic level, on an international level and finally on an inner-Israelite level, Victory and return to Zion, Banquet, Restoration and Purification, YHWH as king, and Fertility.[29]

The main question here concerns the *dating* of these prophetic texts. Beginning from the end, we have examples of full-blown apocalyptic eschatology in texts that can be securely dated by independent factors to the inter-testamental period, such as *1 Enoch* and the Sibylline Oracles. What we do not know, however, is when the change between proto-apocalyptic

---

26   I differentiate between apocalypse as a literary genre, apocalypticism as a social ideology, and apocalyptic eschatology as a set of ideas and motifs that may also be found in other literary genres and social settings. See Collins 1984: 2, with note 4.

27   See further the overview by Doyle 2000: 25–6.

28   See Hanson 1975: 27, who differentiates between the material in Isaiah 40–55 that he calls 'proto-apocalyptic', and the material in Isaiah 56–66; 24–27; Zechariah 9–10 which he calls 'early apocalyptic' (sixth–fifth century). Lastly, in Zechariah 11–14, Hanson traces the transition to full-blown apocalyptic.

29   Petersen 1977: 17.

eschatology and apocalyptic eschatology happened, and, further back in history, when prophetic eschatology gave way to proto-apocalyptic eschatology. Moreover, we lack knowledge as to whether this development was linear or whether proto-apocalyptic eschatology was composed alongside prophetic eschatology. It is often assumed that prophecy gave rise to apocalypse after the loss of national independence and royal patronage following the destruction of Jerusalem in 586 BCE. In this situation, there was an increasing sense that God had revealed his will and purposes in past communications. Therefore, it is assumed that authors/scribes constantly updated earlier texts in search of divine communication relevant for the contemporary situation (*Fortschreibung*). In addition, whole texts were built around allusions to earlier material (e.g. Zechariah 9–14),[30] and theological concepts were transformed. Notably, the idea of 'the Day of the Lord'/'that day'/'these days', evolved from being a historical day when God intervened in the life of Israel (e.g. Amos 5.18-20; Zeph. 1.14-18) into a symbol of final judgement (Joel 2.30-32 [Eng. 3.3-5]).[31]

If we could determine that some of the texts mentioned above were written during the Hellenistic period by means of *independent* factors, e.g. through the existence of Greek loanwords, or through references to political events related to the Hellenistic period, then we could conclude that proto-apocalyptic eschatology is indeed a typical and signifying feature of the biblical literature of the Hellenistic period. If, however, we also found that others of these texts were composed in the Persian period, then we would have to conclude that literature written prior to the Hellenistic period also contains proto-apocalyptic features. Furthermore, we would have to redefine the period that gave birth to proto-apocalyptic texts.[32]

Historical references as indicative of a Hellenistic dating

Finally, we need to determine to what extent historical references in prophetic literature provide proof of dating. As we shall discover, in the case of the prophetic literature, few of these references provide independent evidence of a Hellenistic dating. Rather, they often function as corroboratory confirmations of an already assumed Hellenistic dating. First, scholars investigate the *social situation* presupposed by a given text, for example how it reflects the commercial economy of the surrounding society, and then they enquire how that picture fits in with a Hellenistic dating. Along similar lines, scholars explore the references to *certain ways*

---

30   See, for example, Boda and Floyd 2003.

31   See, e.g. Blenkinsopp (1983: 255–67) who discusses the transformation of eschatological motifs into something more akin to apocalyptic.

32   See especially Cook 1995. In his view, Israelite groups were the main source of Jewish apocalypticm, combined with limited Persian and Hellenistic influence (p. 213).

of thinking or to *human inventions* that are associated with the Hellenistic period.[33] Second, scholars look for *implicit references to persons or events* connected with the Hellenistic period. The study of place names related to Greece and of references to Greece in general falls into this category. Third, exegetes look at the situation in the Ancient Near East, establishing which nations were in ascent and therefore likely to be referred to by the biblical text and vice versa. For instance, the fact that Egypt was weak during most of the Persian period causes more than one exegete to rule out a Persian date for texts referring to Egypt as a major political player.

Our task here is to determine the relative weight of these arguments. Are the references to Greece really signs of the political ascendancy after Alexander the Great or are they better understood as mere geographical references with no political implications? Moreover, is it methodologically correct to date a text to the Hellenistic era just because that text refers to an event that is suggestive of a political, religious or nature-related occurrence that took place during the Hellenistic period? In conjunction with other, non-related, indications of Hellenistic dating, these references may indeed strengthen the case. Often, however, we are dealing with exegetes who are already predisposed to a Hellenistic date, and merely seek historical hints in the text to bolster their claims.

What was it like in Judah during the Hellenistic Period?

We have still a relatively scanty knowledge of early Hellenistic Judah, largely owing to the lack of references to the province of Judah in contemporary Greek sources. We know that Jerusalem was captured four times during the war of succession (321–301 BCE) by Ptolemy I, and we also know that a considerable amount of Jews were deported to Alexandria at that time. For a century following this conquest, Judah belonged to the Ptolemaic province of Syria and Phoenicia (*Coele-Syria*, including Samaria, Galilee, Idumea and Ashdod).[34] The series of Yehud coins from the time of Ptolemy II (282–246 BCE) further suggests that Judah

---

33   The clearest example of this kind of reasoning is whether or not Koheleth's philosophy is influenced by Greek thinking. In the case of human inventions, the type of device mentioned in 2 Chron. 26.15 is a rare example of possible Greek influence in the Chronicler's report. Welten (1973: 111–14) argues that this is a catapult, i.e. an anachronism from the author's own day. Thus, given that the catapult was invented in Syracuse around 400 BCE (Diodorus Siculus 14.42.1), and that they did not develop into the kind of war machines presupposed in Chronicles, this would hint at a Hellenistic date of the author. Erdmann (1977: 80–82) has shown, however, that the Persians may have used some kind of device for hurling stones. Thus, even if the reference is an anachronism, it does not necessarily betray a Hellenistic date.

34   Krüger 2004: 19–20.

was incorporated relatively quickly into the Hellenistic Ptolemaic world of commerce and administration.[35] During the time of the Ptolemaic reign in Judah, the Ptolemies and the Seleucids fought each other regularly (the five Syrian Wars: 274–271, 260–253, 246–241, 221–217, and 201–200/198 BCE), and the people of Judah became familiar with Greek military power. Throughout most of the Hellenistic period, Judah had an extensive political self-administration, through the high priest, the priesthood and the elders: instead of installing a governor in Judah as customary, the Greek authorities seem to have let the reigning high priest fulfil the function.[36]

Examples of dating based on the existence of proto-apocalyptic material and/or on historical allusions

In this section, we shall briefly look at a representative selection of texts (Isaiah 18–23; 24–27; 56–66 and Zechariah 9–14).[37] These texts are often regarded as Hellenistic compositions owing to their proto-apocalyptic character and/or their historical allusions. In the latter case, I shall limit the discussion to those interpretations that claim a Hellenistic setting. Furthermore, I shall refrain from examining the *likelihood* of these interpretations. Rather, I shall focus on evaluating the interpretative criteria.

Isaiah 18–23
The dating of the various oracles against the nations in Isaiah 18–25 is primarily based on the allusions to historical events as found in the texts. Blenkinsopp's interpretations are characteristic of this type of hermeneutics. He sees these oracles as being continuously updated, to meet changing historical situations. For instance, he regards the oracle against Sidon in 23.1-14 to have been extended to include the punishment of Tyre at the hand of Artaxerxes III (343 BCE) and Alexander the Great (332 BCE). The rehabilitation of Tyre 70 years later by Ptolemy II caused even further expansions (23.15-18), influenced by the eschatological teaching about the subjugation of Israel's enemies.[38]

The problematic issue here is not the underlying assumption of *Fortschreibung*. Rather, it is Blenkinsopp's treatment of the so-called historical allusions. A quick glance through the history of interpretation reveals that this is not the only way of interpreting these allusions. That

---

35 Bohlen 1997: 257.
36 Bohlen 1997: 257.
37 The scope of this article does not allow for an exhaustive discussion of all relevant texts.
38 Blenkinsopp 1983: 264–65.

is, in turn, a good indicator that the allusions themselves are too vague to support a certain date unequivocally. Only if it could be argued convincingly that the language and/or the themes of the passage are Hellenistic, would the references to Egypt and to Sidon then refer to events during the Hellenistic period. If this cannot be argued, the references may, of course, still refer to such events, but the interpretation rests on shakier ground. Furthermore, if we accept the claim of the text itself as describing events that, from the perspective of its author, *do not yet exist*, then we do injustice to the same text if we search it for hints that reflect its author's contemporary time. On the contrary, we may actually argue coherently that given that the text predicts a time when Tyre will be destroyed, then this is yet untrue for the author's own time.

Isaiah 24–27
Five factors tend to determine the date of Isaiah 24–27:
1. The view of eschatology *versus* apocalypse
2. The identification of the anonymous city that is destroyed (24.10-12)
3. The interpretation of the destruction of Moab (25.10)
4. The identification of Leviathan and Tannin (27.1)
5. The interpretation of the references to Assyria and Egypt (27.12-13)

In fact, the first issue is often determinative of how the following four criteria are used (see further below). It should be emphasized at this point that although scholars depend on *the same five issues* for determining the date, the results differ widely, ranging from the eighth to the second century BCE.[39] In the present context, we shall limit our discussion to the ways in which these five issues are used for proving a Hellenistic dating.

Eschatology versus apocalypse
Many elements in Isaiah 24–27 are associated with apocalyptic eschatology, e.g. the cataclysmic overthrow of the world order, the dualistic distinction of the end of this age and history (Isaiah 24), the punishment of celestial beings (24.21-22), and the expected imminent end of the time of evil (26.20-21).[40] At the same time, there are significant differences between the eschatology of this text and the apocalypse of Daniel. Hence, most contemporary scholarship has moved away from the notion that Isaiah 24–27 is a full-blown apocalypse and instead sees it as referring to

---

39 Doyle (2000: 30–37) provides a very helpful overview of the various attempts at dating Isaiah 24–27.

40 Doyle 2000: 27.

events of this world. Rudolph, for example, argues that what we have here is a kind of *nationalistisch-partikularistische Eschatologie*:

a. God communicates alone without a middle person to convey the message (e.g. 26.12ff.)
b. There is a sharp distinction between God and his holy dwelling place in Zion and the might of the nations (e.g. 25.1ff.; 10a, 12, 20; 26.1ff.)
c. The overthrow of the world powers is not identical to the annihilation of the Gentiles
d. Israel remains God's chosen people (*Liebling*, e.g. 27.2-5)[41]

Accepting, then, that Isaiah 24–27 is proto-apocalyptic and therefore earlier than the second century book of Daniel, presupposing a linear development, the question remains as to *how much earlier*.

Many scholars prefer to date Isaiah 24–27 to the Hellenistic era, either to the time of the rise of Alexander the Great or to a later period. In general, they place Isaiah 24–27 alongside Ezekiel 38, Joel 4.9-21 (3.9-21) and Zechariah 14. Cheyne, for example, detects three factors that suggest a Hellenistic dating: its *apocalyptic elements*, its *ideas*, especially the promise of the abolition of death (25.8), the resurrection of the individual dead (26.19), and finally its *elevation of the priests* (24.2). He concludes that the writer envisions a bright future in which Alexander's invasion of Persia plays a significant role, against the more oppressive past of Artaxerxes III Ochus' suppression of a Judahite uprising. In particular, Isa. 27.10-11 describes the state of Jerusalem soon after its destruction by Artaxerxes Ochus in 347 BCE. All in all, the writer proclaims that the current upheaval between the Persians and Alexander can be beneficial for the people of Judah if they turn afresh to God and repent of their previous illegal religious practices.[42] Along similar lines, based on the proto-apocalyptic eschatology found in Isaiah 24–27, in particular the reference to the resurrection of the dead (26.13-14, 19) and to the reference to cosmic judgement (24.21), Plöger argues that Isaiah 27 stems from the time of Ezra and Nehemiah while Isaiah 24–26 were written during the Ptolemaic period.[43]

The problem with these arguments can be found within themselves. Cheyne compares the apocalyptic elements in Isaiah 24–27 with those

---

41 Rudolph 1933: 58–60.

42 Cheyne 1895: 150–59. See also Rudolph (1993: 56–8, 61–4) who analyses the text of Isaiah 24–27, and, dividing it into ten sections, argues that with some exceptions (e.g. 25.10b, 11; 26.7-11) the text as a whole was composed by one person during the period 330–300 BCE. See also, Steck (1991: 192) who sees Isa. 13.1–27.12 to be a redactional textual block that was part of what he calls the *Heimkehrredaktion* in 312/11 BCE.

43 Plöger 1968: 77–8.

in Ezek. 38.19, 20; Hag. 2.6-7 (Eng. 2.7-8), 21-22 (Eng. 2.22-23); Joel 4.16; Zech. 14.4, 5. It is, however, preferable to regard these elements as present already in texts from the Persian period, as Haggai certainly does not stem from the Hellenistic period. For instance, we know that the idea of cosmic judgement was present already in the Persian period unless we date Isa. 66.24 to the Hellenistic period (see Steck below). Moreover, as the elevation of the priests can be traced to Zechariah 3, this is again not a convincing indicator of a Hellenistic date. The argument of the resurrection carries more weight, but it is doubtful whether this alone constitutes a convincing reason for dating a text. Instead, we may have to conclude the opposite, i.e. that the issue of resurrection entered into Ancient Israelite faith at an earlier point than previously suspected.[44]

Leviathan and Tannin (27.1), Assyria and Egypt (27.12-13), the destructions of Moab (25.10) and of the anonymous city (24.10-12)
Scholars who are convinced of a given date of a text often seek allusions to historical events that would corroborate with this dating. As mentioned above, there are four references in Isaiah 24–27 that are treated as historical allusions. We shall here look at a few representative arguments that purportedly favour a Hellenistic date.

Blenkinsopp, arguing that Isaiah 24–27 stem from the fourth or the third century BCE, suggests that both the reference to Leviathan and Tannin in 27.1 and the references to Assyria and Egypt in 27.12-13 (cf. Zech. 10.10-11), are code words for the Seleucid and the Ptolemaic empires. He further suggests that 'the city of foolish people', referred to in 27.10-11 (cf. *Sir.* 50. 6), alludes to the fate of Samaria after the Macedonian conquest.[45] In contrast, Mulder focuses on the mention of the destruction of Moab in 25.10 which he understands as referring to its downfall, in particular to the fall of the city Mcdaba (Dibōn) which he identifies through the wordplay of מדמנה / מדמן. As Moab fell to the Nabataeans in the first half of the third century BCE, Mulder dates Isaiah 24–27 to 270 BCE.[46] Lastly, Hengel identifies the anonymous city that is being destroyed in Isa. 24.10-12 with Samaria, suggesting that Isa. 24.1-12 refers to its destruction in 331 BCE.[47]

---

44 See Levenson (2006: 197–216) who argues that the idea of a resurrection of the dead Isaiah 24–27 stands in continuity with earlier texts such as Hosea 13–14. Furthermore, it is unlikely that the idea of resurrection was influenced by Persian and Greek ideas.

45 Blenkinsopp 1983: 266. More recently, Blenkinsopp is open to the possibility that the first draft of Isaiah 24–27 was written at a time quite close to the composition of Isaiah 40–48. See Blenkinsopp 2000: 348.

46 Mulder 1954: 34, 80–93.

47 Hengel 1980: 8–9. We know from the biography of Alexander by the Roman historian Curtius Rufus (60–70 CE – *Historiae Alexandri Magni*) that the Samarians rebelled against

In contrast, Rudolph identifies the city in 24.10 with Babylon, and, as it was conquered twice – once by Cyrus in 539 BCE and once by Alexander the Great in 331 BCE – he argues that what we are dealing with here is the second occasion.[48]

Common to all these suggestions is their *corroborating* character, as they would strengthen an already strong case but cannot stand alone. It is, in fact, symptomatic that virtually all exegetes, regardless of their final verdict pertaining to the date of Isaiah 24–27, look at these four issues and discover places and/or events that fit their dating scheme.[49] As such, only when we can arrive at a plausible date through other, independent, criteria do these allusions carry weight.

Prophetic Fortschreibung
Looking at Isaiah 24–27 from a literary perspective, investigating how it has been influenced by other texts, Scholl argues that Isaiah 24–27 is a product of the time of the Ptolemaic rule (300 BCE and onwards). He argues that the style of Isaiah 24–27 is typical of what he calls 'prophetische Prophetenauslegung'. The various passages in Isaiah 24–27 were never uttered orally but are the result of scribal adaptations of earlier texts. Scholl's dating is thus dependent upon the date of the various passages upon which the authors of Isaiah 24–27 drew. Furthermore, Scholl sees it as part of the final redaction of the book of Isaiah, comparable with Isaiah 56.1-8 and 65–66. Accordingly, as Scholl follows Steck in advocating a Hellenistic dating of this final Isaianic redaction, so must Isaiah 24–27 also be Hellenistic.[50]

This kind of literary critical method of determining which text depends on which is a more reliable way of dating texts than that of seeking to interpret rather vague historical allusions. Nonetheless, it can only result in a *relative* chronology. In this particular case, Scholl's Hellenistic dating of Isaiah 24–27 depends on Steck's dating of Isaiah 56–66. As we shall see shortly, however, Steck's conjecture that the final redaction of the book of Isaiah is a product of the Hellenistic period depends in part on rather

---

Alexander while he was occupied in Egypt, and that he rushed back and executed the leaders of the revolt. This information is further corroborated by the Chronicles of Eusebius, which reports that Alexander destroyed Samaria and turned it into a Macedonian military colony.

48 Rudolph 1933: 62.

49 For an alternative dating scheme, see Duhm 1914: 147–48, who dates Isaiah 24–27 to 135/134 BCE and the siege of Jerusalem by Antiochus Sidetes (ch. 24). Thus, he sees the reference to Leviathan and the Sea monster in 27.1 as symbols of the Parthians, the Syrians and the Egyptians, while 25.1-5, as well as the following 26.1-19, refers to the destruction of Samaria by John Hyrcanus in 107 BCE (cf. Josephus, *Antiq.* 13.280-281). Furthermore, the destruction of Moab (25.9-11) alludes to its conquest by Alexander Jannaeus shortly afterwards. See also Marti 1900: 182–83.

50 Scholl 2000: 218–23, 285–88.

doubtful interpretations of the historical allusions within Isaiah 56–66. It follows that Scholl's interpretation, though methodologically sound, rests on shaky ground.

Conclusion
In conclusion, I find no convincing argument in favour of dating Isaiah 24–27 to the Hellenistic period. It is clearly a relatively late text, as can be seen by its proto-apocalyptic character, but nothing in terms of language and/or historical allusions speaks unequivocally in favour of it being a Hellenistic composition. Accordingly, although the hypothetical possibility of a Hellenistic dating still exists, it must remain a conjecture.

Isaiah 56–66
As hinted at above, parts of Isaiah 56–66 are sometimes being dated to the Hellenistic period, based primarily on literary grounds, including the eschatological flavour of 66.17-24, but also supported by historical allusions.

Blenkinsopp is representative of those scholars who look at the eschatological elements of Isaiah 56–66, noting the general similarity between Isaiah 66.24 and Zechariah 14.12-15. In his view, the final form of the book of Isaiah is the product of the Hellenistic period prior to the Maccabees.[51] As we can see, this argument depends much on the dating of Zechariah 14.12-15. Accordingly, we shall suspend judgement until we have discussed the latter text.

Turning to the historical allusions, one critical issue is whether or not Jerusalem and its temple were destroyed during the Hellenistic period. Therefore, it is important to clarify what the available Greek sources have to say on the matter. The Greek sources are mostly silent about Judah, a small, relatively insignificant temple state in the hill country between the Dead Sea and the coastal plain. We have, however, some data. Notably, the second century historian Agatharichides of Cnidus tells us that Ptolemy I captured Jerusalem on the Sabbath, and that the people of Judah found the Greeks to be hard masters. Along similar lines, Pseudo-Aristeas tells that Ptolemy I, following his capture of Jerusalem, shipped 100 000 Jews to Egypt, 30 000 of them as soldiers and the rest, mostly women and children, as slaves.[52] This conquest of Jerusalem is most likely to have taken place in 302/1 BCE.[53] Likewise, Josephus mentions that Ptolemy I took many

---

51 Blenkinsopp 2000: 85-6.
52 Josephus, *Contra Ap.* i 194, and i 209-210. See also *Antiq.* xii 3-6.
53 Tcherikover 1959: 56-7. Earlier scholars commonly argued that this destruction took place in 312 BCE, in conjunction with Ptolemy I's siege and subsequent conquest of Gaza.

captives from Judah and Samaria and brought them to Egypt.[54] Having said this, however, for a city to be captured does not necessarily equal its destruction. Accordingly, while there is little doubt that Jerusalem was captured multiple times by various Greek rulers,[55] this does not automatically imply that post-exilic biblical texts that speak of Jerusalem's destruction refer to one of these events.

Steck is the chief proponent of a Hellenistic dating of Isaiah 56–66. His dating is based upon his view of the *Formgeschichte* of the book of Isaiah, supported by the reference to the destruction of the temple in Isaiah 64.10 (part of the lament in Isaiah 63.7–64.11), and by the singular character of its expressions (e.g. Isaiah 63.9, 10a, 11, 12, 16, 17; 64.4).[56] He suggests three possible dates for Isa. 63.7–64.11, but settles for a date during the time of Ptolemy I and his capture of Jerusalem in 302/1 BCE on the Sabbath. He finds corroborating evidence for this dating in the emphasis on the keeping of the Sabbath as found in Isa. 56.1 and 66.23, as well as in 58.13-14, a section which Steck considers to be a later addition. Steck is aware that we do not have any archaeological and/or textual evidence of a destruction of the temple at this time, but he regards this lack as due to the scarcity of the available sources. Moreover, Steck suggests that it was a tradition over several centuries to regard any distressing event as a direct continuation of the destruction of Jerusalem in 586 BCE, and to express it in language that mirrored the earlier event. Hence, he sees no need to understand descriptions of destructions in later texts as referring to the catastrophe of 586 BCE. Instead, they are but stereotypical formulas, describing any calamity that befell the Judahite community, including, but not limited to, acts of real destructions. Accordingly, the lament in Isa. 63.7–64.11 does not necessarily testify to an actual destruction of Jerusalem and/or the temple, but might have been triggered by any traumatic event.[57]

---

54   Josephus, *Antiq*. 12.7, 26, 29. See also Olmstead (1936: 243–44) for a discussion of the claim by Hecataeus of Abdera that Jewish soldiers were brought to Egypt by Ptolemy I and given modified citizenship in exchange for their military service.

55   For an overview of possible dates, see Treves 1957: 153.

56   Steck (1991: 30–34, 192) considers the final text of the book of Isaiah to be a product of the time between 312/11 BCE, the date Steck gives to what he labels *Heimkehrredaktion*, and the final redaction of the book of Isaiah as a whole between 302/1 and 270 BCE. Steck divides Isaiah 56–66 into three main parts. Isaiah 60–62 is part of the *Heimkehrredaktion*, while Isa. 56.9–59.21 and 63.1-6, forming one block, and Isa. 56.1-8 and 63.7–66.24, forming another, were composed sometime around 312-302/270 BCE.

57   Steck 1991: 35, 38–40. See especially notes 96, 99, 100 and 101. He also suggests the time of the fight of the *diadochi* and the time of the Maccabees as possible, though less plausible options. Marti (1900: 399–400) already advocated the latter dating, viewing Isa. 63.7-14 and 63.17–64.8 as descriptions of the situation in Jerusalem prior to Nehemiah's arrival, while treating Isa. 63.15-16

Goldenstein, a more recent advocate of a Hellenistic dating of Isa. 63.7–64.11, looks at the issue from a different perspective, focusing more on textual than on historical allusions. He points out that this lament draws upon earlier texts, including Lamentations, Jeramiah 31, and the Deuteronomistic history. As he assigns a late post-exilic date to these texts, Isa. 63.7–64.11 is by necessity later. This, in turn, means that the reference to a destruction of the temple in Isa. 64.10 is likely to be too late to refer to the catastrophe in 586 BCE. Instead, it is more likely to describe a more recent devastating event such as the campaign of Ptolemaios I to Judah in 302/301 BC.[58]

Steck's dating of Isaiah 24–27 is based on a combination of literary arguments and historical allusions, where his view of the formation of the book of Isaiah is influenced by the historical allusions of the text, and vice versa. In the case of Goldenstein, as with Scholl (above), the weighty arguments are those concerning the literary development of the book of Isaiah, while the historical allusions are merely corroborating evidence that can support several dating schemes. In fact, nothing in Isaiah 64.10 itself which demands that it refers to an event other than the destruction of Jerusalem in 586 BCE, and the idea of interpreting references to the destruction of Jerusalem in 586 BCE in later post-exilic material as stereotypical expression suffers from a lack of comparative example. Furthermore, there are no explicit references to any known person or event during the Hellenistic period in all of Isaiah 56–66.[59] In the case of the literary arguments, as with Isaiah 24–27, they can only demonstrate a relative dating. Hence, if it can be argued credibly that Isaiah 56–66 was completed by the end of the fifth century BCE[60], then there is no reason to see Isaiah 56–66 as a Hellenistic text.

Zechariah 9–14

As with the Isaianic material, historical allusions and eschatological motifs are understood as hinting at the date of Zechariah 9–14. The tradition of a Hellenistic or even a Maccabaean date of these chapters goes back to the nineteenth century.[61] In fact, this scholarly consensus has only recently

---

and 64.9-11 as later additions from the time of the Maccabees (*1 Macc.* 4.38). Elliger (1928: 94–5), however, points out that after the Maccabaean revolt in 165 BCE, the temple required purification, not rebuilding.

58   Goldenstein 2001: 236–47.

59   For a more detailed description of my views, see Tiemeyer 2006: 74–80.

60   Smith (1996) argues convincingly that Isa. 56.9–59.21 and 65.1–66.17 were composed by one author in the sixth century BCE, while the surrounding Isa. 56.1-8 and 66.17-24 were created not too long afterwards.

61   See especially Eichhorn 1824: 449–50, and Stade 1882: 299–306.

given way for an earlier, Persian date.[62] Beginning with the latest possible date, Ben Sirah 49.10 refers to 'the book of the twelve', thus suggesting that the book of Zechariah exists in a form as we know it today in 190 BCE.[63] Nonetheless, as it is unclear what exactly Ben Sira included into 'the book of the twelve', a Maccabaean dating cannot be ruled out on this ground alone (see further below).

The historical allusions

It is often assumed that Zechariah 9–14 is full of (alleged) historical allusions (9.1-8; 9.9; 9.13; 10.10-12; 11.1-3; [10.3; 11.4-17; 13.7]; 11.4-17; 12.2 and 12.11), and most exegetes, *regardless of the date that they propose*, seek to anchor these allusions to actual historical events. Those scholars who advocate a Hellenistic dating tend to fit them into one or more of the following five time periods, depending on their view of the formation of the text:

1.   The period of Alexander the Great (immediately following the battle of Issus in 333 BCE)
2.   The wars of the *Diadochi*, i.e. the successors of Alexander who fought to control the empire after Alexander's death (323–278 BCE)
3.   The Ptolemaic province of Judah (311–198 BCE)
4.   The period of the invasion of Judah by Antiochus III and its conquest by him (218–217 BCE)
5.   The age of the Maccabaean wars (165 BCE).

In discussing the most commonly referred to allusions, I shall cite up to five representative scholarly views.

Zech. 9.1-8 – a list of cities and districts: Hamath, Tyre, Sidon, Ashkelon, Gaza, Ekron, the Philistines

While Mitchell contends that the mentioned cities and districts fit Alexander's campaign in 332 BCE,[64] Stade argues that this list of names, together with 11.1-6, best fits the wars between the *Diadochi*.[65] Oesterley and Robinson favour a date from the reign of Antiochus III, as the place

---

62   See Curtis (2006: 118–22) for an overview.

63   Dentan 1956: 1090. It should, however, also be mentioned that some scholars, e.g. Treves (1963: 199–200) date the various poems of Ben Sirah later (165–140 BCE).

64   E.g. Mitchell 1912: 252–55, and Delcor: 1951: 110–24. Elliger (1950: 134) dates what he defines as the basic layer of the book (Zech. 9.1-8; 9.11-17; 10.3b-12; 11.4-16) to the beginning of the Hellenistic period. See also Dentan 1956: 1090–91, Hengel 1980: 9, and Blenkinsopp 1983: 259–60.

65   Stade 1882: 299–306.

names reflect an invasion of Syria in 218 BCE or 199 BCE,[66] while Treves, focusing on the reference to 'our God' (לאלהינו, v. 7), maintains that the king is Judahite and accordingly suggests the time of Jonathan Maccabeus's campaign to annex Ekron in 147–46 BCE (*1 Macc.* 10.84-89).[67]

Zech. 9.13 – the sons of Greece (ועוררתי בניך ציון על בניך יון)
Dentan dates this verse to the time of the *Diadochi*,[68] while Mitchell assigns all of 9.11–11.3 to the reign of Ptolemy III (247–222 BCE).[69] Blenkinsopp regards this verse as a later gloss reflecting the struggle with the Seleucid rulers,[70] while Treves claims that the only time when the sons of Zion fought against the sons of Greece was in the period from 167 to 85 BCE.[71] Finally, Oesterley and Robinson suggest that the reference to the sons of Greece, as well as the reference to the bow of Judah in the same verse, reflects Judas Maccabeus's victory of the Syrian general Apollonius (cf. *1 Macc.* 9.13).[72]

Zech. 10.3; 11.4-17; 13.7 – the division of the society
While Blenkinsopp sees these references as referring to the establishment of the Macedonian colony in Samaria after a failed rebellion in 332 BCE,[73] Mitchell contends that both 11.4-17 and 13.7-9 describe events soon after the battle of Raphia in 217 BCE.[74] From a different angle, Treves ascertains that the lack of a shepherd best fits a time when the high priesthood was vacant or held by individuals considered to be worthless, and accordingly proposes the Maccabaean age and the priestly leaders Jason, Menelaus and Alcimus.[75]

Zech. 12.11 – the mourning over a fallen figure
The public figure, whose death is commemorated in 12.10-14 has been identified with people ranging from king Josiah of Judah (609 BCE –

---

66 Oesterley and Robinson 1934: 420.

67 Treves 1963: 202–3.

68 Dentan 1956: 1090–91. More generally, Stade (1882: 275–90) interprets it as an allusion to the period during which the Greeks controlled Syria-Palestine. He further argues that all of Zechariah 9–14 is a reaction against the conquest of Alexander the Great.

69 Mitchell 1912: 254–59.

70 Blenkinsopp 1983: 260.

71 Treves 1963: 198.

72 Oesterley and Robinson 1934: 421.

73 Blenkinsopp 1983: 261.

74 Mitchell 1912: 258–59.

75 Treves 1963: 198, 201–2. See also Oesterley and Robinson 1934: 423, and Marti 1904: 396–97.

associated with the battle of Megiddo, cf. 2 Chron. 35.25)[76] to Simon
Macabee (134 BCE).[77]

The drawbacks of this method should be obvious by now. The historical
allusions, in particular Zech. 10.3; 11.4-17; 13.7 and 12.11, are far too
vague to provide unequivocal support for any date. Accordingly, they can
also be used to support a non-Hellenistic dating of Zechariah 9–14. In the
case of the list of cities and districts in 9.1-8, the attempt to understand it
to refer to a campaign of an earthly political ruler is questionable. Instead,
rather than seeing it as a historical allusion, it is better understood as the
mythological march of the theophany of YHWH.[78] Finally, in the case
of Zech. 9.13, it is in my view questionable, given the contact between
Judah and Greek mercenaries for centuries (see above), as well as the
political and military interaction between the Persian Empire and the
Greek empire,[79] that a single reference to 'Greece' is enough to support a Hellenistic dating. Therefore, the so-called historical allusions in
Zechariah 9–14 are unlikely to lend support to a Hellenistic dating of the
text.

Eschatological themes
Zechariah 12–14 contains clear eschatological/proto-apocalyptic aspects
(cf. Petersen above). Hence, several exegetes date this material to the
Hellenistic period, arguing that this time period gave rise to these very
aspects. Plöger typifies these scholars. Maintaining that Zechariah 12–14
is slightly earlier than Isaiah 24–27, he regards the Samaritan schism
(350–300 BCE) as the background of the text. Furthermore, he argues that
Zechariah 12–14 constitutes the reply of certain eschatological groups to
the Chronicler's theology of history. He thus advocates a final date for
Zechariah 12–14 in the first decades of the third century.[80] Again, as with
Isaiah 24–27, the crucial question concerns how old proto-apocalypse is.
There is a distinct difference between Zechariah 12–14 and the full-blown
apocalyptic eschatology of the second century BCE.[81] In fact, as Zechariah
12–14 and Isaiah 24–27, as well as Isa. 66.17-24, share many characteristic elements, scholars tend to date these texts to roughly the same time

---

76 Delcor 1953: 67–73. See also Petersen (1995: 122) who compares this passage with the
lament over Josiah in 2 Chron. 35.25.

77 See, e.g. Treves 1963: 200–201, and Oesterley and Robinson 1934: 424–25.

78 Hanson 1973: 37–59 and 1975: 16–324.

79 Curtis 2006: 232–33.

80 Plöger 1968: 94. See also Lutz (1968: 205–16) who, building on Plöger's theory, contends
that Zech. 12.1-8 and 14.1-5 are two contradictory visions of the future, and thus stem from two
different hands brought together by a redactor.

81 Hanson 1975: 400.

period. This means that the arguments for and against a Hellenistic dating of Zechariah 12–14 are the same as those for Isaiah 24–27 (see above).

Ezekiel

The Hellenistic dating of Ezekiel 7 and 28 depends in part on different dating criteria from what we have discussed so far. Although historical allusions, as well as the idea of *Fortschreibung*, do influence the dating, textual criticism plays the most important role. We shall look at two key issues with bearing on the dating, namely the possible stratification of the book of Ezekiel and the chronological relationship between the MT and the LXX. In addition, it must also be mentioned that there are a small number of scholars, although nowadays a clear minority, who view the entire book of Ezekiel as a composition of the Hellenistic era.[82]

First, a number of scholars discern complex stratification in the book of Ezekiel, where some of the textual layers are viewed as stemming from the Hellenistic period. For instance, building upon Schulz's research on the sacred legal terminology in Ezek. 18.5-9,[83] Garscha argues that the book of Ezekiel was composed over several hundred years and only completed around 300 BCE. He postulates three chief layers of the book:

1. The original prophetic book (*VEz*), containing, but not identical to, the words of the prophet Ezekiel (500–485/460 BCE).
2. The deuteronezekielian reworking (*DEz*) (400–350 BCE).
3. The cultic law redaction (*die sakralrechtliche Schicht, SEz*) (300 BCE).

For Garscha, the laments over the king of Tyre (Ezekiel 26–28) provide the key to the final date. As this material refers to the conquest of Tyre by Alexander the Great (332/331 BCE), it follows that the recensions of *VEz* and *DEz* must then be older than 332 BCE, and *SEz* younger.[84]

---

82 See especially Torrey (1930: 83–99) who argues on the basis of, among others, the reference in Ezek. 38.17 to God speaking to prophets 'in old times', the reference to Persia in 27.10 and 38.5, the language – Torrey sees the language of Ezekiel as belonging to the very latest stratum of the literature of the Hebrew Bible, the Aramaic elements in Ezekiel. More specifically, Ezekiel 28 refers to the destruction of Tyre by Alexander the Great, and Ezekiel 38–39 and the reference to Gog is clearly an allusion to Alexander the Great. Lastly, the river of Ezekiel 47 is an apocalyptic motif belonging to the third century BCE. Torrey concludes that Ezekiel dates shortly after Daniel 6 (between Ptolemy III and Sleucus II, i.e. 246–240 BCE) around 230 BCE.

83 Schulz 1969: 163–87.

84 Garscha 1974: 283–311. Along similar lines, Hossfeld (1977) divides the text into seven chronologically consecutive layers, one stemming from the prophet Ezekiel and the following six stemming from the school around his thoughts. Hossfeld, however, refrains from dating these different layers other than relatively.

In this case, we see a mixture of literary and historical arguments, with emphasis on the latter. Garscha regards the content of Ezekiel 26–28 as relating to actual historical situations and accordingly attempts to find the likeliest time period when these chapters would have been composed, in this case when Tyre was destroyed. This methodology is not in itself incorrect. It is, however, based on the assumption that events related to in prophetic texts are directly related to actual historical events happening around the prophet (cf. Isa. 15–23 above). This view is in my view unsustainable. Unless we are dealing with an obvious example of *vaticanus ex eventu*, a prophetic text about the destruction of Tyre does not necessarily presuppose its actual destruction within the author's lifetime. Instead, it may be an example of wishful thinking, implying the very opposite: Tyre is strong and an Israelite prophet wishes for its destruction.

Second, some scholars regard the Hebrew *Vorlage* of the LXX as earlier than the textual ancestor of the MT. The final composition of the MT would then be a product of the Hellenistic period. The LXX, as a translation, clearly stems from the Hellenistic period. It follows that if the MT modifies the Hebrew *Vorlage* of the LXX, it too cannot have been produced much earlier than the Hellenistic period: even though the Hebrew *Vorlage* of the LXX is older than the Hellenistic period, there would have been little point in modifying it before it reached the official status in the Greek translation of the LXX.[85]

Stordalen's treatment of Ezekiel 28 is representative of this view. Stordalen considers the MT of Ezek. 28.11-19 to be a later, Hellenistic emendation of the Hebrew *Vorlage* of the LXX for two reasons. First, the editor of the MT changed the text before him with regard to the character of the king of Tyre. He portrayed him as divine rather than as human in an attempt to harmonize Ezek. 28.11-19 with the apocalyptic tendency of the time (fourth century BC and possibly later) of portraying leaders of nations as angelic or semi-divine (e.g. Dan. 10.13). Secondly, the same editor reduced the link to the high priest (Ezek. 28.13 // Exod. 28.17-20 (// 39.10-13) by removing some of the jewels from the list and scrambling the order of the remaining ones.[86]

Stordalen thus holds the idea of an earthly ruler aspiring to divinity to be a characteristic of apocalyptic eschatology, a supposition that is supported by its attestation in Dan. 10.13, a text of clear Hellenistic dating. Stordalen then continues by claiming that any text containing this idea

---

85 For a discussion of Ezekiel 28, see, e.g. Bogaert 1991: 31–32, and Stordalen 2001: 334–48.

86 Stordalen 2001: 334–48. See also Bogaert 1991: 31–35, who, with regard to the dating of the oracle, argues that the original oracle, directed against the Jerusalem high priest, was reapplied (MT) to Tyre after Alexander's capture of Tyre owing to the resemblance of the cherub with the sea-horse.

cannot have been composed prior to the Hellenistic period. With this latter step, Stordalen moves into less certain grounds, as the idea of divine
rulers is attested throughout the Ancient Near East and Egypt long before
the Hellenistic period. Accordingly, as there is no necessity to regard this
theme as typical of the Hellenistic period, the MT of Ezekiel 28 can be
much older. Regarding the reference to the priests, it is in my opinion far
more likely that the LXX of verse 13 is a harmonizing attempt, with or
without deeper motives, than that a later editor would remove items from
an existing list.[87]

Along similar lines as with Ezekiel 28, Lust and Bogaert argue that
(some of) the differences between Ezekiel 7 in the MT and the LXX are
best explained as the result of intentional editorial additions to the ancestor
of the MT during the Hellenistic era that aimed at introducing a specific
agent of YHWH's judgement. Lust notes that the LXX of 7.7, 10 lacks a
counterpart to צפירה of the MT, a word that he interprets as a reference to
a coming king. He then connects this word with צפיר in Dan. 8.5, 8 (identified later in Dan. 8.21 as 'the king of Greece'), and goes on to suggest
that the Hebrew text has been developed to allude to Alexander the Great.
Accordingly, the Hellenistic editor of Ezekiel and the even later author of
Daniel 8 applied the same image to the Greek people. Furthermore, the
reference in 7.24 to 'I will bring the worst of the nations', absent from the
LXX, is taken by Lust to refer to the Greeks.[88]

The reasoning pertaining to Ezek. 7.7, 10 has a solid foundation in that
we know that the translation into Greek of the Hebrew *Vorlage* of the LXX
happened during the Hellenistic period. It is also text-centred as it seeks to
determine the older text. Even so, the suggestion that there is a conscious
connection between צפירה in Ezek. 7.7, 10 and צפיר in Dan. 8.21 is relatively weak, and the assumption that the scribes responsible for the final
recension of the MT added this word as an allusion to Alexander the Great
is but one possibility among many. Consequently, even though the MT
may be younger than the Hebrew *Vorlage* of the LXX, the fact that צפירה
is lacking the MT is not necessarily a sign that the MT of this particular
passage is a product of the Hellenistic period. In the case of understanding
the phrase 'I will bring the worst of the nations' in Ezek. 7.24 as a reference to the Greeks, this interpretation depends on the prior assumption

---

87   Greenberg 1997: 582. Greenberg instead assumes that the list in the MT has suffered the loss
of one line, i.e. three jewels, in the course of textual transmission. See also Kalman 1964: 35–36.

88   Lust, 1986: 17–20. See also Bogaert (1986: 21–47) in the same book, who identifies the
LXX as 'redaction A' of the book of Ezekiel while the MT is the later 'redaction B'. He guesses
that this latter redaction was inspired by the events during the reign of Antiochus IV Epiphanus,
i.e. in the second century BCE.

that the MT of Ezekiel 7 is the product of the Hellenistic period. At most, it explores the interpretative consequences of such a dating.

In conclusion, there is an ongoing discussion with regard to which of the two Hebrew *Vorlage* (of the LXX or of the MT) of the book of Ezekiel would be the earlier text. There are compelling arguments on both sides. It is indeed possible that some parts of the MT stem from the Hellenistic period. Nonetheless, until we have more conclusive data at our disposal, we need to weigh each case individually. In the two discussed cases, there are no reasons to view the text of the MT as a product of the Hellenistic period.

Conclusion

In conclusion, this article has demonstrated that there are few persuasive reasons for dating any of the discussed prophetic material to the Hellenistic period. The existence of proto-apocalyptic motifs cannot be used as an independent argument in support of such a late dating. In fact, this argument runs the risk of being circular as it depends entirely on the dating of the other texts showing the same motifs. Thus, on this criterion alone, either *all* of Ezekiel 38–39, Joel 3–4, Zechariah 12–14; Isaiah 24–27 and 66.17-24 are likely to be Hellenistic compositions, as they express related views on eschatology, or *all* of them are not. They are clearly post-exilic, as we can trace a certain development towards the type of apocalyptic eschatology attested in the book of Daniel, but we cannot determine with any certainty to what degree these texts are earlier than Daniel. We further have to investigate the arguments favouring the authorial unity of these books, and to determine whether it makes sense or not for Joel 3–4 to have been written in the same situation as Joel 1–2.[89] As for the so-called historical references, given their vagueness, they can at most function as corroboratory evidence. We thus lack conclusive evidence for dating any of the discussed prophetic texts to the Hellenistic period.

89   Cook 1995: 171–209.

BIBLIOGRAPHY

Abel, F. M., 'Alexandre le Grand en Syrie et en Palestine', *RB* 43 (1934/5): 528–45; 44: 42–61.

Abrahams, I., *Campaigns in Palestine from Alexander the Great* (London: British Academy, 1927).

Ackroyd, P. R., *Exile and Restoration: A Study of Hebrew Thought of the Sixth Century BC* (London: SCM Press, 1968).

Aharoni, Y., *The Land of the Bible, A Historical Geography* (Philadelphia: Westminster, 1979).

Aitken, J. K., 'Biblical Interpretation as Political Manifesto: The Seleucid Setting of the Wisdom of Ben Sira', *Journal of Jewish Studies* 51 (2000): 191–208.

—'Hengel's *Judentum und Hellenismus*', *JBL* 123 (2004): 331–41.

Aitken, K. T., 'Proverbs', in J. Barton and J. Muddiman (eds), *The Oxford Bible Commentary* (New York: Oxford University Press, 2001), 405–22.

Albertz, R., *A History of Israelite Religion in the Old Testament Period. Vol. 2: From the Exile to the Maccabees* (OTL; Louisville: Westminster John Knox, 1994).

—'An End to the Confusion? Why the Old Testament Cannot Be a Hellenistic Book!', in L. L. Grabbe (ed.), *Did Moses Speak Attic?* (Sheffield: Sheffield Academic Press, 2001), 30–46.

Albright, W. F., 'Excavations at Jerusalem', *JQR* 21 (1930–31): 163–68.

—'Additional Note', *BASOR* 62 (1936): 25–6.

—'The Beth-Shemesh Tablet in Alphabetic Cuneiform', *BASOR* 173 (1964): 51–3.

Alt, A., 'Judas Gaue unter Josia', *PJ* 21 (1925): 100–16.

—'Das Taltor von Jerusalem', *PJ* 24 (1928): 74–98.

—*Kleine Schriften zur Geschichte des Volkes Israel*, Vol. 2 (München: C. H. Beck, 1953).

Amiran, R. and A. Eitan, 'Excavations in the Courtyard of the Citadel, Jerusalem, 1968–1969 (Preliminary Report)', *IEJ* 20 (1970): 9–17.

Aperghis, G. G., *The Seleukid Royal Economy: the Finances and Financial Administration of the Seleukid Empire* (Cambridge: Cambridge University Press, 2004).

Arbel, Y., 'Lod', *Excavations and Surveys in Israel*, 116 (2004): 40.

Ariel, D. T., 'Imported Stamped Amphora Handles', in D. T. Ariel (ed.), *Excavations at the City of David 1978–1985 Directed by Yigal Shiloh, Vol. II: Imported Stamped Amphora Handles, Coins, Worked Bone and Ivory, and Glass, Qedem* 30 (Jerusalem, 1990), 13–98.

—(ed.), *City of David Excavations: Final Report V, Qedem* 40 (Jerusalem, 2000).

—'Imported Greek Stamped Amphora Handles', in H. Geva (ed.), *Jewish Quarter Excavations in the Old City of Jerusalem Conducted by Nahman Avigad, 1969–1982. Vol. I: Architecture and Stratigraphy: Areas A, W and X-2. Final Report* (Jerusalem, 2003), 267–83.

—'The Stamped Amphora Handles', in A. Mazar, *Excavations at Tel Beth-Shean 1989–1996, Volume I: From the Late Bronze Age IIB to the Medieval Period* (Jerusalem: Israel Exploration Society, 2006), 594–606.

Ariel, D. T., H. Hirschfeld and N. Savir, 'Area D1: Stratigraphic Report', in D. T. Ariel (ed.), *Excavations at the City of David V: Extramural Areas, Qedem* 40 (Jerusalem: The Hebrew University, 2000), 33–72.

Ariel, D. T. and J. Magness, 'Area K', in A. De Groot and D. T. Ariel (eds), *Excavations at the City of David 1978–1985 Vol. III: Stratigraphic, Environmental, and Other Reports, Qedem* 33 (Jerusalem, 1992), 63–97.

Ariel, D. T. and Y. Shoham, 'Locally Stamped Handles and Associated Body Fragments of the Persian and Hellenistic Periods', in D. T. Ariel (ed.), *Excavations at the City of David 1978–1985 VI, Inscriptions, Qedem* 41 (Jerusalem, 2000), 137–71.

Asad, T., *Genealogies of Religion. Discipline and Reasons of Power in Christianity and Islam* (Baltimore and London: The Johns Hopkins University Press, 1993).

Astour, M. C., *Hellenosemitica: An Ethnic and Cultural Study in West Semitic Impact on Mycenaean Greece* (Leiden: Brill, 1965).

Austin, Michel M., 'Hellenistic Kings, War, and the Economy', *CQ* n.s. 36 (1986): 450–66.

—*The Hellenistic World from Alexander to Roman Conquest: A Selection of Ancient Sources in Translation*, 2nd edn (Cambridge: Cambridge University Press, 2006).

Avigad, N., 'Excavations in the Jewish Quarter of the Old City of Jerusalem', 1971, *IEJ* 22 (1972):193–200.

—'Excavations in the Jewish Quarter of the Old City, 1969–1971', in Y. Yadin (ed.), *Jerusalem Revealed: Archaeology in the Holy City 1968–1974* (Jerusalem, 1975), 38–49.

—*The Upper City of Jerusalem* (Jerusalem, 1980).

—*Discovering Jerusalem* (Nashville: T. Nelson, 1983).

—'Jerusalem: The Second Temple Period', *The New Encyclopedia of Archaeological Excavations in the Holy Land* 2 (Jerusalem: Carta, 1993): 717–25.

Avi-Yonah M., *Historical Geography of Palestine from the end of the Babylonian Exile up to the Arab Conquest*, 3rd edn (Jerusalem: The Bialik Institute, 1962).

—*Hellenism and the East: Contacts and Interrelations from Alexander to the Roman Conquest* (Jerusalem: University Microfilms International, 1978).

Badian, Ernst, 'Alexander the Great and the Unity of Mankind', *Historia* 7 (1958): 425–44.

Bagnall, R. S., 'Ptolemaic Foreign Correspondence in *P. Tebt.* 8', *JEA* 61 (1975): 168–80.

—*The Administration of the Ptolemaic Possessions outside Egypt* (Leiden: Brill, 1976).

Bagnall, Roger S., and Peter Derow (eds), *The Hellenistic Period: Historical Sources in Translation*, Blackwell Sourcebooks in Ancient History 1 (Oxford: Blackwell, 2004).

Barag, Dan, 'The Effects of the Tennes Rebellion on Palestine', *BASOR* 183 (1966): 6–12.

—'The Coinage of Yehud and the Ptolemies', *INJ* 13 (1994–99): 27–37.

—'The Mint of Antiochus IV in Jerusalem: Numismatic Evidence on the Prelude to the Maccabean Revolt', *INJ* 14 (2002): 59–77.

Barclay, John M. G., *Against Apion*, trans. Flavius Josephus (Leiden: Brill, 2007).

Barkay, G. and Y. Zweig, 'The Temple Mount Debris Sifting Project: Preliminary Report', in E. Baruch, Z. Greenhut and A. Faust (eds), *New Studies on Jerusalem* 11 (Ramat Gan: Bar Ilan University, 2006): 213–37.

Bar-Kochva, B., *Pseudo-Hecataeus, 'On the Jews': Legitimizing the Jewish Diaspora*, Hellenistic Culture and Society 21 (Berkeley, CA: University of California Press, 1996).

Barr, J., *The Variable Spellings of the Hebrew Bible* (Oxford: Oxford University Press, 1989).

Barstad, H. M., *The Myth of the Empty Land: A Study in the History and Archaeology of Judah during the "Exilic" Period*, Symbolae Osloenses, *Fasciculi Suppletor* 28 (Oslo: Scandinavian University Press, 1996).

Barth, F., 'The Study of Culture in Complex Societies', *Ethnos* 3–4 (1989): 12–42.

Beard, M., North, J., and Price, S., *Religions of Rome* (Cambridge: Cambridge University Press, 1998).

Becking, B., 'Continuity and Community: The Belief System of the Book of Ezra', in B. Becking and M. C. A. Korpel (eds), *The Crisis of Israelite Religion. Transformation of Religious Tradition in Exilic and Post-Exilic Times*, Oudtestamentische Studiën 62 (Leiden, Boston, Köln: E. J. Brill, 1999): 256–75.

—'"We All Returned as One!": Critical Notes on the Myth of the Mass Return', in O. Lipschits and M. Oeming (eds), *Judah and the Judaeans in the Persian Period* (Winona Lake, IN: Eisenbrauns, 2006) 3–18.

Becking, B., and Korpel, M. C. A. (eds), *The Crisis of Israelite Religion. Transformation of Religious Tradition in Exilic and Post-Exilic Times, Oudtestamentische Studiën* 62 (Leiden, Boston, Köln: E. J. Brill, 1999).

Bedford, P. R., 'On Models and Texts: A Response to Blenkinsopp and Petersen', in P. R. Davies (ed.), *Second Temple Studies: 1. Persian Period, JSOT Sup.* 117 (Sheffield: JSOT, 1991) 154–62.

—*Temple Restoration in Early Achaemnid Judah* (Leiden: Brill, 2000).

Bergman, A., 'Soundings at the Supposed Site of Old Testament Anathoth', *BASOR* 62 (1936): 22–25.

Bergren, T. A., 'Nehemiah in 2 Maccabees 1:10-2:18', *Journal for the Study of Judaism* 28 (1997): 249–70.

Bernstein, Moshe J. 'Poetry and prose in 4Q371–373 "Narrative and Poetic Composition" (a, b, c)', in Esther G. Chazon (ed.), *Liturgical Perspectives: Prayer and Poetry in Light of the Dead Sea Scrolls. Proceedings of the Fifth International Symposium of the Orion Center 19–23 January 2000* (Leiden: Brill, 2003), 19–33.

Berquist, Jon L., 'Constructions of Identity in Postcolonial Yehud', in Oded Lipschits (ed.), *Judah and the Judeans in the Persian period* (Winona Lake, IN: Eisenbrauns, 2006) 53–66.

Bertrand, J. M., 'Sur l'inscription d'Hefzibah', *ZPE* 46 (1982): 167–74.

Betlyon, John Wilson, 'A People Transformed Palestine in the Persian Period', *Near Eastern Archaeology* 68 (2005): 47–50.

Bickerman, Elias J., *From Ezra to the Last of the Maccabees: Foundations of post-Biblical Judaism* (New York: Schocken, 1962).

—'La charte séleucide de Jérusalem', *REJ* 100 (1935): 4–35; reprinted in Elias J. Bickerman, *Studies in Jewish and Christian History, AGAJU* 9 (Leiden: Brill, 1980): 44–85.

—'Une proclamation séleucide relative au temple de Jérusalem', *Syria* 25 (1946–48): 67–85; reprinted in Elias J. Bickerman, *Studies in Jewish and Christian History, AGAJU* 9 (Leiden: Brill, 1980): 86–104.

—'Une question d'authenticité les privilèges juifs', in *Mélange Isidore Lévy* Annuaire de l'Institut de philologie et d'histoire orientales et slaves 13 (Brussels: Université de Bruxelles libre, 1955); reprinted in Elias J. Bickerman, *Studies in Jewish and Christian History, AGAJU* 9 (Leiden: Brill, 1980): 24–43.

—*The Jews in the Greek Age* (Cambridge Mass: Harvard University Press, 1988).

Bilde P., T. Engberg-Pedersen, L. Hannestad and J. Zahle (eds), *Religion and Religious Practice in the Seleucid Kingdom* (Aarhus: Aarhus University Press, 1990).

Biran, A., 'Tel Dan', *BA* 37 (1974): 26–51.

—'On the Identification of Anathoth', *Eretz-Israel* 18 (1985): 209–14.

Black, Matthew. *Apocalypsis Henochi Graeci in Pseudepigrapha Veteris Testamenti*, PVTG, 3 (Leiden: Brill, 1970).

—*The Book of Enoch or 1 Enoch*, SVTP 7 (Leiden: Brill, 1985).

Blair, E. P. 'Soundings at 'Anata (Roman Anathoth)', *BASOR* 62 (1936): 18–21.

Blenkinsopp, J., *A History of Prophecy in Israel* (Philadelphia: Westminster, 1983).

—*Ezra/Nehemiah: A Commentary* (Philadelphia: Westminster, 1988).

—'Temple and Society in Achaimenid Judah', in P. R. Davies (ed.), *Second Temple Studies: 1. Persian Period, JSOT Sup.* 117 (Sheffield: JSOT, 1991) 22–53.

—'The Judean Priesthood during the Neo-Babylonian and Achaemenid Periods: A Hypothetical Reconstruction', *CBQ* 60 (1998): 25–43.

—*Isaiah 1–39*, AB, 19 (New York, NY: Doubleday, 2000).

Bliss, F. J. and A. C. Dickie, *Excavations at Jerusalem 1894–1897* (London: Palestine Exploration Fund, 1898).

Bloch-Smith, E. M., 'The Cult of the Dead in Judah: Interpreting the Material Remains', *JBL* 111 (1992): 213–24.

Boda, M. J. and M. H. Floyd (eds), *Bringing Out the Treasure: Inner Biblical Exegesis in Zechariah 9–14, JSOTS* 370 (Sheffield: Continuum, 2003).

Bogaert, P.-M., 'Les deux redactions conserves (LXX et TM) d'Ézéchiel 7', in J. Lust (ed.), *Ezekiel and His Book: Textual and Literary Criticism and their Interrelation* (Leuven: Leuven University Press, 1986) 21–47.

—'Le Chérub de Tyr (Ez 28, 14.16) et l'hippocampe de ses monnaies', in R. Liwak and S. Wagner (eds), *Prophetie und geschichtliche Wirklichkeit im alten Israel. Festschrift S. Herrmann* (Stuttgart: Kohlhammer, 1991), 29–38.

Bohlen, R., 'Kohelet im Kontext hellenisticher Kultur', in L. Schwienhorst-Schönberger (ed.), *Das Buch Kohelet: Studien zur Struktur, Geschichte, Rezeption und Theologie, BZAW* 254 (Berlin: de Gruyter, 1997), 249–68.

Bordreuil, P. and D. Pardee, 'Un abébécédaire du type sud-sémitique découvert en 1988', *CRAIBL* juillet-octobre (1995): 855–60.

—'Textes alphabétiques en ougaritique 8. Abébécédaire (nᵒ 32)', in M. Yon and D. Arnaud (eds), *Etudes ougaritiques I. Travaux 1985–1995* (Paris: Editions recherches sur les civilisations, 2001), 341–48.

Bosworth, Albert B., *Alexander and the East: The Tragedy of Triumph* (Oxford: Clarendon Press, 1996).

Bosworth, Albert B. and Elizabeth J. Baynham, *Alexander the Great in Fact and Fiction* (Oxford: Oxford University Press, 2002).

Brand, E., 'el-Haditha', *Excavations and Surveys in Israel* 19 (1997): 44–46.

—*Salvage Excavation on the Margin of Tel Hadid, Preliminary Report* (Tel Aviv: Institute of Archaeology, Hebrew, 1998).

Briant, P., *Rois, tributs et paysans. Études sur les formations tributaires du Moyen-Orient ancien*, Annales littéraires de l'université de Besançon, 269 (Paris: Les Belles-Lettres, 1982).

—'The Seleucid Kingdom, the Achaemenid Empire and the History of the Near East in the First Millenium BC', in P. Bilde, T. Engberg-Pedersen, L. Hannestad and J. Zahle (eds), *Religion and Religious Practice in the Seleucid Kingdom* (Aarhus: Aarhus University Press, 1990) 40–65.

—*From Cyrus to Alexander: A History of the Persian Empire*, trans. Peter T. Daniels. Winona Lake, IN: Achaemenid History 10 (Leiden, 2002).

Broshi, M., 'Excavations on Mount Zion, 1971–1972 (Preliminary Report)', *IEJ* 26 (1976): 81–8.

Broshi, M. and I. Finkelstein, 'The Population of Palestine in Iron Age II', *BASOR* 287 (1992): 47–60.

Broshi, M. and S. Gibson, 'Excavations along the Western and Southern Walls of the Old City of Jerusalem', in H. Geva (ed.), *Ancient Jerusalem Revealed* (Jerusalem, 1994), 147–55.

Brown, J. P., *The Lebanon and Phoenicia I* (Beirut, 1969).

Browne W. G., *Travels in Africa, Egypt and Syria from the year 1792 to 1798* (London: Cadell and Davies).

Bruneau, Philippe, 'Les Israélites de Délos et la juiverie délienne', *Bulletin Correspondance Hellenique* 106 (1982): 465–504.

Büchler A., 'La relation de Josèphe concernant Alexandre le Grand', *REJ* 36 (1898): 1–26.

Bull R. J., 'The Excavation of Tell er-Ras on Mt. Gerizim', *BA* 31 (1968): 58–72.

Bull R. J. and Wright G. E., 'Newly Discovered Temples on Mt. Gerizim in Jordan', *HTR* 58 (1965): 234–37.

Burckhardt, J. L., *Notes on the Bedouins and Wahabis, collected during his travels in the East* (London: J. Murray, 1830).

Burstein, Stanley M., 'Hecataeus of Abdera's History of Egypt', in Janet H. Johnson (ed.), *Life in a Multi-Cultural Society: Egypt from Cambyses to Constantine and Beyond, Studies in Ancient Oriental Civilization* 51 (Chicago: Oriental Institute of the University of Chicago, 1992), 45–49.

Cahill, J. M., 'The Chalk Assemblages of the Persian/Hellenistic and Early Roman Periods', in A. De Groot, and D. T. Ariel (eds), *Excavations at the City of David 1978–1985 Vol. III: Stratigraphic, Environmental, and Other Reports, Qedem* 33 (Jerusalem, 1992): 190–274.
Cahill, J. M. and D. Tarler, 'Excavations Directed by Yigal Shiloh at the City of David, 1978–1985', in H. Geva (ed.), *Ancient Jerusalem Revealed* (Jerusalem, 1994) 31–45.
Callaway, J. A. and M. B. Nicol, 'A Sounding at Khirbet Hayian', *BASOR* 183 (1966): 12–19.
Camp, C. V. and B. G. Wright, '"Who has been Tested by Gold and Found Perfect?" Ben Sira's Discourses of Riches and Poverty', *Henoch* 23 (2001): 153–74.
Campbell, Edward Fay, *Shechem II, A Portrait of a Hill Country Vale*, The Shechem Regional Survey (Atlanta, GA: Scholars Press, 1991).
—*Shechem III: The Stratigraphy and Architecture of Shechem/Tell Balatah* (Boston, MA: American Schools of Oriental Research, 2002).
Carroll, R. P., 'Jewgreek Greekjew: The Hebrew Bible Is all Greek to Me. Reflections on the Problematics of Dating the Origins of the Bible in Relation to Contemporary Discussions of Biblical Historiography', in L. L. Grabbe (ed.), *Did Moses Speak Attic?* (Sheffield: Sheffield Academic Press, 2001), 91–107.
Carter, C. E., *The Emergence of Yehud in the Persian Period – A Social and Demographic Study*, JSOT Supplement Series 294 (Sheffield, 1999).
—*The Emergence of Yehud in the Persian Period: A Social and Demographic Study* (Sheffield: Academic Press, 1999).
Charles, R. H., *The Book of Enoch or 1 Enoch* (Oxford: Clarendon Press, 1912).
—*Eschatology. The Doctrine of a Future Life in Israel, Judaism and Christianity: A Critical History*, 2nd edn (New York: Schocken Brooks, 1913).
Chartier, R., 'Text, Symbols, and Frenchness', *Journal of Modern History* 57 (1985): 682–95.
Chen, D., S. Margalit and B. Pixner, 'Mount Zion: Discovery of Iron Age Fortifications below the Gate of the Essens', in H. Geva (ed.) *Ancient Jerusalem Revealed* (Jerusalem, 1994), 76–81.
Cheyne, T. K., *Introduction to the Book of Isaiah* (London: Adam and Charles Black, 1895).
Chicago Demotic Dictionary (online). http://oi.chicago.edu/research/pubs/catalog/cdd/
Clarysse, Willy, 'Harmachis, Agent of the Oikonomos. An Archive from the Time of Philopator', *Ancient Society* 7 (1976): 185–207.
—'Greeks and Egyptians in the Ptolemaic Army and Administration', *Aegyptus* 65 (1985): 57–66.
—'Egyptian Scribes Writing Greek', *Chronique d'Égypte* 68 (1993): 186–201.
—'Ptolémées et temples', in D. Valbelle and J. Leclant (eds), *Le Décret de Memphis* (Paris: de Boccard, 1999) 41–65.
Cogan, M. and H. Tadmor, *II Kings* (New York: Doubleday, 1988).
Cohen, A., *Palestine in the 18th Century* (Jerusalem: Magness Press, 1973).
Cohen, G. M., *The Hellenistic Settlements in Europe, the Islands and Asia Minor, Hellenistic Culture and Society* 17 (Berkeley, CA: University of California Press, 1995).
—*The Hellenistic Settlements in Syria, the Red Sea Basin and North Africa, Hellenistic Culture and Society* 46 (Berkeley, CA: University of California Press, 2006).
Cohen, Shaye J. D., 'Alexander the Great and Jaddus the High Priest according to Josephus', *AJS Review* 7–8 (1982–3): 41–68.
—'Conversion to Judaism in Historical Perspective: From Biblical Israel to Post-Biblical Judaism', *Conservative Judaism* 36/4 (1983): 31–45.
—'Crossing the Boundary and Becoming a Jew', *HTR* 82 (1989): 13–33.
—'Religion, Ethnicity and "Hellenism" in the Emergence of Jewish Identity in Maccabean Palestine', in P. Bilde, T. Engberg-Pedersen, L. Hannestad and J. Zahle (eds), *Religion and Religious Practice in the Seleucid Kingdom* (Aarhus: Aarhus University Press, 1990), 204–23.
—*The Beginnings of Jewishness: Boundaries, Varieties, Uncertainties, Hellenistic Culture and Society* 31 (Berkeley, CA: University of California, 1999).

Cohn Eskenazi, T., 'The Missions of Ezra and Nehemiah', in O. Lipschits, and M. Oeming (eds), *Judah and the Judaeans in the Persian Period* (Winona Lake, IN: Eisenbrauns, 2006), 509–29.

Collins, John J., 'Methodological Issues in the Study of 1 Enoch: Reflections on the Articles of P. D. Hanson and G. W. Nickelsburg', in Paul J. Achtemaier (ed.), *Society of Biblical Literature Seminar Papers* 18, Vol. 1 (Missoula, Mt: Scholars Press, 1978), 315–22.

—*The Apocalyptic Imagination* (New York: Crossroad, 1984).

Connelly, B., *Arab Folk Epic and Identity* (Berkeley, CA: University of California Press, 1986).

Cook, S. A., 'Inscribed Jar Handel', *PEFQST* 57 (1925): 91–95.

Cook, S. L., *Prophecy and Apocalypticism. The Postexilic Setting* (Minneapolis: Fortress, 1995).

Corley, Jeremy, *Ben Sira's Teaching on Friendship*, Brown Judaic Studies 316 (Providence, RI: Brown University, 2002).

Cotton, Hannah M. and K. Wörrle, 'Seleukos IV to Heliodoros: A New Dossier of Royal Correspondence from Israel', *ZPE* 159 (2007): 191–205.

Cowley, Arthur Ernest, *Aramaic papyri of the Fifth Century B.C.*, trans. A. Cowley, reprinted (Osnabruck: Otto Zeller, 1967).

Cross, Frank M., 'The Discovery of the Samaria Papyri', *BA*, 26 (1963): 110–12.

—'Aspects of Samaritan and Jewish History in Late Persian and Hellenistic Times', *HTR*, 59 (1966): 201–11.

—'Papyri from the Fourth Century BC from Daliyeh', Freedman D. N, Greenfield J. C (eds), *New Direction in Biblical Archaeology* (Garden City, 1969), 45–69.

—'The Papyri and their Historical Implication', P. W. and L. N. Lapp (eds), *Discoveries in Wadi ed Daliyeh*, (Cambridge MA, 1974), 17–29.

—'A Reconstruction of the Judaean Restoration', in Frank Cross, *From Epic to Canon: History and Literature in Ancient Israel* (Baltimore: Johns Hopkins, 1998), 151–72; revision of Frank Cross, 'A Reconstruction of the Judean Restoration', *JBL* 94 (1975): 4–18/*Int* 29 (1975), 187–203.

—'Samaria and Jerusalem', in Hayim Tadmor (ed.), *The Restoration: The Persian Period*, Vol. 9, The History of the Jewish People (Tel Aviv: Am Oved, 1983): 81–94.

—'A report on the Samaria papyri', *Vetus Testamentum Supplements* (1988): 17–26.

—'Samaria and Jerusalem in the era of the Restoration', revised from Frank Moore Cross, *From Epic to Canon; History and Literature in Ancient Israel* (Baltimore: Johns Hopkins University Press, 1998), 173–202.

—'Samaria and Jerusalem during the Persian Period', in Ephraim, Stern, Hanan Eshel (eds), *The Samaritans* (Jerusalem: Yad Ben Zvi Press, 2002), 45–70.

Crowfoot, John W., *Samaria Sebaste III: The Objects* (London: Palestine Exploration Fund, 1957).

Crowfoot, J. W. and G. M. Fitzgerald, *Excavations in the Tyropoen Valley, Jerusalem*, Palestine Exploration Fund Annual 5 (London: Palestine Exploration Fund, 1929).

Crown, Alan D., 'Another Look at Samaritan Origins', in Alan D. Crown, Lucy Davey (eds), *Essays in Honour of G. D. Sixdenier, New Samaritan Studies* (Sydney: Mandelbaum Pub, 1995): 133–55.

Currid, J. D., *Ancient Egypt and the Old Testament* (Michigan: Baker Books, 1997).

Curtis, B. G., *Up the Steep and Stony Road: The Book of Zechariah in Social Location Trajectory Analysis, SBLAB* 25 (Leiden: Brill, 2006).

Dagan, Y., *The Shephelah during the Period of the Monarchy in Light of Archaeological Excavations and Surveys*, MA thesis (University of Tel Aviv, 1992).

Dandamaev, M., 'State and Temple in Babylonia in the First Millennium B.C.', in E. Lipinski (ed.), *State and Temple Economy in the Ancient Near East II. Proceedings of the International Conference organized by the Katholieke Universiteit Leuven, 10th-14th April 1978*, Orientalia Lovaniensia Analecta, 6, (Leuven: Department Oriëntalistiek, 1979), 589–96.

Darnton, R., *The Great Cat Massacre and Other Episodes in French Cultural History* (New York: Random House, 1984).

Davesne, A. and G. Le Rider, *Le trésor de Meydancikhale (Cilicie Trachée, 1980)* (Paris: Editions recherche sur les civilizations, 1989).

Davies, P. R., 'Scenes from the Early History of Judaism', in D. V. Edelman (ed.), *The Triumph of Elohim: From Yahwisms to Judaisms* (Kampen: Kok Pharos, 1995) 145–82.

—'Biblical Hebrew and the History of Ancient Judah: Typology, Chronology and Common Sense', in I. Young (ed.), *Biblical Hebrew. Studies in Chronology and Typology, JSOTS* 369 (London: T&T Clark, 2003), 150–63.

De Groot, A., 'Jerusalem during the Persian Period', in A. Faust and E. Baruch (eds), *New Studies on Jerusalem, Proceedings of the Seventh Conference* (Ramat Gan: Bar Ilan University, 2001): 77–82.

—'Jerusalem in the Early Hellenistic Period', in E. Baruch and A. Faust (eds), *New Studies on Jerusalem Vol. 10* (Ramat Gan: Bar Ilan University, 2004): 67–70.

—'Excavations in the South of the City of David – Reinterpretation of Former Excavations', *Qadmoniot* 130 (2005): 81–86.

De Groot, A., D. Cohen and A. Caspi, 'Area A1', in A. De Groot and D. T. Ariel (eds), *Excavations at the City of David 1978–1985 Vol. III: Stratigraphic, Environmental, and Other Reports, Qedem* 33 (Jerusalem: The Hebrew University, 1992): 1–29.

De Groot, A. and D. Michaeli, 'Area H – Stratigraphic Report', in A. De Groot and D. T. Ariel (eds), *Excavations at the City of David 1978–1985 Vol. III: Stratigraphic, Environmental, and Other Reports, Qedem* 33 (Jerusalem, 1992), 35–53.

Delcor, M., 'Les Allusions á Alexandre le Grand dans Zech 9:1-8', *VT* 1 (1951): 110–24.

—'Deux passages difficiles: Zacharie 12:11 et 11:13', *VT* 3 (1953): 67–73.

Demsky, A., '*Pelekh* in Nehemiah 3', *IEJ* 33 (1983): 242–44.

Dentan, R., 'Zechariah 9–14', *Interpreter's Bible* 6 (New York: Abingdon-Cokesbury Press, 1956) 1089–114.

de Polignac, F., *Cults, Territory, and the Origins of the Greek City-State*, trans. by J. Lloyd (Chicago: University of Chicago Press, 1995).

Dietrich, M., and O. Loretz, *Die Keilalphabete: Die phönizisch-kanaanäischen und altarabischen Alphabete in Ugarit, ALASP* 1, (Münster: UGARIT-Verlag, 1988).

Dimant, Devorah, '1 Enoch 6–11: A Methodological Perspective', in Paul J. Achtemaier (ed.), *Society of Biblical Literature Seminar Papers* 18 (Missoula, Mt: Scholars Press, 1978), 323–29.

Dinur, U. and N. Feig, 'Eastern Part of the Map of Jerusalem', in I. Finkelstein and Y. Magen (eds), *Archaeological Survey of the Hill Country of Benjamin* (Jerusalem: Israel Antiquities Authority, 1993): 339–427.

Dittenberger, Wilhelm, *Orientis graeci inscriptiones selectae (OGIS)*, 2 vols, reprinted (Hildesheim: Olms, 1960).

Doran, Robert, 'Pseudo-Hecataeus', in James H. Charlesworth, *The Old Testament Pseudepigrapha*, Vol. 2 (New York, NY. Doubleday, 1985), 913–14.

Doyle, B., *The Apocalypse of Isaiah Metaphorically Speaking. A Study of the Use, Function and Significance of Metaphors in Isaiah 24–27* (Leuven: Peeters, 2000).

Driver, G. R., *Semitic Writing: From Pictograph to Alphabet*, revised edn, S. A. Hopkins (ed.) (London: British Academy, 1976).

Duhm, B., *Das Buch Jesaia* (Göttingen: Vandenhoeck & Ruprecht, 1914).

Duncan, J. G., *Digging up Biblical History I-II* (London, 1931).

Durand, Xavier, *Des Grecs en Palestine au IIIᵉ siècle avant Jésus-Christ: Le dossier syrien des archives de Zénon de Caunos (261–252)* (Cahiers de la Revue Biblique 38; Paris: Gabalda, 1997).

Dušek, Jan, *Les manuscrits araméens du Wadi Daliyeh et la Samarie vers 450–332 av. J.-C., CHANE* 30 (Leiden: Brill, 2007).

Edelman, D., 'Introduction', in D. Edelman (ed.) *The Triumph of Elohim: From Yahwisms to Judaisms* (Kampen: Kok Pharos, 1995a), 1–25.

—(ed.) *The Triumph of Elohim: From Yahwisms to Judaisms* (Kampen: Kok Pharos, 1995b).

—*The Origins of the 'Second' Temple: Persian Imperial Policy and the Rebuilding of Jerusalem* (London: Equinox, 2005).

Edgar, Campell Cowan (ed.), *Zenon Papyri I-V [PCZ – P. Cairo Zenon*, Catalogue général antiquités égyptiennes du Musée du Caire 79–84 (Cairo: l'Institut Français d'Archéologie Orientale, 1925–40).

Egger, Rita, *Josephus Flavius und die Samaritanaer: Eine terminologische Untersuchung zur Identitätsklärung der Samaritaner* (Freiburg-Göttingen: Universitätsverlag, 1986).

—'Josephus Flavius and the Samaritans', in Abraham Tal and Moshe Florentin (eds), *First International Congress of the Société d'Études Samaritaines* (Tel Aviv: Chaim Rosenberg School for Jewish Studies, Tel-Aviv University, 1991), 109–14.

Ehrensvärd, M., 'Linguistic Dating of Biblical Texts', in I. Young (ed.), *Biblical Hebrew. Studies in Chronology and Typology, JSOTS* 369 (London: T&T Clark, 2003), 164–88.

Eichhorn, J. G., *Einleitung in das Alte Testament*, 4 (Göttingen: C.E. Rosenbusch, 1824).

Elliger, K., *Die Einheit des Tritojesaia (Jesaia 56–66), BWANT* 3/9 (Stuttgart: W. Kohlhammer, 1928).

—*Das Buch der zwölf kleinen Propheten II. Die Propheten Nahum, Habakuk, Zephanja, Haggai, Zacharja, Maleachi, ATD* 25 (Göttingen: Vandenhoeck & Ruprecht, 1950).

Emerton, J. A., 'A Questionable Theory of Egyptian Influence on a Genre of Hebrew Literature', in G. Khan (ed.), *Semitic Studies in Honour of Edward Ullendorff* (Leiden: Brill, 2005) 189–202.

Eph'al, I., *The Ancient Arabs: Nomads on the border of the Fertile Crescent 9th-5th centuries B.C.* (Jerusalem: Magness Press, 1982).

—'Changes in Palestine During the Persian Period in Light of Epigraphic Sources', *IEJ* 38 (1998): 106–19.

Eph'al, I. and J. Naveh, *Aramaic Ostraca of the Fourth Century BC from Idumaea* (Jerusalem: Magness Press, 1996).

Erdmann, E., *Nordosttor und persische Belagerungsrampe in Alt-Paphos* (Konstanz: Universitätsverlag, 1977).

Erlich, Adi, *The Art of Hellenistic Palestine*, BAR International Series 2010 (Oxford: Archaeopress, 2009).

Erskine, Andrew, 'Life after Death: Alexandria and the Body of Alexander', *Greece and Rome* 49 (2002): 163–79.

Eshel, Hanan, 'Ha-Miqdash ha-Shomroni be-Har Gerizim veha-Mechkar ha-Histori', *Beth Mikra* 39 (1984): 141–55.

—'The Prayer of Joseph, A Papyrus from Masada and the Samaritan Temple on ARGARIZIN', *Zion* 56 (1991): 125–36.

—'The Rulers of Samaria during the Fifth and Fourth Centuries BCE', *Eretz-Israel* 26 (1996a): 8–12 (Heb.), 226 (Eng. summary), 1999.

—'Wadi ed-Daliyeh Papyrus 14 and the Samaritan Temple', *Zion* 61 (1996b): 359–65.

—'Jerusalem under Persian Rule: The City's Layout and the Historical Background', in S. Ahituv and A. Mazar (eds), *The History of Jerusalem, The Biblical Period* (Jerusalem: Yad Ben Zvi, 2000): 327–44.

—'The Onomasticon of Mareshah in the Persian and Hellenistic Periods', in O. Lipschits, G. Knoppers and R. Albertz (eds), *Judah and the Judeans in the Fourth Century B.C.E.* (Winona Lake, IN: Eisenbrauns, 2007), 145–56.

Eshel, E., E. Puech, and A. Kloner, *Aramaic Scribal Exercises of the Hellenistic Period from Maresha: Bowls A and B.*, BASOR 345 (2007): 39–62.

Eshel, H. and A. Kloner, 'An Aramaic Ostracon of an Edomite Marriage from Maresha, dated 176 B.C.E.', *IEJ* 46 (1996): 1–22.

Eskhult, M., 'The Importance of Loanwords for Dating Biblical Hebrew Texts', in I. Young (ed.),

Biblical Hebrew: Studies in Chronology and Typology, JSOTS 369 (London: T&T Clark, 2003), 8–23.

Exum, J. C., *Song of Songs* (Louisville, KY: WJK, 2005).

Falivene, Maria Rosaria, 'Government, Management, Literacy: Aspects of Ptolemaic Administration in the Early Hellenistic Period', *Ancient Society* 22 (1991): 203–27.

Farmer, W. R., *Maccabees, Zealots and Josephus: An Inquiry into Jewish Nationalism in the Greco-Roman Period* (New York: Columbia University Press, 1957).

Feldman, L. H., *Judaism and Hellenism Reconsidered*, Supplements to the Journal for the Study of Judaism 107 (Leiden: Brill, 2006).

Feldstein, A., 1997 'Lod, Neve Yaraq (B)', *Excavations and Surveys in Israel* 19 (1997): 50.

Feldstein, A., G. Kidron, N. Hanin, Y. Kamaisky and D. Eitam, 'Southern Part of the Maps of Ramallah and el-Bireh and Northern Part of the Map of 'Ein Kerem', in I. Finkelstein and Y. Magen (eds), *Archaeological Survey of the Hill Country of Benjamin* (Jerusalem: Israel Antiquities Authority, 1993) 133–264.

Finkelstein, I., 1992 'A Few Notes on Demographic Data from Recent Generations and Ethnoarchaeology', *PEQ* 122 (1992): 47–52.

—'Penelope's Shroud Unraveled: Iron II Date of Gezer's Outer Wall Established', *Tel Aviv* 21 (1994): 276–82.

—'Jerusalem in the Persian (and Early Hellenistic) Period and the Wall of Nehemiah', *JSOT* 32/4 (2008): 501–20.

—'Notes on the Territorial Extension and Population of Yehud/Judea in the Persian and Early Hellenistic Periods' (Jerusalem: Tel Aviv University, forthcoming).

Finkelstein, I., Z. Herzog, L. Singer-Avitz and D. Ussishkin, 'Has King David's Palace been Found in Jerusalem?', *Tel Aviv* 34 (2007): 142–64.

Finkielsztejn, G., 'Hellenistic Jerusalem: The Evidence of the Rhodian Amphora Stamps', in A. Faust and E. Baruch (eds), *New Studies on Jerusalem* (Ramat-Gan: Bar Ilan University Press, 1999), 21–36.

—'L'économie et le roi au Levant sud d'après les sources archéologiques et textuelles', *Topoi, Supplément* 6 (2004): 241–65.

Finley, Moses I., *The Use and Abuse of History* (New York: Viking Press, 1975).

—*Ancient History: Evidence and Models* (London: Chatto & Windus, 1985).

Fischer, T., 'Zur Seleukideninschrift von Hefzibah', *ZPE* 33 (1979): 131–38.

FitzGerald, G. M., *Beth-Shan Excavation 1921–1923: The Arab and Byzantine Levels* (Philadelphia: University Press for the University of Pennsylvania Museum, 1931).

Fox, M. V., *The Song of Songs and the Ancient Egyptian Love Songs* (Madison: University of Wisconsin Press, 1985).

Franken, H. J. and M. L. Steiner, *Excavations in Jerusalem 1961–1967, Vol. II: The Iron Age Extramural Quarter on the South-East Hill* (Oxford: Oxford University Press, 1990).

Fraser, P. M., *Ptolemaic Alexandria*, 3 vols (Oxford: Clarendon Press, 1972).

—*Cities of Alexander the Great* (Oxford: Clarendon Press, 1996).

Fried, L. S., 2006 'The 'am ha'ares in Ezra 4:4 and Persian Imperial Administration', in O. Lipschits, and M. Oeming (eds), *Judah and the Judaeans in the Persian Period* (Winona Lake, IN: Eisenbrauns, 2006), 123–45.

Friedman, J., 'Notes on Culture and Identity in Imperial Worlds', in P. Bilde, T. Engberg-Pedersen, L. Hannestad and J. Zahle (eds), *Religion and Religious Practice in the Seleucid Kingdom* (Aarhus: Aarhus University Press, 1990), 14–39.

Fujita, S., 'The Metaphor of Plant in Jewish Literature of the Intertestamental Period', *JSJ* 7 (1976): 30–45.

Fuks, Gideon, *Scythopolis – A Greek City in Eretz-Israel* (Jerusalem: Yad Izhak Ben-Zvi, 1983).

—*A City of Many Seas: Ashkelon during the Hellenistic and Roman Periods* (Jerusalem: Yad Izhak Ben-Zvi and Sapir College, 2001a).

—'Josephus' Tobiads Again: A Cautionary Note', *Journal of Jewish Studies* 52 (2001b): 354–56.

Funk, R. W., 'The History of Beth-zur with Reference to its Defenses', in O. R. Sellers a.o. (eds), *The 1957 Excavation at Beth-zur*, *AASOR* 38 (Cambridge: American Schools of Oriental Research, 1968): 4–17.

—'Beth-zur', *The New Encyclopedia of Archaeological Excavations in the Holy Land* I (1993): 259–61.

Galili E., *The Battle of Raphia 217 BCE: Tactics, Strategy and Logistic in the Hellenistic Period* (Jerusalem: The Bialik Institute, 1999).

Galling, K., 'The "Gola-List" According to Ezra 2// Nehemiah 7', *JBL* 70 (1951): 149–58.

Garscha, J., *Studien zum Ezechielbuch: Eine Redaktionskritische Untersuchung von Ez 1–39*, Europäische Hochschulschriften, 23.23 (Bern: Herbert Land/ Frankfurt: Peter Land, 1974).

Gatier, P.-L., *Inscriptions de la Jordanie, Vol. 2: Région centrale*, Inscriptions grecques et latines de la Syrie 21 (Paris: Geuthner, 1986).

Gauger, Jörg-Dieter, *Beiträge zur jüdischen Apologetik: Untersuchungen zur Authentizität von Urkunden bei Flavius Josephus und im I. Makkabäerbuch*, Bonner Biblische Beiträge 49 (Cologne/Bonn: Peter Hanstein, 1977).

—'Formalien und Authentizitätsfrage: noch einmal zum Schreiben Antiochos' III. an Zeuxis (Jos. Ant. Jud. 12,148–153) und zu den Antiochos-Urkunden bei Josephus', *Hermes* 121 (1993): 63–9.

Gauthgier H. and H. Sottas, *Un décree trilinguen l'honneur de Ptolémée IV* (Cairo: Institut francais d'archeologie orientale, 1925).

Geertz, C., 'Religion as a Cultural System', in C. Geertz, *The Interpretation of Cultures* (New York: Basic Books, 1973a) 87–125 (orig. in M. Banton [ed.], *Anthropological Approaches to the Study of Religion*, 1966).

—'Thick Description: Towards an Interpretive Theory of Culture', *The Interpretation of Cultures* (New York: Basic Books, 1973b), 3–30.

Geiger, J., 'The Athens of Syria: On Greek Intellectuals in Gadara', *Cathedra* 35 (1985): 3–16.

Gera, Dov, 'Ptolemy son of Thraseas and the Fifth Syrian War', *Ancient Society* 18 (1987): 63–73.

—*Judaea and Mediterranean Politics 219–161 BCE* (Leiden: Brill, 1998).

—'On the Credibility of the History of the Tobiads (Josephus, *Antiquities* 12, 156–222, 228–236)', in A. Kasher, U. Rappaport and G. Fuks (eds), *Greece and Rome in Eretz Israel; Collected Essays* (Jerusalem: Yad Ben Zvi Press, 1990).

—'Olypiodoros, Heliodoros and the Temples of Koilē Syria and Phoinikē', *ZPE* 169 (2009): 125–55.

Geva, H., 'Excavations in the Citadel of Jerusalem, 1979–1980: Preliminary Report', *IEJ* 33 (1983): 55–71.

—'The "First Wall" of Jerusalem during the Second Temple Period – An Architectural-Chronological Note', *Eretz-Israel* 18 (1985): 21–39.

—'Excavations at the Citadel of Jerusalem, 1976–1980', in H. Geva (ed.), *Ancient Jerusalem Revealed* (Jerusalem: Israel Exploration Society, 1994), 156–67.

—'General Introduction to the Excavations in the Jewish Quarter', in H. Geva (ed.), *Jewish Quarter Excavations in the Old City of Jerusalem Conducted by Nahman Avigad, 1969–1982. Vol. I: Architecture and Stratigraphy: Areas A, W and X-2. Final Report* (Jerusalem: Israel Exploration Society, 2000a), 1–31.

—'Excavations at the Citadel of Jerusalem', in H. Geva (ed.), *Ancient Jerusalem Revealed*, reprinted and expanded edition (Jerusalem, 2000b), 156–67.

—'Hellenistic Pottery from Areas W and X-2', in H. Geva (ed.), *Jewish Quarter Excavations in the Old City of Jerusalem Conducted by Nahman Avigad, 1969–1982, volume II: The Finds from Areas A, W and X-2, Final Report* (Jerusalem, 2003a), 113–75.

—'Summary and Discussion of Findings from Areas A, W and X-2', in H. Geva, *Jewish Quarter Excavations in the Old City of Jerusalem II* (Jerusalem: Israel Exploration Society, 2003b), 501–52.

—'Western Jerusalem at the End of the First Temple Period in Light of the Excavations in the Jewish Quarter', in A. G. Vaughn and A. E. Killebrew (eds), *Jerusalem in the Bible and Archaeology: The First Temple Period* (Atlanta: Society of Biblical Literature, 2003c), 183–208.

—'A Chronological Re-evaluation of yehud Stamp Impressions in Paleo-Hebrew Script, Based Upon Findings from the Jewish Quarter Excavations in the Old City of Jerusalem'. *TA* 34(1) (2007a): 92–103.

—'Estimating Jerusalem's Population in Antiquity: A Minimalist View'. *Eretz Israel* 28 (2007b): 50–65.

Geva, H. and N. Avigad, 'Area W – Stratigraphy and Architecture', in H. Geva (ed.), *Jewish Quarter Excavations in the Old City of Jerusalem Conducted by Nahman Avigad, 1969–1982. Vol. I: Architecture and Stratigraphy: Areas A, W and X-2. Final Report* (Jerusalem: Israel Exploration Society, 2000a), 131–97.

—'Area X2 – Stratigraphy and Architecture', in H. Geva (ed.), *Jewish Quarter Excavations in the Old City of Jerusalem Conducted by Nahman Avigad, 1969–1982. Vol. I: Architecture and Stratigraphy: Areas A, W and X-2. Final Report* (Jerusalem: Israel Exploration Society, 2000b) 199–240.

Geva, H. and R. Reich, Area A., 'Stratigraphy and Architecture IIa: Introduction', in H. Geva (ed.), *Jewish Quarter Excavations in the Old City of Jerusalem Conducted by Nahman Avigad, 1969–1982. Vol. I: Architecture and Stratigraphy: Areas A, W and X-2. Final Report* (Jerusalem: Israel Exploration Society, 2000), 37–43.

Geyer, J., 'קצות הארץ – Hellenistic?', *VT* 20 (1970): 87–90.

Gibson, S., 'The 1961–67 Excavations in the Armenian Garden, Jerusalem', *PEQ* 119 (1987): 81–96.

Gitler, H. and C. Lorber, 'A New Chronology for the Ptolemaic Coins of Judah', *American Journal of Numismatics* (2nd Series) 18 (2006): 1–41.

—'A New Chronology for the *Yehizkyah* Coins of Judah', *Swiss Numismatic Review* 87 (2008): 61–82.

Gmirkin, Russell E., *Berossus and Genesis, Manetho and Exodus: Hellenistic Histories and the Date of the Pentateuch*, LHBOTS 433, Copenhagen International Series 15 (New York and London: T&T Clark International, 2006).

Gnuse R., 'The Temple Experience of Jaddus in the Antiquities of Josephus: A Report of Jewish Dream Incubation', *JQR*, 83 (1993): 349–68.

—*Dreams and Dream Reports in the Writings of Josephus* (Leiden: E. J. Brill, 1996).

—'The Temple Theophanies of Jaddus, Hyrcanus, and Zechariah', *Biblica*, 79 (1998): 157 72.

Golan D., 'Josephus, Alexander's Visit to Jerusalem, and Modern Historiography', U. Rappaport (ed.), *Flavius Josephus: Historian of Eretz-Israel in the Hellenistic-Roman Period* (Jerusalem, 1982), 29–55.

Goldenstein, J., *Das Gebet der Gottesknechte. Jesaja 63,7 – 64,11 im Jesajabuch, WMANT* 92 (Neukirchen-Vluyn, Neukirchener Verlag, 2001).

Golding, L., *In the Steps of Moses the Conqueror* (London: Rich & Cowan Ltd., 1938).

Goldstein, J. A., *II Maccabees. A New Translation with Introduction and Commentary*, The Anchor Bible, 41A (Garden City, NY: Doubleday & Co., 1983).

—'Alexander and the Jews', *PAAJR*, 59 (1993): 59–101.

Goldstein, Roni, 'Joshua 22: 9–34: A Priestly Narrative from the Second Temple Period', *Shnaton* 12 (2002): 43–81.

Goodblatt, David, *Elements of Ancient Jewish Nationalism* (Cambridge: Cambridge University Press, 2006).

Goodman, M., *Mission and Conversion. Proselytizing in the Religious History of the Roman Empire* (Oxford: Clarendon Press, 1994).

Gophna, R. and I. Beit-Arieh, *Archaeological Survey of Israel Map of Lod (80)* (Jerusalem: Israel Antiquities Authority, 1997).

Gophna, R., I. Taxel and A. Feldstein, 'A New Identification of Ancient Ono', *Bulletin of the Anglo-Israel Archaeological Society* 23 (2005): 167–76.

Goyon, J.-C., 'Ptolemaic Egypt: Priests and the Traditional Religion', in R. S. Bianchi (ed.), *Cleopatra's Egypt: Age of the Ptolemies* (Brooklyn: The Brooklyn Museum, 1988) 29–39.

Grabbe, Lester L., 'Josephus and the Reconstruction of the Judaean Restoration', *JBL* 106 (1987): 231–46.

—*Ezra-Nehemiah* (London: Routledge, 1998).

—*Judaism from Cyrus to Hadrian* (London: SCM Press, 1994).

—*Judaic Religion in the Second Temple Period: Belief and Practice from the Exile to Yavneh* (London: Routledge, 2000).

—'Jewish Historiography and Scripture in the Hellenistic Period', in Lester L. Grabbe (ed.), *Did Moses Speak Attic? Jewish Historiography and Scripture in the Hellenistic Period JSOT Suppl.* 317 = European seminar in historical methodology 3 (Sheffield: Sheffield Academic Press, 2001), 129–55.

—*A History of the Jews and Judaism in the Second Temple Period 1: Yehud: A History of the Persian Province of Judah* (London/New York: T&T Clark International, 2004).

—'Pinholes or Pinheads in the *Camera Obscura*?: The Task of Writing a History of Persian Period Yehud', in Mario Liverani (ed.), *Recenti tendenze nella ricostruzione della storia antica d'Israele*, Contributi del Centro Linceo Interdisciplinare 'Beniamino Segre' 110 (Rome: Accademia Nazionale dei Lincei, 2005), 157–82.

—'The "Persian Documents" in the Book of Ezra: Are They Authentic?', in Oded Lipschits and Manfred Oeming (eds), *Judah and the Judeans in the Persian Period* (Winona Lake, IN: Eisenbrauns, 2006a), 531–70.

—'Biblical Historiography in the Persian period: or How the Jews Took Over the Empire', in Steven W. Holloway (ed.), *Orientalism, Assyriology and the Bible* (Sheffield: Sheffield Phoenix Press, 2006b), 400–14.

—*A History of the Jews and Judaism in the Second Temple Period 2: The Coming of the Greeks: The Early Hellenistic Period (335–175 BCE)*, LSTS 68 (London/New York: T&T Clark International, 2008).

—'Was Jerusalem a Persian Fortress?', in G. N. Knoppers, L. L. Grabbe and D. N. Fulton (eds), *Exile and Restoration Revisited – Essays on the Babylonian and Persian Periods in Memory of Peter R. Ackroyd* (New York: T&T Clark, 2009), 128–37.

Graetz H., 'Simon der Gerechte und seine Zeit', *MGWJ* 6, Heft 2 (1857): 45–56.

Grainger, John D., *Hellenistic Phoenicia* (Oxford: Clarendon Press, 1991).

Grant, E., 'Beth Shemesh in 1933', *BASOR* 52 (1933): 3–5.

Green, Peter, *Alexander of Macedon: A Historical Biography* (Berkeley, CA: University of California Press, 1992).

—*Alexander to Actium: The Historical Evolution of the Hellenistic Age*, Hellenistic Culture and Society (Berkeley, CA: University of California Press, 1993).

Greenberg, M., *Ezekiel 21–37*, AB, 22A (New York. London: Doubleday, 1997).

Grenfell, Bernard P., *Revenue Laws of Ptolemy Philadelphus, Edited from a Greek Papyrus in the Bodleian Library, with a Translation, Commentary, and Appendices* (Oxford: Clarendon Press, 1896).

Grenfell, Bernard P., Arthur S. Hunt, and J. Gilbart Smyly (eds), *The Tebtunis Papyri, Part I* (London: Henry Frowde, 1902).

Griffith, F. L. and W. M. F. Petrie, *Two Hieroglyphic Papyri from Tanis* (London: Egypt Exploration Fund, 1889).

Griffiths, J. G., *Plutarch's De Iside et Osiride* (Cardiff: University of Wales Press, 1970).

Grintz Y. M., *Sefer Yehudith – A Reconstruction of the Original Hebrew Text with Introduction, Commentary, Appendices and Indices* (Jerusalem: The Bialik Institute, 1957).

Gropp, Douglas M., James VanderKam and Monica Brady, *Wadi Daliyeh II and Qumran Miscellanea: The Samaria Papyri from Wadi Daliyeh* (Oxford: Clarendon, 2001).

Gruen, E. S., 'The Origins and Objectives of Onias' Temple', *Scripta Classica Israelica* 16 (1997): 47–70.

Gubser, P., *Politics and Change in el-Kerak, Jordan* (London: Oxford University Press, 1973).

Gutman Y., 'The Conquests of Alexander Macedon in Eretz-Israel', *Tarbitz*, 11 (1939/40): 271–94.

—*Ha-Sifrut ha-Yehudit ha-Hellenistit* [=*The Beginnings of Jewish-Hellenistic Literature*], 2 vols. (Jerusalem: The Bialik Institute, 1958).

Habicht, C., 'Die herrschende Gesellschaft in den hellenistischen Monarchien', *Vierteljahrschrift Sozial- und Wirtschafsgeschichte* 45 (1958): 1–16.

Hall, Jonathan M., *Ethnic Identity in Greek Antiquity* (Cambridge: Cambridge University Press, 1997).

—*Hellenicity between Ethnicity and Culture* (Chicago and London: University of Chicago Press, 2002).

Hammond, N. G. L., *The Genius of Alexander the Great* (Chapel Hill: University of North Carolina Press, 1997).

Hammond, N. G. L and F. W. Walbank, *A History of Macedonia*, Vol. 3 (Oxford: Clarendon Press, 1988).

Hanson, Paul D., 'Zechariah 9 and the Recapitulation of an Ancient Ritual Pattern', *JBL* 92 (1973): 37–59.

—*The Dawn of Apocalyptic* (Philadelphia: Fortress, 1975).

—'Rebellion in Heaven, Azazel, and Euhemeristic Heroes in 1 Enoch 6–11', *JBL* 96 (1977): 195–233.

Harper, G. M., Jr., 'Tax Contractors and their Relation to Tax Collection in Ptolemaic Egypt', *Aegyptus* 14 (1934): 47–64.

Hauben, Hans, 'Philocles, King of the Sidonians and General of the Ptolemies', in E. Lipiński (ed.), *Phoenicia and the Eastern Mediterranean in the First Millennium B.C.: Proceedings of the Conference Held in Leuven from the 14th to the 16th of November 1985*, Studia Phoenicia 5; OLA 22 (Leuven: Peeters, 1987), 413–27.

—'A Phoenician King in the Service of the Ptolemies: Philocles of Sidon Revisited', *Ancient Society* 34 (2004): 27–44.

Hayes, John H. and Sara R. Mandell, *Jewish People in Classical Antiquity: From Alexander to Bar Kochba* (Louisville: Westminster John Knox, 1998).

Hayward, C. T. R., 'Sacrifice and World Order: Some Observations on Ben Sira's Attitude to the Temple Service', in S. W. Sykes (ed.), *Sacrifice and Redemption: Durham Essays in Theology* (Cambridge: Cambridge University Press, 1991), 22–34.

Hazzard, R. A., 'The Regnal Years of Ptolemy II Philadelphus', *Phoenix* 41 (1987): 140–58.

Hengel, M., *Judentum und Hellenismus. Studien zu ihrer Begegnung unter besonderer Berücksichtigung Palästinas bis zur Mitte des 2. Jh.s v. Chr*, 2nd edn (Tübingen: Mohr Siebeck, 1973).

—*Judaism and Hellenism*, 2 vols. (London: SCM; Philadelphia: Fortress, 1974).

—*Judaism and Hellenism: Studies in Their Encounter in Palestine during the Early Hellenistic Period*, I–II, trans. J. Bowden (London: SCM Press, 1974).

—*Jews, Greeks and Barbarians*, trans. J. Bowden (London: SCM, 1980).

—'Judaism and Hellenism Revisited', *Hellenism in the Land of Israel* in J. Collins and G. E. Sterling (eds), Christianity and Judaism in Antiquity Series 13 (Notre Dame, IN: University of Notre Dame, 2001), 6–37.

Herms, Ronald, *An Apocalypse for the Church and for the World*, BZNW, 143 (Berlin: Walter de Gruyter, 2006).

Hezser, Catherine, *Jewish Literacy in Roman Palestine*, TSAJ, 81 (Tübingen: Mohr Siebeck, 2001).

Higbie, C., *The Lindian Chronicle and the Greek Creation of their Past* (Oxford: Oxford University Press, 2003).

Hill, G. F., *BMC Palestine. Catalogue of the Greek Coins of Palestine (Galilee, Samaria and Judaea)*, 2nd edn (Bologna: A. Forni, 1965).

Hitti P. K., *An Arab-Syrian Gentleman and Warrior in the Period of the Crusades: Memoirs of Usama Ibn-Munqidh* (New York: Columbia University Press, 1929).

Hoglund, K. G., *Achaemenid Imperial Administration in Syria-Palestine and the Missions of Ezra and Nehemiah* (Atlanta: Scholars Press, 1992).

Honeyman, A. M., 'Two Contributions to Canaanite Toponymy', *JTS* 50 (1949): 50–52.

Honigman, S., 'La description de Jérusalem et de la Judée dans la *Lettre d'Aristée*', *Athenaeum* 92 (2004): 73–101.

Hoover, O. D., 'A Seleucid Coinage of Demetrias by the Sea', *INJ* 2 (2007a): 77–87.

—'The Dated Coinage of Gaza in Historical Context (264/3 BC – AD 241/2)', *Swiss Numismatic Review* 86 (2007b): 63–90.

—'Revised Chronology for the Late Seleucids at Antioch (121/0–64 BC)', *Historia* 56 (2007c): 280–301.

—'A Late Hellenistic Lead Coinage of Gaza', *INJ* 2 (2008): 25–35.

Hopkins, K., *Conquerors and Slaves: Sociological Studies in Roman History*, Vol. 1 (Cambridge: Cambridge University Press, 1978).

Hossfeld, F. L., *Untersuchungen zu Komposition und Theologie des Ezechielbuches*, FB, 20 (Würzburg: Echter Verlag, 1977).

Houghton, A., *Coins of the Seleucid Empire from the Collection of Arthur Houghton* (Ancient Coins in North America Collectios 4 (New York: American Numismatic Society, 1983).

—'A Seleucid Mint at Samaria-Sebaste?', *The Celator* 14/7 (2000): 22–5.

Houghton, A., C. Lorber, and O. Hoover, *Seleucid Coins, Part II: Seleucus IV through Antiochus XIII* (New York and Lancaster: American Numismatic Society, 2008).

Houghton, A. and A. Spaer, *Sylloge Nummorum Graecorum, Israel I [SNG Israel I]: The Arnold Spaer Collection of Seleucid Coins* (London: Italo Vecchi, 1998).

Humphreys, S. C., *Anthropology and the Greeks* (London, Henley and Boston: Routledge & Kegan Paul, 1978).

Hunt, Arthur S. and J. Gilbart Smyly (eds), *The Tebtunis Papyri, Volume III, Part I* (London: Humphrey Milford, 1933).

Hurowitz, V., *I Have Built You an Exalted House: Temple Building in the Bible in Light of Mesopotamian and Northwest Semitic Writings*, JSOT Sup. 115 (Sheffield: JSOT Press, 1992).

Hurvitz, A., 'The Historical Quest for "Ancient Israel" and the Linguistic Evidence of the Hebrew Bible', *VT* 47 (1997): 307–15.

—'Can Biblical Texts be Dated Linguistically? Chronological Perspectives in the Historical Study of Biblical Hebrew', in A. Lemaire and M. Sæbø (eds), *Congress Volume. Oslo 1998* (Leiden: Brill, 2000), 143–60.

Huß, Werner, *Ägypten in hellenistischer Zeit, 332–30 v. Chr.* (Munchen Beck, 2001).

Hütteroth W-D. and K. Abdulfattah, *Historical Geography of Palestine, Transjordan and Southern Syria in the Late 16th Century* (Erlangen: Selbstverlag der Fränkischen Geographischen Gesellschaft, 1977).

Imhoof-Blumer, F., *Kleinasiatische Münzen* (Vienna: Österreichisches Archäologisches Institut, 1901–1902).

Iversen, E., *Fragments of a Hieroglyphic Dictionary*, Hist. Filol. Skr. Dan. Vid. Selsk. 3/2 (Copenhagen, 1958).

Jacoby, Felix, *Die Fragmente der griechischen Historiker (FGH)*, parts 1–17 (Berlin: Weidman, 1926–58).

Japhet, S., 'Composition and Chronology in the Book of Ezra–Nehemiah', in T. C. Eskenazi and

K. H. Richards (eds), *Second Temple Studies 2. Temple and Community in the Persian Period*, *JSOT Sup.* 175 (Sheffield: JSOT Press, 1994), 189–216.
—'Periodization between History and Ideology II: Chronology and Ideology in Ezra–Nehemiah', in O. Lipschits, and M. Oeming (eds), *Judah and the Judaeans in the Persian Period* (Winona Lake, IN: Eisenbrauns, 2006), 491–508.
Jenkins, G. K., 'The Monetary Systems in the Early Hellenistic Time with Special Regard to the Economic Policy of the Ptolemaic Kings', in A. Kindler (ed.) *The Patterns of Monetary Development in Phoenicia and Palestine in Antiquity* (Tel Aviv and Jerusalem: Schocken Publication House, 1967), 55–74.
Jeselsohn, D., 'A New Coin Type with Hebrew Inscription', *IEJ* 24 (1974): 77–78.
Ji, Chang-ho C., 'A New Look at the Tobiads in 'Iraq Al-Amir', *Liber Annuus Studii Biblici Franciscani* 48 (1998): 417–40.
Johns, C. N., The Citadel, Jerusalem (A Summary of Work Since 1934), *QDAP* 14 (1950): 121–90.
Johnson, J. H. (ed.), *Life in a Multi-Cultural Society: Egypt from Cambyses to Constantine*, Studies in Ancient Oriental Civilizations 54 (Chicago: The Oriental Institute of the University of Chicago, 1992).
Jones A. H. M., *Cities of the Eastern Roman Provinces* (Oxford: Oxford University Press, 1937).
Kallai, Z., *The Northern Boundaries of Judah* (Jerusalem: The Bialik Institute, 1960).
—'The Land of Benjamin and Mt. Ephraim', in M. Kochavi (ed.), *Judaea, Samaria and the Golan, Archaeological Survey 1967–1968* (Jerusalem: Carta, 1972): 153–95.
Kalman, Y., 'The Dirge over the King of Tyre', *ASTI* 3 (1964): 28–57.
Kasher A., 'The Campaign of Alexander The Great in Eretz-Israel', *Beth Mikra* 20 (1974): 187–208.
—'Milestones in the History of Gaza in the Second Temple Times', *Cathedra* 15 (1980): 21–36.
—'Gaza During the Greco-Roman Era', *The Jerusalem Cathedra* 2 (1982): 63–78.
—*The Jews in Hellenistic and Roman Egypt*, TSAJ 7 (Tübingen: Mohr Siebeck, 1985).
—*Jews and Hellenistic Cities in Eretz-Israel: Relations of the Jews in Eretz-Israel with the Hellenistic Cities during the Second Temple Period 332 BCE–70 CE*, TSAJ 21 (Tübingen: Mohr Siebeck, 1990).
—'The Campaign of Alexander The Great in Eretz-Israel' (revised), in U. Rappaport and I. Ronen (eds), *The Hasmonean State* (Jerusalem – Tel Aviv: Yad Itzhak Ben-Zvi and the Open University, 1993), 13–35.
Katzenstein, H. J., *A History of Tyre* (Jerusalem: Schocken Institute for Jewish Research, 1973).
—'Gaza in the Neo-Babylonian Period (626–539 B.C.E.)' *Transeuphratène* 7 (1994): 35–49.
Kellermann, U., *Nehemia: Quellen Überlieferung und Geschichte* (Berlin: Alfred Töpelmann, 1967).
Kelso, J. L., *The Excavation of Bethel (1934–1960)*, AASOR 39 (Cambridge: American Schools of Oriental Research, 1968).
Kenyon, K. M., *Archaeology in the Holy Land* (London: Ernest Benn, 1960).
—'Excavations in Jerusalem, 1962', *PEQ* 95 (1963): 7–21.
—'Excavations in Jerusalem, 1963', *PEQ* 96 (1964): 7–18.
—'Excavations in Jerusalem, 1964', *PEQ* 97 (1965): 9–20.
—'Excavations in Jerusalem, 1965', *PEQ* 98 (1966): 73–88.
—'Excavations in Jerusalem, 1966', *PEQ* 99 (1967a): 65–71.
—*Jerusalem: Excavating 3000 Years of History* (London: Thames and Hudson, 1967b).
—*Digging Up Jerusalem* (London: Ernest Benn, 1974).
Kessler, J., 'Persia's Loyal Yahwists: Power Identity and Ethnicity in Achaemenid Yehud', in O. Lipschits, and M. Oeming (eds), *Judah and the Judaeans in the Persian Period* (Winona Lake, IN: Eisenbrauns, 2006), 91–121.
Khalaily, H. and A. Gopher, 'Lod', *Excavations and Surveys in Israel* 19 (1997): 51.

Kindler, A., 'Silver Coins Bearing the Name of Judea from the Early Hellenistic Period', *IEJ* 24 (1974): 73–6.

King, P. J. and L. E. Stager, *Life in Biblical Israel* (Louisville: Westminster, 2001).

Kitchen, K. A., *Documentation for Ancient Arabia I* (Liverpool: Liverpool University Press, 1994).

Klausner J., *Historia shel ha-Bayit ha-Sheni*, 2 vols. (Jerusalem: Ahiasaf Publishing House, 1949).

Klinkott, Hilmar, *Die Satrapienregister der Alexander- und Diadochenzeit*, Historia-Einzelschriften 145 (Stuttgart: Franz Steiner Verlag, 2000).

Kloner, A., 'Jerusalem's Environs in the Persian Period', in A. Faust and E. Baruch (eds), *New Studies on Jerusalem, Proceedings of the Seventh Conference* (Ramat Gan: Bar Ilan University, 2001): 91–96.

—*Archaeological Survey of Israel, Survey of Jerusalem: The Northwestern Sector, Introduction and Indices* (Jerusalem: Israel Antiquities Authority, 2003a).

—*Maresha Excavations Final Report I: Subterranean Complexes 21, 44, 70*, IAA Reports 17 (Jerusalem, 2003b).

__ 'Amphorae and Urns as Grave Markers in Idumaea, Judaea, and Nabataea', *Strata: Bulletin of the Anglo-Israel Archaeological Society 28* (2010): 55–78.

Kloner, A., and I. Stern, 'Idumaea in the Late Persian Period (Fourth Century B.C.E.)', in O. Lipschits, G. Knoppers and R. Albertz (eds), *Judah and the Judeans in the Fourth Century B.C.E.* (Winona Lake, IN: Eisenbrauns, 2007), 139–44.

Kloner, A., D. Regev, and U. Rappaport, *A Hellenistic Burial Cave in the Judean Shephelah*. 'Atiqot XXI: 27-50 (1992): 175–77.

Kloner, A., E. Eshel, H. Korzakova, and G. Finkielsztejn, *Maresha Excavations Final Report: Epigraphic Findings from 1989–2000 Seasons*, IAA Reports 45 (Jerusalem: IAA, 2010).

Knibb, Michael A., 'A note on 4Q372 and 4Q390', in F. García Martínez, A. Hilhorst and C. J. Labuschagne (eds), *The Scriptures and the Scrolls; Studies in Honour of A. S. van der Woude* (Leiden: E. J. Brill, 1992): 164–77.

Kochavi, M. (ed.), *Judaea, Samaria and the Golan, Archaeological Survey 1967–1968* (Jerusalem: Carta, 1972).

Koenen, L., 'Die Adaptation ägyptischer Königsideologie am Ptolemäerhof', in E. Van't Dack, P. van Dessel and W. van Gucht (eds), *Egypt and the Hellenistic World. Proceedings of the International Colloquium, Leuven 1982* (Leuven: Leuven University Press, 1983), 143–90.

—'The Ptolemaic King as a Religious Figure', in Anthony Bulloch, Erich S. Gruen, A. A. Long and Andrew Stewart (eds), *Images and Ideologies: Self-definition in the Hellenistic World* (Berkeley, CA: University of California Press, 1993), 25–115.

Kohut, A., *Aruch Completum* (Vienna: Hebräischer Verlag Menorah, 1926).

Kraabel, Alf Thomas, 'New Evidence of the Samaritan Diaspora has been Found on Delos', *Biblical Archaeologist* 47 (1984): 44–6.

Kraeling, C. H. (ed.), *Gerasa: A City of the Decapolis* (New Haven, CT: American Schools of Oriental Research, 1938).

Kramer, Lloyd S., 'Historical Narratives and the Meaning of Nationalism', *Journal of the History of Ideas* 58 (1997): 525–45.

Kratz, Reinhard G., 'The Second Temple of Jeb and of Jerusalem', in Oded Lipschits and Manfred Oeming (eds), *Judah and the Judeans in the Persian Period* (Winona Lake, IN: Eisenbrauns, 2006): 247–64.

Kreissig, H., 'Die Polis in Griechenland und im Orient in der hellenistischen Epoche', in E. C. Welskopf (ed.), *Hellenische Poleis: Krise – Wandlung – Wirkung*, II (Berlin: Akademie-Verlag, 1974), 1074–84.

—'Landed Property in the "Hellenistic" Orient', *Eirene* 15: 5–26. *Wirtschaft und Gesellschaft im Seleukidenreich*: Schriften zur Geschichte und Kultur der Antike, 16 (Berlin: Akademie-Verlag, 1977).

—*Wirtschaft und Gesellschaft im Seleukidenreich: Die Eigentums-und die Abhängigkeitsverhältnisse*, Akademie der Wissenschaften, Schriften zur Geschichte und Kultur der Antike, 16 (Berlin: Akademie, 1978).

Krüger, T., *Qoheleth*, Hermeneia (Philadelphia: Fortress, 2004).

Kugel, James L., *In Potiphar's House: The Interpretive Life of Biblical Texts*, 2nd edn (Cambridge, MA: Harvard University Press, 1994).

Kuhrt, A., 'The Cyrus Cylinder and Achaemenid Imperial Policy', *JSOT* 25 (1983): 83–97.

Kuhrt, A. and S. Sherwin-White, 'Aspects of Seleucid Royal Ideology: The Cylinder of Antiochus I from Borsippa', *Journal of Hellenic Studies* 111 (1991): 71–86.

—*From Samarkhand to Sardis: A New Approach to the Seleucid Empire* (London: Duckworth, 2003).

Kuhs, C., *Das Dorf Samareia im griechisch-römischen Ägypten* (Heidelberg: Eine papyrologische Untersuchung, 1996).

Kushnir-Stein, A., 'Gaza Coinage Dated LIC – A Reappraisal', *Swiss Numismatic Review* 74 (1995a): 49–55.

—'The Predecessor of Caesarea: On the Identification of Demetrias in South Phoenicia', in J. H. Humphrey (ed.), *The Roman and Byzantine Near East: Some Recent Archaeological Research*, Journal of Roman Archaeology, Supplementary Series 14 (Ann Arbor, 1995b), 9–14.

Lackenbacher, S., *Le Roi bâtisseur. Les récits de construction assyriens des origines à Teglat-Phalasar III* (Paris: Éditions Recherche sur les civilisations, 1982).

Lampinen, P., 'A Further Note on the Coins of "Demetrias which is on the Sea"', in K. G. Holum, A. Raban, and J. Patrich (eds), *Caesarea Papers 2: Herod's Temple, the Provincial Governor's Praetorium and Granaries, the Later Harbor, a Gold Coin Hoard, and Other Studies*, Journal of Roman Archaeology, Supplementary Series 35 (Portsmouth, 1999), 358–59.

Landau, Y. H., 'A Greek Inscription Found Near Hefzibah', *IEJ* 16 (1966): 54–70.

Lape, S., *Reproducing Athens: Menander's Comedy, Democratic Culture, and the Hellenistic City* (Princeton: Princeton University Press, 2004).

Lapp, P. W., 'The Excavation of Field II', in O. R. Sellers a.o. (eds), *The 1957 Excavation at Beth-zur*, AASOR 38 (Cambridge: American Schools of Oriental Research, 1968a): 26–34.

—'Bethel Pottery of the Late Hellenistic and Early Roman Periods', in J. L. Kelso *The Excavation of Bethel (1934–1960)*, AASOR 39 (Cambridge: American Schools of Oriental Research, 1968b): 77–80.

Lapp, P. and N. Lapp, 'Iron II – Hellenistic Pottery Groups', in O. R. Sellers a.o. (eds), *The 1957 Excavation at Beth-zur*, AASOR 38 (Cambridge: American Schools of Oriental Research, 1968): 54–79.

—(eds), *Discoveries in the Wadi Ed-Daliyeh* (Cambridge, MA: American Schools of Oriental Research, 1974).

Lawrence, T. E., *Seven Pillars of Wisdom* (London: Penguin Books, 1962 [1926]).

Lee, T. R., *Studies in the Form of Sirach 44–50*, SBL Dissertation Series 75 (Atlanta, GA: Scholar Press, 1986).

Leith, Mary Joan Winn (ed.), *Wadi Daliyeh I: The Wadi Daliyeh Seal Impressions*, DJD 24 (Oxford: Clarendon Press, 1997).

Lemaire, A., 'Populations et territoires de Palestine à l'époque perse'. *Transeuphratène* 3 (1990): 31–74.

—'Le royaume de Tyre dans le second moitie du IV av. J.C.', *Atti del II Congresso Internationale di Studi Fenici e Punici*. Vol. I. Rome (1991): 132–49.

—*Nouvelles inscriptions arameennes d'Idumee du Musee d'Israel, Supplement no. 3a. Transeuphratene* (Paris, 1996).

—*Nouvelles Inscriptions Arameenes D'Idumee II, Supplement no 9a. Transeuphratene* (Paris, 2002).

—'Nabonidus in Arabia and Judah in the Neo-Babylonian Period', in O. Lipschits and J. Blenkinsopp (eds), *Judah and the Judeans in the Neo-Babylonian Period*. Winona Lake, IN: Eisenbrauns, 2003), 285–98.

—'New Aramaic Ostraca from idumea and Their Historical Interpretation', in O. Lipschits and M. Oeming (eds), *Judah and the Judeans in the Persian Period* (Winona Lake, IN: Eisenbrauns, 2006), 413–56.

—'Administration in fourth-Century B.C.E. Judah in Light of Peigraphy and Numismatics', in O. Lipschits, G. Knoppers and R. Albertz (eds), *Judah and the Judeans in the Fourth Century B.C.E* (Winona Lake, IN: Eisenbrauns, 2007), 53–74.

Lemche, N. P., 'The Old Testament – A Hellenistic Book?', revised version in L. L. Grabbe (ed.), *Did Moses Speak Attic?* (Sheffield: Sheffield Academic, 2001), 287–318.

Lenger, Marie-Thérèse, *Corpus des Ordonnances des Ptolémées*, Académie Royale de Belgique, Classe Des Lettres, Mémoires, t. 56/5 (Brussels: Palais des Académies, 1964).

Le Rider, G., *Suse sous les Séleucides et les Parthes: Les trouvailles monétaires et l'histoire de la ville*, Mémoires de la Mission Archéologique en Iran 37 (Paris: P. Geuthner, 1965).

—'La politique monétaire des Séleucides en Coelé Syrie et en Phénicie après 200: Réflexions sur les monnaies d'argent lagides et sur les monnaies d'argent séleucides à l'aigle', *Bulletin de Correspondance Hellénique* 119 (1995): 391–404.

Le Rider, G., and de Callataÿ, F., *Les Séleucides et les Ptolémées. L'héritage monétaire et financier d'Alexandre le Grand* (Paris: éds du Rocher, 2006).

Levenson, J. D., *Resurrection and Restoration of Israel: The Ultimate Victory of the God of Life* (New Haven, CT: Yale University Press, 2006).

Lévi (Levy) I., 'La Légende d'Alexandre dans le Talmud et le Midrasch', *REJ* 7 (1883): 78–83.

—'Alexandre et les Juifs d'après les sources rabbiniquea', in *Gedenkbuch zur Erinnerung an David Kaufman* (Breslau, 1900) 346–54.

—*Olamot Nifgashim: Mehkarim al Ma'amadah shel ha-Yahadut ba-Olam ha-Yevani veha-Romayi* [= *Studies in Jewish Hellenism*] (Jerusalem: The Bialik Institute, 1960).

Levine, L. I., 'A propos de la fondation de la Tour de Straton', *Revue Biblique* 80 (1973): 75–81.

—*Jerusalem, Portrait of the City in the Second Temple Period (538 BCE – 70 CE)* (Philadelphia: Jewish Publication Society, 2002).

Lewis, N., 'The Romanity of Roman Egypt: A Growing Consensus', *Atti del XVII° congresso Internazionale di Papirologia* (Napoli: Centro internazionale per lo studio dei papyri ercolanesi, 1984): 1077–84.

Liddell H. G. and R. Scott, *A Greek-English Lexicon*, 9th edn (Oxford: Oxford University Press, 1968).

Lieberman, S., 'The Halakhic Inscription from the Beth-Shean Valley', *Tarbiz* 45 (1975–76): 54–55.

Liebesny, Herbert, 'Ein Erlass des Königs Ptolemaios II Philadelphos über die Deklaration von Vieh und Sklaven in Syrien und Phonikien (PER Inv. Nr. 24.552 gr.)', *Aegyptus* 16 (1936): 257–91.

Lipschits, O., 'The History of the Benjaminie Region under Babylonian Rule', *Zion* 64 (1999a): 271–310.

—'Nebuchadrezzar's Policy in "☐attu-Land" and the Fate of the Kingdom of Judah', *Ugarit-Forschungen* 30 (1999b): 467–87.

—'Judah, Jerusalem and the Temple (586–539 B.C.)' *Transeuphraténe* 22 (2001a): 129–42.

—'The Policy of the Persian Empire and the Meager Architectural Finds in the Province of Yehud', in A. Faust and E. Baruch (eds), *New Studies in Jerusalem* (Ramat-Gan, 2001b), 45–76.

—'Demographic Changes in Judah between the Seventh and the Fifth Centuries B.C.E.', in O. Lipschits and J. Blenkinsopp (eds), *Judah and the Judeans in the New-Babylonian Period* (Winona Lake, IN: Eisenbrauns, 2003): 323–76.

—'Ammon in Transition from Vassal Kingdom to Babylonian Province', *Bulletin of the American Schools of Oriental Research* 335 (2004): 37–52.

—*The Fall and Rise of Jerusalem* (Winona Lake, IN: Eisenbrauns, 2005).

—'Achaemenid Imperial Policy, Settlement Processes in Palestine, and the Status of Jerusalem in the Middle of the Fifth Century B.C.E.', in O. Lipschits and M. Oeming (eds), *Judah and the Judeans in the Persian Period* (Winona Lake, IN: Eisenbrauns, 2006): 19–52.

—Persian Period Finds from Jerusalem: Facts and Interpretations, *Journal of Hebrew Scriptures* 9 (2009): Article 20.

—Persian Period Finds from Jerusalem: Facts and Interpretations. JHS, forthcoming.

Lipschits, O., and M. Oeming (eds), *Judah and the Judaeans in the Persian Period* (Winona Lake, IN: Eisenbrauns, 2006).

Lipschits, Oded and Oren Tal, 'The Settlement Archaeology of the Province of Judah', in Oded Lipschits, Gary N. Knoppers, and Rainer Albertz (eds), *Judah and the Judeans in the Fourth Century BCE* (Winona Lake, IN: Eisenbrauns, 2007), 33–52.

Lipschits, O. and D. Vanderhooft, 'Jerusalem in the Persian and Hellenistic Periods in Light of the Yehud Stamp Impressions', in Tedi Kolek (ed.), *Eretz Israel – Archaeological, Historical and Geographical Studies* (Jerusalem: Israel Exploration Society, 2007a), 106–15.

—'Yehud Stamp Impressions: History of Discovery and Newly-Published Impressions', *Tel Aviv* 34 (2007b): 3–11.

Lipschits, Oded, Gary N. Knoppers, and Rainer Albertz (eds), *Judah and the Judeans in the Fourth Century B.C.E.* (Winona Lake, IN: Eisenbrauns, 2007).

Llewelyn, S. R. (ed.), *New Documents Illustrating Early Christianity*, Vol. 8: *A review of the Greek Inscriptions and Papyri Published 1984–85* (Grand Rapids and Cambridge: William B. Eerdmans, 1998).

Loundine, A. G., 'L'abécédaire de Beth Shemesh', *Le Muséon* 100 (1987): 243–50.

Lupo, E., 'A New Look at Three Inscriptions from Jaffa, Jerusalem, and Gaza', *SCI* 22 (2003): 193–202.

Lust, J., 'The Use of Textual Witnesses for the Establishment of the Text', in J. Lust (ed.) *Ezekiel and His Book, Textual and Literary Criticism and their Interrelation* (Leuven: Leuven University Press, 1986) 7–20.

Lutz, H.-M., *Jahwe, Jerusalem und die Völker. Zur Vorgeschichte von Sach 12,1-8 und 14,1-5*, WMAMT, 27 (Neukirchen-Vluyn: Neukircherner, 1968).

Ma, J., *Antiochos III and the Cities of Western Asia Minor* (Oxford: Oxford University Press, 2000).

—'Kings', in A. Erskine (ed.), *A Companion to the Hellenistic World* (Oxford: Oxford University Press, 2003), 177–95.

Macalister, R. A. S. and J. G. Duncan, *Excavation on the Hill of Ophel, Jerusalem, 1923–1925* (London: Palestine Exploration Fund, 1926).

Mack, B., *Wisdom and the Hebrew Epic: Ben Sira's Hymn in Praise of the Fathers* (Chicago: University of Chicago Press, 1985).

Magen, Yitzhak, 'A Fortified Town of the Hellenistic Period on Mount Gerizim', *Qadmoniot*, 19 (1986): 91–101.

—'Mount Gerizim – A Temple-City', *Qadmoniot* 23 (1991–92): 70–96.

—'Mount Gerizim – A Hellenistic Temple City', *Judah and Samaria Studies* 1 (1992): 36–60.

—'Mount Gerizim and the Samaritans', in F. Manns and E. Alliata (eds), *Early Christianity in Context: Monuments and Documents* (Jerusalem: Franciscan Printing Press, 1993): 91–148.

—'Mount Gerizim – A Temple-City', *Qadmoniot* 33 (2000): 74–118.

—*Mount Gerizim Excavations: Volume II A Temple City* (Jerusalem: Staff Officer of Archaeology, Civil Administration of Judea and Samaria, 2008a).

—*The Samaritans and the Good Samaritan* (Jerusalem: Staff Officer of Archaeology, Civil Administration of Judea and Samaria, 2008b).

Magen, Yitzhak, Haggai Misgav, and Levana Tsfania, *Mount Gerizim Excavations: Volume 1 The Aramaic, Hebrew and Samaritan Inscriptions* (Jerusalem: Israel Antiquities Authority, 2004).
Manning, J. G., *Land and Power in Ptolemaic Egypt: The Structure of Land Tenure* (Cambridge: Cambridge University Press, 2003).
—*The Last Pharaohs. Egypt under the Ptolemies, 305–30 BC* (Princeton, NJ: Princeton University Press, 2010).
Marcus, Ralph, *Josephus with an English Translation* (Loeb Classical Library), Jewish Antiquities, books 9–11 (Vol. 6), (Cambridge, MA: Harvard University Press, 1937).
—'Notes and appendices' in H. S. J. Thackeray (ed.), *Josephus* (Cambridge, MA: Harvard University Press, 1943).
Marti, K., *Das Buch Jesaja*, KHAT, 10 (Tübingen: J.C.B. Mohr, 1900).
—*Das Dodekapropheton*, KHAT, 13 (Tübingen: J.C.B. Mohr, 1904).
Mattila, Sharon L., 'Ben Sira and the Stoics: A Reexamination of the Evidence', *JBL* 119 (2000): 473–501.
Mazar, B., *The Excavations in the Old City of Jerusalem. Preliminary Report of the First Season 1968* (Jerusalem: Israel Exploration Society, 1969).
—'The Excavations in the Old City of Jerusalem near the Temple Mount – Second Preliminary Report, 1969–1970 Seasons', *Eretz-Israel* 10 (1971): 1–34.
—'Excavations near the Temple Mount', *Qadmoniot* 19–20 (1972): 74–90.
Mazar, E., 'Excavations in the Ophel – The Royal Quarter of Jerusalem during the First Temple Period', *Qadmoniot* 26 (101–102) (1993): 25–32.
—*The Excavations in the City of David, 2005* (Jerusalem: Shoham, Hebrew, 2007a).
—'Excavations at the City of David – Visiting Center (2006–2007)', in E. Baruch, A. Levy-Reifer, and A. Faust (eds), *New Studies on Jerusalem* (Vol. 13), Ramat-Gan (2007b): 7–26.
—'The Steppe Stone Structure in the City of David in Light of the New Excavations in Area G.', in E. Baruch, A. Levy-Reifer, and A. Faust (eds), *New Studies on Jerusalem*, Ramat-Gan, (2008): 25–40.
Mazar, E. and B. Mazar, *Excavations in the South of the Temple Mount, The Ophel of Biblical Jerusalem*, *Qedem* 29 (Jerusalem: The Hebrew University, 1989).
McLean, Bradley Hudson, 'Voluntary Associations and Churches on Delos', in John S. Kloppenborg and Stephen G. Wilson (eds), *Voluntary Associations in the Graeco-Roman World* (London-New York: Routledge, 1996): 186–225.
Mélèze-Modrzejewski, Joseph, 'How to be a Jew in Hellenistic Egypt?', in S. Cohen (ed.), *Diasporas in Antiquity* (Atlanta, GA: Scholars Press, 1993), 65–92.
Mendels, Doron, 'Hecataeus of Abdera and a Jewish "patrios politeia" of the Persian Period (Diodorus Siculus XL, 3)', *ZAW* 95 (1983): 96–110.
—*The Rise and Fall of Jewish Nationalism*, 2nd edn (Grand Rapids, MI; Cambridge: Eerdmans; New York: Doubleday, 1997).
Meshorer, Y., *Jewish Coins of the Second Temple Period* (Tel Aviv: Am Hassefer & Massada, 1967).
—'Again on the Beginning of the Hasmonean Coinage', *Israel Numismatic Journal* 5 (1981): 11–16.
—*The City Coins of Eretz-Israel and the Decapolis in the Roman Period* (Jerusalem: Yad Ben-Zvi, 1984).
—*A Treasury of Jewish Coins: From the Persian Period to Bar Kochba* (New York: Yad Izhak Ben-Zvi and Amphora, 2001).
Meshorer, Ya'akov, and Shraga Qedar, *The Coinage of Samaria in the Fourth Century BCE* (Jerusalem, 1991).
—*Samarian Coinage*, Numismatic Studies and Researches 9 (Jerusalem, 1999).
Meyer, Eduard, *Ursprung und Anfange des Christentums* (Berlin, Stuttgart: J. Cotta'sche Buchhandlung, 1921).
Meyers, C. L. and E. M. Meyers, *Haggai, Zechariah 1–8* (Garden City: Doubleday, 1987).

—*Zechariah 9–14* (New York: Doubleday, 1993).

Middendorp, T., *Die Stellung Jesu Ben Siras zwischen Judentum und Hellenismus* (Leiden: Brill, 1973).

Mildenberg, L., 'Yehud: A Preliminary Study of the Provincial Coinage of Judaea', in O. Mørkholm and N. M. Waggoner (eds), *Greek Numismatics and Archaeology: Essays in Honor of Margaret Thompson* (Wettern: Cultura Press, 1979) 183–96.

Milik, J. T., *The Books of Enoch: Aramaic Fragments from Qumrân Cave 4* (Oxford: Clarendon, 1976).

Millar, F., 'The Phoenician Cities: A Case-Study of Hellenisation', *Proceedings of the Cambridge Philological Society* 209 (1983): 55–71.

—'The Problem of Hellenistic Syria', in A. Kuhrt and S. Sherwin-White, *Hellenism in the East: The Interaction of Greek and Non-Greek Civilizations from Syria to Central Asia after Alexander* (London: Duckworth, 1987) 110–33.

—*Rome, the Greek World, and the East, Volume 3: The Greek World, the Jews and the East* (Chapel Hill, NC: University of North Carolina Press, 2006).

Millard, A. R., 'The Practice of Writing in Ancient Israel', *BA* 35 (1972): 107–08.

Miller, M. C., *Athens and Persia in the Fifth Century B.C.: A Study in Cultural Receptivity* (Cambridge: Cambridge University Press, 1997).

Mitchell, H. G., *A Critical and Exegetical Commentary on Haggai and Zechariah* (Edinburgh: T&T Clark, 1912).

Mitchell, L. G., 'Ethnic Identity and the Community of the Hellenes: A Review (J. M. Hall, *Hellenicity: Between Ethnicity and Culture*)', *Ancient West and East* 4/2 (2006): 409–20.

Momigliano, Arnaldo, 'I Tobiadi nella preistoria del Moto Maccabaico', *Atti della Reale Accademia delle Scienze di Torino* 67 (1931–32): 165–200.

Mooren, Leon, 'On the Jurisdiction of the Nome Strategoi in Ptolemaic Egypt', in *Atti del XVII Congresso Internazionale di Papirologia*, Volume Terzo (Naples: Centro Internazionale per lo Studio dei Papiri Ercolanesi, 1984): 1217–25.

Mor M., *From Samaria to Shechem. The Samaritan Community in Antiquity* (Jerusalem: The Zalman Shazar Center for Jewish Studies, 2003).

—'Putting the Puzzle Together: Papyri, Inscriptions, Coins and Josephus in Relation to Samaritans History in the Persian Period', in Shedadeh Haseeb et al. (eds), *Studies in Memory of Ferdinand Dexinger*, Proceedings of the Fifth International Congress of the Societe d'Etude Samaritaines, Helsinki, August 1–4, 2000 (Paris: Geuthener, 2005): 41–54.

Morag, S., 'Qumran Hebrew: Some Typological Observations', *VT* 38 (1988): 148–64.

Mørkholm, O., 'A Group of Ptolemaic Coins from Phoenicia and Palestine', *Israel Numismatic Journal* 4 (1980): 4–7.

—'Some Coins of Ptolemy V from Palestine', *INJ* 5 (1981): 5–10.

Mowinckel, S., *Studien zu dem Buche Ezra-Nehemia* (Oslo: Universitetsforlaget, 1964).

Muhs, Brian P., *Tax Receipts, Taxpayers, and Taxes in Early Ptolemaic Thebes* (Chicago: Oriental Institute of the University of Chicago, 2005).

Mulder, E. S., *Die Teologie van die Jesaja-Apokalypse. Jesaja 24–27* (Groningen, Djakarta: J. B. Wolters, 1954).

Mulder, O., *Simon the High Priest in Sirach 50: an exegetical study of the significance of Simon the High Priest as climax to the Praise of the Fathers in Ben Sira's Concept of the History of Israel* (Leiden: Brill, 2003).

Müller, Helmut, 'Der Hellenistische Archiereus', *Chiron* 30 (2000): 519–42.

Murphy, R. E., *The Song of Songs* (Hermeneia; Philadelphia: Fortress, 1990).

Musil A., *Northern Nejd: A Topographical Itinerary* (New York: American Geographical Society, 1928).

Myers, J. M., *Ezra Nehemiah* (Garden City: Doubleday, 1965).

Na'aman, N., 'The Kingdom of Judah under Josiah', *Tel Aviv* 18 (1991): 3–71.

—'Shechem and Jerusalem in the Exilic and Restoration Period', *ZION* 58 (1993): 7–32.

Na'aman, N. and R. Zadok, 'Assyrian Deportations to the Province of Samaria in the Light of the Two Cuneiform Tablets from Tel Hadid', *Tel Aviv* 27 (2000): 159–88.

Nagorsky, A., 'el-Haditha', *Excavations and Surveys in Israel* 117 (2005), http://www.hada shotesi.org.il/reports_eng.asp?id=110

Nahlieli, D., 'Settlements in the Late Byzantine and Early Islamic Periods in the Negev, Israel', in E. J. and B. van der Steen, *Saidel: On the Fringe of Society* (2007).

Naveh, Joseph, 'Scripts and Inscriptions in Ancient Samaria', *IEJ* 48 (1998): 91–100.

—'Hebrew and Aramaic Inscriptions' in D. T. Ariel (ed.), *Excavations at the City of David, 1978–1985. Qedem* 41 (Jerusalem, 2000) 1–14.

Netzer, E., *Hasmonean and Herodian Palaces at Jericho I* (Jerusalem: Israel Exploration Society, 2001).

Newell, E. T., *The Coinage of the Western Seleucid Mint: From Seleucus I to Antiochus III* (New York: American Numismatic Society, 1941).

Newman, Hillel I., 'A Hippodrome on the Road to Ephrath', *Biblica* 86 (2005): 213–28.

Newsom, Carol A., 'The Development of 1 Enoch 6–19: Cosmology and Judgment', *CBQ* 42 (1980): 310–29.

Nickelsburg, G. W. E., '1 and 2 Maccabees – Same Story, Different Meaning', in J. Neusner and A. J. Avery-Peck (eds), *George W. E. Nickelsburg in Perspective: An Ongoing Dialogue of Learning*, Vol. 2 (Leiden, Boston, Köln: E. J. Brill, 2003), 659–74.

—'Apocalyptic and Myth in 1 Enoch 6–11', *JBL* 96 (1977): 383–405.

—*Jewish Literature between the Bible and the Mishnah: A Historical and Literary Introduction* (Philadelphia: Fortress Press, 1981).

—*1 Enoch 1: A Commentary* (Minneapolis: Augsburg Fortress, 2001).

Niehr, H., 'Religio-Historical Aspects of the "Early Post-Exilic" Period', in B. Becking and M. C. A. Korpel (eds), *The Crisis of Israelite Religion: Transformation of Religious Tradition in Exilic and Post-Exilic Times*, Oudtestamentische Studiën, 62 (Leiden, Boston, Köln: E. J. Brill, 1999), 228–44.

Noam V., *Megillat Ta'anit – Versions, Interpretation, History with Critical Edition* (Jerusalem: Yad Itzhak Ben-Zvi, 2003).

Norris H. T., 'The Rediscovery of the Ancient Sagas of the Banu Hilal', *Bulletin of the School of Oriental and African Studies* 51/3 (1988): 462–81.

North, J., 'Religious Toleration in Republican Rome', *PCPS* 205 (1979): 85–104.

Ober, J., *Mass and Elite in Democratic Athens: Rhetoric, Ideology, and the Power of the People* (Princeton, NJ: Princeton University Press, 1989).

O'Brien, John, M., *Alexander the Great: The Invisible Enemy* (London: Routledge, 1992).

Oesterley, W. O. E. and T. H. Robinson, *An Introduction to the Books of the Old Testament* (London: SPCK, 1934).

Ofer, A., *The Highland of Judah during the Biblical Period*, PhD thesis (Tel Aviv University, 1993).

Oliphant, L. *The Land of Gilead, with Excursions in the Lebanon* (Edinburgh: William Blackwood and Sons, 1880).

Olmstead, A. T., 'Intertestamental Studies', *JAOS* 56 (1936): 242–57.

Olson, Daniel, *Enoch: A New Translation* (N. Richland Hills, Texas: BibalPress, 2004).

Onn, A. and Y. Rapuano, 1994 'Jerusalem, Khirbet el-Burj', *Excavations and Surveys in Israel* 14 (1994): 88–90.

Oppenheim, A. L., 'Essay on Overland Trade in the First Millennium B. C.', *JCS* 21 (1967): 236–54.

Oppenheim, M., *Die Beduinen, band I* (Leipzig: Harrassowitz, 1939).

—*Die Beduinen, band II* (Leipzig: Harrassowitz, 1943).

Oren, E. D. and Rappaport, U., 'The Necropolis of Maresha-Beth Govrin', *IEJ* 34 (1984) 114–153.

Palmer, L. R., *The Greek Language* (Atlantic Highlands, NJ: Humanities Press, 1980).

Palmisano, Maria Carmela, *"Salvaci, Dio dell'Universo!" Studio dell'eucologia di Sir 36H, 1–17* (AnBib 163; Rome: Pontifical Biblical Institute, 2006).

Pardee, D., 'Arad Ostraca', in W. H. Hallo and K. Lawson Younger, Jr. (eds), *The Context of Scripture, III: Archival Documents from the Biblical World* (Leiden: Brill, 2003), 81–7.

Parker, R. C. T., *Cleomenes on the Acropolis*, inaugural lecture (Oxford, 1998).

Peters, John P. and Hermann Thiersch, *Painted Tombs in the Necropolis of Marissa (Mareshah)* (London: Palestine Exploration Fund, 1905).

Petersen, D. L., *Late Israelite Prophecy*, SBLMS, 23 (Missoula, Mt: Scholars Press, 1977).

—*Zechariah 9–14 & Malachi* (London: SCM, 1995).

Pfister, F., 'Eine jüdische Gründungsgeschichte Alexandrias, mit einem Anhang über Alexanders Besuch in Jerusalem', *Sitzungsberichte der Heidelberger Akademie der Wissenschaften, Philosophisch-historische Klasse* (1914) 1–32.

Piejko, F., 'Antiochus III and Son of Thrasea: The Inscription of Hefzibah Reconsidered', *L'Antiquité Classique* 66 (1991): 245–59.

Plöger, O., *Theocracy and Eschatology*, trans. S. Rudman (Oxford: Blackwell, 1968).

Pollitt, J. J., *Art in the Hellenistic Age* (Cambridge: Cambridge University Press, 1996).

Polzin, R., *Late Biblical Hebrew: Towards an Historical Typology of Biblical Hebrew Prose* (Missoula, Mt: Scholars Press for the Harvard Semitic Museum, 1976).

Pope, M. H., *Song of Songs* (New York: Doubleday, 1985).

Porten, B. and A. Yardeni, *Textbook of Aramaic Documents from Ancient Egypt*: 1–4 (Jerusalem: Hebrew University Press, 1986–89).

—'On Problems of Identity and Chronology in the Idumaean Ostraca', in M. Heltzer and M. Malul (eds), *Teshurot Lavishur Studies in the Bible and the Ancient Near East* (Tel Aviv, 2004) 161–84.

—'Social, Economic, and Onomastic Issues in the Aramaic Ostraca of the Fourth Century B.C.E', in O. Lipschits and M. Oeming (eds), *Judah and the Judeans in the Persian Period* (Winona Lake, IN: Eisenbrauns, 2006), 457–58.

Porten, B., Farber, J. J. et al. *The Elephantine Papyri in English: Three Millennia of Cross-Cultural Continuity and Change* (Leiden: Brill Academic Publishers, 1996).

Prag, K., 'Bethlehem, A Site Assessment', *PEQ* 132 (2000): 169–81.

Préaux, C., 'La singularité de l'Égypte dans le monde gréco-romain', *Chronique d'Égypte* 25 (1950): 110–23.

—'Les raisons de l'originalité de l'Égypte', *Museum Helveticum* 10 (1953): 203–21.

—*Le Monde hellénistique: la Grèce et l'Orient (323–146 av. J.-C.)* (Paris: Presses universitaires de France, 1978).

Preisigke, Friedrich, et al., *Sammelbuch griechischer Urkunden aus Ägypten (SB)*, Vol. 1 (1915).

Price, S. R. F., *Rituals and Power: The Roman Imperial Cult in Asia Minor* (Cambridge: Cambridge University Press, 1986).

—*Religions of the Ancient Greeks* (Cambridge: Cambridge University Press, 1999).

Pritchard, J. B., *Gibeon, Where the Sun Stood Still, The Discovery of the Biblical City* (Princeton: Princeton University Press, 1962).

—*Winery, Defenses and Soundings at Gibeon* (Philadelphia: University Museum, 1964).

—'Gibeon', *The New Encyclopedia of Archaeological Excavations in the Holy Land* 2 (1993): 511–14.

Pucci Ben Zeev, Miriam, *Jewish Rights in the Roman World: The Greek and Roman Documents Quoted by Josephus Flavius* (Tübingen: Mohr Siebeck, 1998).

Pummer, Reinhard, '"Argarizin": A criterion for Samaritan provenance?', *Journal for the Study of Judaism* 18 (1987): 18–25.

—*Early Christian Authors on Samaritans and Samaritanism* (Tübingen: Mohr Siebeck, 2002).

—*The Samaritans in Flavius Josephus* (Tübingen: Mohr Siebeck, 2009).

Quack, J. F., 'Ägyptisches und Südarabisches Alphabet', *REg* 44 (1993): 141–51.

Quirke, S., *Egyptian Literature 1800 BC: Questions and Readings* (London: Golden House Publications, 2004).

Raban, A., 'In Search of Straton's Tower', in R. L. Vann (ed.) *Caesarea Papers: Straton's Tower, Herod's Harbour, and Roman and Byzantine Caesarea* (Ann Arbor, 1992), 7–22.

Rajak, Tessa, *The Jewish Dialogue with Greece and Rome* (Leiden: Brill, 2002a).

—'Hasmonean Kingship and the Invention of Tradition', in *The Jewish Dialogue with Greece and Rome* (Leiden: Brill, 2002b), 39–60.

Rappaport, U., 'The Samaritans in the Hellenistic Period', ZION 55 (1990): 373–96.

—'The Samaritans in the Hellenistic Period', Allan D. Crown, and Lucy Davey (eds), *Essays in Honour of Guy D. Sixdenier, New Samaritan Studies* (Sydney: Mandelbaum Publishing, 1995): 281–88.

—*The First Book of Maccabees* (Jerusalem: Yad Ben Zvi, Hebrew, 2004).

Rappaport, Uriel and Israel Ronen (eds), *The Hasmonean State: the History of the Hasmoneans during the Hellenistic Period—a Collection of Articles* (Jerusalem: Yad Ben-Zvi, 1993).

Ray, J. D., 'Egypt: 525–404 BC', in *Cambridge Ancient History* IV/1 (1987): 254–86.

—'Egyptian Wisdom Literature', in J. Day, R. P. Gordon and H. G. M. Williamson (eds), *Wisdom in Ancient Israel: Essays in Honour of J. A. Emerton* (Cambridge: Cambridge University Press, 1995), 17–29.

Redford, D. B., *Pharaonic King-Lists, Annals and Day-Books* (Missisauga: Benben Publications, 1986).

—*Egypt, Canaan, and Israel in Ancient Times* (Princeton, NJ: Princeton University Press, 1992).

Reich, R., 'The Beth-zur Citadel II – A Persian Residency?', *Tel Aviv* 19 (1992): 113–23.

—'The Ancient Burial Ground in the Mamilla Neighborhood, Jerusalem', in H. Geva (ed.), *Ancient Jerusalem Revealed* (Jerusalem: Israel Exploration Society, 1994), 111–18.

—'Local Seal Impressions of the Hellenistic Period', in H. Geva (ed.), *Jewish Quarter Excavations in the Old City of Jerusalem Conducted by Nahman Avigad, 1969–1982, volume II: The Finds from Areas A, W and X-2, Final Report* (Jerusalem, 2003), 256–62.

Reich, R. and E. Shukron, 'Jerusalem, the City of David', *Excavations and Surveys in Israel* 18 (1998): 91–2.

—'The Urban Development of Jerusalem in the Late Eighth Century B.C.E.', in A. G. Vaughn and A. E. Killebrew (eds), *Jerusalem in the Bible and Archaeology: The First Temple Period* (Atlanta, GA: Society of Biblical Literature, 2003): 209–18.

—'The History of the Gihon Spring in Jerusalem', *Levant* 36 (2004): 211–23.

—'The Yehud Seal Impressions from the 1995–2005 Excavations in the City of David', *Tel Aviv* 34 (2007): 59–65.

Reisner, George Andrew, Clarence Stanley Fisher and David Gordon Lyon, *The Harvard Excavations at Samaria 1908–1910* (Cambridge MA: Harvard University Press, 1924).

Rigsby, Kent J., *Asylia: Territorial Inviolability in the Hellenistic World* (Berkeley, CA: University of California Press, 1996).

Rodd, C. S., 'Psalms', in J. Barton and J. Muddiman (eds), *The Oxford Bible Commentary*, (New York: Oxford University Press, 2001), 355–405.

Rodgers, Zuleika (ed.), *Making History: Josephus and Historical Method* (Leiden: Brill, 2007).

Rogers, H., *Writing Systems: A Linguistic Approach* (Oxford: Blackwells, 2005).

Roller, D. W., 'Straton's Tower: Some Additional Thoughts', in R. L. Vann (ed.) *Caesarea Papers: Straton's Tower, Herod's Harbour, and Roman and Byzantine Caesarea*, Journal of Roman Archaeology, Supplementary Series 5 (Ann Arbor, 1992), 23–5.

Ronen, Y., 'The Weight Standards of the Judean Coinage in the Late Persian and Early Ptolemaic Period', *Near Eastern Archaeology* 61 (1998): 122–26.

—'Some Observations on the Coinage of Yehud', *Israel Numismatic Journal* 15 (2003–06): 28–31.

Rooke, D. W., *Zadok's Heirs: The Role and Development of the High Priesthood in Ancient Israel* (Oxford: Oxford University Press, 2000).

Rooker, M. F., 'The Diachronic Study of Biblical Hebrew', *JNSL* 14 (1988): 199–214.

Rosenberg, G., 'A New Element in the Dating of the Tobyah Inscription at Airaq al-amir in Jordan', *Bulletin of the Anglo-Israel Archaeological Society* 24 (2006): 85–92.

Rosenberger, A. and A. Shavit, 1993 'Lod, Newe Yaraq', *Excavations and Surveys in Israel* 13: 54–56.

Rosenberger, M., 'Two Unpublished Coins of Ashkelon', *Israel Numismatic Journal* 8 (1984–85): 6.

Rostovtzeff, Michael, *The Social and Economic History of the Hellenistic World* (Oxford: Clarendon Press, 1941).

Rowe, A., *The Topography and History of Beth-Shan with Details of the Egyptian and Other Inscriptions Found on the Site* (Philadelphia: University Press for the University of Pennsylvania Museum, 1930).

Rudolph, W., *Jesaja 24–27*, BWANT, 4/10 (Stuttgart: Kohlhammer, 1933).

Ryle, H. E., *Ezra and Nehemiah* (Cambridge: Cambridge University Press, 1907).

Sadleir, G. F., *Diary of a Journey Across Arabia* (Cambridge/New York: Oleander Press, 1866/1977).

Sáenz-Badillos, A., *A History of the Hebrew Language*, trans. J. Elwolde (Cambridge: Cambridge University Press, 1993).

Saïd, S., 'The Discourse of Identity in Greek Rhetoric from Isocrates to Aristides', in I. Malkin, (ed.), *Ancient Perceptions of Greek Ethnicity* (Cambridge, MA: Harvard University Press, 2001) 275–99.

Samuel, Alan E., 'The Internal Organization of the Nomarch's Bureau in the Third Century B.C.', in *Essays in Honor of C. Bradford Welles* (New Haven, CT: American Society of Papyrologists, 1966), 213–29.

—'The Greek Element in the Ptolemaic Bureaucracy', in Deborah H. Samuel (ed.), *Proceedings of the Twelfth International Congress of Papyrology* (Toronto: A. M. Hakkert, 1970), 443–53.

Sanders, Jack T., *Ben Sira and Demotic Wisdom* (Chico, CA: Scholars Press, 1983).

Sanders, S., 'Beth Shemesh 1: Alphabetic Cuneiform Abecedary', in W. Horowitz and T. Oshima (eds), *Cuneiform in Canaan: Cuneiform Sources From the Land of Canaan in Ancient Times* (Jerusalem: Israel Exploration Society, 2006), 157–60.

Satlow, M. L., *Jewish Marriage in Antiquity* (Princeton, NJ: Princeton University Press, 2001).

Schachermeyr, Fitz, *Alexander, der Grosse. Ingenium und Macht* (Pustet, Graz–Salzburg–Wien, 1949).

Schalit A., 'Pereq be-Toldot Milhemet ha-Miflagot bi-Yerushalayim be-Sof ha-Meah ha-Hamishit ubi-Tehilat ha-Meah ha-Reviyit Lifnei ha-Sefirah', in M. Schwabe and Y. Gutman (eds), *Memorial Volume to Johanan Levi* (Jerusalem: The Magnes Press, The Hebrew University, 1949): 252–72.

—'The Letter of Antiochus III to Zeuxis regarding the Establishment of Jewish Military Colonies in Phrygia and Lydia', *JQR* 50 (1959/60): 289–318.

—'Alexander', *Encyclopaedia Hebraica*, 3 (1966): cols. 635–655.

Schaper, J., 'The Jerusalem Temple as an Instrument of the Achaemenid Fiscal Administration', *Vetus Testamentum* 45/4 (1995): 328–39.

—'The Temple Treasury Committee in the Times of Nehemiah and Ezra', *Vetus Testamentum* 47/2 (1997): 200–206.

Scheid, J., *Religion et piété à Rome*, 2nd edn (Paris: Albin Michel, 2001).

—*Quand faire, c'est croire. Les rites sacrificiels des Romains* (Paris: Aubier, 2005).

Schlange-Schöningen, Heinrich, 'Alexandria-Memphis-Siwa: wo liegt Alexander der Grosse begraben?', *Antike Welt* 27 (1996): 109–19.

Schmitt-Pantel, P., and L. Bruit-Zaidman, *Religion in the Ancient Greek City* (Cambridge: Cambridge University Press, 1992).

Schniedewind, W., 'Jerusalem, the Late Judaean Monarchy and the Composition of the Biblical Texts', in A. G. Vaughn and A. E. Killebrew (eds), *Jerusalem in the Bible and Archaeology: The First Temple Period* (Atlanta: Society of Biblical Literature, 2003): 375–94.
—*How the Bible Became a Book: The Textualization of Ancient Israel* (Cambridge: Cambridge University Press, 2004).
Scholl, R., *Die Elenden in Gottes Thronrat* (Berlin: de Gruyter, 2000).
Schuller, Eileen M., '4Q372 1: A text about Joseph', *Revue de Qumran* 14 (1990): 349–76.
—'A preliminary study of 4Q373 and some related(?) fragments [4Q371, 4Q372]', in Julio Trebolle Barrera and J. Vegas Montaner L. (eds), *The Madrid Qumran Congress; Proceedings of the International Congress on the Dead Sea Scrolls, March 1991*, Vol. I–II (Leiden: E. J. Brill, 1992a): 515–30.
—'The Psalm of 4Q372 1 within the context of Second Temple Prayer', *Catholic Biblical Quarterly* 54 (1992b): 67–79.
—*Discoveries in the Judaean Desert*, Vol. XXVIII (Oxford: Clarendon Press, 2001).
Schulz, H., 'Das Todesrecht im Alten Testament: Studien zur Rechtsform der Mot-Jumat-Sätze' (Berlin: de Gruyter, 1969).
Schumacher G., *The Jaulan* (London: Richard Bentley and Son, 1888).
Schürer, E., *Geschichte des jüdischen Volkes im Zeitalter Jesu Christi* (Leipzig [Göttingen]: Georg Holms Hildesheim 1967).
—*The History of the Jewish People in the Age of Jesus Christ* (Edinburgh: T&T Clark, 1973).
—*The History of the Jewish People in the Age of Jesus Christ (175 B.C.–A.D. 135)*, A New English Version Revised and Edited by G. Vermes and F. Millar (Edinburgh: T&T Clark, 1973), Vol. 1.
—*The History of the Jewish People in the Age of Jesus Christ (175 B.C.–A.D. 135)*, Vol. 3 (Edinburgh: T&T Clark, 1973).
Schwartz, Daniel R., 'Some papyri and Josephus' sources and chronology for the Persian period', *Journal for the Study of Judaism* 21 (1990): 175–99.
—'Josephus' Tobiads: Back to the Second Century?', in Martin Goodman (ed.), *Jews in the Graeco-Roman World* (Oxford: Clarendon Press, 1998): 47–61.
—'Once Again on Tobiad Chronology: Should We Let a Stated Anomaly Be Anomalous? A Response to Gideon Fuks', *Journal of Jewish Studies* 53 (2002): 146–51.
Schwartz, D. S., *Studies in the Jewish Background of Christianity* (Tübingen: J. C. B. Mohr-Paul Siebeck, 1992).
—'On Something Biblical about 2 Maccabees', in M. E. Stone and E. G. Chazon (eds), *Biblical Perspectives: Early Use and Interpretation of the Bible in Light of the Dead Sea Scrolls* (Leiden, Boston, Köln: E. J. Brill, 1998): 223–32.
Schwartz, Seth, 'John Hyrcanus I's Destruction of the Gerizim Temple and Judaean-Samaritan Relations', *Jewish History* 7 (1993): 9–25.
—'On the Autonomy of Judaea in the Fourth and Third Centuries B.C.E.', *JJS* 45 (1994): 157–68.
—*Imperialism and Jewish Society, 200 B.C.E. to 640 C.E.* (Princeton, NJ: Princeton University Press, 2001).
—'Conversion to Judaism in the Second Temple Period: A Functionalist Approach', in Shaye J. D. Cohen and Joshua J. Schwartz (eds), *Studies in Josephus and the Varieties of Ancient Judaism, Louis H. Feldman Jubilee Volume* (Leiden: Brill, 2007), 224–36.
Seetzen U. J., *Reisen durch Syrien, Palaestina, Phoenizien, die Trans-Jordan länder, Arabia-Petraea und Unter Ägypten* (Berlin: G. Reimer, 1854–59).
Sellers O. R., *The Citadel of Beth-Zur* (Philadelphia: Westminster, 1933).
—'Coins of the 1960 Excavations at Shechem', *Biblical Archaeologist* 25 (1962): 87–96.
Sellers, O. R., R. W. Funk, J. L. McKenzie, P. Lapp and N. Lapp, *The 1957 Excavation at Beth-zur, AASOR* 38 (Cambridge: American Schools of Oriental Research, 1968).

Seow, C. L., 'Linguistic Evidence and the Dating of Qohelet', *JBL* 115 (1996): 643–66.
Sérandour, A., 'Les récits bibliques de la construction du second temple: leurs enjeux',
     Transeuphratène 11 (1996): 9–32.
Seyrig H., *Notes on Syrian Coins*, Numismatic Notes and Monographs 119 (New York: American
     Numismatic Society, 1950a).
—'Antiquités syriennes 43. Démétrias de Phénicie', *Syria* 27 (1950b): 50–6.
—'Antiquités Syriennes: Sur une prétendue ère Tyrienne', *Syria*, 34 (1957): 93–7.
—'Temples, Cultes et Souvenirs Historiques de la Décapole', *Syria*, 36 (1959): 60–78.
—'Alexander le Grand Fondateur de Gerasas', *Syria*, 42 (1965): 25–28.
Sharon, I., 'Phoenician and Greek Ashlar Construction Techniques at Tell Dor', *Bulletin of the
     American Schools of Oriental Research* 267 (1987): 21–42.
—'The Fortifications of Dor and the Transcription from the Israeli-Syrian concept of Defense to
     the Greek Concept', *Qadmoniot* 24 (1991): 105–13.
Sherwin White, S. and A. Kuhrt, *From Samarkhand to Sardis: A New Approach to the Seleucid
     Empire* (London: Duckworth, 1993).
Shiloh, Y., *Excavations at the City of David* I, *Qedem* 19 (Jerusalem: The Hebrew University, 1984).
—'Stratigraphical Introduction to Parts I and II', in D. T. Ariel (ed.), *Excavations at the City of
     David 1978–1985 Directed by Yigal Shiloh, Vol. II: Imported Stamped Amphora Handles,
     Coins, Worked Bone and Ivory, and Glass, Qedem* 30 (Jerusalem, 1990) 1–12.
Shryock, A., *Nationalism and the Genealogical Imagination: Oral history and Textual Authority
     in Tribal Jordan* (Berkeley, CA: University of California Press, 1997).
Shukron, E. and R. Reich, 'Jerusalem, City of David, the Givʿati Car Park', *Hadashot
     Arkheologiot – Excavations and Surveys in Israel* 117 (2005): 7–9.
Simon, M. and A. Benoît, *Le Judaïsme et le christianisme antique d'Antiochus Epiphanie à
     Constantin* (Paris: Presses Universitaires de France, 1968).
Sivan, R. and G. Solar, 'Excavations in the Jerusalem Citadel, 1980–1988', in H. Geva (ed.).
     Ancient Jerusalem Revealed (Jerusalem: Israel Exploration Society, 1994): 168–76.
Skeat, T. C. (ed.), *Greek Papyri in the British Museum (now in the British Library): VII The
     Zenon Archive* (London: British Museum Publications, 1974).
Skehan, P. W. and A. A. Di Lella, *The Wisdom of Ben Sira: A New Translation with Notes by
     P. W. Skehan; Introduction and Commentary by A. A. di Lella*, Anchor Bible, 39 (New York:
     Doubleday, 1987).
Smelik, K. A. D., '"Who Knows not what Monsters Demented Egypt Worships?" Opinions on
     Egyptian Animal Worship in Antiquity as Part of the Ancient Conception of Egypt', *ANRW* II
     17.3 (Berlin and New York: W. de Gruyter, 1984): 1852–2000.
Smend, R., *Die Weisheit des Jesus Sirach, erklärt* (Berlin: George Reimer, 1906).
Smith, H. S., and W. J. Tait, *Saqqâra Demotic Papyri I* (London: Egypt Exploration Society,
     1983).
Smith, Morton, 'The Gentiles in Judaism 125 BCE-CE 66', in William Horbury, W. D. Davies
     and John Sturdy (eds), *Cambridge History of Judaism*, III: *The Early Roman Period*
     (Cambridge: Cambridge University Press, 1999), 192–249.
Smith, P. A., *Rhetoric and Redaction in Trito-Isaiah: The Structure, Growth and Authorship of
     Isaiah 56–66*, VTSup, 62 (Leiden: Brill, 1996).
Smith, R. R. R., 'Kings and Philosophers', in Anthony Bulloch, Erich S. Gruen, A. A. Long
     and Andrew Stewart (eds), *Images and Ideologies: Self-definition in the Hellenistic World*
     (Berkeley, CA: University of California Press, 1993), 202–11.
Snaith, J. G., *Song of Songs*, NCBC (London: Marshall Pickering, 1993).
Sourvinou-Inwood, C., 'What is *Polis* Religion?', in O. Murray and S. Price (eds), *The Greek City
     from Homer to Alexander* (Oxford: Clarendon Press, 1990), 295–322.
Spak I., *Der Bericht der Josephus über Alexander den Grossen* (Diss., Königsberg: Pr.
     Hartungsche Buchdruckerei, 1911).

Spencer, Diana, *The Roman Alexander: Reading a Cultural Myth* (Exeter: University of Exeter Press, 2002).

Stade, B., 'Deuterosacharja. Eine kritische Studie, III', *ZAW* 2 (1882): 275–309.

Stadelmann, Helge, *Ben Sira als Schriftgelehrter: Eine Untersuchung zum Berufsbild des vor–Makkabäischen Sofer unter Berücksichtigung seines Verhältnisses zu Priester–, Propheten– und Weisheitslehretum*, WUNT 2/6 (Tübingen: J. C. B. Mohr, 1981).

Stark K. B., *Gaza und die philistäische Küste* (Jena: Friedrich Mauke, 1852).

Steck, O. H., *Studien zu Tritojesaja*, BZAW, 203 (Berlin/ New York: de Gruyter, 1991).

Steiner, R. C., 'The Aramaic Text in Demotic Script, The Liturgy of a New Year's Festival Imported from Bethel to Syene by Exiles from Rash', *JAOS* 111 (1991): 362–63.

Sterling, Gregory E., *Historiography and Self-Definition: Josephus, Luke-Acts and Apologetic Historiography* (Leiden: Brill, 1992).

Stern, E., *The Material Culture of the Land of the Bible in the Persian Period 538–332 BCE* (Jerusalem: The Bialik Institute, 1973).

—'Achaemenian Tombs at Shechem', *Qadmoniot* 13 (1980a): 101–103.

—'Achaemenian Tombs from Shechem', *Levant* 12 (1980b): 90–111.

—*Material Culture of the Land of the Bible in the Persian Period, 538–332 B.C.* (Warminster: Aris and Phillips, 1982).

—'The Beginning of the Greek Settlement in Palestine in Light of the Excavations at Tel Dor', in S. Gitin and W. G. Dever (eds), *Recent Excavations in Israel; Studies in Iron Age Archaeology, Annual of the American Schools of Oriental Research* 49 (1990): 107–24, The Dor Province in the Persian Period in the Light of the Recent Excavations at Dor, *Transeuphratène* 2 (1989): 147–55.

—'The Phoenician Architectural Elements in Palestine during the Late Iron Age and Persian Period', in A. Kempinski and R. Reich (eds), *The Architecture of Ancient Israel: From the Prehistoric to the Persian Periods* (Jerusalem: Biblical Archaeology Society, 1992), 302–309.

—*Archaeology of the Land of the Bible Vol. II: The Assyrian, Babylonian, and Persian Periods (732–332 B.C.E.)* (New York: Doubleday, 2001).

Stern M., *The Documents on the History of the Hasmonaean Revolt with a Commentary and Introductions* (Tel-Aviv: Hakibbutz Hameuchad Publishing House Ltd., 1965).

—*Greek and Latin Authors on Jews and Judaism* (Jerusalem: The Israel Academy of Sciences and Humanities, 1974).

—*Studies in Jewish History: The Second Temple Period* (Jerusalem: Yad Izhak Ben-Zvi, 1991).

Stieglitz, R. R., 'Stratonos Pyrgos – Migdal Śar – Sebastos: History and Archaeology', in A. Raban and K. G. Holum, *Caesarea Maritima: A Prospective after Two Millennia* (Leiden: E. J. Brill, 1996), 593–608.

Stone, Michael E. and David Satran, *Emerging Judaism: Studies on the Fourth and Third Centuries BCE* (Minneapolis: Augsburg-Fortress Press, 1989).

Stordalen, T., *Echoes of Eden, Genesis 2–3 and Symbolism of the Garden in Biblical Hebrew Literature* (Leuven: Peeters, 2001).

Stuckenbruck, Loren T., 'The "Angels" and "Giants" of Genesis 6:1-4 in Second and Third Century BCE Jewish Interpretation: Reflections on the Posture of Early Apocalyptic Traditions', *DSD* 7 no. 3 (2000): 354–77.

—'Giant Mythology and Demonology: From the Ancient Near East to the Dead Sea Scrolls', in A. Lange, H. Lichtenberger and K. T. Diethard Römheld (eds), *Die Dämonen: Demons* (Tübingen: Mohr Siebeck, 2003), 318–38.

—*Commentary on 1 Enoch 91–108* (Berlin: Walter de Gruyter, 2007).

Sussmann, Y., 'A Halakhic Inscription from the Beth-Shean Valley', *Tarbiz* 43 (1973–74): 88–158.

Suter, David, 'Fallen Angels, Fallen Priests', *HUCA* 50 (1979): 115–35.

Svoronos, J. N., *T□ Νομίσματα το□ Κράτους τ□ν Πτολεμαίων* (Athens: P. D. Sakellarios, 1904–08).

Swarup, P. N. W., *The Self-Understanding of the Dead Sea Scrolls Community: An Eternal Planting, A House of Holiness* (London: T&T Clark, 2006).

Syon, D., 'Numismatic Evidence of Jewish Presence in Galilee before the Hasmonean Annexation?' *INJ* 1 (2006): 21–4.

Tal, O., 'On the Origin and Concept of the Loculi Tombs of Hellenistic Palestine', *Ancient West and East* 2/2 (2003): 288–307.

—'Some Remarks on the Coastal Plain of Palestine under Achaemenid Rule – An Archaeological Synopsis', *Persika* 6 (2005): 71–96.

—*The Archaeology of Hellenistic Palestine: Between Tradition and Renewal* (Jerusalem: The Bialik Institute, 2006).

—'Cult in Transition from Achaemenid to Greek Rule: The Contribution of Achaemenid-Ptolemaic Temples of Palestine', *Transeuphratène* 36 (2008): 165–83.

Talmon, S., 'A Masada Fragment of Samaritan Origin', *Israel Exploration Journal* 47 (1997): 220–32.

Talshir, D., 'The Habitat and History of Hebrew during the Second Temple Period', in I. Young (ed.), *Biblical Hebrew: Studies in Chronology and Typology, JSOTS* 369 (London: T&T Clark, 2003), 251–75.

Tarn, W. W., and G. T. Griffith, *Hellenistic Civilization*, 3rd edn (London: St. Martins, 1952).

Tcherikover, V., *Die hellenistischen Stadtegründungen von Alexander dem Grossen bis auf die Römezeit* (Leipzig: Philologus, 1927).

—'Palestine under the Ptolemies (A Contribution to the Study of the Zenon Papyri)', *Mizraim* 4–5 (1937): 9–90.

—*Corpus Papyrorum Judaicarum* (Cambridge MA: Harvard University Press, 1957).

—*Hellenistic Civilization and the Jews* (New York: JPS, 1959).

—*The Jews and Greeks in the Hellenistic Period* (Tel Aviv: Dvir, 1963).

—*The Jews in the Graeco-Roman World* [A Collection of His Studies], 2nd edn (Tel Aviv: M. Newman, 1974).

—*Hellenistic Civilization and the Jews* trans. S. Applebaum (New York: Atheneum, 1977).

Tcherikover, V. A., A. Fuks, and M. Stern (eds), *Corpus Papyrorum Judaicarum (CPJ)*, 3 vols. (Cambridge, MA: Harvard; Jerusalem: Magnes, 1957–64).

Tepper, Y. 'A Basilica at Beth Yeraḥ? Beth Yeraḥ Revisited', *Tel Aviv* 26 (1999): 271–82.

Thackeray H. St. J., *Josephus with an English Translation*, Vol. 1 (Cambridge MA: Harvard University Press, 1926).

Thackeray, H. St. J., Marcus, Wikgren and Feldman (eds), *Josephus* (London: Heinemann, 1926).

Thomas, J. David, *The epistrategos in Ptolemaic and Roman Egypt: Part 1 The Ptolemaic epistrategos* (Opladen: Westdeutscher Verlag, 1975).

—'Aspects of the Ptolemaic Civil Service: The Dioiketes and the Nomarch', in Herwig Maehler and Volker Michael Strocka (eds), *Das ptolemäische Ägypten: Akten des Internationalen Symposions 27.-29. September 1976 in Berlin* (Mainz: Zabern, 1978), 187–94.

—*The epistrategos in Ptolemaic and Roman Egypt: Part 2 The Roman epistrategos* (Opladen: Westdeutscher Verlag, 1982).

Thompson, Dorothy J., 'The Idumaeans of Memphis and the Ptolemaic *Politeumata*', in *Atti del XVII Congresso Internazionale di Papirologia*, Volume Terzo (Naples: Centro Internazionale per lo Studio dei Papiri Ercolanesi, 1984), 1069–75.

Thompson, T. L., 'The Bible and Hellenism: A Response', in L. L. Grabbe (ed.), *Did Moses Speak Attic?* (Sheffield: Sheffield Academic Press, 2001), 274–86.

Throntveit, M. A., *Ezra-Nehemiah* (Louisville: J. Knox, 1992).

Tiemeyer, L.-S., *Priestly Rites and Prophetic Rage: Post-Exilic Prophetic Critique of the Priesthood* (Tübingen: Mohr Siebeck, 2006).

Tiller, Patrick, *A Commentary on the Animal Apocalypse of* 1 Enoch, SBL Early Judaism and Its Literature, 4 (Atlanta, GA: Scholars Press, 1993).
—'The "Eternal Planting" in the Dead Sea Scrolls', *Dead Sea Discoveries* 4.3 (1997): 312–35.
Torrey, C. C., *The Composition and Historical Value of Ezra-Nehemiah* (Giessen: J. Kicker'sche Buchhandlung, 1896).
—*Ezra Studies* (Chicago: University of Chicago, 1910).
—'Sanballat "The Horonit"', *JBL*, 47 (1928): 380–89.
—*Pseudo-Ezekiel and the Original Prophecy* (New Haven, CT: Yale University Press, 1930).
—'The Walls of Jerusalem in the Period of Nehemiah', *Cathedra* 4 (1977): 31–42..
Tov, E., *Textual Criticism of the Hebrew Bible* (Minneapolis, MN: Fortress, 1992).
Treves, M., 'Conjectures Concerning the Date and Authorship of Zechariah ix-xiv', *VT* 13 (1963): 196–207.
Trotter, James M., 'The Second Jerusalem Temple a Primarily Persian Project?', *Scandinavian Journal of Old Testament* 15 (2000): 276–93.
Tsafrir, Y., 'The Walls of Jerusalem in the Period of Nehemiah', *Cathedra* 4 (1977): 31–42.
Tsafrir, Y., L. Di Segni and J. Green, *Tabula Imperii Romani Judaea Palastina, Maps and Gazetteer* (Jerusalem: Israel Academy of Sciences and Humanities, 1994).
Tushingham, A. D., 'Armenian Garden', *PEQ* 99 (1967): 71–3.
—*Excavations in Jerusalem, 1961–1967, Vol. I: Excavations in the Armenian Garden, on the Western Hill.* (Toronto: Royal Ontario Museum, 1985).
Uhlig, Siebert, *Jüdische Schriften aus hellenistisch-römischer Zeit. Band V: Apocalypsen: Lieferung 6: Das Äthiopische Henochbuch* (Gütersloh: Gütersloher Verlagshaus, 1984).
Ussishkin, D., 'The Borders and *De Facto* Size of Jerusalem in the Persian Period', in O. Lipschits and M. Oeming (eds), *Judah and the Judeans in the Persian Period* (Winona Lake, IN: Eisenbrauns, 2006): 147–66.
Vanderhooft, D. S., *The Neo-Babylonian Empire and Babylon in the Latter Prophets.* (Atlanta, GA: Harvard Semitic Museum Monographs, 1999).
Vanderhooft, D. and O. Lipschits, 'A New Typology of the Yehud Stamp Impressions', *Tel Aviv* 34 (2007): 12–37.
VanderKam, James C, 'Jewish High Priests of the Persian period: Is it Complete?', in G. Anderson and S. Olyan (eds), *Priesthood and Cult in Ancient Israel* (Sheffield: Sheffield Academic Press, 1991) 67–91.
Van der Steen, E. J., 1998. What happened to Arab-Geometric pottery in Beirut? *ARAM* 9–10 (1998): 121–27.
—'Town and Countryside of the Kerak Plateau', in E. J. van der Steen and B. Saidel (eds), *On the Fringe of Society: Archaeological and Ethnoarchaeological Perspectives on Pastoral and Agricultural Societies*, BAR International Series 1657 (Oxford: Archeopress, 2007).
—'Tribal States in History: The Emirate of Ibn Rashid as a Case Study', in B. Saidel and E. J. van der Steen (eds), *The Archaeology of the Ottoman and Mandate periods in the Levant* (forthcoming).
van Henten, J. W., *The Maccabean Martyrs as Saviours of the Jewish People: A Study of 2 and 4 Maccabees* (Leiden, Boston, Köln: E. J. Brill, 1997).
—'2 Maccabees as a History of Liberation', in M. Mor et al. (eds), *Jews and Gentiles in the Holy Land in the Days of the Second Temple, the Mishnah and the Talmud: A Collection of Articles* (Jerusalem: Yad Ben-Zvi Press, 2003): 62–86.
Van't Dack, E., W. Clarysse, G. Cohen, J. Quaegebeur and J. K. Winnicki, *The Judean-Syrian-Egyptian Conflict of 103–101 B.C.: A Multilingual Dossier Concerning a 'War of Sceptres'* (Brussels: Publikatie van het Comité Klassieke Studies, 1989).
Vermes, G., F. Millar, and M. Goodman, *The History of the Jewish People in the Age of Jesus Christ* (London: T&T Clark, 1986–87).
Vriezen, K. J. H., 'Hirbet Kefire – eine Oberflächenuntersuchung', *ZDPV* 91 (1975): 135–58.

Walbank, F. W., *The Hellenistic World* (London: Fontana, 1992).

—'Two Hellenistic Processions: A Matter of Self-Definition', in F. W. Walbank, *Polybius, Rome and the Hellenistic World. Essays and Reflections* (Cambridge: Cambridge University Press, 2002): 79–90.

Wallace-Hadrill, A., '*Mutatio morum*: The idea of a Cultural Revolution', in T. Habinek and A. Schiesaro (eds), *The Roman Cultural Revolution* (Cambridge: Cambridge University Press, 1997), 3–22.

—'*Mutatas Formas*: The Augustan Transformation of Roman Knowledge', in K. Galinsky (ed.), *The Cambridge Companion to the Age of Augustus* (Cambridge: Cambridge University Press, 2005), 55–84.

Wansbrough, J., 'The decolonization of North African History', *Journal of African history* 9/4 (1968): 643–50.

Weill, R., *La Cité de David* (Paris, 1920).

Weinberg, Joel, *The Citizen-Temple Community*, trans. D. L. Smith-Christopher. JSOT Suppl. 151 (Sheffield: Sheffield Academic Press, 1992).

—'Jerusalem in the Persian Period', in S. Ahituv and A. Mazar (eds), *The History of Jerusalem, The Biblical Period* (Jerusalem: Yad Ben Zvi, 2000): 307–26.

Weisman, D. J., 'Babylonia 605–539 B.C.', *The Cambridge Ancient History*, Vol. III/2 (1991): 229–51.

Welles, C. Bradford, 'The Ptolemaic Administration in Egypt', *Journal of Juristic Papyrology* 3 (1949): 21–47.

—'The Role of the Egyptians under the First Ptolemies', in Deborah H. Samuel (ed.), *Proceedings of the Twelfth International Congress of Papyrology*, American Studies in Papyrology 7 (Toronto: A. M. Hakkert, 1970), 505–10.

Welten, P., *Geschichte und Geschichtsdarstellung in den Chronikbüchern* (Neukirchen-Vluyn: Neukirchener, 1973).

Whiston W., *The Genuine Works of Flavius Josephus* (London: Printed by W. Bowyer, 1737 (1980).

White L. M., 'The Delos Synagogue Revisited: Recent Fieldwork in the Graeco-Roman Diaspora', *Harvard Theological Review* 80 (1987): 133–60.

Wightman, G. J., *The Walls of Jerusalem: From the Canaanites to the Mamluks* (Sydney: Meditarch, 1993).

Wilcken, U., *Alexander der Grosse* (Leipzig: Quelle und Meyer, 1931).

Will, Wolfgang, *Alexander der Große* (Stuttgart: Kohlhammer, 1986).

Williams, R. J., 'The alleged Semitic original of the Wisdom of Amenemope', *JEA* 47 (1961): 100–106.

Williamson, H. G. M., *Ezra, Nehemiah* (Waco: World Books, 1985).

—*Studies in Persian Period History and Historiography*, FAT, 38 (Tübingen: Mohr Siebeck, 2004).

Willrich H., *Juden und Griechen vor der makakabäuschen Erhebung* (Göttingen: Vandenhoeck und Ruprecht, 1895).

—*Judaica: Forschung zur hellenistisch-jüdischen Geschichte und Literatur* (Göttingen: Vandenhoeck und Ruprecht, 1900).

Wischmeyer, O., *Die Kultur des Buches Jesus Sirach*, BZNW 77 (Berlin/New York: de Gruyter, 1995).

Wise, M. O., 'Accidents and Accidence: A Scribal View of the Linguistic Dating of the Aramaic Scrolls from Qumran', in T. Muraoka (ed.), *Studies in Qumran Aramaic* (Abr-Nahrain Suppl. 3; Louvain: Peeters, 1992), 124–67.

Worthington, Ian (ed.), *Alexander the Great: A Reader* (London: Routledge, 2003).

Wright, B. G., 'Fear the Lord and Honor the Priest: Ben Sira as Defender of the Jerusalem Priesthood', in P. C. Beentjes (ed.), *The Book of Ben Sira in Modern Research*, BZAW 255 (Berlin: Walter de Gruyter, 1997), 189–222.

—'Ben Sira on Kings and Kingship', in T. Rajak, S. Pearce, J. Aitken and J. Dines (eds), *Jewish Perspectives on Hellenistic Rulers* (Berkeley, CA: University of California Press, 2007), 76–91.

Wright, G. E., *Shechem: The Biography of a Biblical City* (New York: McGraw-Hill, 1965).

Wright, J. L., *Rebuilding Identity: The Nehemiah Memoir and its Earliest Readers* (Berlin: Walter de Gruyter, 2004).

Wright, J. W., 'Remapping Yehud: The Borders of Yehud and the Genealogies of Chronicles', in O. Lipschits, and M. Oeming (eds), *Judah and the Judaeans in the Persian Period* (Winona Lake, IN: Eisenbrauns, 2006) 67–89.

Wright, N. T., *The New Testament and the People of God* (London: SPCK, 1992).

Yadin, Y., 'Four Epigraphical Queries', *IEJ* 24 (1974): 30–36.

Yassif, Eli, 'The Hebrew Traditions about Alexander the Great: Narrative Models and their Meaning in the Middle Ages', *TARBIZ* 75 (2006): 359–407.

Yeivin, S., 'The Benjaminite Settlement in the Western Part of their Territory', *IEJ* 21 (1971): 141–54.

Young, I. M., *Diversity in Pre-exilic Hebrew*, FAT, 5 (Tübingen: Mohr-Siebeck, 1993).

—'Israelite Literacy: Interpreting the Evidence: Part 1', *VT* 48 (1998): 239–53.

—(ed.), *Biblical Hebrew. Studies in Chronology and Typology*, JSOTS 369 (London: T&T Clark, 2003a), 338–40.

—'Late Biblical Hebrew and Hebrew Inscriptions', in I. Young (ed.), *Biblical Hebrew: Studies in Chronology and Typology*, JSOTS 369 (London: T&T Clark, 2003b) 276–311.

—'Concluding Reflections', *Biblical Hebrew: Studies in Chronology and Typology* in I. Young (ed.), *Biblical Hebrew. Studies in Chronology and Typology*, JSOTS 369 (London: T&T Clark, 2003c), 312–17.

Zedaka, Benyamim, *Summary of the History of the Israeli-Samaritans* (Holon, 2001).

Zevit, Ziony, 'Dating Ruth: Legal, Linguistic and Historical Observations', *ZAW* 117 (2005): 574–600.

Zorn, J. R., 'Estimating the Population Size of Ancient Settlements: Methods, Problems, Solutions, and a Case Study', *BASOR* 295 (1994): 31–48.

Zwickel, W., 'Jerusalem und Samaria zur Zeit Nehemias: Ein Vergleich', *Biblische Zeitschrift* 52 (2) (2008): 201–22.

INDEX

CPSIA information can be obtained at www.ICGtesting.com
Printed in the USA
LVOW10s1555171013

357417LV00006B/385/P